AF771314

ROUTLEDGE HANDBOOK OF HIGH-PERFORMANCE WORKPLACES

This timely book focuses on an overview of the fundamentals behind high-performance workplaces underpinning occupants' satisfaction, health, and productivity. To this end, it covers human, environmental, and organisational aspects proven to be of great relevance to the design of high-performance workplaces. Perhaps most significantly it looks at these characteristics both before and after the start of the COVID-19 pandemic.

From the exodus from private offices to the rise of open-plan workplaces, where, how, and when people work was changing rapidly pre-COVID. Post-COVID, pandemic-imposed restrictions banished workers from offices into their homes fast, leaving organisations scrambling to keep workers functioning away from HQ. After the immediate shockwaves set by the pandemic, workers and organisations have had time to learn about the positive and negative aspects of remote working, with the vast majority now questioning the need to go back to HQ and the purpose of offices. In this book, the contributors share and discuss lessons learned from research conducted in workplaces pre- and post-2020 with a view to providing a clear picture about what high-performance workplaces are about, including the key drivers behind workers' satisfaction, health, and productivity. This handbook builds on a programme of applied research conducted in workplaces led by the editors over the last decade which is aimed at understanding the synergies between the design, performance, and experience of spaces. It examines ergonomics, biophilic design, acoustics, indoor air quality, thermal comfort, diversity, leadership, psychological safety, culture, and much more.

Research findings are presented side-by-side with case studies selected from the research database led by the editors. Industry experts add to the academic voice, reinforcing the authenticity of this book and its relevance to other stakeholders found outside the academic arena, including the property and design industry, students, government, and the community in general.

Christhina Candido directs the SHE (Sustainable and Healthy Environments) Lab at the University of Melbourne Faculty of Architecture, Building and Planning. She leads a program of applied and interdisciplinary research aimed at advancing knowledge about the design, performance, and experience of the built environment. She has led Post-Occupancy Evaluation surveys in 250 workplaces located in five continents. Findings from her work in workspaces have been used to inform changes in design and operational practices around the world. She is member of expert advisory groups with the International WELL Building Institute (IWBI), WELL Faculty, the Green Building Council of Australia (GBCA), and the National Australian Building Rating System (NABERS).

Iva Durakovic is a lecturer and interior designer with over 10 years' experience working on high-profile, award-winning workplace design projects. She holds a Bachelor of Interior Architecture Hons from the University of New South Wales. Her research focuses on behavioural impacts and phenomenology of high-performance workplaces, evaluating the environments and their cultures to understand the human factors at play across individual, physical, and organisational levels, particularly within emergent post 2020 workplace contexts. Her projects blend research, industry, and work-integrated learning to foster knowledge exchange between leading practitioners, academics, and next-generation designers.

Samin Marzban is a lecturer with the School of Civil, Mining, Environmental and Architectural Engineering at the University of Wollongong, Australia. She is an architect by training and holds a PhD in Built Environment from the University of New South Wales, Sydney. Her research focuses on indoor environmental quality, with a particular focus on post-occupancy evaluation and workspace well-being. She is also interested and skilled in multi-disciplinary building-related research, including performance-based design, optimisation, and energy efficiency.

TRANSDISCIPLINARY WORKPLACE RESEARCH AND MANAGEMENT

Series Editors: Rianne Appel-Meulenbroek and Vitalija Danivska

A HANDBOOK OF THEORIES ON DESIGNING ALIGNMENT BETWEEN PEOPLE AND THE OFFICE ENVIRONMENT
Rianne Appel-Meulenbroek and Vitalija Danivska

A HANDBOOK OF MANAGEMENT THEORIES AND MODELS FOR OFFICE ENVIRONMENTS AND SERVICES
Rianne Appel-Meulenbroek and Vitalija Danivska

METHODOLOGICAL APPROACHES FOR WORKPLACE RESEARCH AND MANAGEMENT
Edited by Chiara Tagliaro, Marko Orel and Ying Hua

ROUTLEDGE HANDBOOK OF HIGH-PERFORMANCE WORKPLACES
Edited By Christhina Candido, Iva Durakovic, and Samin Marzban

For more information about this series, please visit: www.routledge.com/

ROUTLEDGE HANDBOOK OF HIGH-PERFORMANCE WORKPLACES

Edited by Christhina Candido, Iva Durakovic, and Samin Marzban

Routledge
Taylor & Francis Group
LONDON AND NEW YORK

Designed cover image: B:Hive. Architecture and Interior Design by BVN Architecture. Photography by John Gollings

First published 2024
by Routledge
4 Park Square, Milton Park, Abingdon, Oxon OX14 4RN

and by Routledge
605 Third Avenue, New York, NY 10158

Routledge is an imprint of the Taylor & Francis Group, an informa business

© 2024 selection and editorial matter, Christhina Candido, Iva Durakovic, and Samin Marzban; individual chapters, the contributors

The right of Christhina Candido, Iva Durakovic, and Samin Marzban to be identified as the authors of the editorial material, and of the authors for their individual chapters, has been asserted in accordance with sections 77 and 78 of the Copyright, Designs and Patents Act 1988.

The Open Access version of this book, available at www.taylorfrancis.com, has been made available under a Creative Commons Attribution-Non Commercial-No Derivatives (CC-BY-NC-ND) 4.0 International license.
Funded by Body/Bodies University of Melbourne; and The Transdisciplinary Workplace Research (TWR) network.

Trademark notice: Product or corporate names may be trademarks or registered trademarks, and are used only for identification and explanation without intent to infringe.

British Library Cataloguing-in-Publication Data
A catalogue record for this book is available from the British Library

Library of Congress Cataloging-in-Publication Data
Names: Candido, Christhina, editor. | Durakovic, Iva, editor. | Marzban, Samin, editor.
Title: Routledge handbook of high-performance workplaces / edited by Christhina Candido, Iva Durakovic and Samin Marzban.
Description: Abingdon, Oxon ; New York, NY : Routledge, 2024. | Includes bibliographical references and index.
Identifiers: LCCN 2023059283 (print) | LCCN 2023059284 (ebook) | ISBN 9781032358130 (hbk) | ISBN 9781032358147 (pbk) | ISBN 9781003328728 (ebk)
Subjects: LCSH: Work environment. | Organizational behavior. | Employee motivation.
Classification: LCC HD7261 .R69 2024 (print) | LCC HD7261 (ebook) | DDC 658.3/12—dc23/eng/20240220
LC record available at https://lccn.loc.gov/2023059283
LC ebook record available at https://lccn.loc.gov/2023059284

ISBN: 978-1-032-35813-0 (hbk)
ISBN: 978-1-032-35814-7 (pbk)
ISBN: 978-1-003-32872-8 (ebk)

DOI: 10.1201/9781003328728

Typeset in Times New Roman
by Apex CoVantage, LLC

To all out there committed to making workplaces beautifully designed and functional spaces that can make a positive contribution to individuals, organisations, and the community. And all the women trailblazers making it happen.

CONTENTS

CONTRIBUTORS

Evodia Alaterou, HASSELL Studio, Australia

Prof Rianne Appel-Meulenbroek, Eindhoven University of Technology, Netherlands

Dr Behnaz Avazpour, University of Melbourne, Australia

Laurie Aznavoorian, University of Melbourne, Australia

A/Prof Arianna Brambilla, University of Sydney, Australia

Dr Kirsten Brown, Australia

A/Prof Densil Cabrera, University of Sydney, Australia

A/Prof Christhina Candido, University of Melbourne, Australia

Dr Vitalija Danivska, Delft University of Technology, Netherlands

Dr Kirsten Day, University of Melbourne, Australia

Iva Durakovic, UNSW, Australia

Dr Lina Engelen, University of Wollongong, Australia

Prof Peter Gahan, University of Melbourne, Australia

Dr Ozgur Gocer, University of Sydney, Australia

Eoin Higgins, Veldhoen + Company, Australia

Imogen Howe, University of Melbourne, Australia

Dr Wenye Hu, University of Sydney, Australia

Annabel Khoo, Athena Blue Global, Australia

Dr Maryam Khoshbakht, Griffith University, Australia

Ivy Li, Velhoen + Company, Australia

Dr Yaolin Lin, Shanghai University of Engineering Science, China

Dr Angela Loder, Greening the City, USA

A/Prof Martin Mackey, University of Sydney, Australia

Dr Andrew Martel, University of Melbourne, Australia

Dr Samin Marzban, University Wollongong, Australia

Lisa Munao, FreeHand Studio, Australia

Jack Noonan, International WELL Building Institute, Australia

Christian Pistauer, Athena Blue Global, Australia

Dr Victor Sojo, University of Melbourne, Australia

Prof Leena Thomas, UTS, Australia

Prof Dian Tjondronegoro, Griffith University, Australia

Niranjika Wijesooriya, University of Sydney, Australia

Dr Manuj Yadav, RWTH Aachen University, Germany

Dr Fan Zhang, Griffith University, Australia

ABOUT THE TRANSDISCIPLINARY WORKPLACE RESEARCH AND MANAGEMENT SERIES

In recent years workplace research and management topics became even more relevant due to many changes that our societies experience. Businesses started to see the hidden value that thoughtful management of workplaces can bring to organisations and people. More research is conducted providing evidence of the impact that workplace interventions create. People more freely express their preferences in the working environments they want to have.

We capture this growing interest for better workplaces also through our book series titled 'Transdisciplinary Workplace Research and Management'. This is already the fourth book in our book series since we started in 2021. Our aim as editors with this series is to bundle important insights from the many different disciplinary fields that are involved in researching or managing work environments and the workers using these spaces. Our first two books identified 40 important workplace-related theories from many fields and integrated them into two holistic models. Book 3 presented an overview of workplace research methodologies that help collect essential information on workplace design, use, and experience in practice. This fourth handbook again has a unique contribution for everybody involved in studying, designing, or managing workplaces and/or their users. Where Book 3, on methods, perhaps was more beneficial to researchers, this fourth book provides a strong overview of the state of the art in scientific research for practitioners and workplace researchers alike.

Every chapter provides valuable advice on how to create a high-performance workplace from many different important design angles. First the physical environment is discussed regarding both spatial design–related and indoor environmental quality factors, ranging from layout or biophilic design to air quality and acoustic quality. What we particularly like is the complementarity of that with the second section on human factors, where the authors try to clarify the 'one-size-does-NOT-fit-all' problem of workplace design and management. Last, several case studies add insights on how office organisations are trying to adjust their work environments to the 'new normal' of hybrid working.

The first books already proved to be a success among researchers and practitioners. So, we are delighted to add this fourth book to our series. We hope the transdisciplinary and holistic angle will help create the high-performance workplaces that all workers worldwide deserve. We thank the editors and authors of the fourth book for all their work and wish its readers many insights for future studies and workplace projects. As you will see, this time most of the authors and the provided case examples are from the Pacific Rim region. But the issues discussed in the book are no different from office workplaces in the rest of the world. It is a great example of how workplaces, employees, and organisations across the globe are concerned about the same things. So, the findings provided here and discussions of international literature will be beneficial to everyone worldwide. We support and encourage the development of an international community of researchers and practitioners that focuses on developing workplaces further. To download the first three books in the series, visit https://www.routledge.com/Transdisciplinary-Workplace-Research-and-Management/book-series/TWR and look for the free download or order a print version.

Rianne Apple-Meulenbroek and Vitalija Danivska

ABOUT THE EDITORS

The relationship between workers and the workplace is undergoing the most profound shift seen in decades. Combined pressures of the COVID-19 pandemic, a global mental health crisis, and increased pressure on organisations to report their social and environmental impact are challenging long-standing assumptions about where, when, and how we work. Workplaces that did not prioritise well-being – for example with marginal indoor air quality and a lack of daylight – may have found it challenging to convince workers to head back to the office. If they worked in a poorly designed open-plan office, the chances of bringing them back are even lower. Evidence to date has shown that home offices on average are better suited to the focused work most knowledge workers spend a large percentage of their time doing (Gensler, n.d.), highlighting long-standing complaints about workplaces that fail to meet the health and performance needs of their workers (de Oliveira et al., 2023). All of these pressures have renewed attention on workplaces that are successful. The stakes are high, with implications not only for the individual workplaces but for real estate portfolios, urban planning, public health, and social and community impact. Given that we spend approximately 90% of our time indoors, and much of our waking hours working, workplaces have the potential to profoundly influence our health, well-being, and performance. Understanding *how* they can do this is the focus of this book, and it could not be more timely or relevant.

From the early 2000s, Australian workplaces have been leaders globally regarding the design of high-quality physical office spaces. This has largely been thanks to the emergence of the green building movement and maturing industry associations, which created a mainstreaming of design factors that raised the bar for the air, light, acoustics, and thermal comfort conditions for many workplaces. In the 2010s, the focus of these physical factors shifted beyond design to measurement and performance, thus setting Australian workplaces up well to make environmental, social, and governance (ESG) disclosures. Other factors that have helped drive an increased national focus on sustainability leadership include a highly competitive local property industry which is open to collaboration, a willingness of building owners to go above and beyond in providing amenities and experience to their tenants, and various standards and rating tools to drive different parts of the market. Australia's leadership in high-quality physical office spaces, combined with their current focus on measurement and performance, makes them an excellent example for other regions wrestling with how to address current health and sustainability issues in the workplace.

As evidenced by the fallout of the pandemic, however, a workplace consists of more than the physical office and leadership in environmental design. Organisational culture, leadership, and social relationships are crucial factors that can influence the health, well-being, and performance of both employees and the organisation as a whole. Global data indicates that factors such as psychological safety, diversity, equity, and inclusion, and an environment of care and support, are also emerging as critical factors in the workplace (Abid et al., 2016; Office of the U.S. Surgeon General, 2022; Platform on Sustainable Finance, 2022; Rozovsky, 2015). Despite an appreciation for much of the physical workplace factors by Australian industry, including psychosocial and organisational factors in the understanding of high-performing workplaces has not been mainstream. This is a missed opportunity to understand the full range of factors that impact health, well-being, and performance in Australian workplaces. Understanding how our workplaces and our organisational structures can support the health and well-being of our workforce can potentially drive both short- and long-term public health outcomes and lead to a happier, healthier, and more engaged and inclusive workforce.

A/Prof. Christhina Candido, Iva Durakovic, and Dr Samin Marzban have been working to understand these global and local factors impacting workplaces for over a decade. Their pioneering work in Australian and international workplaces has bridged research and industry and provided concrete data exploring multiple facets of the worker–organisation office relationship. A/Prof. Candido's work on post-occupancy evaluation in particular has evolved over the last decade from overseeing some of Australia's first research-led post-occupancy evaluation surveys focused on indoor environment quality (IEQ) to more recently being able to show links between IEQ factors and self-reported health, engagement, and productivity outcomes (Candido et al., 2019). As a pre-approved survey provider for the International WELL Building Institute (IWBI) and the first research lab teaching WELL coursework, she and her team have provided essential datapoints and evidence to support the global WELL Building standard, including the largest case studies to date of WELL Certified buildings within the APAC region (Candido et al., 2020; Marzban et al., 2023).

The national leadership of all three editors is also evidenced by their ongoing contributions to standards and rating tools across Australia. Internationally, they have been selected to participate in IWBI's advisories of global experts, tasked to inform the development of the WELL Building Standard, and identify current trends in research and industry. These have ranged from identification of key research and implementation gaps for healthy buildings in the *Global Research Agenda* to strategies for tracking, measuring, and reporting health across scales in the *12 Competencies for Measuring Health and Well-being for Human and Social Capital*. Importantly, all three editors recognise the significant opportunity of improving our workplaces to be environments where people can thrive and are recognised globally for their expertise.

Given this level of expertise, it is not surprising that this book addresses key gaps in knowledge using a holistic approach to high-performance workplaces that blends evidence on the physical *and* psychosocial work environments. This approach is essential to understand what constitutes a high-performance workplace. It is also needed to translate those findings into the kinds of data industry needs to show that an investment in high-performing workplaces can lead to financial, health, and social benefits for organisations and communities. Given the current pressures on real estate, organisations, and workers themselves to balance performance with social impact and well-being, this contribution to the field of workplaces studies could not be better timed.

Angela Loder and Jack Noonan

References

Abid, G., Zahra, I., & Ahmed, A. (2016). Promoting thriving at work and waning turnover intention: A relational perspective. *Future Business Journal*, *2*(2), 127–137.

Candido, C., Marzban, S., Haddad, S., Mackey, M., & Loder, A. (2020). Designing healthy workspaces: Results from Australian certified open-plan offices, facilities, *39*(5/6), 411–433. https://doi.org/10.1108/F-02-2020-0018

Candido, C., Thomas, L., Haddad, S., Zhang, F., Mackey, M., & Ye, W. (2019). Designing activity-based workspaces: Satisfaction, productivity and physical activity. *Building Research & Information*, *47*(3), 275–289.

de Oliveira, S. F. C., Aletta, F., & Kang, J. (2023). Self-rated health implications of noise for open-plan office workers: An overview of the literature. *Building Acoustics*, *30*(2), 1351010X231152841. https://doi.org/10.1177/1351010X231152841

Gensler. (n.d.). *What we've learned about focus in the workplace*. https://www.gensler.com/doc/download-what-weve-learned-about-focus-in-the-workplace-pdf.pdf

Marzban, S., Candido, C., Avazpour, B., Mackey, M., Zhang, F., Engelen, L., & Tjondronegoro, D. (2023). The potential of high-performance workplaces for boosting worker productivity, health, and creativity: A comparison between WELL and non-WELL certified environments. *Building and Environment*, *243*(7), 110708. https://www.sciencedirect.com/science/article/pii/S0360132323007357

Office of the U.S. Surgeon General. (2022). *Workplace mental health and well-being*. Office of the U.S. Surgeon General. Retrieved November 23, from https://www.hhs.gov/sites/default/files/workplace-mental-health-well-being.pdf

Platform on Sustainable Finance. (2022). *Final report on social taxonomy*. Retrieved October 4, 2023, from https://finance.ec.europa.eu/system/files/2022-08/220228-sustainable-finance-platform-finance-report-social-taxonomy_en.pdf

Rozovsky, J. (2015). *The five keys to a successful Google team*. Google rework. Retrieved November 22, from https://rework.withgoogle.com/blog/five-keys-to-a-successful-google-team/

ABOUT THIS BOOK

Workplaces are complex ecosystems, playing a critical role in the success of organisations and workers. Workplace experience, well-being, and sustained human performance have been key priorities for organisations, with workplaces striving to create the optimal physical, cultural, and operational environments for people to thrive. Decades of research documenting the evolution and transformation have shown that culture, leadership, and social capital are key to sustaining organisational talent, innovation, and productivity. Places where people work from enable, support, and represent these critical elements by providing the physical and digital infrastructure needed by workers to perform their activities.

The pandemic has challenged them all, highlighting the inadequacies of ways of working and workplaces that were already fast emerging and accelerating trends around increased flexibility, health and well-being, and workspace design and performance. The collective experiences during the pandemic have fundamentally challenged a decades-long business model built around a 9–5 work week able to bring masses of people to our cities – everyday, rain or shine, they would be there. This deterministic approach to a static, spatial-temporal work arrangement has profound ramifications to workers' financial commitments (mortgages, childcare), health and well-being (commute times, stress, burn-out) and overall work–life balance (or lack thereof). Further, this model also greatly influenced cities' infrastructure and their subsequent environmental footprint, liveability, and the business ecosystems built around central business districts (CBDs). Having workers returning to centralised offices is pivotal to the economic recovery of cities, and therein lies the challenge of closing the great divide between thriving, resilient workplaces discussed in this book and the workplaces which some have called the age of 9–5 office obsolescence.

From a way of working perspective, the forced disconnection from the physical workplace experienced by knowledge workers globally has illuminated how critical intangible factors are to the success of our ways of working, and the value physical workspace holds in supporting the physiological and psychological functions of employees. In many ways, the appetite for more flexibility and autonomy was already there, being constantly captured in academic and especially industry-led research focusing on workforce needs from different generations. For instance, millennials, the first digital natives, were under the spotlight because of their expectations, attitudes, and beliefs towards work, including an unapologetic need for flexibility and wiliness to change jobs to find a position with better work–life balance. Not surprisingly, when faced with the prospect of fulfilling their needs for flexibility, as the global working from home and elsewhere experiment enabled, many are finding it difficult to let go. Whilst asymmetrical and country-specific, our collective experiences have raised awareness of the importance of communities, work or otherwise, to our psychological well-being, sense of safety, and resilience. For employees, the disconnection from the office has illuminated its role in supporting their professional identities, social connections, and daily transition rituals, diminishing their sense of purpose and belonging, leaving simply the work itself exposed bare for evaluation. By allowing workers to have more control of when they work, they managed to better balance their individual needs whilst maintaining their productivity, though this has sometimes come at a cost to their health and well-being due to the increased time spent seated and attending online meetings, challenges in consolidating a routine, and other aspects. At the same time, managers are challenged to find an approach for navigating the new ways of working and reconciling individual, team, and organisational needs.

From a physical environment perspective, the pandemic prompted generations of open-plan office natives to experience the benefits of cellular offices when it comes to creating a bespoke environment that suits their needs. This hyper-personalisation made an average home equal and sometimes better than a premium-graded office in delivering people with environments they can concentrate in and perform individual work. This has fundamentally shifted workers' expectations when returning to the office and with it the baseline of performance – what was deemed a nice thing to have before is now very much a must have when it comes to experience and performance of workspaces. The pandemic is the biggest disruptor in workplace history since the internet. At this stage, the evidence shows that the very need of workplaces is not going away, but its shape and size is likely to change, and the type of office people would like to go back to (if at all) will receive further thought. In the evolving landscape of ways of working, leaders need to find approaches to effectively navigate and manage the flexible parameters of when, where, and how people want and need to work, to be truly inclusive of an ever diverse, connected, and globalised workforce. We now find ourselves in a landscape where workers hold organisations accountable to action and decisions which deliver positive impact on people, society, environment, and economy. The understanding of what makes workplaces high-performance is more important than ever before.

Design is a powerful problem solver and critical conduit for the translation of knowledge (research), needs (organisational, functional, and experiential/human) and requirements (performance) into tangible physical places we occupy. Workplaces are powerful tools of work for organisations, teams, and individuals enabling professional networks, communities, identities, and cultures to thrive, but without skilful design solutions to fit the puzzle pieces together they cannot function effectively. By understanding the factors critical to high-performance workplaces and the mechanisms through which they interact with human motivations, behaviours, and experience, we can more effectively apply this knowledge to create the responsive, supportive, resilient, and sustainable environments that the broader issues of society, economy, and planet demand now and in the future.

This book introduces the fundamentals behind high-performance workplaces and the challenges of harnessing human, environmental, and organisational aspects that can make a positive contribution to workers' satisfaction, productivity, and health. This publication builds on a programme of applied research led by authors which is aimed at understanding the synergies between the design, performance, and experience of spaces; knowledge which is pertinent and applicable to workplace researchers, designers, and organisations globally. When combined, chapters provide a road map to achieve high-performance in static, untethered, and adaptive workplaces, including reflections on the needs of the unshackled workforce post-pandemic. This book places research findings and case studies under the spotlight, celebrating the work of Australian-based academics and industry professionals, especially women from diverse backgrounds. The combination of industry and academic voices reinforces the authenticity of this book and its relevance to other stakeholders from the property and design industry, students, government, and the community in general. It is the fourth publication of the Transdisciplinary Workplace Research and Management Series led by Prof. Rianne Appel-Meulenbroek and Dr Vitalija Danivska.

The book is structured around four parts: physical environment factors, human factors, organisational management factors, and case studies. The first three focus on introducing fundamentals behind each factor, why they matter, and how they contribute to achieving a high-performance workplace from the workers' perspective, including reflections around productivity, health, and well-being. The fourth and final part of the book focuses on selected case studies of workplaces built and occupied before or after the pandemic, demonstrating how high-performance workplaces can be achieved in practice.

Christhina Candido, Iva Durakovic, and Samin Marzban

ABOUT WAYS OF WORKING

'Ways of working' can be understood as the manner in which work is done by teams and individuals to meet organisational priorities and needs. The evolution of the contemporary workplace where such work has been conducted has been well documented, especially in its transformation from factory production to the intensively paper-based administration of colonial mercantile and banking settings through to the open-plan landscape of the offices of 50 years ago. The invention of the lift, air-conditioning, and the elevator simultaneously led to the possibility of stackable deep floor plans contained within office towers as symbols of corporate image and identity. Since the turn of the century, workers' mobility prompted by advances in technology has enabled further changes in the location, purpose, and design of the contemporary workplace. Throughout these phases, there has been a symbiotic relationship between the development of ways of working within the office, organisations, and the design and development of workplaces, with important consequences for the overall performance of workplaces.

Adoption of various models of working have far-reaching implications that go beyond the physical workplace to include individuals, culture, and the broader environment and as such requires careful consideration. Indeed, at the organisational level, a high-performance workplace is not only functional and fit for the purpose of facilitating the way in which work needs to be carried out, but one that affords and supports workers' productivity and health whilst enabling a business to achieve their environmental, social, and governance (ESG) ambitions. Additionally, at the worker level, ways of working can have a tremendous impact on how workers interact with other colleagues and where they work from and when. To be effective, the adoption of any way of working requires a negotiation of the interests of all parties involved.

The recent pandemic has resulted in a step change or evolution in how and where work is done – there has been a significant shift from focus on the central physical workplace to the formal workplace becoming part of an ecosystem of places to conduct one's daily work-related tasks. Pandemic-related restrictions prompted a seismic shift in ways of working: knowledge workers were forced out of office headquarters and into their homes or elsewhere. Since then, workers experienced changes in where, when, and how they worked, enabled by synchronous and asynchronous ways of communicating with colleagues at a scale and pace never seen before. Once unshackled from a '9–5', centralised office routine, workers have been reluctant to relinquish the freedom of choice to work from where and when suits them best. This new chapter in ways of working invites organisations to revisit the purpose of their 'purpose-built' office premises and reconcile individual and collective needs.

This introduction commences with some background and highlights the drivers of change regarding new ways of working. The evolution in ways of working and change is described, commencing with the fixed address and fixed desking models through to the current practice of hybrid and distributed working. Through the evolution of ways of working both in the international and the Australian workplace contexts, we have seen many organisations seize the opportunity to address key agenda items of sustainability and the health and well-being of employees. As such, implications and impacts of ways of working models are presented in this introduction through the lenses of individual well-being, organisational impacts, and the broader environment. Finally, recommendations offering practical considerations for the way forward are also discussed.

Evolution of the workplace landscape

While individual organisations may prioritise different aspects – key considerations in relation to workplace location have typically related to effective utilisation of resources, including the physical footprint of the office space, rental and real estate costs, tapping into better city or precinct scale infrastructure, getting the best out of employee time, and managing office rents, as well as ensuring employee retention. Additionally, ambitions for a high-performance workplace mean that it is imperative to consider how ways of working influence communication and connection, utilisation of resources, leadership, team collaboration, worker flexibility and choice, worker health and well-being, staff learning and development, and social cohesion and inclusion (see Figure 0.1). In this section we consider how the evolution of ways of working have altered the workplace landscape to raise challenges and opportunities for high-performance workplaces into the future.

Static working

The static way of working where people are bound to a specific location and undertake work mostly synchronously with their colleagues has been present from the birth of the office. This discreet spatio-temporal nature of the office has had significant impact on how the built environment of our cities is designed and experienced by people, with long-lasting ramifications to where people work and live, their commute times, and the overall urban infrastructure needed to support and get people in and out of central business districts (CBDs).

Indeed, the early CBD office workplace was characterised as the go-to location where work was undertaken. The physical location, as well as the nature of the place where work is undertaken, has been inextricably linked to the ways of working within organisations at multiple scales, and a number of shifts have occurred in recent years. In Australia, the drive to distribute employment centres around transport nodes, reduce commuting for employees, attendant CO_2 emissions (Thomas et al., 2015), and attract workers and companies with better infrastructure has also seen the development of a number of work precincts and technology and innovation hubs in major metropolitan cities and regional centres.

In addition to a fixed geographical address, settings within the office were developed on the assumption of continuous desk-based tasks and the allocation of one desk for every employee. At the office fit-out scale, static working styles means that people are bound to a given location and they develop their work mostly from this same location. This way of working is often observed in cellular offices and earlier versions of open-plan offices. These localised workplaces are often

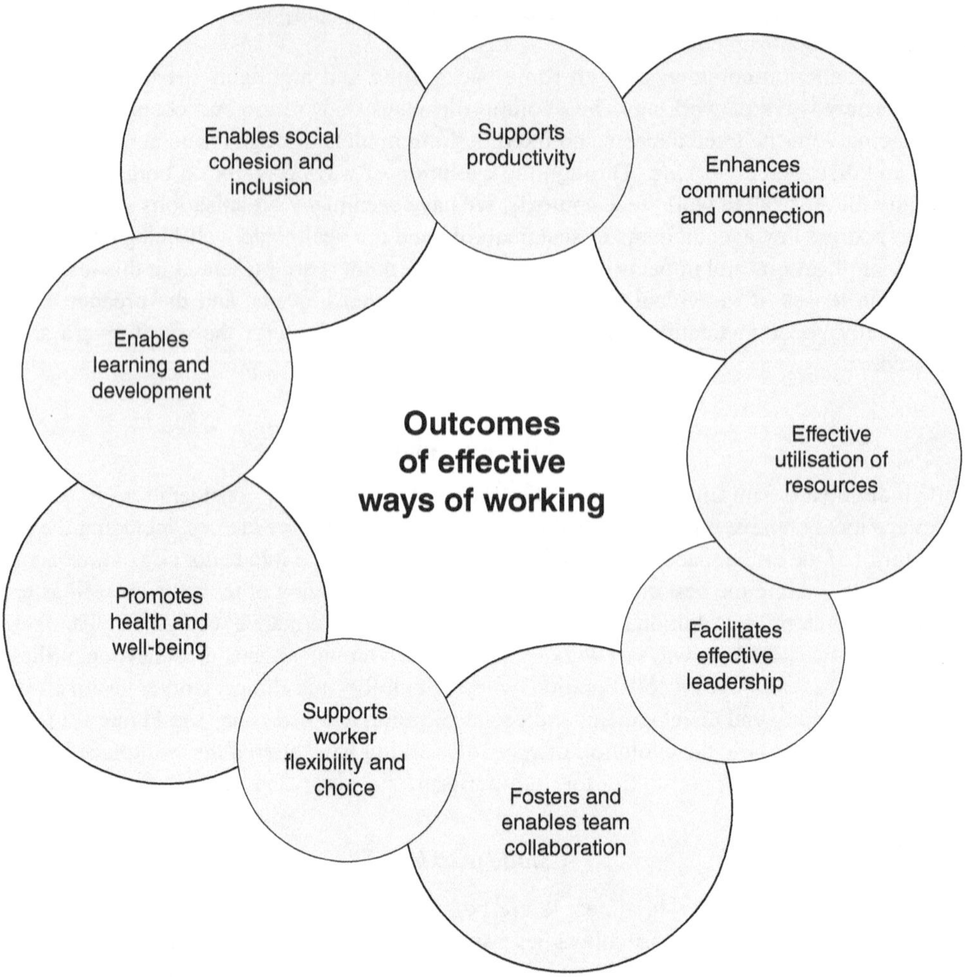

Figure 0.1 High-performance outcomes of effective ways of working.

characterised by clocking in and clocking out at fixed times, extensive paperwork, and tasks completed in person alongside other colleagues.

By performing several working tasks from the same location, workers and organisations maintained the expectation that work completed within a 'line of sight' and heightened co-ordination would yield better performance. However, with the mainstreaming of open-plan offices, there was also the rise of the evidence of the unsuitability of these open-plan offices to support organisational and individual needs. These included concerns of noise and distractions on the one hand and the need to facilitate collaboration on the other, which led to the need for customisation of space to suit tasks. Moreover, as more of the workforce engaged in both casual and formal meetings and off-site tasks away from one's desk, it has been estimated that desk occupancy is often as low as 60–70% in offices designed to support static ways of working. This raises several questions about the cost-effectiveness and resource utilisation from a space perspective.

The reliance on office-bound and synchronous communications raises challenges when implementing diverse and inclusive workplaces. By having to commute to office headquarters every day or most days at set schedules, workers have had to arrange their lives around the time they are expected to be at the office. This could be challenging for primary carers, people with disabilities, and many other workers, with some finding static ways of working a barrier to their participation in the paid workforce.

Whilst many forms of flexible working arrangements, technology, and ways of working and collaborating remotely are not new, working practices did not change enough to allow workers to have more autonomy about when and where they work within some organisations. The expectation of workers being tethered to office headquarters remains the backbone of static ways of working as adopted by many organisations and leaders. As discussed next, the pandemic has been a catalyst for questioning this assumption. However, static ways of working are likely to still be prevalent, either through mandates, workers' preferences, and/or other motivators. Unless fully subscribed, static open-plan offices as we have known them are likely to underperform and will need to be reconceptualised to be more adaptable to changing needs to maintain currency.

Untethered working

The decoupling of the employee from a 'fixed address' also facilitated alternate ways of conceptualising work. Untethered ways of working shift the focus from location to tasks. Whilst workers may be still bound to the temporal aspects of office headquarters, they are free to choose to work from a setting or space that is best suited to their task at hand. Going beyond the undistinguished model of 'hot-desking' that was developed primarily as a space-efficiency measure to combat the aforementioned low occupancy rates of static offices, Activity-Based Working (ABW) environments are developed to align the various workplace activities with the most supportive tools and spaces, with the focus on team needs rather than individual work points. This type of flexible working enhances workers' autonomy and empowers the individual. However, some find it difficult to adapt to this 'free address' model, as it can reduce the sense of belonging, and the perceived loss of line of sight poses challenges to mentoring and team building if not implemented and managed effectively.

Research undertaken through a host of Post-Occupancy Evaluation (POE) studies indicated the best outcomes for productivity are achieved with an integrated design approach to workplaces that is cognisant of user needs for getting their work done effectively. For example, research undertaken at the University of Technology Sydney between 2009 and 2011 tracked over 2,500 employees as they moved from a conventional open-plan office into their new high-performance office and sites of one of Australia's first ABW environments (GBCA, 2013). The transition was managed through pilots, mockups, and focus groups to communicate and co-design shifts from private offices to open plan, removal of fixed addressing, and introduction of ABW. Participants in the study showed an average of 15% net increase in perceived productivity for employees who had moved into the new building. Importantly the research also underlined the need to continue the user-responsive approach during the ongoing management of the workplace once it is in operation to gain the best results for a high-performance workplace. The case study in Chapter 20 also highlights how adoption of ABW as part of a holistic workplace strategy that allows for evolving work and workstyles can enable resilience and HPW.

As more organisations test and customise the activity-based environments, many are finding a hybrid model of neighbourhoods within the office efficient, as it enables better approaches for team building and collaboration. For example, employees in a department may remain grouped together but with flexible seating and shared amenities, such as project-based spaces, libraries, and breakout spaces. Careful design and management of the physical space that supports this way of working is critical and discussed in detail in Chapter 1, 'Office Layout'. Other aspects that are critical relate to the provision of enabling infrastructure via digital technology and space management as well as the development of workplace culture and practices to foster more collaborative ways of working while also mitigating unwanted interruption (Candido et al., 2021).

Adaptive working and implications of ways of working post-COVID

Even before the onset of COVID-19, new ways of working wherein 'employees are able to work independent of time, place and organisation, supported by a flexible work environment which is facilitated by information technologies' (de Leede, 2016) were already gaining traction as an effective way of procuring a workforce. In addition to the simple distinction between working from home and in the 'office', a number of alternate work locations have evolved in most Australian cities. These range from the neighbourhood café and co-working sites with shared amenities, to carefully curated hub and spokes models where the spokes are envisioned as bespoke satellite work locations aimed at attracting workforces from a wider geographical pool.

Nonetheless, accelerated by the government lockdown restrictions during the pandemic, workers and organisations experienced the large-scale potential of untethered working and the transformation of the workplace from being a primary or central location for all employees to attend to one that is greatly distributed or decentralised. In its wake, many organisations have adopted varied blended or hybrid arrangements where their employees work partly in the office or remotely from home or other locations.

In 2023 many organisations are juggling to balance organisational goals with individual needs of employees in an uncertain and somewhat 'post-COVID' environment. Notwithstanding the flexibility and autonomy discussed earlier that untethered working offers employees, the shift from synchronous (online or face-to-face) modes of working to asynchronous modes results in a loss of immediacy and a risk to overall effectiveness.

As many organisations shift to adopt some form of hybrid and blended ways of working, they are grappling to achieve the right balance between face-to-face interactions and enabling potential for remote working, and to develop the technology and infrastructure to support this. Forward-thinking companies have begun trialling different models of working – some are real estate led with set days in the office, while others are more flexible as individuals are empowered to nominate the location that best supports their work requirements.

It is widely accepted that some form or type of hybrid working is now 'standard practice' and now part of the working week for professional workers. These models will have mixed impacts which require careful consideration to ensure both the organisation and individuals are supported and can thrive as part of a high-performance workplace.

Studies (Rothe, 2020) suggest many respondents report they are more productive working from home than in the office. It is now recognised that many individual tasks and some processing work can be done anywhere and anytime. Advances in technology for communication, record keeping, and digital storage have meant that many tasks can equally or more effectively be done in virtual or remote settings. Research has also suggested virtual and digital ways of working offer potential health benefits and improved employee satisfaction.

Although not entirely written off, as feared by some (Berliner, 2020), the purpose of the physical office has fundamentally changed because of this distributed or hybrid way of working. It has been recognised that team and collective work can be most effective when conducted in the office. In relation to supporting effective ways of working, face-to-face interactions at the workplace are noted to be critical for ensuring social connectedness, effective collaboration, staff development, mentoring, and team building (see Chapter 16 for more on sense of belonging and professional identity), as well as certain types of work, especially creative and strategic negotiations. Research on individual needs within the office has also illustrated the need for quiet or private spaces for concentrative work or virtual calls.

Technology tools that support and enable this new hybrid or distributed working are yet to fully adapt. There is a clear need for software and hardware that allows users to have an effective and equal experience for those in the office and those that are remote. Industry research by consultants Six Ideas by Dexus and Warren and Mahoney found that current tech hardware is limiting the benefits of effective hybrid collaboration. In addition to inadequate tools and spaces that have not yet adapted, it has been identified that skills to use technology and interact in a hybrid format are limited.

Ways of working: key considerations

The evolution of workplaces has shown there are varied and diverse influences that impact the effectiveness and success of a high-performance workplace. It is recognised that post-COVID, for many organisations high-performance workplaces will continue to involve a purpose-built physical office location. For those adopting hybrid and distributed working it becomes necessary to pay attention to the wider ecosystem that constitutes the high-performance workplace. The following section focuses on factors from the human to global perspective. Current ways of working have well-documented impacts on health and well-being. A more distributed workforce brings new challenges for organisations to ensure collaboration, knowledge transfer, and a cohesive culture remain effective. Both of these individual and organisational considerations are part of the wider environmental impacts requiring attention and holistic solutions.

Health and well-being impacts

Hybrid or distributed working presents new challenges and opportunities when it comes to health and well-being, as employees are less 'visible' to their peers and managers and the remote working environment is difficult to control and monitor (Ekpanyaskul & Padungtod, 2021). A recent study of 1009 full-time Australian Workers (The Wellbeing Lab, 2022) reports that workers' resilience has waned, with 68.5% feeling like they were burning out at work. In 2021, 53.1% ticked the set response of 'living well despite struggles', which has reduced to 43% in Sept. 2022. In addition, 62.4% of hybrid workers reported the psychosocial hazard of 'unachievable job demands' (The Wellbeing Lab, 2022). A negative outcome of being distributed is the inability to physically see if employees are feeling overwhelmed by workload or other work factors which could be addressed by intentional and empathetic leadership. This report emphasises the need for multi-professional approaches to workplace well-being and the need to recognise that perceptions, experiences, and behaviours are diverse.

It is well-documented that the number of knowledge workers increases relative to other sectors of the economy These include the health implications of sedentary work indoors (Sugiyama et al.,

2020) as well as a number of measures adopted to promote active/health-focused ways of working, including sit to stand; encouraging movement within the workday through change in location, use of stairs, and access to nature'; emphasising the benefits of indoor environmental quality, such as access to fresh air and natural light, all of which are noted to improve worker health and satisfaction (Aristizabal et al., 2019). Many of these elements are discussed throughout Chapters 4–10 of this book. Whereas these aspects were solely addressed within the purview of purpose-built offices until now, the shift to working from home and other locations calls for better education and a shared responsibility between employees and the organisation to ensure safe and healthy working practices wherever work is undertaken. Ways of working can also play an instrumental role in work–life balance and autonomy of time. The reduction in the daily commute with the advent of hybrid or remote working allows many to engage with their families and have time for health-promotive activities (Figure 0.2). However, evidence suggests that people are replacing the commute time with longer working hours (Davis & Green, 2020). Blurring the line between work and home life has inherent pitfalls; health may be impacted because working from home can reduce social contact and cause social isolation, a risk factor for many health conditions (Meister, 2019). Remote working means that some employees need to balance their caring responsibilities in their homes, disproportionally affecting women (McPhail, 2020; Meister, 2019; Figure 0.3).

Hybrid working has also increased the levels of individual autonomy for many. Better outcomes have been observed where employees perceived to have greater control over the physical workplace, especially when things are not working well. From a strict control on working hours where requisite hours were meticulously clocked, workplaces had already recognised the flexibility in work hours, job sharing, and potential for some level of remote working. The pandemic has created a further shift in workplaces underlining the development of trust and empowerment of employees to undertake their tasks without having to be seen to be supervised or managed and where autonomy over time is also highly valued.

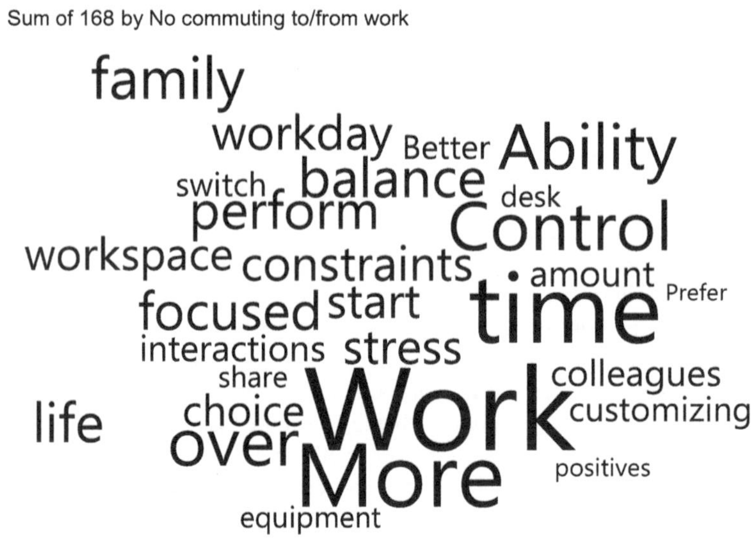

Figure 0.2 Word frequency count of 'Best aspects of flexible working arrangements during the COVID-19 pandemic'.

Source: SHE COVID survey database, 2023. Not published

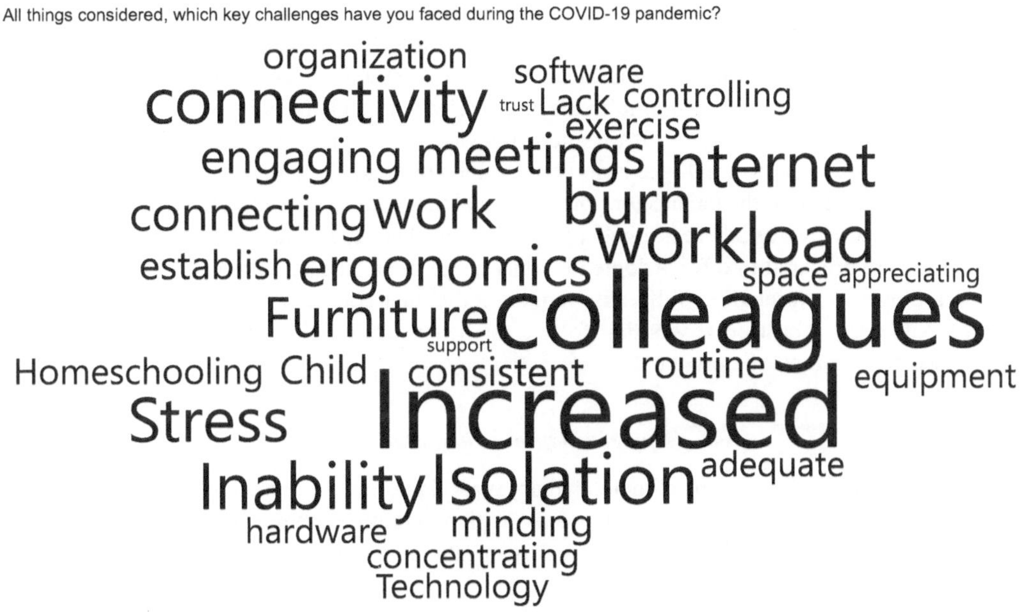

Figure 0.3 Word frequency count of 'Challenges of flexible working arrangements during the COVID-19 pandemic'.

Source: SHE COVID survey database, 2023. Not published

Organisational impacts

The challenge to develop communication and collaboration in relation to virtual ways of working is evident. Not only is there the equity and access issues in relation to network connectivity and ability to use tools provided (Jain et al., 2021) but also the need to create alternate approaches for social connections and participation. This is increasingly important as organisations seek to create truly diverse and inclusive workplaces in the absence of full-time face to face.

There are also concerns that company culture and team cohesion is negatively impacted when individuals are remote for extended periods of time. Tech organisations such as Atlassian have adopted their 'Work Anywhere' strategy, allowing individuals to work from any location for up to 90 days at a time. However, it recognises the value of teams to be together in a structured and organised manner. Atlassian has established a programme for teams to organise and host purposeful engagements. Team leaders are provided with skills, suggested formats, and budgets to host varied team events from social connection to problem-solving workshops (Atlassian Presents: Work Life).

These new ways of working or models require a different set of management and leadership skills. If teams are distributed, ensuring engagement and cohesion remains within a team and across an organisation requires thoughtful planning and an empathetic approach. Some leaders have highlighted the need to move from 'line-of-sight' management to leadership centred on outcomes and trust. It is now recognised that high-value work and tasks can be completed in a supportive home or remote environment, while activities such as mentoring and ideating are more effective in person.

Pioneering work in post-occupancy evaluation in green buildings in Australia (Leaman et al., 2007; Candido et al, 2016) established a longstanding culture of understanding and providing for employee needs and priorities in relation to the ways of working and high-performance workplaces. Research in Australian workplaces over this period (Candido et al., 2018; Candido et al., 2021) has repeatedly shown the value of user participation and consultation/co-design between organisations, design teams, and employees, especially where changes in working models were envisaged. Such approaches are all the more relevant in the present unchartered post-COVID scenario. The voice of the employee is arguably valued more today than ever, and many organisations are seeking to find the balance or optimal model that addresses the needs of the organisation and individuals. However, there is a widening disconnect between what employees want and what companies are prepared to offer. Adopted models range from office-focused, structured, or team-based arrangement through to fully autonomous individual choice. Ultimately, an agile culture with flexible and robust processes that fosters resilience while being nimble to adapt to future unforeseen changes will be pivotal.

Environmental considerations

In the contemporary context of climate change, workplaces need to be environmentally sustainable, resilient, and adaptable to changing needs. With numerous extreme weather events, concerns have also been heightened post-COVID as organisations compete for the hearts and minds of environmentally savvy millennials.

Until recently, designing and operating workplaces to respond to environmental aspects and to ways of working have largely occurred in isolation of each other. Attention with respect to sustainable ways of working within a workplace has typically been limited to organisational office practices, such as the use of paper, waste recycling, food composting, and reduction of travel miles for work/meetings.

Attention to the size of the office footprint and consequential impact on embodied/operation carbon and CO_2/employee has meant that efficiency of the floorplate is also recognised as a significant factor. While untethered forms of working offer a reduction in floor plate, the low utilisation of offices post-COVID poses further challenges. Low utilisation of space, especially within a fully air-conditioned contiguous floor plate, indicates the further challenge hybrid ways of working place on resource efficiency and sustainability of the physical office building.

Post-pandemic, the churn and environmental impacts from changing fit outs, especially where customised layouts are highly inflexible, is also exacerbated. Varied activities such as casual interactions, taking breaks, and some forms of desk working, meeting, and collaboration no longer require stringent environmental conditions compared to concentrated work. This recognition, coupled with the ability of employees to exercise adaptive practices such as relocating work location and adjusting clothing has enabled Atlassian to propose a drastically low-energy solution where 10% of its office tower net lettable area (NLA) will be outdoor protected parks, and a further 15% will be naturally ventilated spaces, while still offering regulated environment across 55% of its NLA (Holcim, 2021).

Conclusion

Over the past decades, we have witnessed a sea change in the workplace and ways in which work is undertaken. Organisations have evolved from fixed locations with hierarchical management focused on productivity and organisational gains to an ecosystem of places that encompass individual needs, with leadership focused on outcomes rather than process.

It is clear that the rapid changes of the pandemic years have meant many organisations have had to navigate uncharted territory. Embracing change and adopting best practice when designing and implementing a high-performance workplace relies on a strategic foundation or framework that is holistic and flexible for continuous evolution and adaptation. This framework encompasses all aspects of the workplace, including the people, the spaces where they work, and the tools required to support a resilient organisation today and in the future.

Whether in determining particular modes of working or adapting to further and inevitable changes in the workplace landscape, there is a need for employers to understand their employees' needs and interrogate assumptions. The necessity for robust research and collaboration between researchers and the industry to understand the ramifications of changes and collaborate to share knowledge and insights is now more important than ever. As practitioners and researchers in the field, we believe a collaborative approach built on evidence from the ground and robust research is critical to creating resilient responsive and supportive high-performance workplaces.

When developing a framework for effective ways of working focused on resilience and agility in a high-performance workplace, consider the following:

Leena Thomas and Kirsten Brown

References

Aristizabal, S., Porter, P., Clements, N., Campanella, C., Zhang, R., Hovde, K., & Lam, C. (2019). Conducting human-centered building science at the well living lab. *Technology Architecture + Design*, *3*(2), 161–173. https://doi.org/10.1080/24751448.2019.1640535

Atlassian presents: Work life. Retrieved March 29, 2023, from https://events.atlassian.com/worklife.

Berliner, U. (2020). *Get a comfortable chair: Permanent work from home is coming*. Retrieved March 2, 2022, from https://www.npr.org/2020/06/22/870029658/get-a-comfortable-chair-permanent-work-from-home-is-coming

Candido, C., Gocer, O., Marzban, S., Gocer, K., Thomas, L., Zhang, F., Gou, Z., Mackey, M., Engelen, L., & Tjondronegoro, D. (2021). Occupants' satisfaction and perceived productivity in open-plan offices designed to support activity-based working: Findings from different industry sectors. *Journal of Corporate Real Estate*, *23*(2), 106–129. https://doi.org/10.1108/JCRE-06-2020-0027

Candido, C., Thomas, L. E., Zhang, F., Haddad, S., & Mackey, M. (2018). The unvarnished truth about ABW. *EcoLibrium(R)*, *17*(6), 46–49. https://www.airah.org.au/EcoLibrium/2018/Ecolibrium_July_2018.aspx

Candido, C. M., Kim, J., de Dear, R., & Thomas, L. (2016). BOSSA: A multidimensional post-occupancy evaluation tool. *Building Research and Information (Print)*, *44*(2), 214–228.

Davis, M. F., & Green, J. (2020). *Three hours longer, the pandemic workday has obliterated work-life balance*. Retrieved November 20, 2020, from https://www.bloomberg.com/news/articles/2020-04-23/working-from-home-in-covid-era-means-three-more-hours-on-the-job

de Leede, J. (2016). *New ways of working practices: Antecedents and outcomes*. Emerald Publishing Limited.

Ekpanyaskul, C., & Padungtod, C. (2021). Occupational health problems and lifestyle changes among novice working-from-home workers amid the COVID-19 pandemic. *Safety and Health at Work*, *12*(3), 384–389. https://doi.org/10.1016/j.shaw.2021.01.010

GBCA Green Building Council Australia. (2013). *Evolution – A year in sustainable building* (pp. 17, 45). https://www.gbca.org.au/docs/evolution2013.pdf

Holcim. (2021). *Global Holcim awards entry – High-performance tower in Australia*. https://d1f6o4licw9har.cloudfront.net/flip/A21/High-Performance-Tower-in-Australia/index.html

Jain, T., Currie, G., & Aston, L. (2022). COVID and working from home: Long-term impacts and psychosocial determinants. *Transportation Research Part A: Policy and Practice*, *156*, 52–68. https//doi.org/10.1016/j.tra.2021.12.007

Leaman, A., Thomas, L. E., & Vandenberg, M. (2007). 'Green' buildings: What Australian users are saying. *EcoLibrium(R)*, *6*, 22–30.

McPhail, R. (2020). *Workplaces after COVID-19: Impacts of working from home on people, productivity and the planet*. https://www.griffith.edu.au/griffith-business-school/new-thinking-for-the-new-economy/blog/post-covid-workplaces

Meister, J. C. (2019). *Survey: What employees want most from their workspaces*. Retrieved March 29, 2023, from https://hbr.org/2019/08/survey-what-employees-want-most-from-their-workspaces

Rothe, P. (2020, August 2). The wellbeing imperative. *The Leesman Review*, *29*. Retrieved July 2020, from https://www.leesmanindex.com/the-wellbeing-imperative/

SHE POE dataset. (2023). *Sustainable and healthy environments post-occupancy evaluation dataset*. SHE Lab (not published).

Sugiyama, T., Hadgraft, N., Clark, B. K., Dunstan, D. W., & Owen, N. (2020). Sitting at work & waist circumference – A cross-sectional study of Australian workers. *Preventive Medicine*, *141*, 106243–106243. https://doi.org/10.1016/j.ypmed.2020.106243

Thomas, L. E., Rickwood, P., & Dilevska, J. (2015). The carbon cost of work-impacts of office building and commuting energy in Sydney workplaces. *Urban Policy and Research*, *33*(3), 340–361. https://doi.org/10.1080/08111146.2015.1029119

The Wellbeing Lab. (2022). *Workplace report: The state of wellbeing in Australian workplaces*. https://www.ahri.com.au/wp-content/uploads/wellbeinglab_workplace_report_australia_2019-2021.pdf

PART I

Physical environment considerations

DOI: 10.1201/9781003328728-1
This chapter has been made available under a CC-BY-NC-ND 4.0 license.

1
OFFICE DESIGN

Christhina Candido, Behnaz Avazpour, and Iva Durakovic

> If the average home can support workers better than a premium-graded workplace, we know the baseline needs to be lifted.
>
> – *Authors*

Introduction

There is no denying that office design and layout have dramatically changed over the years. This transformation was facilitated by advances in technology, including Wi-Fi, computers and mobile devices, which then enabled workers to be unshackled from where and when they work, working from anywhere, anytime, in office or elsewhere. These changes did not happen overnight, and workers had to progressively transition and adapt to office layouts as they transformed.

First versions of open-plan offices were largely hierarchical, adopting a layout that identified and segregated workers depending on their position within the food chain. Junior workers would be assigned a desk at small, non-private, open environments. Mid-level workers would be assigned a cubicle, likely with high partitions to allow for some visual privacy and sense of ownership over their desk and space within the office. Finally, senior staff would be allocated an office, with a door and walls, often a nice view and the opportunity to organise and furnish the space to suit their preferences and needs – top dog gets the corner office kind of thing. This design segregated workers and the once abundance of physical barriers (i.e. partitions or wall) were deemed not to be conducive to learning, collaborative and innovative exchanges between workers. The response was to remove physical barriers and individual offices to introduce open-plan layouts that could facilitate a permanent flow of incidental opportunities for work, to learn from one another, collaborate, and ultimately innovate.

At a later stage, open plan became multizonal, landscaped layouts intended to support a variety of work tasks and activities. By keeping desk ownership intact, these layouts seem to provide a middle-ground transition between full to no ownership of space. More recently, these contemporary open-plan office landscapes were subject to even more curation, and desk ownership was removed to support the activity-based working mindset.

In practice, these changes in office configuration were asymmetrical and were not absorbed by all industry sectors at the same time, hence refraining from mentioning specific dates or decades.

DOI: 10.1201/9781003328728-2

This chapter has been made available under a CC-BY-NC-ND 4.0 license.

Whilst a significant portion of the workforce can be considered open-plan office natives, having never worked from an assigned desk or individual office before the pandemic, many knowledge workers have not transitioned into open-plan configurations yet. As a result, many types and variations of office layouts and landscapes are still present in buildings, and these spaces are likely to continue to evolve, especially after the changes in ways of working and space and use needs after the pandemic.

This chapter explores these changes in workplace layouts over time, from the inception of open-plan office until today. It focuses on how workers use and engage with workplaces from a mobility perspective, exploring the various workstyles and space still present at the time this book was written. Authors explore the concept of workplaces as static, untethered, and adaptive, including the challenges of harnessing the physical infrastructure to achieve high-performance layouts that can make a positive contribution to workers' satisfaction, productivity and health.

The physical evolution of open-plan offices: from static to untethered and then adaptive

Office layouts must support, and are primarily driven by, the functional requirements of the work being done. As such they both closely reflect and impact the ways of working of occupants, their workflows and patterns of movement and interaction within the workplace environment having direct effect on workers' satisfaction, productivity and health. The planning, design and increasing mix of space types/typologies these environments offer is discussed in relation to the evolution of workstyles from static to adaptive in open-plan offices as well as their associated challenges with respect to indoor environmental quality (IEQ), management, occupant satisfaction, productivity and health. Whether static, untethered or adaptive, layouts must continually be allowed to evolve to best support the work tasks intended and reflect the proportions of spaces the workstyles/teams need.

Static

Static offices are those where workers are physically bound to the same location (a room or a desk), thereby expecting to perform their work activities mostly from the same location. These types of offices can be designed as cellular or open plan, and spaces are shared by multiple workers. Open-plan layouts where people work from the same desk are the epitome of static offices. Open-plan offices became the norm for large portions of the workforce over the last few decades. The removal of physical barriers observed in open-plan office landscapes intended to foster incidental collaboration, learning and innovation, with emphasis placed on creating opportunities for interaction and socialization. Since its inception, open-plan office layouts changed through time, moving away from cubicle farms to incorporate multizonal landscapes that could better cater for work activities and tasks, giving rise to a plethora of informal and formal meeting rooms, spaces for concentration, break-out spaces, call booths and other zones. But despite the changes in the physical configuration of these workplaces, one aspect remains intact and that workers are bound to the same location, usually a desk, performing a considerable number of their work tasks from there. And that's perhaps one of the biggest issues when it comes to these offices – when multiple workers attempt to work from a shared space and location clashes will inevitably happen.

The shortcomings of static offices are well known around the globe – just type open-plan office in your browser and see the types of articles returned. Several studies have extensively documented issues around workers' inability to concentrate for sustained periods of time greatly stemming from interruptions from other colleagues (Hodzic et al., 2021; Kaarlela-Tuomaala et al., 2009) and speech intelligibility (Lee & Aletta, 2019; Jahncke & Hallman, 2020). Studies also show the negative effects of lack of visual and acoustic privacy may have on workers' overall dissatisfaction, stress levels and anxiety. Further, dissatisfaction about thermal comfort, glare and Indoor Air Quality are also common. Not surprisingly, research has also documented decrease in perceived productivity (Di Blasio et al., 2019), job satisfaction (Keller et al., 2020) and overall health and well-being (Muzaffar et al., 2020).

Open plan has been used as an umbrella term for as long as the research in this space has been conducted. This needs to change if we ought to address the shortcomings of these environments. Further, despite a wealth of knowledge about issues observed in open-plan offices, shortcomings of the static behaviour are often mute. Understanding and then reporting the layout configuration of the space where findings are coming from is key to move the needle of these spaces. To improve satisfaction in these offices, the overall quality of the interior design and layout is key (Candido, Thomas, et al., 2019). If workers are still bound to the same desk, there should be clarity around the rules of engagement with tasks that can be performed from the workers' desk. Activities that are deemed unsuitable to be performed from their desk should be performed elsewhere, but the layout needs to clearly cater for them, which often does not happen, or workers do not engage with the multiple zones available to them. As such, static layouts need to be checked from time to time to fine-tune work zones and workers' behaviour and needs. Zoning is crucial, and the curation of a multizonal office landscape needs to be considerate of the amount of time people spend at their desk and create appropriate locations for zones that won't prompt clashes (i.e. concentration zones next to a collaborative space).

Untethered

Untethered offices are open-plan landscapes where desk ownership is removed, and workers are required to find the best location to perform their task at hand. These offices are commonly designed to support activity-based working (ABW) and have been another sore point in the history of workplaces from inception (again, just try the words on your browser and see what comes out). Layouts cater for a variety of work tasks and activities, very much like those observed in contemporary, landscaped open-plan offices. Some may have neighbourhoods implemented to allow for teams, departments, etc. to work together from the same area within a floor.

Untethered workplace layouts have been extensively researched (and loathed by workers), especially from a desk-ownership removal perspective (Babapour et al., 2018; Gao et al., 2022; Rolfö, 2018a). Desk-ownership removal can be confronting to many, and understandably so as they are the very last piece of m2 allocated to a person for their exclusive use since the birth of open-plan offices. Similarly to the issues raised earlier about the lack of contextual information about where the research was conducted, the change in management process and how people engage with the space need to be rectified in order to improve the design and performance of untethered workplaces. A recent literature review focusing on research conducted between 2010 and 2020 concluded that key shortcomings transpire from the way of working implementation and/or transition and how workers engage with it (Marzban et al., 2023). Despite the polarised nature of discussion around untethered ways of working, findings are not in agreement, with some evidence of positive impacts on workers coming from an interior design perspective (Rolfö, 2018b; Forooraghi et al., 2023) and the negatives coming from an IEQ (Pollard et al., 2022), design and health perspective (Engelen et al., 2017, 2019).

Untethered environments can work if they are designed to allow workers the freedom to find places within the office that cater for their needs and preferences in terms of space supporting work tasks, Indoor Environmental Quality, increased ability to concentrate and reduce their time spent seated (Candido et al., 2021a, 2021b). Research focusing on comparative analysis before and after relocation to untethered offices found that these spaces can outperform static office layouts in terms of worker satisfaction, perceived productivity and health if there is a structured change in management process, authentic buy-in from leadership and workers, ongoing championing/training of the way of working and careful curation of landscapes informed by evidence to achieve a fit between work and space (Bauer, 2020; Finch & Aranda-Mena, 2019; Khanna & New, 2008; Morrison & Smollan, 2020; Wohlers & Hertel, 2016). Research also shows that the implementation of neighbourhoods increases workers' satisfaction with the space and way of working as it facilitates communication and overall visibility of teammates, also grounding them to a location, diminishing the sense of territoriality loss from desk removal (Ayoko & Härtel, 2003; Gao et al., 2022; Zak & Barraza, 2013). Further, the use of prototyping to expose workers to new spaces and ways of working, early in the engagement if paired with (i) data from workers and other sources and (ii) clear articulation of how this data will then inform changes in the final design can also lift overall satisfaction with the space post-relocation (Cobaleda-Cordero et al., 2023; Sanders & Stappers, 2014).

Adaptive

At the time this chapter was written, workplaces and corporate real estate (CRE) were being shaken up by the pandemic, which was the most significant event since the internet. For the first time in workplace history workers hold the power of choosing when and where they want to work. The pandemic is a catalyst for change and acceleration, prompting a significant expansion of the digital infrastructure needed to facilitate information flow, efficiency and productivity of distributed teams, making location less of a constraint, unshackling people from the office from a space and time perspective. Research found that managers expressed concerns about decreased efficiency, workplace culture and workplace safety and health during the pandemic-induced lockdowns. However, workers expressed concerns about their lack of social connections, internet connectivity and increased work demands (and burn-out) (Marzban et al., 2021). Interacting with colleagues in person was the primary reason for workers to return to the office HQ (Marzban et al., 2021; Durakovic et al., 2023a). Nonetheless, both organisations and workers reported a high level of trust and appreciation for one another. There is also a consistent increase in appreciation for health and well-being in terms of overall ergonomics of homemade office set-ups, increase in time spent seated, cognitive demands from constant engagement via videoconferencing, inconsistency in routine and increased reporting of burn-out (Hayes et al., 2021; Niebuhr et al., 2022).

From a workspace perspective, the pandemic has posed significant challenges in terms of asset management and provision of office space because of pronounced fluctuations in utilisation needs. With people and teams coming to the office to socialise at an average of two or three days a week, workspace layout needs to *adapt* to accommodate fluctuations in space demands, expanding or shrinking in size and shape from one day to another, which is challenging considering the static nature of fit-out and base-building provisions (power points, HVAC systems, etc.). Further, this adaptive office layout should allow workers to modify the space in a way that can cater for their work needs at different points in time during the week. Finally, this workspace can and should consider how the infrastructure can be adapted to be used by permanent and non-permanent residents of the office with the goal of maximising the use of the space and reactivating at the same time, which is likely to generate a much needed 'vibe' and pull to the office.

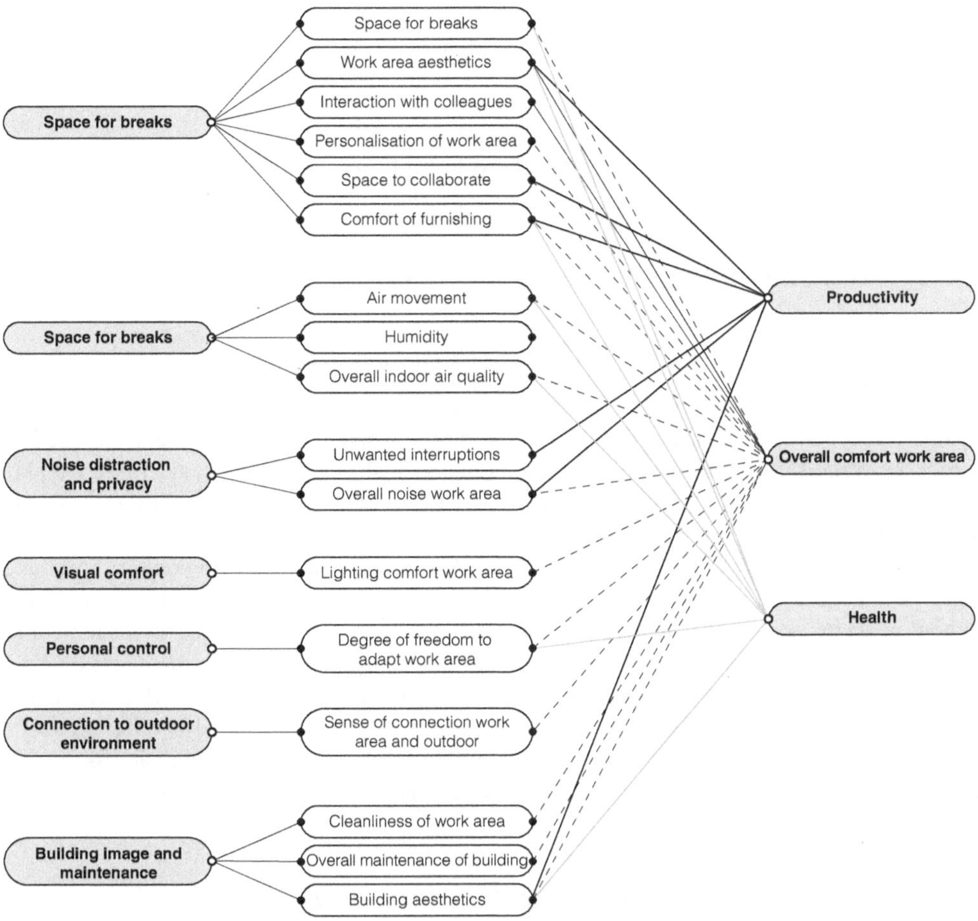

Figure 1.1 Links between interior design and performance aspects and considerations to workers' satisfaction, perceived productivity and health. (Adapted from Candido, Chakraborty and Tjondronegoro, 2019)

Novel research in collaboration with industry before the pandemic has shown the potential of using robotic fabrication to generate ceiling-mounted structures that could address cabling issues within an existing fit-out whilst helping to generate improved acoustic performance (Reinhardt et al., 2019). This pre-pandemic research was already trying to respond to the clash between the needs of an organisation around space reconfigurability and the fixed nature of an office fit-out and base-building provision. Fast tracking post-pandemic, research conducted of a pilot workspace, designed specifically for the hybrid worker and their teams' workstyles, reinforced the need for responsive and dynamic environments free of the limitations of fixed power, data and furniture, allowing occupants to 'hack' their workspaces. This test and learn approach to workspace layout revealed that providing tools not available elsewhere organically increased and strengthened demand for returning to work in the office by enabling spaces and tools to be utilised to maximum benefit in connecting teams and aiding connective work for occupants (Durakovic et al., 2023b). These early days in the chapter of adaptive workspaces are likely to perform well from the workers and teams' perspective if they can constantly adapt to respond to their needs. Experimentation guided by evidence from data is key in fine-tuning space needs in this ever-evolving phase of workplaces.

Key design attributes observed in high-performance fit-outs

High-performance workplaces are those that can harness the design, performance and experience of the workspace to positively impact workers' satisfaction, perceived productivity and health. From an interior design perspective, these spaces share the following:

Responsive, landscaped layouts

Office fit-outs must provide workers with spaces that can adequately support them whilst performing different types of work tasks. The freedom to choose where to work from can have a powerful impact on workers' satisfaction and motivation (Gagne et al., 1997; Ilardi et al., 1993; Durakovic et al., 2023b; Marzban et al., 2021), productivity (Baard et al., 2004) and health (Haapakangas et al., 2018; Rolfö, 2018b). By allowing them to seek spaces to concentrate for sustained periods of time without interruptions (Wohlers & Hertel, 2016), that suit their thermal comfort preferences, engage and collaborate with colleagues (in person or virtually) (Appel-Meulenbroek et al., 2021) without concerns around disrupting others, to make/take a call, take a break to recharge and/or simply work from a space that has a 'vibe' that matches their mood at that moment in time. Spaces need to be zoned in such way that do not clash in terms of tasks performed. The layout should be reconfigurable in at least some parts to allow zones to change to respond to different uses and appropriation of space. The spaces also ride the wave of sensing technology to harness the power of data to inform changes based on the evidence coming from actual use and performance of the layout over time.

Brings the digital and physical tribes together

With workers working from different locations inside and outside 'the office', layouts need to cater for the increased need for spaces that can support and bring the tribes of workers together physically and virtually seamlessly. From a space perspective, this means an increased need for spaces that can support teleconferencing of individuals and groups. This needs to consider spaces that provide people with proper acoustic performance, seamless connection, and necessary infrastructure to allow meetings to take place in hybrid fashion that can deliver good experiences to those attending in person and online. Further, spaces need to allow visual access to greenery and daylight, sit-stand workstations and ergonomic furniture.

Healthy and environmentally conscious

The health and well-being of workers has been front-of-mind due to the recognition of the effect of workplace design and performance on people. Spaces that achieve high levels of workers' satisfaction, perceived productivity and health incorporate ergonomic, biophilic, active and universal design principles. They take a user-centred approach that prioritises users' well-being from inception. These spaces also leverage data to inform design decisions and then check results to fine-tune results post-occupancy. The rapid uptake of the health and well-being certification globally reflects the appetite to lift performance up to deliver healthy environments for people to work from on the back of the understanding of the tangible and intangible benefits to individuals, businesses and communities. Post-pandemic, healthy (and safe) environments are a must have.

In addition to prioritising health and well-being, workers also value organisations that consider its impact on the environment and society. From a space perspective, overall layout specifications, operational practices, provision for e-waste collection/recycle options, provision of food in situ, end of trip facilities to support green travel and other practices can have a significant impact on an office's overall environmental footprint.

Conclusion

Workplaces are organisms that exist in a permanent state of metamorphosis, forever changing to respond to ways of working. The physical environment of a workplace is a blueprint to workers about an organization's values, culture and brand. Choices about the interior design of an office also encapsulates work hierarchy and work styles from organisational leaders. Combined, these intangible aspects of workplaces led to interior design choices and office landscapes intended to support and influence the way people work, where they work and who they work with. As a result, for decades workers had to adapt their way of working to the in-office infrastructure available to them, regardless of if it suited their individual/team preferences and expectations and/or needs. In addition, a mismatch between the in-office infrastructure available to workers and the way they are expected to use and appropriate the space can also happen. These two issues can be used to explain major workplace underperformance in terms of workers' satisfaction, perceived productivity and health, including the well-known backlash against static and untethered offices.

The pandemic prompted generations of open-plan office natives to experience the advantages and challenges of choosing where and when they would like to work. Setting up their own workplaces at home (or elsewhere) meant that a portion of the workforce was able to come up with bespoke solutions that suited their own needs in terms of office overall physical set-up and, most importantly, control over interruptions, interactions and ability to concentrate. On the flip side, workers also gained renewed appreciation of in-office exchanges and work activities better performed whilst people are together at the same time and place, with this ringing true especially for teams. Combined, these recent experiences have placed pressure to lift the baseline of fit-outs to improve in-office experience for workers of all walks of life and can deliver a seamless experience when bridging the digital and physical reams. Fit-outs need to adapt and respond to pronounced fluctuations in utilisation over time and to provide workers with healthy and environmentally conscious environments they can thrive in and strive to return to (albeit not every day).

A 'high-performance' checklist for conceptualising layouts is provided here:

Principle	*Description*
RESPONSIVE LANDSCAPED LAYOUTS	□ User-centred, evidence-based approach to interior design is crucial to deliver high-performance and experience of spaces □ Curated, multizonal landscapes able to support a variety of work tasks and styles □ Layouts should be able to respond to changes in space needs over times □ Data must be harnessed to fine-tune changes over time by responding to needs

(*Continued*)

(Continued)

Principle	*Description*
BRINGS THE DIGITAL AND PHYSICAL TRIBES TOGETHER	□ Workspaces needs to support the needs of the digital and physical tribes through seamless interactions
HEALTHY AND ENVIRONMENTALLY CONSCIOUS	□ Healthy and environmentally conscious workspaces are a 'must have' and need to respond to the rise in expectations from workers and the society more broadly

References

Appel-Meulenbroek, R., Steps, S., Wenmaekers, R., & Arentze, T. (2021). Coping strategies and perceived productivity in open-plan offices with noise problems. *Journal of Managerial Psychology*, *36*(4), 400–414. https://doi.org/10.1108/JMP-09-2019-0526

Ayoko, O. B., & Härtel, C. E. J. (2003). The role of space as both a conflict trigger and a conflict control mechanism in culturally heterogeneous workgroups. *Applied Psychology*, *52*(3), 383–412.

Baard, P. P., Deci, E. L., & Ryan, R. M. (2004). Intrinsic need satisfaction: A motivational basis of performance and well-being in two work settings. *Journal of Applied Social Psychology*, *34*(10), 2045–2068. https//doi.org/10.1111/j.1559-1816.2004.tb02690.x

Babapour, M., Karlsson, M., & Osvalder, A. L. (2018). Appropriation of an activity-based flexible office in daily work. *Nordic Journal of Working Life Studies*, *8*. https://doi.org/10.18291/njwls.v8iS3.105277

Bauer, A. (2020). Pride and productivity: Post occupancy evaluation of the healing office design concept. *Journal of Corporate Real Estate*, *22*(4), 313–340. https//doi.org/10.1108/JCRE-02-2019-0012

Candido, C., Chakraborty, P., & Tjondronegoro, D. (2019). The rise of office design in high-performance, open-plan environments [article]. *Buildings*, *9*(4), 100. https://doi.org/10.3390/buildings9040100

Candido, C., Gocer, O., Marzban, S., Gocer, K., Thomas, L., Zhang, F., Gou, Z., Mackey, M., Engelen, L., & Tjondronegoro, D. (2021a). Occupants' satisfaction and perceived productivity in open-plan offices designed to support activity-based working: Findings from different industry sectors [Article]. *Journal of Corporate Real Estate*, *23*(2), 106–129. https://doi.org/10.1108/JCRE-06-2020-0027

Candido, C., Marzban, S., Haddad, S., Mackey, M., & Loder, A. (2021b). Designing healthy workspaces: Results from Australian certified open-plan offices. *Facilities*, *39*(5–6), 411–433. https://doi.org/10.1108/F-02-2020-0018

Candido, C., Thomas, L., Haddad, S., Zhang, F., Mackey, M., & Ye, W. (2019). Designing activity-based workspaces: Satisfaction, productivity and physical activity [Article]. *Building Research and Information*, *47*(3), 275–289. https://doi.org/10.1080/09613218.2018.1476372

Cobaleda-Cordero, A., Karlsson, M., & Chafi, M. B. (2023). Design for user experience of control with flexible office environments-explorative user tests with prototypes. *International Journal of Human Factors and Ergonomics*, *10*(2), 165–186.

Di Blasio, S., Shtrepi, L., Puglisi, G. E., & Astolfi, A. (2019). A cross-sectional survey on the impact of irrelevant speech noise on annoyance, mental health and well-being, performance and occupants' behavior in shared and open-plan offices. *International Journal of Environmental Research and Public Health*, *16*(2), 280. https://doi.org/10.3390/ijerph16020280

Durakovic, I., Aznavoorian, L., & Candido, C. (2023a). Togetherness and (work)Place: Insights from workers and managers during Australian COVID-induced lockdowns. *Sustainability*, *15*(1), 94. https://doi.org/10.3390/su15010094

Durakovic, I., Munao, L., & Finlayson, S. (2023b). *Supporting social capital in an omni-channel workforce. Research report*. Alastair Swayn Foundation Open Research, First published: June 1, 2023.

Engelen, L., Chau, J., Bohn-Goldbaum, E., Young, S., Hespe, D., & Bauman, A. (2017). Is active design changing the workplace? A natural pre-post experiment looking at health behaviour and workplace perceptions. *Work*, *56*, 229–237. https//doi.org/10.3233/WOR-172483

Engelen, L., Chau, J., Young, S., Mackey, M., Jeyapalan, D., & Bauman, A. (2019). Is activity-based working impacting health, work performance and perceptions? A systematic review. *Building Research & Information*, *47*(4), 468–479. https//doi.org/10.1080/09613218.2018.1440958

Finch, E., & Aranda-Mena, G. (2019). *Creating emotionally intelligent workspaces: A design guide to office chemistry*. Routledge.

Forooraghi, M., Miedema, E., Ryd, N., Wallbaum, H., & Babapour Chafi, M. (2023). Relationship between the design characteristics of activity-based flexible offices and users' perceptions of privacy and social interactions. *Building Research & Information*, 1–17.

Gagne, M., Senecal, C. B., & Koestner, R. (1997). Proximal job characteristics, feelings of empowerment, and intrinsic motivation: A multidimensional model. *Journal of Applied Social Psychology*, *27*(14), 1222–1240. https//doi.org/10.1111/j.1559-1816.1997.tb01803.x

Gao, S., Low, S. P., & Gong, H. Q. (2022). Effects of activity-based workspaces on employee belongingness. *Facilities*, *40*(1/2), 98–117. https://doi.org/10.1108/F-08-2020-0093

Haapakangas, A., Hallman, D. M., Mathiassen, S. E., & Jahncke, H. (2018). Self-rated productivity and employee well-being in activity-based offices: The role of environmental perceptions and workspace use. *Building and Environment*, *145*, 115–124.

Hayes, S. W., Priestley, J. L., Moore, B. A., & Ray, H. E. (2021). Perceived stress, work-related burnout, and working from home before and during COVID-19: An examination of workers in the United States. *Sage Open*, *11*(4), 21582440211058193. https://doi.org/10.1177/21582440211058193?

Hodzic, S., Kubicek, B., Uhlig, L., & Korunka, C. (2021). Activity-based flexible offices: Effects on work-related outcomes in a longitudinal study. *Ergonomics*, *64*(4), 455–473. https://doi.org/10.1080/00140139.2020.1850882

Ilardi, B. C., Leone, D. L., Kasser, T., & Ryan, R. M. (1993). Employee and supervisor ratings of motivation: Main effects and discrepancies associated with job satisfaction and adjustment in a factory setting. *Journal of Applied Social Psychology*, *23*(21), 1789–1805.

Jahncke, H., & Hallman, D. M. (2020). Objective measures of cognitive performance in activity-based workplaces and traditional office types. *Journal of Environmental Psychology*, *72*, 101503.

Kaarlela-Tuomaala, A., Helenius, R., Keskinen, E., & Hongisto, V. (2009). Effects of acoustic environment on work in private office rooms and open-plan offices–longitudinal study during relocation. *Ergonomics*, *52*(11), 1423–1444. https://doi.org/10.1080/00140130903154579

Keller, A. C., Meier, L. L., Elfering, A., & Semmer, N. K. (2020). Please wait until I am done! Longitudinal effects of work interruptions on employee well-being. *Work & Stress*, *34*(2), 148–167. https://doi.org/10.1080/02678373.2019.1579266

Khanna, S., & New, J. R. (2008). Revolutionizing the workplace: A case study of the future of work program at Capital One. *Human Resource Management*, *47*(4), 795–808. https://doi.org/10.1002/hrm.20245

Lee, Y., & Aletta, F. (2019). Acoustical planning for workplace health and well-being: A case study in four open-plan offices. *Building Acoustics*, *26*(3), 207–220. https://doi.org/10.1080/00140130600679142

Marzban, S., Candido, C., Mackey, M., Engelen, L., Zhang, F., & Tjondronegoro, D. (2023). A review of research in activity-based working over the last ten years: Lessons for the post-COVID workplace [Review]. *Journal of Facilities Management*, *21*(3), 313–333. https://doi.org/10.1108/JFM-08-2021-0081

Marzban, S., Durakovic, I., Candido, C., & Mackey, M. (2021). Learning to work from home: Experience of Australian workers and organizational representatives during the first Covid-19 lockdowns [Article]. *Journal of Corporate Real Estate*, *23*(3), 203–222. https://doi.org/10.1108/JCRE-10-2020-0049

Morrison, R. L., & Smollan, R. K. (2020). Open plan office space? If you're going to do it, do it right: A fourteen-month longitudinal case study. *Applied Ergonomics*, *82*, 1–18, https//doi.org/10.1016/j.apergo.2019.102933

Muzaffar, A., Noor, P. N., & Mahmud, S. A. (2020). A comparative study on the impacts of open plan and closed office layout towards employees' perceived productivity. *Journal Penyelidikan Sains Sosial (JOSSR)*, *3*(6), 49–58.

Niebuhr, F., Borle, P., Börner-Zobel, F., & Voelter-Mahlknecht, S. (2022). Healthy and happy working from home? Effects of working from home on employee health and job satisfaction. *International Journal of Environmental Research and Public Health*, *19*(3), 1122. https://doi.org/10.3390/ijerph19031122

Pollard, B., Engelen, L., Held, F., Van Buskirk, J., Spinney, R., & de Dear, R. (2022). Associations between spatial attributes, IEQ exposures and occupant movement behaviour in an open-plan office. *Building and Environment*, *212*, 108812. https://doi.org/10.1016/j.buildenv.2022.108812

Reinhardt, D., Watt, R., Wozniak-OConnor, D., Candido, C., Cabrera, D., Titchkosky, N., Bickerton, C., & Bohnernberger, S. (2019). Towards on-site, modular robotic carbon-fiber winding for an integrated ceiling structure. *Construction Robotics*, *3*, 23–40.

Rolfö, L. (2018a). *Activity-based flexible office work environments. Design and implementation processes and outcomes*. Stockholm, KTH Royal Institute of Technology (TRITA-CBH-FOU, 2018: 52).

Rolfö, L. V. (2018b). Relocation to an activity-based flexible office–design processes and outcomes. *Applied Ergonomics*, *73*, 141–150. https://doi.org/10.1016/j.apergo.2018.05.017

Sanders, E. B. N., & Stappers, P. J. (2014). Probes, toolkits and prototypes: Three approaches to making in codesigning. *CoDesign*, *10*(1), 5–14.

Wohlers, C., & Hertel, G. (2016). Choosing where to work at work towards a theoretical model of benefits and risks of activity-based flexible offices. *Ergonomics*, *60*(4), 467–486.

Zak, P. J., & Barraza, J. A. (2013). The neurobiology of collective action. *Frontiers in Neuroscience*, *7*, 211.

2
UNIVERSAL DESIGN

Imogen Howe and Andrew Martel

The universal design approach aspires to create spaces that are not just accessible or usable, but inclusive for everyone.

– Authors

Introduction

The United Nations Convention on the Rights of Persons with Disabilities (UNCRPD) (2006) establishes that parties to the convention recognise persons with disabilities' right to work on an equal basis and that parties will promote the realisation of this right to work. To actively support increased employment, many workplaces will require upgrades enabling access and ensuring the building is a safe and inclusive place where people can focus on performing their work tasks well. When considering design for disability, it is worth keeping in mind that disability can be temporary or permanent and can be experienced at any stage of life, either gradually or suddenly. Disability is a natural part of human diversity, and people's lived experiences can provide valuable insights and rich creative opportunities for design.

There is a trend to create more inclusive workplaces (Moody et al., 2017), and as business owners seek to upgrade offices to welcome a diverse workforce, designers require skills and knowledge to ensure they can deliver high-quality spaces that are truly inclusive. Design to code compliance is not the same as quality (or even adequate) design. Disability advocates generally agree that high-quality outcomes result when inclusive design thinking is implemented from the very beginning of project conception and integral to the design process throughout (Boys, 2014; Mace, 1985) and that problems often come from assumptions made by designers about building users (Imrie, 1996; Reeve, 2019). To design for diversity, we need to be open-minded about the breadth of diversity in the population. For example, inclusive spaces might consider people with physical mobility or sensory disabilities, neurodiverse or psycho-social conditions, dexterity impairment and chronic illnesses, arthritis, ageing or post-surgery impairments. The principles of universal design (UD) can provide a framework to assist designers to develop these inclusive design skills and generate a greater understanding of diverse lived experiences.

This chapter explains the UD framework developed by the Center for UD in 1997, and how it differs from accessibility and usability. It breaks down each of the seven principles of UD (Connell et al.,

DOI: 10.1201/9781003328728-3

This chapter has been made available under a CC-BY-NC-ND 4.0 license.

1997) in detail, showing how they could be applied in workplaces. The chapter concludes with reflections on some of the contemporary issues surrounding disability and inclusion that might bear relevance to a UD approach today.

What is universal design?

UD was initially conceived in the 1980s by architect Ronald Mace through his work in disability studies. Mace argued that the built environment is used by a diverse group of individuals of varied ages, abilities and identities and therefore should be designed to be usable by everyone, accommodating their differences. Mace and other experts established the Center for Universal Design (CUD) at North Carolina State University, where they focussed on the development of key principles of UD to assist and guide designers in the creation of inclusive places. In 1997 the CUD published the seven principles for UD: equitable use, flexibility in use, simple and intuitive use, perceptible information, tolerance for error, low physical effort, size and space for approach and use, along with guidelines for implementation (Connell et al., 1997). It is these seven principles that form the framework for UD explored here.

How does universal design differ from accessibility or usability?

The concepts of accessibility, usability and UD are representative of different world views regarding designing for disabilities, even though they are often used interchangeably. A key aspect of their difference is the association of these concepts with historical disability models (Jackson, 2018) and the consideration of individuals in their development and application. These considerations result in either objective or subjective approaches.

Accessibility is generally associated with the medical model of disability. It is premised on a largely objective approach, seeking compliance of an object or environment with official documents which are measured against norms[1] and standards (Iwarsson & Ståhl, 2003). Iwarsson and Ståhl (2003) argue that a key problem with this approach is that these norms have not been developed systematically and subsequently many are considered invalid. Hamraie's work (2017) shows that historically many of these norms or 'normates' were developed from idealised individuals, typically white, youthful and male; as such, they deal only with the capacities of the individuals from which these standards were developed and are not broadly representative.

The concept of usability is like accessibility but introduces a further component, the evaluation and subjective judgements of the performance of an object or space in use. The concept implies that the environment should be fit-for-purpose, usually described as the 'person-environment fit', and able to be optimally used by the target individual or group (Appel-Meulenbroek et al., 2019; Iwarsson & Ståhl, 2003). Common critiques of both accessibility and usability are that these approaches do not recognise issues beyond access or functionality. An accessible or usable adjustment may comply but can nevertheless be distressing to use and create psycho-emotional barriers to inclusion (Reeve, 2019).

While a key tenet of UD is to create products and environments that are usable, the concept is broader than that of usability. UD was borne out of the social model of disability and is premised on a more democratic, equitable approach to design. UD employs principles that encourage a change of mindset, assisting designers to use their creativity and ingenuity when designing for disabilities but also to consider the broadest possible range of users. For workers with undisclosed or invisible disabilities, the decision to disclose can be difficult even though disclosure is necessary to enable accommodations to be made (Prince, 2017). If a workplace employs UD principles in the design process and in operations, it may reduce the need for accommodations or adjustments.

UD seeks to enable designs that go beyond the minimum standards of access and functionality to create inclusive solutions for everyone.

Universal design in the workplace

This section explains the concept of UD in detail and how it applies to workplace design. By providing a detailed breakdown we endeavour to demystify the UD process and its principles often criticised as vague (Alterator et al., 2019). The incorporation of built-environment-specific descriptions and examples in workplace design can expand how we understand and include disability concerning spatial planning and design. The UD principles apply to assistive technology, tools, organisational or operational decisions, as well as the physical space of the workplace, and integration of this approach can benefit all workers (Harpur, 2019). In addition, the seven principles are not mutually exclusive, and a particular design solution may cover several of them. Appropriate design solutions can be multipurpose and multifunctional but can be used to make the workplace more suitable for all workers, including those with invisible or undisclosed disabilities.

Equity ensures that resources are distributed where needed, resulting in an equal outcome. An equitable work environment would ensure that everyone could perform their work equally well. This might mean that more thought is put into the design at the beginning, to plan for and support a broad diversity of workers. An equitable workplace would also be a place where everyone feels they belong and are included regardless of their ability. Such solutions can benefit all people, not

Figure 2.1 An inclusive reception desk for use by people of different heights or mobility.

Credit: Gordon Howe

Figure 2.2 A blind person trying to use a handrail that is situated on the same side of their body as their guide dog. This is difficult and dangerous for the handler. Installing handrails on both sides of a stair gives the user options for descent.

Credit: Imogen Howe

only those with disabilities (Miralles et al., 2011). The principle of equitable use describes equity beyond issues of functionality or access to consider whether the design is appealing to all users. This may include ensuring that areas like accessible bathrooms, ramps and lifts are as beautiful and well-considered as their non-accessible counterparts. To make all design features equitable, think about ease of use, movement, beauty, privacy and dignity for all parts of the design.

Flexible use means that spaces or objects can be used in many ways. Creating a workplace that is flexible from the outset reduces the need for adaptations for employees and allows for flexibility if any employee's needs change (Pinna et al., 2020). For example, a handrail on both sides of a stair enables people to grab a rail on either side of the body. This helps people with one-hand bias or someone with a guide dog to grasp the rail. Such a minor consideration can make a remarkable difference to a person's everyday life by creating *ease* in acts of daily living, reducing the frustration or lost time experienced in trying to work around these restrictions or relying on others for assistance. This is important even in fire stairs to give people independence in their movement.

Workplaces usually contain several cues that indicate how they should be used. These can be harnessed to enable simple and intuitive use. Meeting rooms tend to be enclosed, acoustically protected spaces. Kitchens are typically smooth and easily cleaned. All spaces can be designed to make their use more intuitive. The logical proximity of uses can also assist with making workspaces simple and intuitive to use – for example, locating waste points near print rooms or kitchens. Consider some simple things you could include in the design that provide intuitive clues to

Figure 2.3 Airport wayfinding signage showing that signs can be simple and clear and often mostly pictorial.

Credit: Imogen Howe

Figure 2.4 A typical 'Norman Door' where the handle suggests it should be pulled to open, so a sign is required to tell the user to push. Design for intuitive use could remove confusion.

Credit: Imogen Howe

navigate the space and indicate its use. These adjustments would help many employees, including newcomers, to learn where things are without needing to ask.

To be perceptible, information needs to be provided in several different formats, including audible, tactile and visual modes. To make a space legible, it requires one to consider how it might be understood, interpreted or navigated by people with different sensory requirements. Designs should also be considered for how they enable or foster different methods of communication; for example, consider how contrast background colours might assist the legibility of sign language (Edwards & Harold, 2014) or whether permanent signage is legible against the substrate it is fixed to.

Figure 2.5 Students at the University of Melbourne (Yizhi Zhao, Zhilin Mo, Ziyue Zhou, Xinyi Zhang, Miki Ueda, Wenjie Sun) created tactile floor plans enabling the layout of their buildings to be understood by someone with low vision.

Credit: Imogen Howe

Figure 2.6 Illegible room signage and glare from lighting make for difficult navigation and uncomfortable work conditions. This signage is difficult to read against the background of the room.

Credit: Imogen Howe

Unexpected adjustments are bound to be required as workplaces evolve and our communities change. Therefore, it is essential to incorporate flexibility into your design, enabling it to accommodate retrofit solutions, adjustments or adaptations to meet changing needs.

Figure 2.7 Adjustable-height workstations allow for flexibility and tolerance for different user requirements.
Credit: Imogen Howe

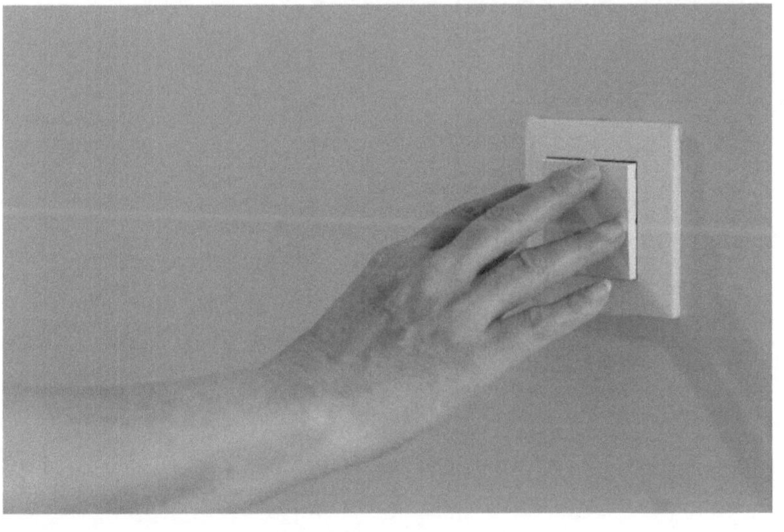

Figure 2.8 Large rocker switches for lights and power outlets allow tolerance in use.
Credit: nkeskin

A workplace of low physical effort is easy to move about and use, but also does not contribute undue sensory stress or strain. This includes doors that can be easily opened with easy-grip handles or automation but also includes comfortable light levels and targeted acoustic treatments. These additional measures can make it easier for people to focus on their work. These distractions can often be designed out with attention to artificial lighting design, natural light control, and acoustic treatment as well as the functionality of doors, drawers, windows, blinds, locks and the like for people with low grasp or limited mobility. When applied to workplace design, this principle would ensure that workplaces are spacious enough to enable movement throughout the office, as well as within key areas, but also that furniture, fixtures and equipment are designed and installed to accommodate users of varied sizes and reach.

Forty years on – what can we add to universal design?

The global pandemic has impacted and changed workplaces across the globe. In many instances, workers were required to work from home and were unable to attend their regular workplace. This

Figure 2.9 Heavy doors like this can be difficult and tiring to open.

Credit: Imogen Howe

Figure 2.10 Vision Australia Headquarters, Kooyong. Clear sightlines and wide circulation spaces allow two people, or a person with a guide dog, to walk side by side.

Credit: Nicole Reed Photography

change exposed existing, but previously concealed, household inequalities, including internet connection and speed; workspace size (linked to dwelling size) and capacity to accommodate work; and workstation issues, including ergonomics and workplace equipment such as access to computers and phones (Adams-Prassl et al., 2020; Messacar et al., 2020). Where previously these physical and technological responsibilities were the employer's, including the provision and maintenance of space and equipment, as well as footing the bill for phone and internet services, suddenly the burden was placed on individual employees and their homes. For persons with disability, this was further complicated by being at high risk of COVID-19 infection due to the nature of disability support work. Isolation and segregation, an already fraught issue for this community, was also exacerbated (Bolisani et al., 2020). However, for many people, the change to work from home brought convenience by removing the struggle with daily commutes and spatial workarounds. As work was moved online, people had access to opportunities previously unavailable to them. With the ability to work from home, people could work at their own pace to manage energy levels and capacity to work, a major plus for many workers with chronic conditions or disabilities. While remote work has expanded opportunities for some people, we must recognise that providing work from home opportunities for people with disabilities does not equal inclusion or equity in the workplace. People with disabilities have a right to work from the office as well as a right to work from home, as we all do (Martel et al., 2021).

The concept of UD is now over forty years old. During this time, ideas about disability and inclusion have advanced. Since its introduction, many scholars and advocates have argued that the term 'universal design' is embedded in an outdated mode of thinking which relies on a belief that there may be or could be a 'universal' experience, rather than recognising and celebrating difference.

Scholar Aimi Hamraie provides an in-depth political-historical background of the critiques and contentions around UD. Hamraie (2016) identifies that some narratives that universalise difference feed into post-disability ideologies premised on the belief that through design and technology disability can be eliminated. Post-disability ideologies are highly problematic, as they are premised on ableist beliefs that a preferable life is one without disability. Such beliefs fail to recognise the value of disability or the unique cultural identities of disability communities, such as the Deaf community. Hamraie also argues that UD does not go far enough, as it fails to tackle this pervasive ableism embedded within society but also in our design processes and building codes. Historian David Gissen (2022) pushes instead for a 'practice of disability' as a more empowered way for people with disabilities to directly engage with the built environment, which he sees as a locus for constructing impairment and disability and challenging its spatial relationships (Gissen, 2022).

These concerns deserve careful attention, but they do not render UD irrelevant. Ensuring its ongoing relevance requires an agile and reflexive approach, to enable UD to evolve in response to the social-cultural advancements. Today, the United Nations promotes a twin-track approach to disability-inclusive development, combining both mainstream and targeted initiatives for people with disabilities (United Nations, 2019). This twin-track approach combines both the social model and human rights model approaches to disability. This might be a way forward for UD. A similar approach could be taken when implementing UD, recognising that it is only one tool in a suite of approaches to design inclusively for people with disabilities and that both mainstream and targeted solutions are required.

Conclusion

Despite earlier restrictions during the pandemic, offices have now mostly reopened to workers, and many businesses have introduced flexible work arrangements that allow employees to periodically work from home. These types of arrangements will likely be a permanent change to workplace operations for many businesses. Regardless of the perceived positives and negatives of flexible and work from home arrangements, it is now clear that efficient and productive work is not limited to office buildings in urban areas but can be networked across large territories that include the home as a fundamental part of the workplace. Research shows that diversity adds value to the workplace and that besides legal compliance, there are financial, productivity and cultural incentives to hiring and retaining people with disabilities (Lindsay et al., 2018). The number of workplace inclusion policies that are publicly available shows that employers recognise this value. UD is a way that employers can ensure their workplace is considered by people with diverse needs when seeking work (Leber et al., 2018).

The UD principles explained in this chapter can assist designers with the implementation of inclusive thinking in their designs. Implementing these principles early in the design process is inexpensive and can result in more flexible, sustainable buildings that benefit all users (Harpur, 2019; Pinna et al., 2020; Rostamiasl & Jrade, 2022). Armed with these principles, designers can confidently and creatively design high-performance, inclusive workplaces within and beyond the office.

Designing for disability in the workplace should not be a compliance-based box-ticking exercise. We must recognise the equal rights of people with disabilities, including their right to dignity, joy, high-performance and wellness in good design. By adopting an inclusive and open mindset, designers have the responsibility and opportunity to impact the everyday experience of individuals, to create a more equitable and just society where anyone can enjoy their work in a space where they feel they belong.

A 'high-performance' checklist for UD is provided here:

Principle	*Description*
THE SPACE IS DESIGNED TO BE EQUITABLE	• Entrances should be designed so that everyone can enter the building the same way. Minimise or eliminate changes in level (e.g. steps) by locating the lobby on grade or sloping the terrain to provide level access. • Reception counters must accommodate people of different heights and reach without the need to twist or strain. • Consider how to accommodate service animals in the space, including toileting areas and how to keep them close to a worker while off-harness to remove the need for prolonged restraint. • Bathrooms must be readily available. Many people who require an accessible bathroom can need it urgently. It should be easy to find and quick to access. An alternative option should be available if needed during maintenance or if occupied. • Accessible solutions should be dignified. A bathroom design should consider privacy and discretion. A ramp or lift should be as joyful to use as the stair. • Ramps and elevators can be beautiful too. Where a grand staircase is introduced, an equally beautiful lift or ramp must be introduced nearby.
THE SPACE IS DESIGNED FOR COMFORT, EFFICIENCY AND MINIMAL STRAIN	• Heavy doors can be difficult to negotiate and painful to move. Ensure doors are well hung with sufficient hinges to reduce their weight, do not require twisting or are automated. • Introduce clear, easy-to-read and consistent wayfinding signage. • Poor lighting design and glare can cause issues including sensory overload, eye strain, irritation and migraines. • Reduce reverberant, audible noise by introducing soft furnishings and acoustic surface treatments throughout the workplace. This is important for people who use text-to-speech or screen-reading software to complete their daily work (e.g. JAWS, Window Eyes).
THE SPACE IS DESIGNED FOR EASE OF USE AND MOVEMENT	• Circulation pathways should be generous to accommodate two people side by side (e.g. people using sign language to communicate), people with guide dogs, wheelchairs, scooters or other mobility devices. • Ensure there are clear sightlines on pathways or within the space to see people approaching when you cannot hear them. • Ensure that appropriate handles are installed for easy use on all doors, windows and drawers, including cabinetry. • Design cupboards, benches and desks to be used by people of different statures and mobility by making them adjustable or locating equipment at reachable heights. For example, install kettles or boiler taps instead of wall boiler units. Cups, plates, coffee, tea and snacks can be stored at a reachable height. • Provide sufficient storage and waste collection to ensure a clear and tidy space for approach and use is maintained.

Note

1 This touches on a key issue of discussion within disability studies and advocacy, which is the railing against the process of normalisation. It is generally understood within disability studies that normalisation is a reductionist notion that does not allow for difference or diversity, but instead perpetuates othering when a body does not conform to the norm and the construction of disability as deviation (Davis, 2017; Imrie, 1996). As such, accessibility is problematic and can only deal with limited aspects of the problems of exclusion within the built environment.

References

Adams-Prassl, A., Boneva, T., Golin, M., & Rauh, C. (2020). Inequality in the impact of the coronavirus shock: Evidence from real time surveys. *Journal of Public Economics*, *189*, 104245. https://doi.org/10.1016/j.jpubeco.2020.104245

Alterator, S., Cleveland, B., & Boys, J. (2019, December 3). Students with disabilities need inclusive buildings. We can learn from what's already working. *The Conversation*.

Appel-Meulenbroek, R., Le Blanc, P., & de Kort, Y. (2019). Person-environment fit: Optimizing the physical work environment. In O. B. Ayoko & N. M. Ashkanasy (Eds.), *Organizational behaviour and the physical environment* (1st ed.). Routledge. https://doi.org/10.4324/9781315167237

Bolisani, E., Scarso, E., Ipsen, C., Kirchner, K., & Hansen, J. P. (2020). Working from home during COVID-19 pandemic: Lessons learned and issues. *Management & Marketing. Challenges for the Knowledge Society*, *15*(s1), 458–476. https://doi.org/10.2478/mmcks-2020-0027

Boys, J. (2014). *Doing disability differently: An alternative handbook on architecture, dis/ability and designing for everyday life*. Routledge.

Connell, B. R., Jones, M., Mace, R., Mueller, J., Mullick, A., Ostroff, E., Sanford, J., Steinfeld, E., Story, M., & Vanderheiden, G. (1997). *The principles of universal design* [Poster].

Davis, L. J. (Ed.). (2017). Introduction. In *The disability studies reader* (5th ed.). Routledge, Taylor & Francis Group.

Edwards, C., & Harold, G. (2014). DeafSpace and the principles of universal design. *Disability and Rehabilitation*, *36*(16), 1350–1359. https://doi.org/10.3109/09638288.2014.913710

Gissen, D. (2022). *The architecture of disability: Buildings, cities, and landscapes beyond access*. University of Minnesota Press.

Hamraie, A. (2016). Universal design and the problem of "post-disability" ideology. *Design and Culture*, *8*(3), 285–309. https://doi.org/10.1080/17547075.2016.1218714

Hamraie, A. (2017). *Building access: Universal design and the politics of disability*. University of Minnesota Press.

Harpur, P. D. (2019). *Ableism at work: Disablement and hierarchies of impairment* (1st ed.). Cambridge University Press. https://doi.org/10.1017/9781108667371

Imrie, R. (1996). *Disability and the city: International perspectives*. Paul Chapman.

Iwarsson, S., & Ståhl, A. (2003). Accessibility, usability and universal design – Positioning and definition of concepts describing person-environment relationships. *Disability and Rehabilitation*, *25*(2), 57–66.

Jackson, M. A. (2018). Models of disability and human rights: Informing the improvement of built environment accessibility for people with disability at neighborhood scale? *Laws*, *7*(1), 10. https://doi.org/10.3390/laws7010010

Leber, M., Bastic, M., Moody, L., & Schmidt Krajnc, M. (2018). A study of the impact of ergonomically designed workplaces on employee productivity. *Advances in Production Engineering & Management*, *13*(1), 107–117. https://doi.org/10.14743/apem2018.1.277

Lindsay, S., Cagliostro, E., Albarico, M., Mortaji, N., & Karon, L. (2018). A systematic review of the benefits of hiring people with disabilities. *Journal of Occupational Rehabilitation*, *28*(4), 634–655. https://doi.org/10.1007/s10926-018-9756-z

Mace, R. L. (1985). Universal design, barrier-free environments for everyone. *Designers West*, *33*(1), 147–152.

Martel, A., Day, K., Jackson, M. A., & Kaushik, S. (2021). Beyond the pandemic: The role of the built environment in supporting people with disabilities work life. *Archnet-IJAR: International Journal of Architectural Research*, *15*(1), 98–112. https://doi.org/10.1108/ARCH-10-2020-0225

Messacar, D., Morissette, R., & Deng, Z. (2020). *Inequality in the feasibility of working from home during and after COVID-19*. Statistics Canada.

Miralles, C., Holt, R., Marin-Garcia, J. A., & Canos-Daros, L. (2011). Universal design of workplaces through the use of Poka-Yokes: Case study and implications. *Journal of Industrial Engineering and Management*, *4*(3), 436–452.

Moody, L., Saunders, J., Leber, M., Wójcik-Augustyniak, M., Szajczyk, M., & Rebernik, N. (2017). An exploratory study of barriers to inclusion in the European workplace. *Disability and Rehabilitation*, *39*(20), 2047–2054. https://doi.org/10.1080/09638288.2016.1217072

Pinna, F., Garau, C., Maltinti, F., & Coni, M. (2020). Beyond architectural barriers: Building a bridge between disability and universal design. In O. Gervasi, B. Murgante, S. Misra, C. Garau, I. Blečić, D. Taniar, B. O. Apduhan, A. M. A. C. Rocha, E. Tarantino, C. M. Torre, & Y. Karaca (Eds.), *Computational science and its applications – ICCSA 2020* (Vol. 12255, pp. 706–721). Springer International Publishing. https://doi.org/10.1007/978-3-030-58820-5_51

Prince, M. J. (2017). Persons with invisible disabilities and workplace accommodation: Findings from a scoping literature review. *Journal of Vocational Rehabilitation*, *46*(1), 75–86. https://doi.org/10.3233/JVR-160844

Reeve, D. (2019). Part of the problem or part of the solution? How far do 'reasonable adjustments' guarantee 'inclusive access for disabled customers'? In *Disability, spaces and places of policy exclusion*. Routledge.

Rostamiasl, V., & Jrade, A. (2022). Integrating universal design standards and building information modeling at the conceptual design stage of buildings. *Open Journal of Civil Engineering*, *12*(4), 492–523. https://doi.org/10.4236/ojce.2022.124028

United Nations. (2019). *Disability inclusion strategy*. UN. https://www.un.org/en/content/disabilitystrategy/

United Nations General Assembly. (2006, December 13). *Convention on the rights of persons with disabilities. A/RES/61/106*. https://undocs.org/en/A/RES/61/106

3
ACTIVE DESIGN

Lina Engelen

> Active Design refers to the integration of physical activity into buildings, workspaces and urban environments through thoughtful design.
>
> – *Author*

Introduction

Active design refers to the integration of physical activity into buildings, workspaces and urban environments through thoughtful design. As a set of architectural principles and workplace strategies, Active design creates spaces that encourage and support health and well-being.

Active design strategies that facilitate and provide opportunities for physical activity, particularly for incidental movement integrated into usual daily work practices, are increasingly being incorporated into public health and urban planning guidelines in many countries (The City of New York, 2010; Heart Foundation, 2015; Sport England, 2015). These guidelines contain a set of recommendations around stair, lobby and lift design, as well as for internal walking routes, strategic placement of amenities within buildings and provision of facilities such as bicycle storage, locker rooms and shower rooms to encourage activity (The City of New york, 2010).

Active design hence works on the basis that behaviour can be influenced at an individual and population level by altering the environments within which people make choices (choice architecture). Choice architecture refers to the design of the environment and presentation of options that influence people's decisions. In the office setting, choice architecture can be used to encourage physical activity by making it easier and more appealing for employees to engage in physical activities during the workday, and thus may accomplish two things: it may make it easier for the user/building occupant to navigate complex choices, but it may also influence the choices they make. It is proposed that interventions, such as thoughtful design, provision and placement of stairs, and kitchens typically require little conscious engagement on the part of the individual to realise their intended effects, mainly working via non-conscious psychological processes (Hofmann et al., 2008; Marteau et al., 2011; Marteau et al., 2012).

The term Active design has been used differently in diverse disciplines. In architecture, the term would refer to the structural elements and design of a building and might be called "building programming and design", while in pssychology the concept refers to the environmental and

DOI: 10.1201/9781003328728-4
This chapter has been made available under a CC-BY-NC-ND 4.0 license.

organisational psychology of how people perceive spaces; and in the public health discipline the term often encompasses physical activity interventions and sitting-reduction interventions (Zimring et al., 2005; Nicoll & Zimring, 2009; Vischer, 2011). Each of these disciplines highlights important aspects of the concept; however, in isolation, none of them are sufficient in applying Active design principles across multiple levels effectively. The concept of Active design in the office environment is hence a holistic approach that incorporates the structural design elements necessary for promoting physical activity and well-being, as well as the policies, workplace cultures, work styles and personal factors that promote these.

This chapter aims to explore the advantages of active design and its potential to enhance workplace performances, whether in conventional office buildings or non-traditional settings. Additionally, practical suggestions for integrating active design principles into these spaces are presented.

Why do we need active design?

Many people in developed nations spend up to 90% of their day inside buildings (Athes, 2016), and much of that time is spent in inactive or low-active pursuits. Physical activity has a range of great proven benefits to physical and mental health. Conversely, individuals who do not meet the daily recommended levels of physical activity (called physical inactivity) have a greater risk of developing obesity, chronic disease and premature death (Australian Institute of Health and Welfare, 2018; World Health Organization, 2018). The annual estimated cost from physical inactivity to health care systems is in the billions.

Excessive sitting has been found to be a risk factor for ill health and mortality (Bauman et al., 2013; Giles-Corti et al., 2016). Both physical inactivity and sedentary behaviour are problems exacerbated by modern work practices and workplaces, driven by rapid technological change over the last 50 years (Buckley et al., 2015; Straker et al., 2016). We could reverse the trend by exercising on a daily basis, but not everyone has the required time or discipline to do so. Luckily, our daily routines offer plenty of opportunities to enhance physical activity and reduce sitting time. Non-exercise energy expenditure (also called NEAT; activities we undertake in our daily life, such as walking, lifting, household chores and shopping) contributes to the largest additional daily energy expenditure (above the basal metabolic rate), even among avid exercisers (Levine, 2002); hence there are good reasons to target increases in NEAT during otherwise sedentary work time. Research shows that office workers only walk on average 2.4 min/h at work (Spinney et al., 2015) and that sedentary time in office workers at work is around 6h/workday (Chau et al., 2013; Shrestha et al., 2016). There is clearly scope for increased movement during work time. Even high-intensity short-duration activities, such as stair climbing, can confer health benefits at work (Halsey et al., 2012).

The World Health Organization (WHO) recognises the workplace as a key setting for interventions to improve physical activity levels and advocates for changes in the built environment that support healthier lifestyles and well-being (Quintiliani et al., 2007). Buildings are a good place to start to make small changes in our daily routines; after all, this is where most people spend the vast majority of their time. However, architecture has been anything but instrumental for the active lifestyle. Modernity has brought us an architecture dominated by the efficient allocation of (economic) resources, rather than by the physiological or psychological needs of the human being. A human-centred design approach, on the other hand, makes us identify human needs and allows us to nudge towards healthy behaviour. The approach towards active design in offices can be divided into two lines: discouraging sedentary behaviour and encouraging active behaviour.

In addition, national building/construction codes and accreditation systems generally do not directly support incidental physical activity within the building (e.g., restricted access to fire stairs). In the current accreditation systems, a building with a premium quality lift (elevator) ride receives a Premium rating, but the accreditation system does not reward an accessible, high-capacity staircase. Although the construction codes do not prescribe requirements for structures that support physical activity, building owners and/or tenants can opt for one of the several voluntary certification systems currently on the market that aim to create healthy, sustainable and productive environments for occupants (such as Fitwel, WELL, etc.). These certifications have a strong focus on health and well-being and require a number of structures and strategies related to active design in order to grant certifications. The increased interest in these voluntary certifications by organisations sends a clear signal to employees and building owners that support for health and well-being is prioritised.

One could ask if an increase in incidental physical activity during work time would make any substantial difference to health. I would say that it does. For the majority of adults who do not meet the recommended guidelines for health, every active minute counts, and every opportunity to be engaged in a less sedentary and more active lifestyle is likely to be beneficial. Stair climbing is particularly beneficial, as it is a short-duration, high-intensity physical activity (Skelly et al., 2014). Walking and standing both may have benefits through reducing prolonged sitting and leading to reduced musculoskeletal symptoms (Thorp et al., 2014) and a reduced risk of chronic disease (Stamatakis et al., 2015). For many, movement that can be integrated in the normal workday and that does not require sport gear or special equipment is a feasible method for incremental accumulation of daily activity.

How can we implement active design in workplaces?

Many progressive organisations want their staff to feel healthier and more well by being at work. One way towards this is to implement the active design principles. A building's physical structure, including its physical footprint and the number of floors, can influence the way the building is used. In an active design environment, the built structure of the workplace provides employees with the facilities necessary to undertake and encourage incidental and recreational physical activity. The building's characteristics (facilities, layout, interior design, fit-out and technology) can serve to either encourage incidental activity, such as a central and open stairwell, or discourage activity through a lack of access (Zimring et al., 2005). When considering active design principles in the office setting, it is important to consider creating destinations that are worth changing locations for.

The layout of the workplace is a contributing factor to the accumulation of incidental physical activity and interruption of prolonged sitting time. Restructuring the physical layout of the floor plan by providing more opportunities for incidental physical activity, in particular the number and location of destinations, such as meeting rooms, printers, bathrooms and kitchens, may influence walking time and characteristics of sedentary time (Smith et al., 2013). Communal areas, such as central coffee places, eating areas and atria can influence incidental physical activity and social networks through increased employee connectedness and interaction.

Stair climbing is an efficient way to engage in physical activity in everyday life. It is considered vigorous physical activity, and taking the stairs can contribute to the daily physical activity recommendations. In accordance with the active design guidelines and building codes, it is recommended that buildings have accessible (not just fire egress), conveniently located staircases in easy to find locations. Improved stair design is associated with increased stair use, where attractive, open and well-lit staircases with outside views are used far more often than concealed, enclosed fire stairs. However, it is not always sufficient just to provide the facility (in this case the stairs) itself. Even in a building that provides centrally located, open, bright and attractive staircases (such as in the Charles Perkins Centre at the University of Sydney), we found that the stair-to-lift ratio was only 0.45, hence the lifts were used more than twice as often per day than the stairs were (Engelen et al., 2019). When we introduced nudges in the form of signs, AV screen notifications, and gamification, the stair-to-lift ratio increased to 0.55. This represents an increase of daily stair climbing of 15%, illustrating the importance of the provision of a well-designed and strategically located structure together with prompts and nudges for increasing physical activity.

When studying movement patterns of office workers, the main reasons for moving around were found to be to complete paperwork tasks, such as printing, to access food/drink, and to be with others. Centralised facility placement is hence a useful active design strategy to increase incidental movement. This could include toilets, printers and bins that hit the sweet spot of being located far enough from most workstations to contribute to incidental physical activity, while still being considered conveniently located. Studies have found that if printers and bins are placed too far away from workstations, workers save up rubbish and/or print jobs and limit trips to once a day, defeating the purpose. Interviews have also revealed that toilets located too far away from workstations (more than 60–70 m) have resulted in some drinking less water and hot drinks so as to reduce the need for the bathroom. It is hence important to balance distance with convenience when designing and fitting out active design workplaces.

Other facilities, such as cafes or kitchen/dining areas, can be located a further distance away from workstations if they are attractive and practical, as these can become destinations worth walking to for meeting and spending time with people in. Movement patterns inside offices have indeed been found to depend on, amongst other things, providing office destinations and well-integrated spaces and thoughtfully designed corridors. Office destinations for collaboration and socialising have become even more important post-COVID return-to-office, where remote and hybrid working have highlighted the importance of human contact and creating a sense of belonging at work.

Activity-based working (ABW) is a modern office design philosophy that prioritises flexibility and collaboration in the workplace, by allowing employees to choose where and how they work best (see Ways of Working). A workplace that supports ABW typically has design features such as team desks, sit-stand workstations, quiet rooms, break-out and collaboration areas, meeting rooms and lounge areas in ratios suitable to the organisation. In an ABW setting, a variation in work tasks would lead to performing these tasks in various work settings. ABW and active design are related, as work settings for the various work tasks are located in different areas, or floors of the office, and this can promote incidental physical activity and reduce prolonged sitting. In recent literature reviews (Engelen et al., 2019; Marzban et al., 2022) we report that ABW environments are associated with greater opportunities for movement and have beneficial associations with healthy behaviour and well-being.

Creating outdoor spaces for employees to take breaks and move around can help improve their physical and mental well-being. It is imperative that these patios and green spaces are accessible and provide a sheltered environment for relaxation and social interactions. Another important aspect of active design is the provision of end-of-trip facilities with showers, change rooms, lockers and secure spaces to store bicycles and sport/exercise items. This supports active transport to and from work, as well as physical activity during lunch or other break times.

The overall quality of the precinct in which we work also needs to be considered for health and well-being. Access to nature, outdoor spaces and biophilia in the workplace is related to lower levels of perceived job stress and higher levels of job satisfaction (Largo-Wight et al., 2011).

Buildings in more walkable locations have been shown to foster improved health by increasing opportunities for regular physical activity, social interactions and access to amenities. In addition, use of public transport is associated with an increase in physical activity, stress reduction, injury prevention and equity (Saelens et al., 2014). When deciding on a location for an organisation's offices, it is of great importance to take the interior, as well as the precinct quality and possibilities, into consideration.

A systems-based approach to active design

A systems-based approach to active design considers the interplay between physical, socio-cultural and behavioural factors in creating environments that support and encourage physical activity. It considers the design of buildings and spaces, as well as the policies and programmes that support active living.

Efforts to change behaviour are more likely to be successful when multiple levels of influence are addressed at the same time. The general principle of systems-based models of behaviour is that the environment facilitates the range of behaviour by promoting and sometimes demanding certain actions and discouraging or prohibiting other behaviours. They posit that intrapersonal variables, interpersonal and cultural factors and physical environments can all influence behaviour (Sallis et al., 2006).

Literature on best practices in active design identified nine interactive dimensions for implementing active workplace strategies (leadership, relevance, partnership, comprehensiveness, implementation, engagement, communications, being data-driven and compliance) (Pronk, 2014, 2015). A study examined themes for active buildings and showed that overlaying the physical workplace design are multiple layers of spatial, managerial and cultural influences that affect workers and their reasons for movement (McGann et al., 2014).

The socio-cultural environment is equally important as the physical environment in producing sustainable health behaviour changes (Yancey et al., 2004). The organisational culture of a workplace creates a social environment for its employees. In this context, the social environment may drive the overall workplace culture towards wellness and creates the social norms around workplace physical activity and sedentary behaviours (Quintiliani et al., 2007). An organisational culture that normalises, supports and facilitates active design principles may influence the health and well-being of the entire organisation, such that workers feel movement and not being seen at their desk are acceptable.

Managers have identified that it is necessary to underpin the push for workplace activity strategies (including active design), with solid evidence for efficacy relating to health outcomes, as well as for cost-effectiveness relating to productivity and work performance outcomes. In this way decision-makers can be swayed to support changes in the face of limited resources and competing demands. Active design depends greatly upon the willingness of business leaders to hold long-term visions and advocate for multisectoral collaboration, supported by policy and regulatory measures.

By taking a systems-based approach to active design, we are more likely to be successful in creating office environments that are convenient, accessible and appealing for adoption and maintenance of movement.

Implementation of active design for hybrid working

As a result of the pandemic that started in late 2019, many organisations shifted to remote work starting in 2020 and continuing into the current year for the safety of employees. During this prolonged period of remote working, it became clear that collaboration, interactions and sense of belonging with colleagues suffered. Therefore, in mid- to late-2022, many organisations encouraged staff to return to the office, at least for a few days a week. This hybrid working, a combination of remote and on-site work, offers several benefits, including work–life balance, higher sense of control and often higher productivity.

Some studies have shown that people have more time for physical activity during remote working due to a reduction in commute time, while others have shown that remote work can lead to a more sedentary lifestyle. Hence, an organisation's office buildings still play an important role in providing opportunities for physical activity through active design, as discussed in the previous sections. However, with hybrid working likely being here for the foreseeable future, are there ways we can implement active design in a more localised fashion? Many organisations have home office checklists that must be complied with; however, these traditionally focus on reduction of hazards, such as trip hazards from cables, and reduction of musculoskeletal issues through good ergonomics (see Chapter 4), rather than on active design strategies to increase movement. It would be beneficial to introduce active design checklists for remote working that could include opportunities to implement similar strategies in the home setting, such as:

- placing waste baskets or snacks and drinks in a location farther away from the workstation.
- designating areas in the home that encourage physical activity, such as yoga or stretching, and make it a part of the daily routine.
- encourage outdoor activities in outdoor spaces that are functional and enjoyable, or scheduled regular walks.
- height-adjustable tables to support variation in posture and reducing prolonged sitting time.
- under-desk treadmills (walking pads). These have become increasingly popular. Walking at low speed (2–2.5 km/h), it is still very possible to type and read, and at slightly higher speeds to have online meetings.

As hybrid working has become a well-established work practice, strategies for active design in the office building, as well as in the remote work location should be considered.

What are the benefits of active design to the organisation?

The refurbishment of a workplace is costly, and the change in organisational policy and culture can be hard to implement. So, what would the incentive be for an organisation to go through this exercise and support active design? Increased physical activity has physical and psycho-social health benefits and is related to reduced absenteeism and reduced presenteeism, and to increased productivity (Pronk et al., 2004; Block et al., 2008; Brown et al., 2011; Amlani & Munir, 2014). In addition, employees who are satisfied with their work environment generally produce better work outcomes through improved productivity. A strong interest and investment in staff contributes to employees feeling valued (Zafar et al., 2014), which can improve staff morale and retention rates in a workplace. Data from the Sustainable and Healthy Environments (SHE) survey (SHE POE, 2023) showed that 87% of the participants were satisfied with the ability to be physically active during their working days (Figure 3.1). A global survey revealed that improving morale/engagement, reducing employee absences and improving productivity/presenteeism all scored in the top four reasons why employers choose to engage in wellness strategies (Buck consultants, 2014). Hence, strategies that are initially designed to support physical activity also have the potential to support social interaction, collaboration and staff retention.

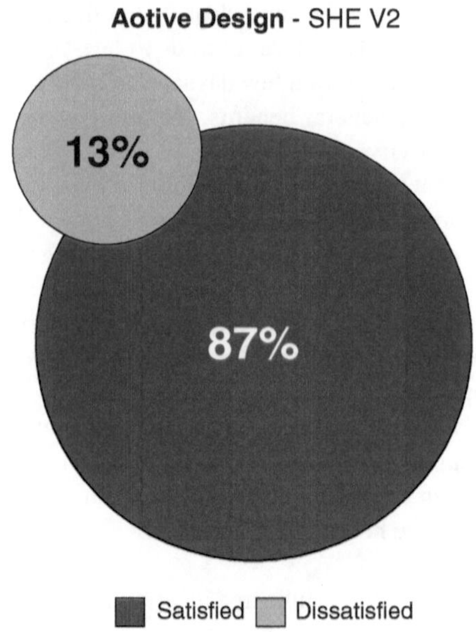

Figure 3.1 Percentage of satisfied and dissatisfied workers with being active during their workdays according to the SHE POE dataset.

Source: SHE POE dataset, 2023

The benefits of active design for an organisation hence include:

- Improved Employee Health and Wellness: active design can improve the health of employees through physical activity, reducing the risk of sedentary lifestyle–related illnesses and injuries.
- Increased Productivity: Studies have shown that physical activity can improve cognitive function and overall well-being, leading to increased productivity.
- Enhanced Work Environment: active design can create a more engaging and dynamic work environment, promoting a sense of community and improving overall employee satisfaction.
- Cost Savings: Implementing active design can reduce health care costs, improve employee retention and lower absenteeism, resulting in significant cost savings for the organisation.
- Improved Sustainability: active design can promote sustainability by encouraging the use of alternative transportation options, such as cycling or walking, reducing carbon emissions.

In a pre-post occupancy evaluation study (Engelen et al., 2017), where more than 100 participants moved from traditional office buildings to a new active design building, we found that standing increased, while sitting and lower back pain decreased, in the new building. We also found that the participants were finding work more motivating and were looking forward to going to work more in the new building. These results support the notion that active design has positive effects of well-being-related behaviour and outcomes, as well as benefits for productivity-related outcomes.

Conclusion

This chapter has covered a range of aspects of active design as an integral part of the high-performing office. Overall, incorporating active design principles into workplace design can create a healthier, more productive and more sustainable work environment for the occupants and the organisations. By adopting a systems-based approach to active design, the chance of realising all the potential benefits of active design is greatly enhanced.

A "high-performance" checklist for active design is provided here:

Principle	*Description*
PROVIDE STRUCTURES AND LAYOUTS ALIGNING TO ACTIVE DESIGN	☐ Open, well-lit staircases
CENTRALISE FACILITIES	☐ Placing bins and printers away (but within 20–30 m) from workstations ☐ Placing toilets and kitchen facilities away (but within 50–60 m) from workstations
CREATE DESTINATIONS	☐ Dining or collaboration areas that are attractive and comfortable and conducive to social interactions
PROVIDE ACCESSIBLE END-OF-TRIP FACILITIES	☐ Bicycle storage, lockers and showers promote physical activity and active transport to work
INCLUDE GREEN AND OUTDOOR AREAS	☐ Outdoor patios providing sheltered environments for breaks and social interactions
ESTABLISH SUPPORTIVE WORKPLACE CULTURE, POLICIES AND PROCEDURES	☐ Make stairs and outdoor areas accessible and useable ☐ Normalise physical movement at work and working away from a workstation

References

Athes, E. (2016, September 22). The office experiment. *Nature*, *537*, 294–296.

Australian Institute of Health and Welfare. (2018). *Australia's health 2018.* Retrieved March 02, 2023, from https://www.aihw.gov.au/reports/australias-health/australias-health-2018/contents/table-of-contents

Bauman, A. E., Chau, J. Y., Ding, D., & Bennie, J. (2013). Too much sitting and cardio-metabolic risk: An update of epidemiological evidence. *Current Cardiovascular Risk Reports*, *7*(4), 293–298. https//doi.org/10.1007/s12170-013-0316-y

Buckley, J. P., Hedge, A., Yates, T., Copeland, R. J., Loosemore, M., Hamer, M., Bradley, G., & Dunstan, D. W. (2015). The sedentary office: An expert statement on the growing case for change towards better health and productivity. *British Journal of Sports Medicine*, *49*(21), 1357–1362. https//doi.org/10.1136/bjsports-2015-094618

Chau, J. Y., Grunseit, A. C., Chey, T., Stamatakis, E., Brown, W. J., Matthews, C. E., Bauman, A. E., & Van Der Ploeg, H. P. (2013). Daily sitting time and all-cause mortality: A meta-analysis. *PloS One*. Edited by O. Y. Gorlova. Public Library of Science, *8*(11), e80000. https//doi.org/10.1371/journal.pone.0080000

The City of New york. (2010). *Active design guidelines: Promoting physical activity and health in design.* Retrieved March 02, 2023, from https://centerforactivedesign.org/guidelines/

Engelen, L. et al. (2017). 'Is active design changing the workplace? A natural pre-post experiment looking at health behaviour and workplace perceptions. *Work (Reading, Mass.)*, *56*(2), 229–237.

Engelen, L., Chau, J., Young, S., Mackey, M., Jeyapalan, D., & Bauman, A. (2019a). Is activity-based working impacting health, work performance and perceptions? A systematic review. In *Building research & information* (pp. 1–12). Routledge. https//doi.org/10.1080/09613218.2018.1440958

Engelen, L., Gale, J., & Bauman, A. E. (2019b). Beyond posters: Stairtember-evaluating the effectiveness of a multicomponent intervention to promote stair climbing. *Journal of Occupational and Environmental Medicine*, *61*(9), 743–746. https//doi.org/10.1097/JOM.0000000000001651

Giles-Corti, B., Vernez-Moudon, A., Reis, R., Turrell, G., Dannenberg, A. L., Badland, H., Foster, S., Lowe, M., Sallis, J. F., Stevenson, M., & Owen, N. (2016). City planning and population health: A global challenge. *The Lancet*, *388*(10062), 2912–2924. https//doi.org/10.1016/S0140-6736(16)30066-6

Halsey, L. G., Watkins, D. A. R., & Duggan, B. M. (2012). The energy expenditure of stair climbing one step and two steps at a time: Estimations from measures of heart rate. *PloS One*. Public Library of Science, *7*(12), e51213. https//doi.org/10.1371/journal.pone.0051213.

Heart Foundation. (2015). *Healthy active by design*. Retrieved June 12, 2019, from https://www.healthy activebydesign.com.au

Hofmann, W., Friese, M., & Wiers, R. W. (2008). Impulsive versus reflective influences on health behavior: A theoretical framework and empirical review. *Health Psychology Review*. Taylor & Francis Group, *2*(2), 111–137. https//doi.org/10.1080/17437190802617668

Largo-Wight, E., Chen, W. W., Dodd, V., & Weiler, R. (2011). Healthy workplaces: The effects of nature contact at work on employee stress and health. *Public Health Reports*, *126*(SUPPL. 1), 124–126. https//doi.org/10.1177/00333549111260s116

Levine, J. A. (2002). Non-exercise activity thermogenesis (NEAT). *Best Practice & Research. Clinical Endocrinology & Metabolism*, *16*(4), 679–702. Retrieved January 19, 2016, from http://www.ncbi.nlm.nih.gov/pubmed/12468415

Marteau, T. M., Hollands, G. J., & Fletcher, P. C. (2012). Changing human behavior to prevent disease: The importance of targeting automatic processes. *Science*, *337*(6101), 1492–1495. https//doi.org/10.1126/science.1226918

Marteau, T. M., Ogilvie, D., Roland, M., Suhrcke, M., & Kelly, M. P. (2011). Judging nudging: Can nudging improve population health? *BMJ*, *342*(3), d228–d228. https//doi.org/10.1136/bmj.d228

Marzban, S., Candido, C., Mackey, M., Engelen, L., Zhang, F., & Tjondronegoro, D. (2022). A review of research in activity-based working over the last ten years: Lessons for the post-COVID workplace. *Journal of Facilities Management*, *21*(3), 313–333. https://doi.org/10.1108/JFM-08-2021-0081

McGann, S. et al. (2014). Stationary in the office: Emerging themes for active buildings. *Architectural Science Review*. Taylor and Francis Ltd., *57*(4), 260–270. https//doi.org/10.1080/00038628.2014.958127

Nicoll, G., & Zimring, C. (2009). Effect of innovative building design on physical activity. *Journal of public health policy*. Nature Publishing Group, 30(Suppl 1), S111–S123. https//doi.org/10.1057/jphp.2008.55

Quintiliani, L., Sattelmair, J., & Sorensen, G. (2007). The workplace as a setting for interventions to improve diet and promote physical activity. *World Health Organization*, pp. 1–36.

Saelens, B. E., Vernez Moudon, A., Kang, B., Hurvitz, P. M., & Zhou, C. (2014). Relation between higher physical activity and public transit use. *American Journal of Public Health*, *104*(5), 854–859. https//doi.org/10.2105/AJPH.2013.301696

Sallis, J. F., Cervero, R. B., Ascher, W., Henderson, K. A., Kraft, M. K., & Kerr, J. (2006). An ecological approach to creating active living communities. *Annual Review of Public Health*, *27*(1), 297–322. https//doi.org/10.1146/annurev.publhealth.27.021405.102100

Skelly, L. E., Andrews, P. C., Gillen, J. B., Martin, B. J., Percival, M. E., & Gibala, M. J. (2014). High-intensity interval exercise induces 24-h energy expenditure similar to traditional endurance exercise despite reduced time commitment. *Applied Physiology, Nutrition, and Metabolism = Physiologie appliquée, nutrition et métabolisme*. NRC Research Press, *39*(7), 845–848. https//doi.org/10.1139/apnm-2013-0562

Smith, L., Ucci, M., Marmot, A., Spinney, R., Laskowski, M., Sawyer, A., Konstantatou, M., Hamer, M., Ambler, G., Wardle, J., & Fisher, A. (2013). Active buildings: Modelling physical activity and movement in office buildings. An observational study protocol. *BMJ Open*, *3*(11), e004103. https//doi.org/10.1136/bmjopen-2013-004103

Spinney, R., Smith, L., Ucci, M., Fisher, A., Konstantatou, M., Sawyer, A., Wardle, J., & Marmot, A. (2015). Indoor tracking to understand physical activity and sedentary behaviour: Exploratory study in UK office buildings. *PLoS One*. Edited by J. Shaman. Public Library of Science, *10*(5), e0127688. https//doi.org/10.1371/journal.pone.0127688

Sport England. (2015). *Active design: Planning for health and wellbeing through sport and physical activity*. Retrieved June 12, 2019, from https://www.sportengland.org/media/3426/spe003-active-design-published-october-2015-email-2.pdf

Stamatakis, E., Rogers, K., Ding, D., Berrigan, D., Chau, J., Hamer, M., & Bauman, A. (2015). All-cause mortality effects of replacing sedentary time with physical activity and sleeping using an isotemporal substitution model: A prospective study of 201,129 mid-aged and older adults. *The International Journal of Behavioral Nutrition and Physical Activity*. BioMed Central, *12*(1), 121. https//doi.org/10.1186/s12966-015-0280-7

Straker, L., Dunstan, D., Gilson, N., & Healy, G. (2016). *Sedentary work: Evidence on an emergent work health and safety issue*. Retrieved June 12, 2019, from https://www.safeworkaustralia.gov.au/system/files/documents/1702/literature-review-of-the-hazards-of-sedentary-work.pdf

Thorp, A. A., Kingwell, B. A., Owen, N., & Dunstan, D. W. (2014). Breaking up workplace sitting time with intermittent standing bouts improves fatigue and musculoskeletal discomfort in overweight/obese office workers. *Occupational and Environmental Medicine*, *71*(11), 765–771. https//doi.org/10.1136/oemed-2014-102348

Vischer, J. C. (2011). Towards an environmental psychology of workspace: How people are affected by environments for work. *Architectural Science Review*, *51*(2), 97–108. https//doi.org/10.3763/asre.2008.5114

World Health Organization. (2018). *Global action plan on physical activity 2018–2030: More active people for a healthier world.* Retrieved March 01, 2023, from https://www.who.int/publications/i/item/9789241514187

Yancey, A. K., McCarthy, W. J., Taylor, W. C., Merlo, A., Gewa, C., Weber, M. D., & Fielding, J. E. (2004). The Los Angeles Lift Off: A sociocultural environmental change intervention to integrate physical activity into the workplace. *Preventive Medicine*, *38*(6), 848–856. https//doi.org/10.1016/j.ypmed.2003.12.019

Zimring, C., Joseph, A., Nicoll, G. L., & Tsepas, S. (2005). Influences of building design and site design on physical activity: Research and intervention opportunities. *American Journal of Preventive Medicine*. Elsevier, *28*(2 Suppl 2), 186–193. https//doi.org/10.1016/j.amepre.2004.10.025

4
ERGONOMIC DESIGN

Martin Mackey

> The science and practice of ergonomics focusses on the worker as the most important element of the office and adapts the office components, environment, and work systems to the workers involved to optimise their health and safety, productivity, efficiency, acceptance, and ultimately quality of life.
>
> – *Kroemer & Kroemer, 2001; van der Voordt, 2003*

Introduction

Office work as a proportion of all occupations has increased markedly in the last century. In the USA, office workers increased three-fold from 18% in 1900 to 60% of employees in 2010 (Cenedella, 2010). In Australia, the most common occupations during 2018–19 were professionals (18.8%), clerical and administrative workers (11.3%) and managers (10.8%), many of whom would be categorised as office workers (ABS, 2020). As the proportion of office work being undertaken has grown, so has the revolution in microcomputing and information technology over the last 40 years, which has led to most knowledge workers using a computer for at least part of their work activities, either in the office, in the home, in transport, or other locations of choice. This rapid evolution in the computerisation of work, and more recently an IT-driven greater flexibility to conduct office work remotely, has led to an increased importance of understanding ergonomic principles to inform the design of the 'office' workplace, work systems and the work environment to optimise the musculoskeletal health and productivity of knowledge workers no matter the work setting (Hedge, 2017b; Pereira et al., 2017). This chapter explores how the science and practice of ergonomics can support the design of high-performing office workplaces by placing the worker at the centre of consideration and adapt the office (tasks, settings, systems and environment) to the knowledge worker to enhance their health and safety, productivity and well-being. (McAtamney et al., 2017). In doing so, this chapter will define the elements of ergonomics, discuss the challenges to the musculoskeletal health of knowledge workers in the computerised office environment and the potential impact on health-related productivity. The chapter will also explore the evidence for implementing ergonomic solutions to these challenges, reflect on the implications for the post-COVID office workplace, including the home office environment, and provide an ergonomic checklist for a high-performance office.

DOI: 10.1201/9781003328728-5
This chapter has been made available under a CC-BY-NC-ND 4.0 license.

Domains of ergonomics

The term 'ergonomics' (or human factors), derived from the Greek words 'ergon' (work) and 'nomos' (laws), is the scientific discipline concerned with the understanding of interactions among humans and other elements of a work system, and one which uses the scientific method to design work and workplaces in order to optimize human well-being and overall work system performance (IEA, 2000). The discipline of ergonomics consists of several domains, including physical, cognitive and organisational factors (Hedge, 2017a) (see Figure 4.1). Physical ergonomics concerns the impact of working postures, materials handling, repetitive movements and workplace layout on the health, safety and productivity of workers. Cognitive ergonomics concerns the impact of mental workload, decision-making, skilled performance, human–computer interaction, work stress and training, as these relate to human–work system design. Organizational ergonomics is concerned with communication, scheduling and working times, teamwork, participatory design, new work paradigms and virtual and telework (IEA, 2000). For example, if the design or use of a computer workstation results in a worker adopting habitual awkward or constrained sitting postures, their musculoskeletal comfort and resultant work performance will be negatively impacted. Equally, an imbalance between the work demands and a worker's control over scheduling or work hours may lead to increased stress, errors, physical and mental ill health, and ultimately lost productivity.

However, in addition to these three key ergonomic domains, we also need to consider the design of the physical work environment (such as the indoor ventilation, lighting, visual and auditory acoustic conditions) on the health and productivity of the knowledge worker. For example, if the internal ambient temperature, airflow, lighting and noise levels are each not optimally designed, worker health, performance and job satisfaction will decline. Similarly, if the physical layout and adaptability of workplace settings (workstations, collaborative meeting and social spaces) is sub-optimal, work postures, teamwork and communication may be affected, impacting health and work performance. Thus, the work environment should be rightly regarded as an essential fourth domain of the ergonomic work system design process (Hedge, 2017a). Each of these four ergonomic domains can impact, independently and synergistically, on musculoskeletal health, productivity and job satisfaction in office workers.

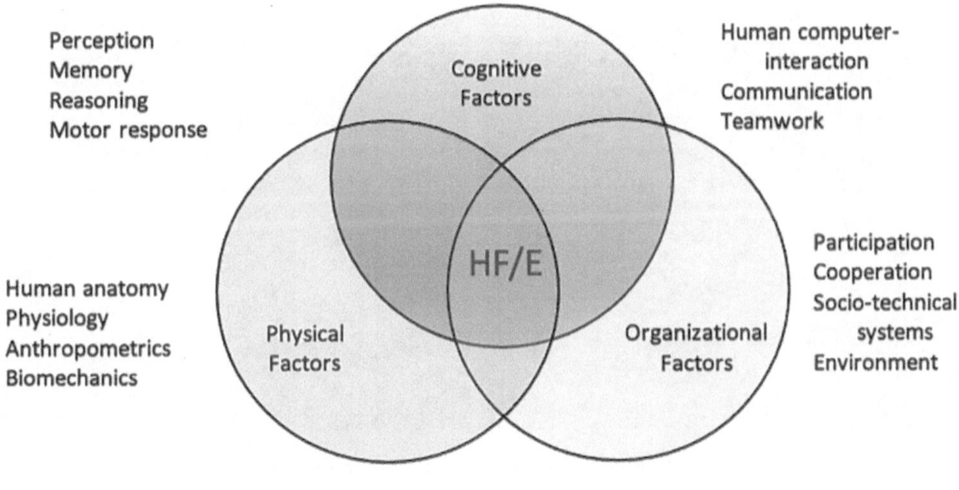

Figure 4.1 Domains of ergonomics.

Source: What Is Ergonomics (HFE)? | International Ergonomics Association https://iea.cc/what-is-ergonomics/ (with permission)

Computer-based office work and musculoskeletal disorders

Microcomputers have become synonymous with the way of working in the modern office since their introduction as an essential component of knowledge work in the 1980s. The ubiquity of microcomputers has enabled knowledge workers to operate in a variety of office layouts ranging from one-person rooms/cells to two–six-persons rooms to open plan, each typically found in a traditional office environment, and where each worker is usually allocated their own personal computer workstation. In the last 20 years newer, more flexible office designs have emerged, such as combi-offices (Figure 4.2), providing for a variety of workspace areas where focussed work is possible, and other open areas in which communication and collaborative or creative tasks may be undertaken (Vink et al., 2017). In combi-offices it is more common that knowledge workers are not allocated their own computer workstation but move between work areas to suit the nature of tasks they are performing, typified by activity-based working (ABW) office environments (Candido et al., 2019; Marzban et al., 2022). In ABW environments knowledge workers generally have access to a portable computerised devise (laptop or tablet), which may be operated independently in a variety of work areas or connected to a desktop workstation screen and keyboard.

Since the technology shift from paper- to computer-based office work in the 1980s, workers began to experience work-related musculoskeletal disorders, due in part to the poor design of office work and workspaces (Hedge, 2017b). Risk factors associated with the development of musculoskeletal disorders (MSD) in office workers are manifold but include prolonged exposure to biomechanical risks, such as sustained and awkward sitting postures; poor work systems, such as inadequate task variation, communication and teamwork; and psychosocial risks, such as excessive workload demands. The association between the 12-month prevalence of musculoskeletal symptoms with computer-based work was investigated in a cross-sectional study of over 900 public service office workers from six government departments (Griffiths et al., 2012). The duration of daily computer work had a significant, positive linear association with a higher prevalence of musculoskeletal symptoms in the neck and upper extremity regions (Griffiths et al., 2012), with employees in higher-level management and professional occupational groups at greater risk

Figure 4.2 Example of a combi-office comprising focussed areas for concentrated work; open areas for lower focussed work; open and closed meeting areas for collaboration, creative and project work and eating and social areas for rest and casual engagement.

Source: personal images

than those in administration and secretarial occupational groups due to their greater exposure to computer work (6–8 hours per day) (Griffiths et al., 2012). Similarly, a recent systematic review investigating the association of exposure to screen work with neck and upper extremity symptoms from 12 prospective studies (total of 18,538 participants) found an 11% increased relative risk of musculoskeletal symptoms with larger exposure to screen work (Coenen et al., 2019), though this risk was weaker when screen work was assessed objectively compared to self-report.

Computerised office work not only has important implications for worker health, but also for work productivity and job satisfaction. The relationship between individual and work-related factors with health-related productivity in 700 office workers, employed by 14 large public and private organizations, was investigated in a recent study (Pereira et al., 2017). The research found health-related productivity loss was more likely in those with lower job satisfaction, psychological well-being and musculoskeletal pain, and that financial burden to the organisations of overall health-related productivity loss was predominately driven by the costs of presenteeism (Pereira et al., 2017). The barriers and enablers to achieving greater productivity in offices has been the subject of extensive research (van der Voordt, 2003). For knowledge workers evidence is emerging that health-related productivity is optimised when the ergonomic office design caters for a variety of workspaces where workers can perform specific tasks such as focussed work, creative and collaborative work and casual and social engagement, typified by ABW office environments (Candido et al., 2021a; Candido et al., 2021b; Vink et al., 2017).

Further, ergonomics is most successfully integrated into high-performance offices to optimise worker health, productivity and job satisfaction when the office environment and work organisation are designed to meet the workers' 'fit' and functional needs and without them being conscious of it (McAtamney et al., 2017). Moreover, application of ergonomic principles in designing office workspaces and work practices have emerged as a means not only of rehabilitating injured workers but also as a means of preventing future work injuries (Hedge, 2017b). Key amongst these principles is to design computerised work so it can be performed with the body (and body parts) positioned in a neutral posture, to minimise repetitive movements, and to avoid a requirement for excessive muscle activation force. Working with a neutral body posture means that no parts of the body are bent, twisted or contorted away from a normal, relaxed comfortable position (Hedge, 2017b).

Office ergonomic design principles

The neutral posture

Guidelines for assuming a neutral posture during computerised office work have been well documented in numerous occupational ergonomic texts (Grandjean & Kroemer, 1997; Hedge, 2017b; Kroemer & Kroemer, 2001). In summary, for the upper body, this means the neck is balanced and aligned on top of the spine with minimal bending or twisting; the spine is erect with normal 'S' shape curvature but in a slightly reclined posture supported by a suitable back support such as an ergonomic chair; the shoulders are relaxed and are not lifted upward towards the neck; the upper arms are relaxed and rest close beside the upper body; the elbows are relaxed beside the upper body, bent close to a right angle and not lifted upward and/or outward away from the upper body; the forearms are not twisted; and wrists and hands are straight and level (see Figure 4.3). For the lower body, the thighs (when seated) should be close to horizontal or slightly dropped, supported and comfortable, and when standing, vertically aligned without twisting. The knees, when seated, should be at a right angle or greater to prevent tissue compression, and the lower leg is close to vertical so the feet lie ahead of the knees. When standing, the knees should not be uncomfortably

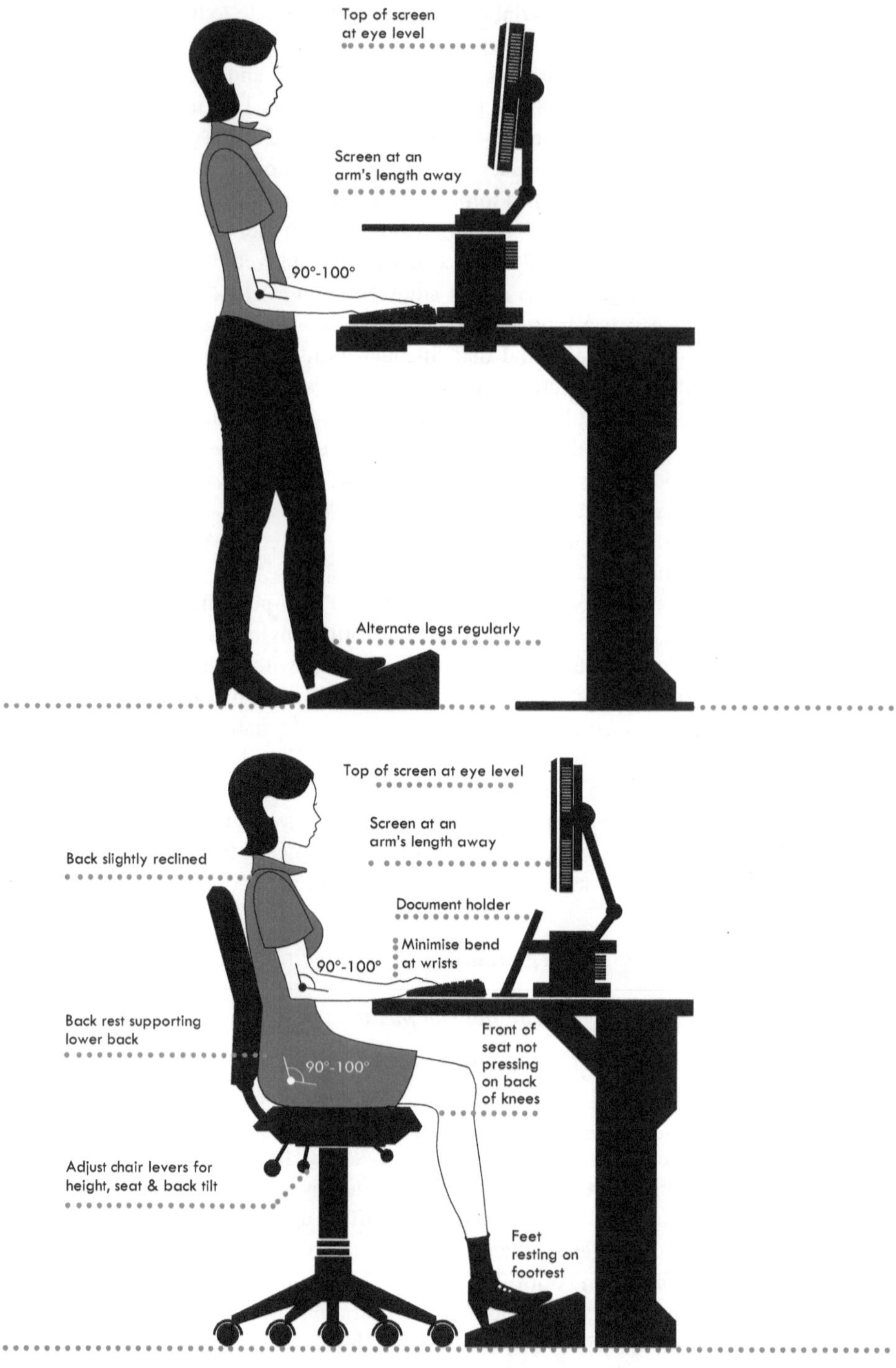

Figure 4.3 Neutral posture for computer-based work in sitting and standing.

Source: University of Sydney https://intranet.sydney.edu.au/services/safety-wellbeing/standards-guidelines/office-ergonomics.html (with permission)

bent, and lower legs should be vertically aligned with the ankles positioned so the feet are flat on the floor or on an inclined foot support (Hedge, 2017b; Vink et al., 2017). In addition to these recommended postures ergonomic design principles need to consider the requirement for, and ease of adjustability of workstations and computer/IT hardware to suit the characteristics of the end-use, such as the worker's size and shape, their frequency and duration of use, their accessibility and mobility, if single or multiple users are being designed for, and whether the keyboard is embedded or separate to the computer device (Australian Government Department of Health, 2017).

There is ample evidence from research (Hagberg et al., 1995) that optimising musculoskeletal function by enabling individuals to work in settings designed to promote a neutral posture of the body and body parts can eliminate pain and discomfort to a large extent (Hedge, 2017b). In practice, however, this objective of 'fitting the task to the human' has proven to be difficult to attain consistently. Over the last 20 years the variety of office furniture and equipment, including workstations, desks, chairs and screen raisers, have increased substantially in response to changes to the design and function of office work and workspaces, including the rapid uptake of mobile devices (phones, notebooks, tablets/laptops), the use of sit-to-stand workstations and the growth in ABW environments in preference to standard cell-based and open-plan office space (McAtamney et al., 2017). However, design standards for office workstations, desks and chairs are prescriptive and have not kept pace with the design changes in work environments, equipment and technology to adequately meet the needs of human end users (McAtamney et al., 2017). Nonetheless, while the same ergonomic principles relating to posture and sightlines still apply regardless of the changing technology (McAtamney et al., 2017), additional ergonomic design solutions are needed to respond to the changing environment. These include providing opportunities for postural variation and greater movement in the office environment.

Postural variation

A major risk of office work is sustained sedentary behaviour and insufficient physical activity during the working day. Objective measurement of sitting has shown that office workers spend around three-quarters of their working hours sitting (Straker et al., 2016). The duration of workplace sitting adds to the overall daily exposure to sedentariness acquired in the home, in leisure and in transport. In addition to any negative impact of excessive sitting on musculoskeletal health (Gupta et al., 2015), a growing body of recent evidence links high volumes of sitting time to a risk of premature mortality and major chronic illness, such as cardiovascular disease, type 2 diabetes, obesity, depression and some forms of cancer (Katzmarzyk et al., 2019). A recent meta-analysis of studies comprising more than 1 million adults (Ekelund et al., 2016) found that only very high volumes of moderate-to-vigorous intensity physical activity (≥60 min per day), achieved by less than 5% of the population, can attenuate the risk of premature death associated with high sitting time. Therefore, national physical activity and health guidelines now include recommendations that we should move more and sit less (Australian Government Department of Health, 2017).

Studies have shown that the risk to health is not only associated with the total duration of sitting but how sitting time is accumulated, with much of this sitting time accrued in prolonged, unbroken bouts of 30 minutes or longer (Healy et al., 2016), potentially increasing the risk of cardiometabolic disease (Dunstan et al., 2012) and low back pain (Gupta et al., 2015). Consequently, occupational health regulators have acknowledged that prolonged workplace sitting is an emergent work health and safety issue (Straker et al., 2016). It is recommended that workers take brief breaks from seated computerised work every 30 minutes, during which they can stand and walk around; engage in alternate work tasks, such as collecting documents from a remote printer; or get some refreshment from the kitchen. These sitting breaks can help provide relative rest to the neck and upper limb muscles while exercising the large sedentary lower limb muscles to improve blood circulation and reduce musculoskeletal discomfort and pain (Straker et al., 2016).

On the other hand, standing for long periods of the day can also be deleterious for health, with studies showing an increased risk of varicose leg veins, lower back and foot pain and premature birth (Vink et al., 2017). Prolonged standing has been associated with low back symptoms in epidemiological studies (Coenen et al., 2016), and in laboratory studies 40–71% of asymptomatic individuals without a history of low back pain (LBP) developed LBP within 120 minutes of standing that did not resolve with resumed sitting (Johnston et al., 2019). Thus, a growing body of evidence concerning the risks of sustained sitting or standing in working life has led to the development of numerous innovative interventions in office workplaces to encourage variation of posture throughout the working day (Johnston et al., 2019; Neuhaus et al., 2014; Radas et al., 2013; Straker et al., 2013).

Sit-stand workstations

One possible strategy to promote variation of posture throughout the working day is to encourage office workers to use an ergonomically designed sit-stand workstation to perform their work in sitting for part of the time and in standing for part of the time (Figure 4.3). Sit-stand workstations appear to have positive effects on sitting time. Radas et al. (2013) conducted a randomised controlled trial to determine whether providing 60 university office workers with an adjustable sit-stand ergonomic workstation together with a targeted education programme (https://www.happybodyatwork.com.au/), or targeted education alone, would lead to changes in sedentary behaviour at work compared with no intervention. The study found large (Cohen's D) effect size differences between the groups favouring the combined education/sit-stand workstation intervention for subjectively measured sitting time per workday (65 min less), and per work week (369 mins less) (Mackey et al., 2015). This effect in sitting time at work was similar to that reported in a systematic review and metanalysis of the impact of activity-permissive workstations on sedentary time and work performance in office workplaces, which found a pooled effect size of 77 minutes of less sitting over an 8-hour day (95% CI 120 to -35 min), without compromising work performance (Neuhaus et al., 2014). A later study which examined the impact of three sit-stand protocols found sitting time reduced by almost two hours and standing increased by 1.5 hours over the workday, without significantly impacting leisure-time physical activity or sleep time (Li et al., 2017). The use of sit-stand desks and awareness of the importance of postural variation and breaks were associated with an altered pattern of sedentary behaviour amongst 131 call-centre office workers (Straker et al., 2013). The study found that working at a sit-stand desk (90 operators), as opposed to a sit desk (41 operators), was associated with significantly lower daily proportion of the time seated (79% vs 84%), and less time to accumulate 5 minutes of standing/walking (36 vs 46 min). However, neither sitting episode length nor the number of switches between sitting and standing/walking per hour differed between the two groups. Interestingly, ergonomics awareness was not associated with any sedentary pattern variable among those using a sit-stand desk (Straker et al., 2013).

Health and productivity effects of sit-stand workstation use have also been examined. In a recent randomised controlled study, Johnston et al. (2019) compared the feasibility and impact of sit-stand workstations plus advice, with or without 4-weeks progressive resistance exercise training, on back pain and sitting time in university office workers at risk of LBP. The study found that the intervention had good acceptability and small but significant reduction in LBP severity (mean difference of -1.3 [-2.0, -0.6]) and workplace sitting time (82.7–99.3 min/8-hr workday reduction) in both groups without affecting productivity-related presenteeism (Johnston et al., 2019).

Recently, a large cluster randomised trial examined the effectiveness of a multicomponent intervention, with and without a height-adjustable desk, on daily sitting time, on physical behaviours and work-related health and performance outcomes in 756 desk-based council office workers (Edwardson et al., 2022). The multicomponent SMArT Work And Life (SWAL) intervention trialled in this study, built on an earlier successful intervention (Stand More AT Work [SMArT Work]), by focussing on a whole-day approach to reducing sitting time, facilitated by trained workplace champions within each organisation, and enabling evaluation of the real-world implementation of the intervention. The research team found that while both SWAL and SWAL plus desk were associated with a significant reduction in sitting time at 3- and 12-month follow-ups, the addition of a height-adjustable desk was found to be three times more effective. In addition, both intervention groups were associated with small improvements in stress, well-being and vigour, and the SWAL plus desk group was associated with improvements in pain in the lower extremities (Edwardson et al., 2022).

The question often arises as to how often office workers should change their posture between sitting and standing at an adjustable workstation. A recent study measured participant responses to different sit:stand ratios (30:0, 27:3, 24:6, 21:9, 18:12 and 15:15) within 30-minute cycles and facilitated by height-adjustable workstations for a 4-week period, amongst 16 computer-user university academics in their normal office environment (Black et al., 2022). The research team found that the presence and severity of musculoskeletal discomfort (across 11 body areas) were both significantly reduced following exposure to the sit-stand ratios, a finding consistent with earlier research. Interestingly, preferred standing durations were generally longer (between 24:6 and 15:15 ratios) and shorter ones were least liked. Standing at least 6 minutes improved perceptions most overall (Black et al., 2022). However, some cynicism still lingers over the long-term impact of sit-stand desks in field studies (Vink et al., 2017). For instance, one study of 90 office workers across four organisations found that after one month 60% of workers did not adjust their workstations (Wilks et al., 2006).

Treadmill and stationary cycle computer workstations in office environments have been investigated as a means of achieving desirable postural variation from chair sitting but also with an added benefit of being more physically active than that provided by sit-stand workstations (Vink et al., 2017). Workstations allowing office workers to walk or cycle while performing computer tasks have been shown to demand sufficient energy expenditure to result in significant health benefits (Levine & Miller, 2007); however, the impact on work performance was unclear. Straker and colleagues (2009) investigated the effects of these types of active computer workstations on keyboard and mouse performance in 30 office workers. Their study found that computer task performance was lower when walking and slightly lower when cycling compared with chair sitting, but mouse performance was more affected than typing performance, indicating that active workstations may be less suitable for mouse-intensive work (Straker et al., 2009).

However, the ways of office working are not static phenomena. Changes in technology have created new ways of working beyond the traditional office. Over the last 10 years much research attention has been focussed by industry and academia as to whether ABW office environments may also be a means of providing sedentary knowledge workers with greater opportunities for regular postural change and health-enhancing physical activity, in addition to their impact on worker productivity and job satisfaction (Candido et al., 2021; Engelen et al., 2018; Marzban et al., 2022).

ABW environments

ABW is an emerging way of working based on a holistic approach to work style that harnesses the intersection of the people (behavioural environment), place (physical environment) and technology, including knowledge sharing (virtual environment) (Engelen et al., 2018; Veldhoen & Company, 2018). An ABW environment facilitates the ability of knowledge workers to periodically move between work areas that best supports the performance of the tasks or 'activities' at hand. An office workplace that supports ABW, such as the combi-office, typically has design features such as quiet areas/rooms for concentrated or focused tasks; adjustable sit-stand workstations; open and closed meeting areas of variable occupant capacity for collaborative, project and creative tasks; team desks; standing desks; break-out areas; telephone booths for quiet areas and lounge and kitchen areas for rest and social engagement (see Figure 4.2). Workers are not allocated their own seating or desktop workstations, although teams or project groups may be allocated their own neighbourhood or home area in the office to facilitate communication. Instead, knowledge workers in an ABW environment may be allocated or 'bring their own' mobile 'smart' device, such as a laptop, tablet or phone, that is IT capable and internet accessible, so they can either dock onto an ergonomic workstation with screen, keyboard and mouse and/or use the device independently on a desktop anywhere in the office or even remotely, best suited to the task at hand.

However, the emergence of ABW as a new way of working has led to challenges for organisations in maintaining safe working conditions such as optimal ergonomic practice and infection control as workers move between different work and social areas to meet the task at hand. The latter infection risk has become particularly apparent to ABW office managers and knowledge workers in the post-COVID lockdown period, as workers return to the office and move between different workstations/areas during the day. This has necessitated additional work health and safety (WHS) strategies, such as regular and 'just in time' cleaning protocols of work surfaces, computer devices and multi-user equipment. In ABW, knowledge workers need to be educated on, and routinely practise, adjustment of the various workstations and seats they move to and between during the workday to maintain an optimal seated or standing neutral posture (Figure 4.3). Furthermore, if using a laptop or tablet on a work surface, it will be generally too low to maintain a safe neutral posture of the operator's neck, upper limb and trunk, which can create a risk for musculoskeletal health if the posture and associated excessive muscle activation is maintained for longer periods. If a laptop is replacing an adjustable desktop, it is recommended that a laptop riser is used to elevate the screen to a comfortable viewing height (Figure 4.3) and use a wireless keyboard and mouse so that an optimal neck posture and keying performance can be maintained (Hedge, 2017b).

Several recent state-of-the-art reviews on the effects of ABW have been published. A systematic review of the ABW literature comprising 17 studies involving 36,039 participants (Engelen et al., 2018) reported that ABW had positive impacts on knowledge workers' interaction, communication, control of time and space and satisfaction with the workspace; however, it was unfavourable for concentration and privacy, a finding frequently cited in the ABW literature (Candido et al., 2021a; Marzban et al., 2022). Two studies included in this review provided limited and mixed evidence that working in an ABW environment impacted employees' self-reported musculoskeletal complaints or discomfort (Engelen et al., 2018). In one included study, knowledge workers reported less LBP when working in an ABW trial space compared with the usual office, but no changes in discomfort of other body parts (Foley et al., 2016). An earlier study reported musculoskeletal discomfort over eight body parts was significantly reduced among employees after six months working in a new flexible office workspace with added ergonomics training (Robertson et al., 2008), a finding highlighting that when employees transition from a traditional office to an ABW design environment, enhanced induction for workers on how to best utilise the flexible workspace is necessary. For physical and mental health, Engelen et al. (2018) found the evidence was equivocal, recommending more high-quality research was needed.

A more recent review of research into ABW over the last 10 years (Marzban et al., 2022) focussed on the organizational, human and physical environment impacts of ABW. The review found that ABW office environments had positive impacts on the satisfaction of knowledge workers with the interior office design, but ABW was inclined to be more unfavourable for occupants' satisfaction with indoor environmental quality, productivity, distraction and privacy. Importantly, the review contended that satisfaction with ABW was a function of how this 'way of working' was implemented and how occupants use it, rather than the concept itself, supporting the earlier research finding by Robertson et al., 2008. Further, the review found that a partial uptake of ABW was more likely to lead to occupants' dissatisfaction, lower productivity and lower well-being, while a holistic uptake increased the chance of success. Additionally, after relocation to an ABW environment, ongoing monitoring and enhancement of the design features, supporting technology and behavioural etiquettes was required to allow settings to be adjusted by the organisation in response to the changing needs and preferences of occupants (Marzban et al., 2022).

The findings of this latter review appear to be consistent between industry sectors. A cross-industry comparison of occupants' satisfaction and perceived productivity in open-plan offices designed to support ABW office workspaces was conducted by appraising 2,090 post-occupancy evaluation (POE) surveys conducted in five industry sectors (tertiary education, finance, construction, property/asset management and design/engineering) (Candido et al., 2021a). The study found biophilic and interior design features of the premises were consistently rated the highest by occupants from all industry sectors, while distraction and privacy rated the lowest level of satisfaction (Candido et al., 2021a). Furthermore, knowledge workers from the construction industry were the most satisfied, followed by finance and tertiary education, then occupant satisfaction, with interior design found to be the strongest predictor for perceived productivity across all industry sectors (Candido et al., 2021a). There is also evidence that office design that attempts to link the built environment with human health through compliance with certification tools such as the 'WELL Building Standard' (International WELL Building Institute, 2015) optimises occupants' satisfaction and productivity. For example, a recent study comparing WELL-certified office premises with non-WELL premises found that occupants' overall satisfaction, work ability, productivity and health were highest in the WELL-certified premises (Candido et al., 2021a). Further, open-plan offices designed to support ABW outperformed traditional offices on most ergonomic design features, including spatial comfort, personal control, comfort of furniture, adjustability of the work areas and ability to collaborate, with the best-performing offices prioritising overall ergonomics and providing a range of spaces designed to support a variety of work activities (Candido et al., 2021a).

However, the places where knowledge work can be conducted is now ubiquitous in modern society, in response to technology advancements and cultural change. Indeed, the COVID-19-induced lockdowns throughout 2020–21 disrupted workplaces globally by forcing knowledge workers out of the office and into their own homes (Marzban et al., 2021). For instance, by May 2020, 57% of public service employees were reportedly working from home (Duckett & Stobart, 2020). Numerous published studies have been conducted to evaluate the experience of knowledge workers of working from home during the COVID-19 lockdown and have lessons for the emerging ways of working in the post-COVID work culture, with increasing proportions of those workers choosing to remain working from other locations, including the home 'office', for at least for part of their work hours (Davis et al., 2020; Harrington & Walker, 2004; Marzban et al., 2021; Oakman et al., 2020; Oakman et al., 2022; Weale et al., 2022; Wutschert et al., 2022).

The home office

A recent cross-sectional study contributed to this research knowledge by identifying positive and negative aspects of working from home (WFH), from the perspectives of both organisations (n=28) and knowledge workers (n=301) across numerous industry sectors during the first wave of COVID-19-induced lockdowns, examining the human, organisational and environmental considerations of the WFH experience (Marzban et al., 2021). Physical environment considerations of WFH included the varied, but often sub-optimal, 'ergonomics' of the home 'office' (Davis et al., 2020), including working in shared spaces, with potential negative impacts on musculoskeletal health and productivity (see Figure 4.4). In addition, the available digital infrastructure and internet connectivity were also important environmental considerations of the WFH experience. Key challenges experienced by employees in their WFH arrangements included poor internet connectivity, increased workload, poor home office furniture ergonomics or set-up and increased stress and burnout. In addition, employees generally reported a decline in both physical and mental health, a finding supported by another cross-sectional survey study of WFH arrangements (Oakman et al., 2022). In contrast, key challenges from the organisational perspective included WHS concerns, knowledge sharing and maintaining work culture and productivity. Despite this latter concern, 75% of employees rated their productivity as the 'same or better than before', and 65% indicated that they could do their job as effectively remotely as in the office, a finding also reflective of their perspectives on their connectedness and to a lesser extent team cohesion and knowledge sharing whilst WFH (Marzban et al., 2021).

Davis et al. (2020) conducted a quality improvement evaluation of the ergonomic features of the home 'office' set-up amongst 46 academic and professional university staff in the early stages of the COVID-19 pandemic lockdown in the USA (Davis et al., 2020). Common ergonomic problems found in the home 'offices' of these university knowledge workers included sitting for sustained periods on fixed, non-adjustable-height stools and chairs and/or chairs with no lumbar spine support; working at table and desk surfaces which were too high, requiring elevation of shoulders and arms which necessitated excessive postural muscle activation; desk surfaces with hard edges putting pressure on wrists during keyboard and mouse operation; regular viewing of external monitors positioned off to the side, requiring sustained neck rotation, or

Figure 4.4 Examples of common ergonomic posture problems found in home offices.

using laptop monitors positioned too low on work surfaces including on the thighs, requiring sustained excessive neck flexion; and walking on a treadmill at a computer workstation with the risk of tripping or falling (Davis et al., 2020). Several of these ergonomic problems are illustrated in Figure 4.4.

In terms of home office seating and desk issues identified in the Davis et al. (2020) study, ergonomic recommendations for chair and workstation requirements are available in relevant standards. However, using personal resources to fund an ergonomic chair and workstation for use in a dedicated home office space may be outside the budget for many knowledge workers, particularly younger workers or those with families or those in shared accommodations. Therefore, potential solutions may include using a cushion to elevate the seat height while ensuring the feet remain supported, using a rolled-up towel to provide lumbar support and avoiding or removing chair arm rests to facilitate closer access to the desk surface. If using an external computer screen in the home office, the monitor should be elevated on books to ensure the top is at eye height, and if using dual monitors, the primary monitor should be positioned directly in front of the operator with the secondary monitor off to the side. If using a laptop or tablet it should be positioned on a desk or table and ideally used for short periods. However, if the laptop or tablet is replacing a desktop computer, a docking station could be used to link it to a larger external screen. If being used independently for long periods, a laptop riser should be used to elevate the screen to a comfortable viewing height and integrated with a wireless keyboard and mouse to reduce neck flexion and improve keying performance. Continuous use of a laptop while positioned on a couch, bed or floor should be avoided to minimise awkward and sustained postures and resultant musculoskeletal discomfort. Changing postures from seated work in the home office by taking regular standing or walking rest breaks, task variation and rotating between sitting and standing for online meetings, telephone calls and possibly computer operation are also recommended. In the absence of the capacity to purchase costly sit-stand ergonomic workstations, some suggestions for simple makeshift standing workstations for short use in the home include placing a laptop on an elevated stable ironing board, on top of a piano, or on top of a box. Glare is another concern that accompanies workstations in homes due to sunlight exposure through untreated glass. As such the desk should be oriented so that computer screens are positioned perpendicularly to the window.

A recent systemic review examining the working conditions and work-related musculoskeletal disorders amongst WFH teleworkers found a lack of ergonomically sound working arrangements in the home office (Wutschert et al., 2022), supporting the earlier research by Davis et al. (2020) and Marzban et al. (2021). The study also found that most of the included studies reported teleworkers who had experienced musculoskeletal issues, and additionally they reported a lack of awareness amongst the organisations regarding the existence of WFH-based policies, ergonomics training programmes for employees and the health-related consequences associated with the absence of ergonomic support (Wutschert et al., 2022). This is a concerning finding, especially as earlier research indicated that ergonomics training significantly improved the knowledge, attitudes and practices of teleworkers, and in some cases, the pain and discomfort they had experienced was eliminated or reduced as a result of the training (Harrington & Walker, 2004).

In future, many organisations will likely prefer their employees return to the office on a regular basis to control optimal ergonomic office conditions, maintain work culture, build trust and knowledge sharing and create organic, incidental opportunities for learning, collaboration and innovation. In contrast, many knowledge workers have enjoyed the flexibility of WFH and may prefer to only return to the office part-time.

Conclusion

While ergonomic design criteria applicable to office and workstations will still have utility in future, these principles may not always provide guidance for managing the risks in many of the new ways of working in the post-COVID-19 environment. This creates challenges for organisations and knowledge workers on how person-centred ergonomic principles are best implemented considering the varied environments, technologies, work patterns and ways of collaborations (McAtamney et al., 2017). However, this chapter provides an overview of key evidence-based recommendations for ergonomic design in high-performing offices to optimise health, productivity and job satisfaction.

A 'high-performance' checklist for ergonomic design is provided here:

Principle	*Description*
WORKSTATIONS Work areas, workstations and computer equipment should be set up to allow the operator to maintain a neutral posture of the body and body parts	• Provision of sit-stand and activity-permissible workstations in the office to facilitate regular posture change and health-enhancing physical activity
WORKPLACE Open offices should be designed to facilitate an ABW environment	• ABW provides workers with a variety of spaces based on the task.
TRAINING Organisations should provide ergonomic training to, and monitor safe work practices, for their office workers	• Workers should be provided with ergonomic training and guidelines for setting up and working in a home office or other remote work environment
ENCOURAGING BREAKS Workers should be encouraged to take frequent, brief rest breaks during the workday	• Looking away from the screen every 20 minutes to reduce eye strain and fatigue • Microbreaks from typing for less than 2 minutes by standing up, stretching, making a phone call, moving around and doing a different work task, such as walking to the printer • Engage in gentle exercise or incidental physical activity (walking) breaks every 1–2 hours • Workers should be encouraged to change their posture regularly
FLEXIBLE WORKING ARRANGEMENT	• In the post-COVID-19 work environment, a participatory approach by organisations and employees is recommended to negotiate and manage flexible work arrangements

References

ABS. (2020). *6160.0 – Jobs in Australia, 2014–15 to 2018–19: Key statistics*. Australian Bureau of Statistics. https://www.abs.gov.au/statistics/labour/jobs/jobs-australia/latest-release

Australian Government Department of Health. (2017). *Australia's physical activity and sedentary behaviour guidelines*. http://www.health.gov.au/internet/main/publishing.nsf/Content/fs-18-64years

Black, N. L., Tremblay, M., & Ranaivosoa, F. (2022). Different sit: Stand time ratios within a 30-minute cycle change perceptions related to musculoskeletal disorders. *Applied Ergonomics*, *99*, 103605. https//doi.org/10.1016/j.apergo.2021.103605

Candido, C., Gocer, O., Marzban, S., Gocer, K., Thomas, L., Zhang, F., Gou, Z., Mackey, M., Engelen, L., & Tjondronegoro, D. (2021a). Occupants' satisfaction and perceived productivity in open-plan offices designed to support activity-based working: Findings from different industry sectors [Article]. *Journal of Corporate Real Estate*, *23*(2), 106–129. https://doi.org/10.1108/JCRE-06-2020-0027

Candido, C., Marzban, S., Haddad, S., Mackey, M., & Loder, A. (2021b). Designing healthy workspaces: Results from Australian certified open-plan offices [Article]. *Facilities*, *39*(5–6), 411–433. https://doi.org/10.1108/F-02-2020-0018

Candido, C., Thomas, L., Haddad, S., Zhang, F., Mackey, M., & Ye, W. (2019). Designing activity-based workspaces: Satisfaction, productivity and physical activity [Article]. *Building Research and Information*, *47*(3), 275–289. https://doi.org/10.1080/09613218.2018.1476372

Cenedella, M. (2010). Great news! We've become a white-collar nation. *Business Insider*. https://www.businessinsider.com/great-news-weve-become-a-white-collar-nation-2010-1

Coenen, P., van der Molen, H. F., Burdorf, A., Huysmans, M. A., Straker, L., Frings-Dresen, M. H., & van der Beek, A. J. (2019). Associations of screen work with neck and upper extremity symptoms: A systematic review with meta-analysis. *Occupational & Environmental Medicine*, *76*(7), 502–509. https//doi.org/10.1136/oemed-2018-105553

Coenen, P., Willenberg, L., Parry, S., Shi, J. W., Romero, L., Blackwood, D. M., Maher, C. G., Healy, G. N., Dunstan, D. W., & Straker, L. M. (2016). Associations of occupational standing with musculoskeletal symptoms: A systematic review with meta-analysis. *British Journal of Sports Medicine*, *52*(3), 176–183.

Davis, K. G., Kotowski, S. E., Daniel, D., Gerding, T., Naylor, J., & Syck, M. (2020). The home office: Ergonomic lessons from the 'new normal'. *Ergonomics in Design: The Quarterly of Human Factors Applications*, *28*(4), 4–10.

Duckett, S., & Stobart, A. (2020). *Australia's COVID-19 response: The story so far*. Retrieved October 13, 2020, from https://grattan.edu.au/news/australias-covid-19-response-the-story-so-far/

Dunstan, D., Kingwell, B., Larsen, R., Healy, G., Cerin, E., Hamilton, M., Shaw, J., Bertovic, D., Zimmet, P., Salmon, J., & Owen, N. (2012). Breaking up prolonged sitting reduces postprandial glucose and insulin responses. *Diabetes Care*, *35*(5), 976–983. https//doi.org/10.2337/dc11–1931

Edwardson, C., Biddle, S., Clemes, S., Davies, M. J., Dunstan, D., Eborall, H., Granat, M., Gray, L., Healy, G., Jaicim, M., Lawton, S., Maylor, B., Munir, F., Richardson, G., Yates, T., & A. M., C.-C. (2022). Effectiveness of an intervention for reducing sitting time and improving health in office workers: Three arm cluster randomised controlled trial. *BMJ*, *378*, e069288. https//doi.org/10.1136/bmj-2021-069288

Ekelund, U., Steene-Johannessen, J., Brown, W. J., Fagerland, M., Owen, N., Powell, K., Bauman, A., Lee, I., & Lancet Physical Activity Series 2 Executive Committee Lancet Sedentary Behaviour Working Group. (2016). Does physical activity attenuate, or even eliminate, the detrimental association of sitting time with mortality? A harmonised meta-analysis of data from more than 1 million men and women. *Lancet*, *388*(10051), 1302–1310. https//doi.org/10.1016/S0140–6736(16)30370–1

Engelen, L., Chau, J., Young, S., Mackey, M., Jeyapalan, D., & Bauman, A. (2018). Is activity-based working impacting health, work performance and perceptions? A systematic review. *Building Research & Information*, *47*, 468–479. https://doi.org/10.1080/09613218.2018.1440958

Foley, B., Engelen, L., Gale, J., Bauman, A., & Mackey, M. (2016). Sedentary behaviour and musculoskeletal discomfort is reduced when office workers trial an Activity Based Work (ABW) environment. *Journal of Occupational and Environmental Medicine*, *58*(9), 924–931.

Grandjean, E., & Kroemer, K. H. E. (1997). *Fitting the task to the human: A textbook of occupational ergonomics* (5th ed.). CRC Press.

Griffiths, K. L., Mackey, M. G., Adamson, B. J., & Pepper, K. L. (2012). Prevalence and risk factors for musculoskeletal symptoms with computer based work across occupations. *Work*, *42*(4), 533–541. https//doi.org/10.3233/WOR-2012-1396

Gupta, N., Christiansen, C., Hallman, D., Korshøj, M., Carneiro, I., & Holtermann, A. (2015). Is objectively measured sitting time associated with low back pain? A cross-sectional investigation in the NOMAD study. *PLoS One*, *10*(3), e0121159. https//doi.org/10.1371/journal.pone.0121159

Hagberg, M., Silverstein, B., Wells, R., Smith, W., Hendrick, H., & Carayon, P., & Perusse, M. (1995). *Work Related Musculoskeletal Disorders (WMSDs): A reference book for prevention*. Taylor and Francis.

Harrington, S., & Walker, B. L. (2004). The effects of ergonomics training on the knowledge, attitudes, and practices of teleworkers. *Journal of Safety Research*, *35*(1), 13–22.

Healy, G., Eakin, E., Owen, N., LaMontagne, A., Moodie, M., Winkler, E., Fjeldsoe, B., Wiesner, G., Willenberg, L., & Dunstan, D. (2016). A cluster randomized controlled trial to reduce office workers' sitting time: Effect on activity outcomes. *Medicine & Science in Sports & Exercise*, *48*(9), 1787–1797. https//doi.org/10.1249/MSS.0000000000000972

Hedge, A. (2017a). Introduction to workplace ergonomics and issues of health and productivity in computer work settings. In A. Hedge (Ed.), *Ergonomic workplace design for health wellness and productivity*. CRC Press, Taylor & Francis Group.
Hedge, A. (Ed.). (2017b). *Ergonomic workplace design of health, wellness, and productivity*. CRC Press, Taylor & Francis Group.
IEA. (2000). What is ergonomics. *International Ergonomics Association*. https://iea.cc/what-is-ergonomics/
International WELL Building Institute. (2015). *The WELL building standard*. Retrieved November 3, 2022 from https://www.wellcertified.com/
Johnston, V., Gane, E. M., Brown, W., Vicenzino, B., Healy, G. N., Gilson, N., & Smith, M. D. (2019). Feasibility and impact of sit-stand workstations with and without exercise in office workers at risk of low back pain: A pilot comparative effectiveness trial. *Applied Ergonomics*, *76*, 82–89. https//doi.org/10.1016/j.apergo.2018.12.006
Katzmarzyk, P., Powell, K., Jakicic, J., Troiano, R., Piercy, K., Tennant, B., & COMMITTEE*, P. A. G. A. (2019). Sedentary behavior and health: Update from the 2018 Physical Activity Guidelines Advisory Committee. *Medicine & Science in Sports & Exercise*, *51*(6), 1227–1241. https//doi.org/10.1249/MSS.0000000000001935
Kroemer, K. H. E., & Kroemer, A. D. (2001). *Office ergonomics*. Taylor and Francis Ltd.
Levine, J., & Miller, J. (2007). The energy expenditure of using a "walk-and-work" desk for office workers with obesity. *British Journal of Sports Medicine*, *41*, 558–561. https//doi.org/10.1136/bjsm.2006.032755
Li, I., Mackey, M. G., Foley, B., Pappas, E., Edwards, K., Chau, J. Y., Engelen, L., Voukelatos, A., Whelan, A., Bauman, A., Winkler, E., & Stamatakis, E. (2017). Reducing office workers' sitting time at work using sit-stand protocols: Results from a pilot randomized controlled trial. *Journal of Occupational and Environmental Medicine*, *59*(6), 543–549.
Mackey, M., Leaver, A., Radas, A., Shirley, D., Bouvier, A.-L., Chau, J., Engelen, L., Gale, J., & Bauman, A. (2015). Do ergonomic and education interventions reduce prolonged occupational sitting? A randomised controlled trial. *Physiotherapy*, *101*, e844.
Marzban, S., Candido, C., Mackey, M., Engelen, L., Zhang, F., & Tjondronegoro, D. (2022). A review of research in activity-based working over the last ten years: Lessons for the post-COVID workplace [Review]. *Journal of Facilities Management*, *21*(3), 313–333. https://doi.org/10.1108/JFM-08-2021-0081
Marzban, S., Durakovic, I., Candido, C., & Mackey, M. (2021). Learning to work from home: Experience of Australian workers and organizational representatives during the first Covid-19 lockdowns [Article]. *Journal of Corporate Real Estate*, *23*(3), 203–222. https://doi.org/10.1108/JCRE-10-2020-0049
McAtamney, L., Aickin, C., Caple, D. C, Caponecchia, C. D., & Mackey, M. (2017). Challenges and future research opportunities with new ways of working. In A. Hedge (Ed.), *Ergonomic workplace design of health, wellness, and productivity* (pp. 353–370). CRC Press Taylor & Francis Group.
Neuhaus, M., Eakin, E. G., Straker, L., Owen, N., Dunstan, D. W., Reid, N., & Healy, G. N. (2014). Reducing occupational sedentary time: A systematic review and meta-analysis of evidence on activity-permissive workstations. *Obesity Reviews*, *15*(10), 822–838. https//doi.org/10.1111/obr.12201
Oakman, J., Kinsman, N., Lambert, K., Stuckey, R., Graham, M., & Weale, V. (2022). Working from home in Australia during the COVID-19 pandemic: Cross-sectional results from the Employees Working From Home (EWFH) study [Research Support, Non-U.S. Gov't]. *BMJ Open*, *12*(4), e052733. https//doi.org/10.1136/bmjopen-2021-052733
Oakman, J., Kinsman, N., Stuckey, R., Graham, M., & Weale, V. (2020). A rapid review of mental and physical health effects of working at home: How do we optimise health? [Review]. *BMC Public Health*, *20*(1), 1825. https//doi.org/10.1186/s12889-020-09875-z
Pereira, M. J., Johnston, V., Straker, L. M., Sjogaard, G., Melloh, M., O'Leary, S. P., & Comans, T. A. (2017). An investigation of self-reported health-related productivity loss in office workers and associations with individual and work-related factors using an employer's perspective [Research Support, Non-U.S. Gov't]. *Journal of Occupational & Environmental Medicine*, *59*(7), e138–e144. https//doi.org/10.1097/JOM.0000000000001043
Radas, A., Mackey, M., Leaver, A., Bouvier, A. L., Chau, J. Y., Shirley, D., & Bauman, A. (2013). Evaluation of ergonomic and education interventions to reduce occupational sitting in office-based university workers: Study protocol for a randomized controlled trial. *Trials*, *14*, 330. https//doi.org/10.1186/1745-6215-14-330
Robertson, M., Huang, Y., O'Neill, M., & Schleifer, L. (2008). Flexible workspace design and ergonomics training: Impacts on the psychosocial work environment, musculoskeletal health, and work effectiveness among knowledge workers. *Applied Ergonomics*, *39*(4), 482–494. https//doi.org/10.1016/j.apergo.2008.02.022

Straker, L., Abbott, R. A., Heiden, M., Mathiassen, S. E., & Toomingas, A. (2013). Sit-stand desks in call centres: Associations of use and ergonomics awareness with sedentary behavior [Research Support, Non-U.S. Gov't]. *Applied Ergonomics, 44*(4), 517–522. https//doi.org/10.1016/j.apergo.2012.11.001

Straker, L., Coenen, P., Dunstan, D., Gilson, N., & Healy, G. (2016). *Sedentary work – Evidence on an emergent work health and safety issue – final report*. Retrieved March 01, 2023, from https://www.safetyconsultantsaustralia.com.au/sedentary-work-evidence-on-an-emergent-work-health-and-safety-issue/#:~:text=Sedentary%20Work%20–%20Evidence%20on%20an%20Emergent%20Work%20Health%20and%20Safety%20Issue&text=The%20harm%20associated%20with%20prolonged,variety%2C%20and%20diminished%20gravitational%20resistance

Straker, L., Levine, J., & Campbell, A. (2009). The effects of walking and cycling computer workstations on keyboard and mouse performance. *Human Factors, 51*(6), 831–844. https://doi.org/doi/10.1177/0018720810362079

Van der Voordt, T. J. M. (2003). *Costs and benefits of innovative workplace design*. Center for People and Building.

Vink, P., Bakker, I., & Groenestejin, L. (2017). Office workplaces. In A. Hedge (Ed.), *Ergonomic workplace design for health, wellness, and productivity*. CRC Press, Taylor & Francis Group.

Weale, V., Lambert, K. A., Stuckey, R., Graham, M., Cooklin, A., & Oakman, J. (2022). Working from home during COVID-19: Does work-family conflict mediate the relationship between workplace characteristics, job satisfaction and general health? *Journal of Occupational & Environmental Medicine, 19*, 19. https//doi.org/10.1097/JOM.0000000000002635

Wilks, S., Mortimer, M., & Nylénd, P. (2006). The introduction of sit–stand worktables; Aspects of attitudes, compliance and satisfaction. *Applied Ergonomics 37*(3), 359–365.

Wutschert, M. S., Romano-Pereira, D., Suter, L., Schulze, H., & Elfering, A. (2022). A systematic review of working conditions and occupational health in home office. *Work, 72*(3), 839–852. https://doi.org/10.3233/WOR-205239

5
BIOPHILIC DESIGN

Niranjika Wijesooriya and Arianna Brambilla

> Integrating nature into the workplace through biophilic design has the power to improve our well-being, productivity, and creativity, creating a more harmonious and sustainable connection between humans and the natural world.
>
> – *Authors*

Introduction

The demands of the modern lifestyle and socio-economic context require many individuals to work in office environments. These indoor spaces have been extensively researched, with studies highlighting the impact that indoor environmental quality (IEQ) can have on the occupants.

The factors of indoor environmental quality (IEQ) that have been identified to impact human performance include indoor air quality, lighting, thermal conditions, acoustics, layout design, biophilic design elements, nature views, visual appearance, location, and amenities. Like IEQ factors, human performance in the workplace can be broadly categorized into several aspects, including cognitive performance, comfort, and psychological well-being (van der Voordt & Jensen, 2021). Indeed, IEQ factors have been found to affect cognitive functions and psychological well-being, with discomfort in lighting, thermal, acoustic, and air quality being potential stressors that distract workers, decrease performance, and increase dissatisfaction among occupants (Sanchez et al., 2018).

Modern office workers face a range of factors that can negatively affect their mental well-being and productivity, creating mental fatigue and stress. To address these concerns, designers have looked at various design considerations, studying the impact on health and well-being in the workplace. By creating healthy workplaces, workers can enjoy a positive work experience while avoiding negative impacts on performance (van der Voordt & Jensen, 2021; Douglas et al., 2022). Regenerative architecture has emerged as a key design approach to harness health and well-being benefits, with biophilic design (BD) as a strategy that draws upon the human affinity to connect with nature. The concept of biophilia has been gaining attention for its restorative benefits, including attention restoration, stress reduction, and mood improvement (Kaplan, 1995; Lopes et al., 2020). These psychological benefits can potentially lead to increased workplace productivity and improved occupant health and well-being.

DOI: 10.1201/9781003328728-6
This chapter has been made available under a CC-BY-NC-ND 4.0 license.

BD has numerous benefits that can potentially synergize to result in a high-performance workplace. While studies have reported on these benefits individually, there is a lack of research on the association between high-performance workspaces and BD. Candido et al. (2019) found that high-performing open-plan offices often included BD principles in their design. Thus, the aim of this chapter is to provide an overview of the benefits of adopting BD principles and their potential contribution towards designing a high-performance workspace.

This chapter will synthesize the existing literature on BD benefits, drawing upon recent reviews, and further examine how BD has influenced cognitive performance, comfort, and well-being in workplace settings.

Benefits of biophilic design

> Although we spend 95% of our time indoors, we are really outdoor animals.
>
> (Baker, 2006)

Biophilia, introduced by biologist Edward Wilson (1984) and later developed as a design approach by biologist Stephen Kellert, is based on the premise that humans have an inherent affinity for connecting with nature (Kellert et al., 2008). However, modern lifestyles and urbanization have significantly reduced opportunities for such contact (Kayıhan, 2018). Biophilic design (BD) has gained attention as a means of bridging the gap between the built environment and nature within architecture (Wijesooriya et al., 2020).

Consulting firms such as Terrapin Bright Green and Interface Flooring have championed the concept of BD, with the former publishing various white papers on the subject and the latter creating the Human Spaces website to promote discussion. In addition, many green building rating systems have recently incorporated BD into their certification schemes, with the Living Building Challenge providing a design guide and having the highest focus on this aspect (Wijesooriya et al., 2021; ILFI, 2016).

Wijesooriya and Brambilla (2021) conducted a SWOT analysis on BD for sustainable design, revealing several strengths and opportunities that offer overall benefits for human well-being. The analysis showed the strongest evidence for health and well-being aspects. Figure 5.1 summarizes the benefits based on the identified strengths and opportunities.

BD for workplaces offers benefits in four main categories:

- Cognitive impacts: BD can enhance productivity, creativity, mnemonic capacity (capacity to acquire, store, and retrieve information from the past), and academic capacity (Nieuwenhuis et al., 2014; Evensen et al., 2017; Douglas et al., 2022).
- Emotional impacts: BD can induce happiness, relaxation, higher self-esteem, and more generally, positive emotions (Ibrahim et al., 2021; Yin et al., 2019; Evensen et al., 2017).
- Health and well-being: BD has restorative potential and has been linked to reduction in anxiety, improved recovery, reduced stress, and lower blood pressure (Zhu et al., 2015; Yin et al., 2019).

The current approach to implementing BD in design is largely guided by frameworks that outline specific principles for incorporating nature into built environments. One notable example is Stephen Kellert's six principles and 70 attributes for BD (Kellert et al., 2008). The 14 patterns of BD, developed by Terrapin Bright Green, is also a widely used guide in this area. In practice, BD involves incorporating natural elements directly into spaces or through their representation, even

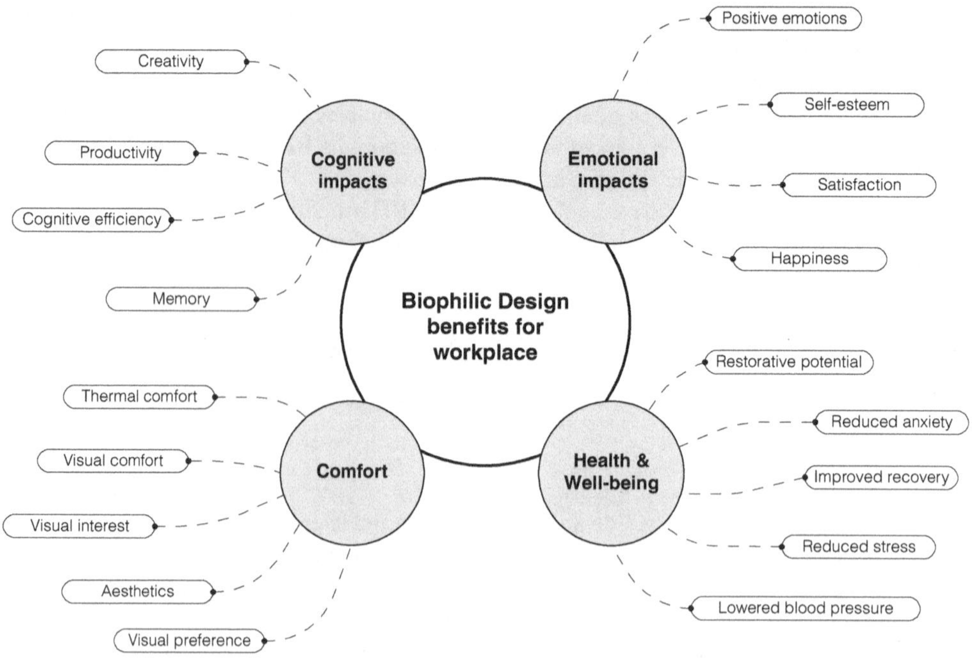

Figure 5.1 Benefits of biophilic design adapted from Wijesooriya and Brambilla (2021).

in confined areas, to enhance occupants' experiences of nature. This allows individuals to access the benefits of nature even in indoor environments.

The use of green walls is the more common approach where water is used for aesthetics and psychological effect. These elements could be coupled for enhanced thermal performance of the building that could bring multiple benefits to the interior. The water feature used as a roof in One Central Park mall in Sydney, Australia, is one such instance where the biophilic element aesthetically enhances the space, brings daylight, improves thermal performance in the building envelope, and enhances psychological well-being.

These identified benefits and design elements were seen across different building types, and further exploration of the use of BD in workplaces identified specific impacts for high-performance workspaces as detailed in the following section.

Exploring biophilic design for high-performance workplaces: lessons from the literature

The study of the benefits of nature experience originated in the field of environmental psychology, with attention restoration theory focusing on replenishing human attentional capacity, and stress recovery theory focusing on reducing psychophysiological stress and improving mood (Kaplan, 1995; Ulrich et al., 1991). The central concept of BD is integrating natural experiences into the built environment, encompassing various sensory domains such as visual attributes, sounds, natural airflow, sunlight, and natural fragrances (Heerwagen & Gregory, 2013; Kellert & Calabrese, 2015). Recent research has explored the association between BD elements and restorative benefits to building occupants, particularly in the design and construction of workplace environments.

The impact of biophilic design on workplaces can be categorized into three main areas: cognitive performance, comfort, and psychological well-being.

Cognitive performance

Cognitive performance is an essential component of workplace tasks that can benefit both workers and organizations in achieving their objectives efficiently. Productivity is perceived as a key parameter in work environments that contributes to achieving given targets. Several studies have explored the impact of BD on cognitive performance in the workplace. There is a consensus about the pivotal role that plants can play within an office, which can be associated with increased productivity (Nieuwenhuis et al., 2014; Evensen et al., 2017). Additionally, indoor plants have the potential to improve perceived creativity among office workers. Exposure to natural materials and windows has also been found to increase divergent creativity among occupants (Douglas et al., 2022).

The sensory experience represented in the workplace, including sounds from nature, can have a positive impact on cognitive performance. Studies have shown that bird songs and water sounds can enhance cognition and task performance in open-office settings (Ratcliffe et al., 2018; Ma & Shú, 2018). Lei et al. (2021) found that adding edible plants to small, confined spaces, such as modern office spaces, could increase cognitive performance.

BD utilizes natural elements and processes that are physically integrated into the workplace design. However, studies have also shown that virtual reality (VR) can be used to expose individuals to BD elements and demonstrate better memory performance, creativity, and shorter reaction time (Yin et al., 2019).

Overall, the evidence suggests that workplaces with BD can positively impact cognitive performance, productivity, and creativity through the use of various design elements.

Comfort

Ensuring physiological comfort is crucial for individuals spending significant time indoors, particularly in work environments where it can impact satisfaction and performance levels. This comfort can be experienced through thermal, visual, and acoustic means.

The benefits of natural airflow on thermal comfort and human performance have been extensively investigated (Zhu et al., 2015), while recent studies have also explored the relationship between thermal pleasure, restorative benefits, and BD in semi-outdoor workspaces (Lyu et al., 2023). Biophilic visual qualities, including views of nature and daylight, have also been shown to enhance thermal comfort, potentially through psychological adaptation or improvements in mood (Ibrahim et al., 2021). Similarly, studies have found that incorporating natural elements into indoor spaces can enhance visual and auditory comfort (Evensen et al., 2017; Mangone et al., 2017). Overall, BD can improve the aesthetic of indoor spaces and increase occupants' perceived comfort levels.

Psychological impact

BD is becoming increasingly important in contemporary architecture, especially in designing healthy and restorative spaces. The need for incorporating BD elements into workplace design is supported by numerous studies that have shown their potential for improving psychological well-being.

Research has extensively studied the visual attributes of greenery and nature views, which have been found to have significant benefits for cognitive performance, stress reduction, and mood (Yin et al., 2019). Even the presence of living plants, as demonstrated in a study by Lei et al. (2022) using strawberry plants in a small space, has been found to enhance psychophysiological health.

Incorporating BD elements into workplace design has also been shown to result in improved satisfaction and reduced stress and anxiety levels. For instance, Yin et al. (2019) conducted an experiment using VR technology, where participants experienced higher levels of stress reduction in office designs with BD elements, such as living walls and potted plants, and natural materials and shapes. Additionally, incorporating natural light through windows has been found to reduce drowsiness and perceived workload, improving satisfaction (Sanchez et al., 2018).

Studies have also shown that incorporating plants into the workplace can reduce complaints regarding the environment, leading to improved satisfaction (Evensen et al., 2013; Nieuwenhuis et al., 2014) and even positive emotions (Evensen et al., 2017). The use of natural elements and materials, such as wooden finishes, has also been found to significantly reduce stress levels (Douglas et al., 2022).

Overall, the numerous studies linking BD elements with psychological impacts highlight the importance of incorporating natural elements, materials, and simulated nature into workplace design to improve satisfaction, reduce stress and anxiety, and promote positive emotions.

Discussion: designing biophilic and healthy workplaces

By incorporating nature into workplace design, BD can offer numerous benefits that can transform a workplace into a high-performance workplace. By leveraging the innate human affinity for living entities, BD can positively impact cognitive performance, productivity, and creativity, thereby enhancing overall human performance – a key attribute of a high-performance workspace. In addition to improving performance, BD interventions can also enhance occupant comfort, resulting in a more satisfied workforce.

Perhaps the most significant benefit of BD is its potential to create a restorative environment that promotes psychological well-being, reduces stress levels, and improves mood. These positive implications of BD interventions further position biophilic office spaces as exemplary high-performance workspaces that support enhanced performance and well-being.

Exploring several BD frameworks (Kellert et al., 2008; Wijesooriya et al., 2022), it is possible to outline key strategies that can be applied to workplace design, with a focus on incorporating biophilic elements.

Connectivity to direct nature

The prominent biophilic element utilized in workplace design is plants, including both ornamental and edible varieties, as well as indoor green walls. Fitzgerald and Danner (2012) argued that incorporating plants into indoor environments can bridge the gap between our evolutionary need for nature connectivity and modern interiors that often lack such elements, leading to increased job satisfaction and overall performance. Additionally, plants have been shown to release negative air ions that can improve both mental and physical health (Yan et al., 2015).

While water is also a key biophilic element, studies on workplace design have primarily adapted it in virtual reality simulations, rather than incorporating it into physical spaces. Natural sounds, such as those of birds (Ratcliffe et al., 2018) or water (Ma & Shu, 2018), can also add to the sensory experience and improve occupant well-being.

Natural materials

The use of natural materials is a crucial aspect of BD that aims to depict nature and create a more visually appealing environment. The BD frameworks strongly advocate for the incorporation of natural materials in their original colours and textures (Kellert et al., 2008; Kellert & Calabrese, 2015). Among the most used natural materials, wooden finishes have gained significant attention and were extensively studied for their psychological impact. Indeed, wooden finishes can have significant positive impacts on the occupants' psychological well-being. The use of wood in the workplace is associated with reduced stress levels and improved productivity. Furthermore, wooden finishes create a warm and welcoming atmosphere, improving the overall aesthetic of the workspace (Burnard & Kutnar, 2020).

In addition to wood, other natural materials such as stone, bamboo, and cork can also be used in BDs. These materials not only provide aesthetic appeal but also have a positive impact on the indoor environment. For instance, stone can regulate temperature and humidity levels, while bamboo is known for its fast-growing and sustainable properties.

Incorporating natural materials into workplace design can enhance the overall biophilic experience, create a more pleasant and visually appealing environment, and promote a sense of connection with nature among the occupants.

Daylight, windows, and views

The incorporation of views of nature in biophilic workplace design has been shown to have a significant impact on the well-being and productivity of occupants. By including elements of nature, such as trees, grass, and water, in outdoor views, biophilic workplaces provide a sense of connection to the natural environment, which has been shown to reduce stress and improve mood. In addition to the visual benefits, exposure to natural daylight has also been linked to improved cognitive function and mood, as well as better sleep quality.

Studies have shown that views of nature are an important aspect of biophilic workplace design. For example, Yin et al. (2020) conducted an experiment on the effects of BD elements on stress and anxiety reduction using VR technology. They found that a simulation scenario that included outdoor views containing trees, grass, water, and daylight over a large distance was associated with higher levels of recovery compared to a non-BD scenario.

Overall, the incorporation of views of nature is an essential aspect of biophilic workplace design, providing a sense of connection to the natural environment that has been shown to have numerous benefits for occupant well-being and productivity.

Representations of nature

The use of VR experiences to recreate natural settings is a recent development in biophilic workplace design. Research has shown that such experiences can produce similar results to actual nature experiences. This is significant because it suggests that even representations of nature, such as augmented reality or images, could be used in offices where direct access to nature is not possible (Yin et al., 2019).

In addition to VR, other forms of representations of nature, such as biomorphic shapes, have also been found to enhance the occupant's connectivity to nature. Biomorphic shapes refer to shapes that resemble those found in nature, such as the curve of a leaf or the pattern of a spider's web. These shapes have been found to have a calming effect on the occupants and can help to reduce stress levels.

The use of virtual and augmented reality (AR), as well as biomorphic shapes, are important tools for biophilic workplace design because they offer a way to bring the benefits of nature into the workplace in a way that is practical and accessible. They also provide a way to incorporate BD elements into existing buildings, without the need for major structural changes.

Multisensory experience

Research and design of workplace environments have historically been focused on the visual aspects of the space. However, the visual attributes of greenery and nature have gained increasing attention due to the extensive studies demonstrating their benefits on cognitive performance, stress level, and mood. Previous studies have looked at these elements separately, but recent research suggests that the design elements and outcomes are interrelated.

In addition, recent studies have shown that the combined benefits of visual and auditory naturalness can bring even more benefits to the workplace. These studies reveal that the multisensory approach to workplace design is crucial and that current design approaches have predominantly focused on eliminating indoor sensory impressions other than visual perception. The combination of visual and auditory naturalness significantly improves cognitive performance and mood among building occupants (Zhao et al., 2018).

Biophilic design elements for high-performance workplaces

The design framework depicted in Figure 5.2 outlines the various design elements that can be implemented to create biophilic office spaces that foster high-performance. The framework also highlights the potential impacts of these design elements on the occupants.

The framework summarizes the potential impacts and design elements that could be used to create biophilic office spaces that promote high-performance. The high-performance workspace is characterized by three key attributes: high cognitive performance, enhanced comfort, and a restorative environment. Studies examining the use of BD in workplaces have shown that productivity, cognitive efficiency, creativity, and memory can be improved through the integration of BD elements. Enhanced comfort is achieved by addressing a range of factors, including thermal comfort, visual comfort, aesthetics, and visual preference. The use of BD elements also has the potential to create a restorative environment that induces positive emotions, increases satisfaction, reduces stress, improves recovery, and reduces anxiety.

The current practices of using BD in workplace design have mainly focused on incorporating elements such as plants, green walls, water, daylight, outdoor views, natural shapes, virtual reality, natural materials, and natural sounds. However, there are numerous other BD elements and criteria that could be further explored and integrated into this initial framework. By incorporating a wider range of BD elements, workplaces could become even more effective in enhancing the health, well-being, and performance of occupants.

Conclusion

This chapter indicates that incorporating biophilic design (BD) elements in workplaces can have a positive impact on cognitive performance, productivity, and creativity, leading to higher workplace performance. The use of natural elements such as plants, water, and daylight enhances the comfort of the workspace and creates visually appealing spaces. Biophilic offices are restorative environments that promote positive emotions, increase satisfaction, reduce stress, improve

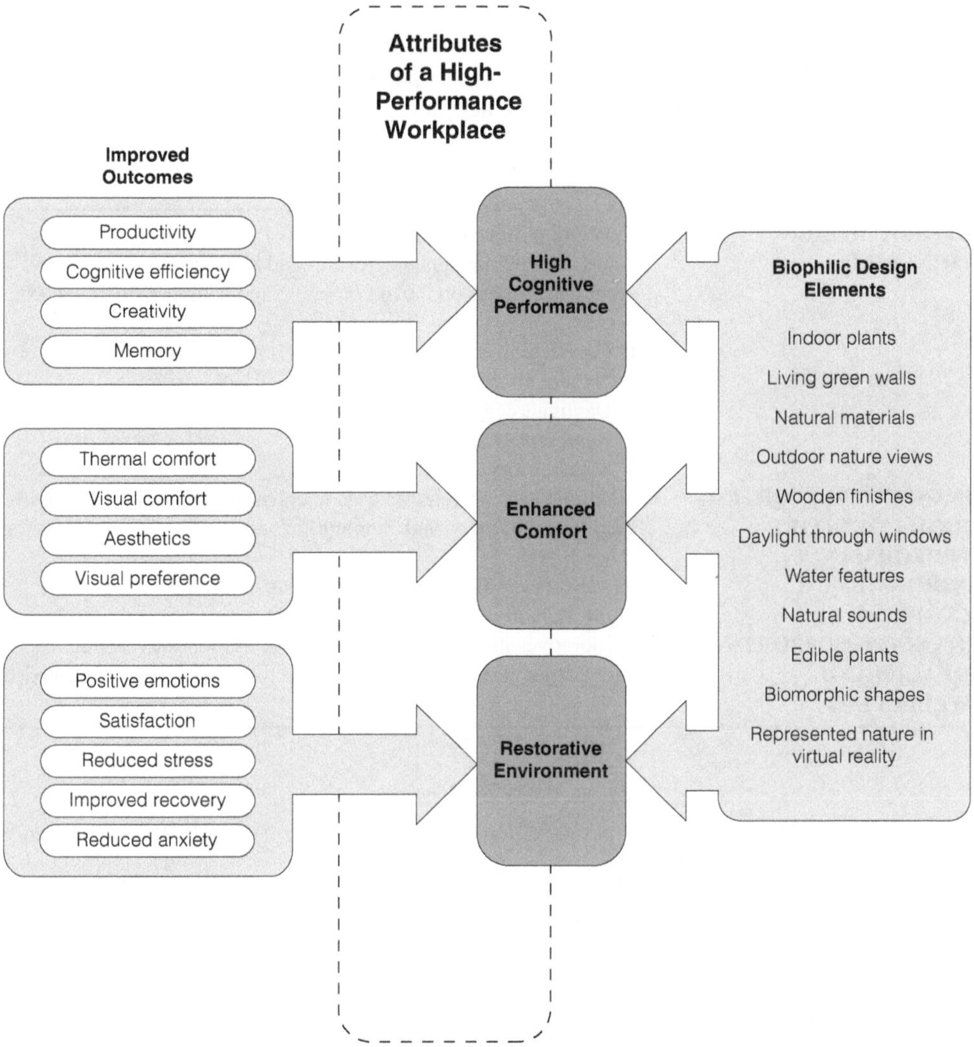

Figure 5.2 Biophilic design framework for high-performing workplaces.

recovery, and reduce anxiety among occupants. These features make biophilic offices exceed the expectations of a typical high-performance workplace.

While visual experience plays a crucial role in BD, there is a need to design for multisensory spaces that can strengthen the impact. The application of auditory, olfactory, and tactile elements within workplaces can be interesting areas for future studies.

The developed framework provides a starting point for systematically applying BD to create high-performing workplaces. However, the study only investigated a limited number of design elements, and there are many other natural elements that can be explored further. Research has shown that evidence from many features in other typologies can be applied to workplaces with adequate studies.

The COVID-19 pandemic has demonstrated the need for nature in indoor environments and how humans' natural affinity can influence overall health and well-being. In this context, adopting a biophilic approach is a design imperative for the post-pandemic workplace.

A "high-performance" checklist for biophilic design is provided here:

Principle	*Description*
BIOPHILIC DESIGN PRINCPILES	• Core principles applied to the design of workplaces to deliver improved environmental outcomes and high-performance workspaces focus on the use of nature and natural elements. These include: 1. Connectivity to direct nature 2. Natural materials 3. Daylight, windows, and views 4. Representations of nature 5. Multisensory experience
EHNANCING/SUPPORTING HIGH COGNITIVE PERFORMANCE	• Biophilic design strategies used to enhance productivity, creativity, cognitive efficiency, and memory include:
ENVIRONMENTAL COMFORT	• Enhanced comfort outcomes, including thermal comfort, visual comfort, aesthetics, and visual preference
ENHANCING/SUPPORTING HEALTH AND WELLBEING	• Restorative environment outcomes, including positive emotions, satisfaction, reduced stress, improved recovery, and reduced anxiety

References

Baker, N. (2006). Cultural responses to primitive needs. *WIT Transactions on The Built Environment, 86*. https//doi.org/10.2495/ARC060011

Bergefurt, L., Weijs-Perrée, M., Appel-Meulenbroek, R., & Arentze, T. (2022). The physical office workplace as a resource for mental health – A systematic scoping review. *Building and Environment, 207*, 108505, https://doi.org/10.1016/j. buildenv.2021.108505

Burnard, M. D., & Kutnar, A. (2020). Human stress responses in office-like environments with wood furniture. *Building Research & Information*. 48, 316–330. https://doi.org/10.1080/09613218.2019.1660609

Candido, C., Chakraborty, P., & Tjondronegoro, D. (2019). The rise of office design in high-performance, open-plan environments. *Buildings*, *9*(4), 100.

Douglas, I. P., Murnane, E. L., Bencharit, L. Z., Altaf, B., dos Reis Costa, J. M., Yang, J. . . . Billington, S. L. (2022). Physical workplaces and human well-being: A mixed-methods study to quantify the effects of materials, windows, and representation on biobehavioral outcomes. *Building and Environment, 224*, 109516.

Evensen, K. H., Raanaas, R. K., Hägerhäll, C. M., Johansson, M., & Patil, G. G. (2017) Nature in the office: An environmental assessment study. *Journal of Architectural and Planning Research on JSTOR, 34*, 133–146.

Evensen, K. H., Raanaas, R. K., Patil, G. G. (2013). Potential health benefits of nature-based interventions in the work environment during winter. A case study. *Psyecology, 4*, 67–88. https://doi.org/10.1174/217119713805088315

Heerwagen, J., & Gregory, B. (2013). Biophilia and sensory aesthetics. In S. R. Kellert, J. Heerwagen, & M. Mador (Eds.), *Biophilic design: The theory, science and practice of bringing buildings to life* (p. 16). John Wiley & Sons, Incorporated.

Ibrahim, A., Ali, H., Zghoul, A., & Jaradat, S. (2021). Mood state and human evaluation of the thermal environment using virtual settings. *Indoor and Built Environment, 30*(1), 70–86. https://doi.org/10.1177/1420326X19880325

ILFI International Living Future Institute. (2016). *Living building challenge V3.1. Vol. 3.1*. https://www2.living-future.org/LBC4.0?RD_Scheduler=LBC4

Kaplan, S. (1995). The restorative benefits of nature: Toward an integrative framework. *Journal of Environmental Psychology*, *15*(3), 169–182.

Kayıhan, K. S. (2018). Examination of Biophilia Phenomenon in the context of sustainable architecture. In *International sustainable buildings symposium* (pp. 80–101). Springer. https://doi.org/10.1007/978-3-319-63709-9_7

Kellert, S., Heerwagen, J., & Mador, M. (2008). *Biophilic design: The theory, science and practice of brining buildings to life*. John Wiley and Sons Ltd.

Kellert, S. R., & Calabrese, E. F. (2015). *The practice of biophilic design*. https://www.academia.edu/18646355/The_Practice_of_Biophilic_Design

Lei, Q., Yuan, C., & Lau, S. S. Y. (2021). A quantitative study for indoor workplace biophilic design to improve health and productivity performance. *Journal of Cleaner Production*, *324*, 129168.

Lopes, S., Lima, M., & Silva, K. (2020). Nature can get it out of your mind: The rumination reducing effects of contact with nature and the mediating role of awe and mood. *Journal of Environmental Psychology*, *71*, 101489. https://doi.org/10.1016/j.jenvp.2020.101489

Lyu, K., Brambilla, A., Globa, A., & de Dear, R. (2023). An immersive multisensory virtual reality approach to the study of human-built environment interactions. *Automation in Construction*, *150*, art. no. 104836. https://doi.org/10.1016/j.autcon.2023.104836

Ma, H., & Shu, S. (2018). An experimental study: The restorative effect of soundscape elements in a simulated open-plan office. *Acta Acustica United with Acustica*, *104*(1), 106–115.

Mangone, G., Capaldi, C. A., van Allen, Z. M., & Luscuere, P. G. (2017). Bringing nature to work: Preferences and perceptions of constructed indoor and natural outdoor workspaces. *Urban Forestry & Urban Greening*, *23*, 1–12 https://doi.org/10.1016/j.ufug.2017.02.009

Nieuwenhuis, M., Knight, C., Postmes, T., Haslam, S. A. (2014). The relative benefits of green versus lean office space: Three field experiments. *Journal of Experimental Psychology Applied*, *20*, 199–214. https://doi.org/10.1037/xap0000024

Ratcliffe, E., Gatersleben, B., & Sowden, P. T. (2018). Predicting the perceived restorative potential of bird sounds through acoustics and aesthetics. *Environment and Behavior*, *52*(4), 371–400. https://doi.org/10.1177/0013916518806952

Sanchez, J. A., Ikaga, T., & Sanchez, S. V. (2018). Quantitative improvement in workplace performance through biophilic design: A pilot experiment case study. *Energy and Buildings*, *177*, 316–328.

Ulrich, R. S., Simons, R. F., Losito, B. D., Fiorito, E., Miles, M. A., & Zelson, M. (1991). Stress recovery during exposure to natural and urban environments. *Journal of Environmental Psychology*, *11*(3), 201–230.

van der Voordt, P. A. J., & Jensen, P. A. (2021). The impact of healthy workplaces on employee satisfaction, productivity and costs. *Journal of Corporate Real Estate*. https://doi.org/10.1108/JCRE-03-2021-0012, ahead-of-print.

Wijesooriya, N., & Brambilla, A. (2021). Bridging biophilic design and environmentally sustainable design. *Journal of Cleaner Production*, *283*, art. no. 124591.

Wijesooriya, N., Brambilla, A., & Markauskaite, L. (2021). Biophilic water criteira: Exploring a technique to develop an environmentally sustainable biophilic design framework. In *Advanced studies in efficient environmental design and city planning* (pp. 437–447). Springer International Publishing.

Wilson, E. (1984). The drive to discovery: An essay from biophilia. *American Scholar*, *53*(4), 447–464.

Yin, J., Arfaei, N., MacNaughton, P., Catalano, P. J., Allen, J. G., Spengler, J. D. (2019). Effects of biophilic interventions in office on stress reaction and cognitive function: A randomized crossover study in virtual reality. *Indoor Air*, *29*, 1028–1039. https://doi.org/10.1111/ina.12593

Yin, J., Yuan, J., Arfaei, N., Catalano, P. J., Allen, J. G., & Spengler, J. D. (2020). Effects of biophilic indoor environment on stress and anxiety recovery: A between-subjects experiment in virtual reality. *Environment International*, *136*, 105427.

Zhao, J., Xu, W., & Ye, L. (2018). Effects of auditory-visual combinations on perceived restorative potential of urban green space. *Applied Acoustics*, *141*, 169–177. https://doi.org/10.1016/j.apacoust.2018.07.001

Zhu, Y., Luo, M., Ouyang, Q., Huang, L., & Cao, B. (2015). Dynamic characteristics and comfort assessment of airflows in indoor environments: A review. Building and Environment, *91*, 5–14. https://doi.org/10.1016/j.buildenv.2015.03.032

6
THERMAL COMFORT

Wei Yang, Yaolin Lin, and Dorsa Fatourehchi

> We need to move away from a static approach to thermal comfort and embrace thermal variability to create environments people actually enjoy being in.
>
> *– Authors*

Introduction

Indoor thermal comfort greatly impacts the well-being and performance of occupants in a workplace. In a comfortable office environment, occupants have a higher sense of happiness, and their work efficiency can increase by 15–20% (Thayer et al., 2010). Thermal discomfort can seriously impact a worker's overall morale and work performance (Kaushik et al., 2020). Prolonged exposure can lead to fatigue and lowered concentration and productivity (Lan et al., 2011). In addition, worker complaints and absenteeism can increase (Lan et al., 2011).

Space heating and cooling are typically provided by means of centralised heating, ventilation and air conditioning (HVAC) systems, therefore delivering comfortable and healthy offices is often done in an energy-intensive manner, leading to increasing cooling and heating demand globally. For a typical office building, the HVAC system accounts for 40% of the building's energy consumption (Residovic, 2017). Although the energy consumption of HVAC systems is very high, the thermal comfort satisfaction rate in air-conditioned office buildings continues to be stubbornly low. The results from a survey of 351 office buildings and 2980 occupants in the US show that only 38% of the respondents are satisfied with the thermal comfort level in their workplace (Caroline et al., 2018). In Australia, results from surveys also show that occupants' satisfaction in NABERS (National Australian Built Environment Rating System) certified buildings was not within the expected 90% satisfaction, with being too cold/hot as the main source of dissatisfaction (Marzban et al., 2022). One of the major reasons for the low satisfaction with thermal comfort in air-conditioned office buildings is that the HVAC system is designed to deliver static conditions indoors where occupants are not expected to attenuate it or interact significantly with their environment. The lack of opportunity to adjust their immediate setting to suit their thermal preferences and slow the adoption of personal control systems further explain dissatisfaction scores observed in controlled environments.

DOI: 10.1201/9781003328728-7
This chapter has been made available under a CC-BY-NC-ND 4.0 license.

How to provide a thermally comfortable indoor environment without too much energy consumption is still a big challenge for air-conditioned office buildings around the world. Climate change and the COVID-19 pandemic environment worsen the problem. The rising temperatures, more frequent and extreme weather, population growth and urbanisation are expected to lead to an unprecedented heating and cooling demand in all types of buildings in the future. Under the pandemic environment, 100% fresh air supply was recommended for the HVAC system to stop the spread of the virus, which led to huge energy consumption in office buildings (Lin et al., 2022). Mixed-mode ventilation may be a good solution, as mixed-mode buildings have been found to be more resilient regarding thermal comfort, energy, health, coping with future pandemics and accommodating individual needs as compared to HVAC buildings (Shahzad & Rijal, 2022).

This chapter mainly discusses thermal comfort–related issues in the workplace. Factors affection thermal comfort are identified, and thermal comfort models that have been used in the workplace are discussed. Findings of thermal comfort studies from both static and adaptive environments in office buildings are presented. A high-performance checklist is provided at the end of this chapter for delivering a thermally comfortable workplace in office buildings.

Thermal comfort in buildings

Thermal comfort is defined as "that condition of mind which expresses satisfaction with the thermal environment" (ASHRAE, 2020). Factors affecting thermal comfort can be divided into two categories: environmental factors and personal factors. Environmental factors include air temperature, air humidity, radiant temperature and air movement. Personal factors include metabolic rate (level of activity), clothing, physical fitness and acclimatisation.

A suitable thermal comfort environment can maintain a certain temperature range and satisfy 80% of users (ASHRAE, 2020). However, some studies have shown that many people are still dissatisfied with the thermal environment and suffer from sick building syndrome (SBS) even under constant temperature conditions (Yan et al., 2008). Thermal comfort, as a subjective feeling of human beings, is a dynamic and comfortable state. The current practice of supplying a constant-temperature indoor environment with small fluctuations ignores the dynamic characteristics of human thermal comfort and does not consider the individual differences of building users. It also leads to overheating or overcooling and thus unnecessary waste in heating and cooling energy consumption. Therefore, it is crucial to fully consider the individual differences and time-dependent characteristics of human thermal comfort in the HVAC design and operation stages to provide building users with a flexible, comfortable and sustainable thermal comfort environment.

A particular factor that should be considered in the workplace is the age factor. As pointed out in a study by Cleary et al. (2019), it is not uncommon for people who are more than 65 years to still be in the workplace; therefore, their needs should also be considered. The attention of older residents to personal issues related to thermal comfort linked to physical and mental health emphasise the importance of concerns regarding mobility, nursing care and autonomy, which makes thermal comfort for elderly people more complicated.

Thermal comfort models

In the research history of thermal comfort studies, there are many indices used to assess thermal comfort, including effective temperature index ET, new effective temperature ET*, standard effective temperature SET* and PMV-PPD model (Fanger, 1970; ASHRAE, 2020). Fanger's PMV-PPD model has been the most widely used index in indoor thermal environment evaluation in air-conditioned buildings. In recent decades, the adaptive comfort model proposed by de Dear and Brager (1998) has become the most popular model in the thermal comfort research paradigm for naturally ventilated and mixed-mode buildings.

Static model

The static model is based on the thermal balance that the human body undergoes with the environment, under the same air-conditioning conditions throughout the study, where thermal comfort is evaluated by the predicted mean vote (PMV) (Fanger, 1970; Mamani et al., 2022). The PMV index predicts the mean response of a large group of people on the ASHRAE seven-point thermal sensation scale, which consists of seven verbal anchors: "cold", "cool", "slightly cool", "neutral", "slightly warm", "warm" and "hot" (ASHRAE, 2020).

The application of the PMV model for the evaluation of thermal comfort within air-conditioned office environments has been extensively explored by several researchers. The PMV model serves as a standardised method to quantify and predict the thermal sensation experienced by individuals in indoor spaces, with a consideration of factors such as air temperature, relative humidity, air velocity and clothing insulation.

While the PMV model has demonstrated certain advantages in assessing thermal comfort, researchers have identified limitations associated with accommodating the diverse needs of occupants. A research study conducted by Cheung et al. (2019) demonstrated a prediction accuracy of 34%, showing a two out of three times inaccurate thermal sensation prediction. Another study by Kiki et al. (2020) revealed that the PMV model underestimated the adaptability of the occupants to relatively high comfort temperatures in an air-conditioned office in a humid tropical climate. Moreover, it has been indicated that such a static model could lead to an increase of energy consumption, in locations where adequate levels of thermal comfort could primarily be obtained through the consideration of natural ventilation (García et al., 2019).

This could be due to the variances in individual preferences as well as their psychological and physiological characteristics, which could in turn impact their thermal comfort responses on different occasions (Wang et al., 2020). Studies also showed that spatial attributes in office buildings (e.g., location, orientation, interior arrangements) can play a significant role in affecting the prediction accuracy of the classic models (Song et al., 2022). Therefore, relying solely on the PMV model to determine the optimal environmental conditions for thermal comfort may not fully result in accurate results.

Such differences in results have made researchers to consider the PMV model as a rather general framework in their studies than viewing it as a representative model for the occupants' comfort levels. To overcome these limitations, several studies have proposed incorporating additional parameters and subjective feedback mechanisms into the evaluation process. These may include factors such as thermal preference surveys, occupants' feedback on their thermal comfort and personalised adaptive control systems. With this approach, researchers have expanded the model's application through the consideration of individual parameters to enhance their understanding of occupants' thermal comfort. For instance, Omidvar and Kim (2020) hace improved the classic model through the modification of regulatory sweating heat loss for an office building case study. In addition, revised PMV models were proposed by some researchers with the aim of broadening the application range (Du et al., 2022). In another study, Zhang et al. (2020) proposed calibration methods for activity level and clothing insulation to improve the PMV model. The studies within air-conditioned offices demonstrated that the recognition of subjective feedback could be necessary for a more personalised environment.

Adaptive model

It has long been recognised that the experience of thermal comfort is more complex than the steady-state heat balance which strives simply to achieve "thermal neutrality" (Parkinson & de Dear, 2015). Therefore, the adaptive model becomes more acceptable to researchers, engineers and architects who work in the human thermal comfort area. A study implemented by de Dear et al. (1998) showed that the PMV model provided few opportunities for the environments where occupants adapt themselves for thermal comfort, especially for naturally ventilated settings. Therefore, there demonstrated the need for an adaptive model for such settings. For the adaptive model, the occupant is an active actor who interacts with their environment, adapting it according to their preferences and comfort, considering that environmental conditions can vary and do not remain static, giving way to naturally ventilated spaces (de Dear & Brager, 1998; Mamani et al., 2022). The ultimate goal of the adaptive model is to achieve thermal neutrality, where individuals neither feel too hot nor too cold. This balance is crucial for promoting productivity and well-being among office occupants. By providing a degree of control and customisation over the thermal environment, the adaptive model encourages occupants to actively engage in managing their thermal comfort, leading to enhanced satisfaction and performance. The adaptive model has provided a more realistic approach to assessing thermal comfort by considering the dynamic interactions between occupants and their environment. The model hypothesises that the contextual factors, such as environmental controllability and past thermal history, can affect building occupants' thermal expectations and preferences (de dear & Brager, 1998). Therefore, it recognises that individuals could achieve thermal neutrality through the implementation of adaptive behaviours, such as individual (e.g., clothing) or technological adjustments (e.g., personalised fans). This model aims to create an environment where occupants can achieve thermal comfort without solely relying on mechanical systems for heating and cooling. Therefore, considering adaptability of occupants within their built environment, providing personal control over environmental parameters in both mixed-mode and naturally ventilated buildings, such as opening windows or adjusting blinds, occupants have the flexibility to tailor their immediate surroundings to meet their thermal needs.

As a result of this recognition, this model has garnered significant attention from researchers to evaluate thermal comfort within mixed-mode and naturally ventilated office environments. Many researchers have analysed occupants' feedback and behaviours to gain insights into the key factors affecting occupants' comfort while reaching to an understanding of the strategies to maintain thermal neutrality in different climates and office environments. It can be concluded from previous studies regarding adaptive models that the interrelationship between occupants' thermal sensation, their behaviour and environmental conditions plays a significant role in these types of studies.

The studies conducted in different climatic regions pointed out that adaptive models are necessary for the optimisation of indoor thermal environment and thus energy use reductions for both mixed-mode and naturally ventilated office buildings. Therefore, numerous studies have been conducted for both naturally and mixed-mode ventilated buildings since studies concluded that buildings' ventilation type (natural mode or mixed mode) can affect occupants' thermal sensitivity variations (Rupp et al., 2022).

In terms of naturally ventilated office buildings, studies revealed that the occupants' thermal comfort preferences and behaviours varied with respect to local weather conditions, their culture and the opportunities provided in the office buildings (Sharma et al., 2021; Lamsal et al., 2023).

While the adaptive model concept is mostly applied to naturally ventilated buildings, a study conducted by Parkinson et al. (2020) demonstrated that adaptive comfort processes can be applicable to the occupants of all buildings, including air-conditioned ones, since the thermal environmental exposures occur indoors where most of the time is being spent. Therefore, several studies have been conducted regarding mixed-mode buildings. For example, a study by Wu et al. (2019a) pointed out that compared to the PMV model, the adaptive model was more applicable to the split air-conditioned office buildings in China.

The research thus far has shed light on the factors influencing occupant comfort and the strategies employed to create environments that facilitate optimal thermal conditions for individuals in these settings. The adaptive model can be further refined and expanded upon to create a personalised and responsive environment. Advances in sensor technology and building automation systems could enable more precise monitoring and control of indoor conditions, allowing for real-time adjustments based on occupants' preferences and thermal comfort thresholds. In addition, the integration of machine learning and artificial intelligence algorithms can improve the adaptive model's capability by continuously learning from occupants' feedback (Liu et al., 2021).

In the future, the widespread application of adaptive comfort models in office buildings has the potential to revolutionise traditional HVAC systems, enhance occupants' well-being and contribute to sustainable and energy-efficient applications.

Thermal alliesthesia

As mentioned earlier, the recent mainstreaming of "adaptive comfort" begins to recognise the dynamic complexity of thermal comfort. However, "thermal alliesthesia" goes beyond this, proposing that the hedonic qualities of the thermal environment (qualities of pleasantness or unpleasantness, or "the pleasure principle") are determined as much by the general thermal state of the subject as by the environment itself. In its simplest form, cold stimuli will be perceived as pleasant by someone who is warm; whilst warm stimuli will be experienced as pleasant by someone who is cold (Parkinson & de Dear, 2015).

Thermal alliesthesia has gained attention form researchers as an evolving approach to understanding human thermal perception. Building upon the foundations established by the adaptive model mentioned earlier, researchers have explored the potential of incorporating thermal alliesthesia into the assessment of thermal comfort. Studies have pointed out that dynamic thermal environments can deliver higher levels of occupant satisfaction than static indoor environments (Parkinson et al., 2012). Parkinson et al. (2016) has shown experimental data exploring alliesthesia in non-steady-state conditions in occupants' different physiological conditions, including the thermoneutral zone. Their findings suggested a potential to increase thermal comfort by means of personally controlled systems to force local skin temperatures against the dominant mean skin temperature trend. In another research conducted by Parkinson and de Dear (2017) showed that the thermal pleasure can be experienced by individuals due to the local air-velocity profiles which could affect thermal boundary of the comfort zone. Their research pointed out that positive thermal pleasure can be achieved through the establishment of contrast relationships between global and local skin temperatures trends.

While the concept of thermal alliesthesia holds promise in deepening our understanding of thermal comfort, its practical application is yet to be fully realised. Therefore, more research is needed translating the theoretical framework of thermal alliesthesia into applicable methodologies for evaluating and designing thermal environments. One of the primary hurdles is the lack of standardised methods to measure and quantify thermal alliesthesia. Currently, there is a dearth of practical tools and techniques to objectively assess an individual's physiological state and incorporate it into the assessment of thermal comfort (Son & Chun, 2018). As a result, the utilisation of thermal alliesthesia in real-world settings needs to be further explored in terms of thermal comfort (Li et al., 2022).

Moreover, the complex nature of thermal alliesthesia and its interplay with various individual and environmental factors presents a significant challenge in developing universally applicable guidelines or models. The subjective nature of thermal perception and the personalised responses to thermal stimuli make it difficult to establish standardised thresholds or benchmarks for thermal alliesthesia–based evaluations.

Despite these challenges, ongoing research continues to explore the potential of incorporating thermal alliesthesia into the assessment of thermal comfort. Researchers are investigating innovative approaches such as wearable sensors (Tartarini et al., 2022), physiological monitoring (Yang et al., 2020) and subjective feedback mechanisms (Wu et al., 2019b; Zheng et al., 2022) to gather data on individuals' thermal responses and tailor environmental conditions accordingly.

Findings from static and adaptive environments

Air-conditioned workplaces

Under normal conditions, the goal of HVAC systems is to create a good indoor environment for buildings and consume as little energy as possible. However, in a pandemic environment, pandemic prevention should be the core concern of the HVAC system (Pan et al., 2021). To reduce the spread of COVID-19, the World Health Organization (WHO) recommended increasing the rate of air change, reducing recirculation and increasing outdoor air intake. For public spaces and buildings (such as offices and schools), it provided more detailed advice, including using economy modes to increase the percentage of outside air, disabling demand-control ventilation controls, improving filtration, running systems at maximum outdoor airflow two hours before and after spaces are occupied and making sure that air flows from clean to less-clean areas (Vendor, 2020).

Each occupant in a shared office space often has different indoor temperature requirements due to sitting in different locations with changes in the angle of direct sunlight and differences in their own temperature preferences. It is difficult for a traditional HVAC system, such as constant air volume (CAV), variable air volume (VAV), demand-controlled ventilation (DCV) and fan coil unit (FCU), to satisfy the individual thermal comfort requirements of all the occupants. Therefore, there is a need for a paradigm shift from a uniform indoor environment to a non-uniform indoor environment accommodating various individual preferences (Yan et al., 2008; Nicol & Roaf, 2017; Lin et al., 2022). The target should be to control local conditions when a person is at the workplace. There is also a need to introduce more advanced systems where users can influence their own local micro-environment. The development of more advanced smart systems should be introduced to improve indoor climate conditions for all the occupants of a space. Personalised ventilation can be considered as an acceptable way to accommodate various individual thermal comfort preferences. Another strategy is to think about flexible layouts that could be hacked to suit people's thermal comfort needs and enable thermal variability (as in slightly warmer/cooler zones) that people could drift towards. A rethink of HVAC systems to embrace mixed-mode ventilation should also be considered.

Data from the Sustainable and Healthy Environments (SHE) survey show that 70% of the respondents from Australian workplaces feel satisfied with thermal comfort (voted somewhat satisfied, satisfied and extremely satisfied) in their buildings (as shown in Figure 6.1). There is still

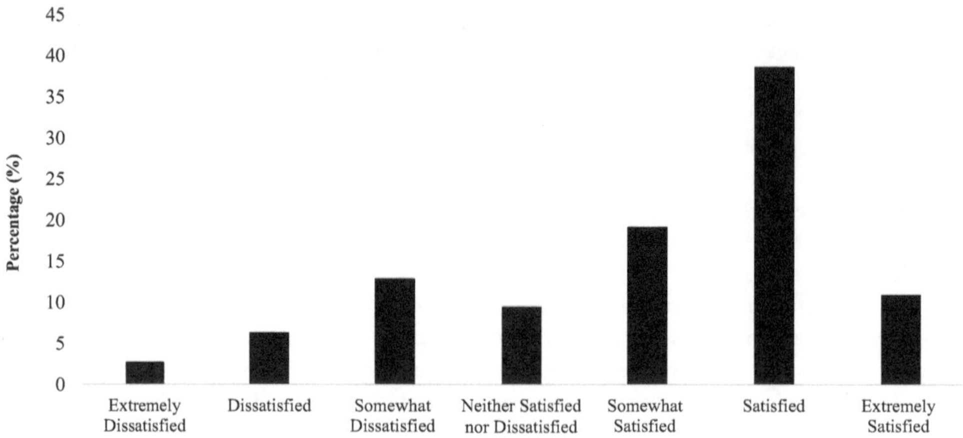

Figure 6.1 Percentage of people who feel satisfied with thermal comfort.

quite a large percentage of respondents (30%) who feel unsatisfied with thermal comfort even though all the offices were fully air-conditioned and the setpoints were following the Australian typical temperature range of 21–24.9°C based on the NABERS guide. The result highlights again the problem with static indoor conditions provided by the HVAC system. The HVAC industry, therefore, needs to define "comfort" in terms of the physical variables that could be controlled using the HVAC system (Nicol & Roaf, 2017). Figure 6.2a presents some of the main dissatisfaction reasons of thermal comfort in the SHE post-occupancy evaluation (POE) dataset, and Figure 6.2b indicates the percentages of satisfied and dissatisfied with thermal comfort across the SHE POE dataset.

Workplaces with mixed-mode ventilation

Mixed ventilation refers to making full use of the respective advantages of mechanical ventilation and natural ventilation, in different seasons or different times of the day, according to outdoor weather conditions, using the control system to reasonably switch between the mechanical ventilation mode and the natural ventilation mode or combined operation. Mixed-mode ventilation can provide comfortable indoor environments and minimise reliance on energy-intensive HVAC systems (Deuble & de Dear, 2012; Kim et al., 2019).

Mixed-mode ventilation was found to be better than air-conditioned offices for resilient comfort. The mixed-mode building had 16% higher overall comfort and 32% satisfaction and health conditions, as compared to the HVAC building. However, extra care is needed in designing mixed-mode buildings and user-friendly thermal controls, as they have the potential to be energy-efficient by using natural ventilation and a variety of adaptive opportunities to achieve comfort. Overall, mixed-mode buildings were found to be more resilient regarding thermal comfort, energy, health, coping with future pandemics and accommodating individual needs, as compared to HVAC buildings (Shahzad & Rijal, 2022).

Kim et al. (2019) conducted a study to investigate how different modes of operation in a mixed-mode building in Wollongong, Australia, affect indoor thermal environmental conditions and occupant perceptions of thermal comfort. They found that occupants of the mixed-mode building

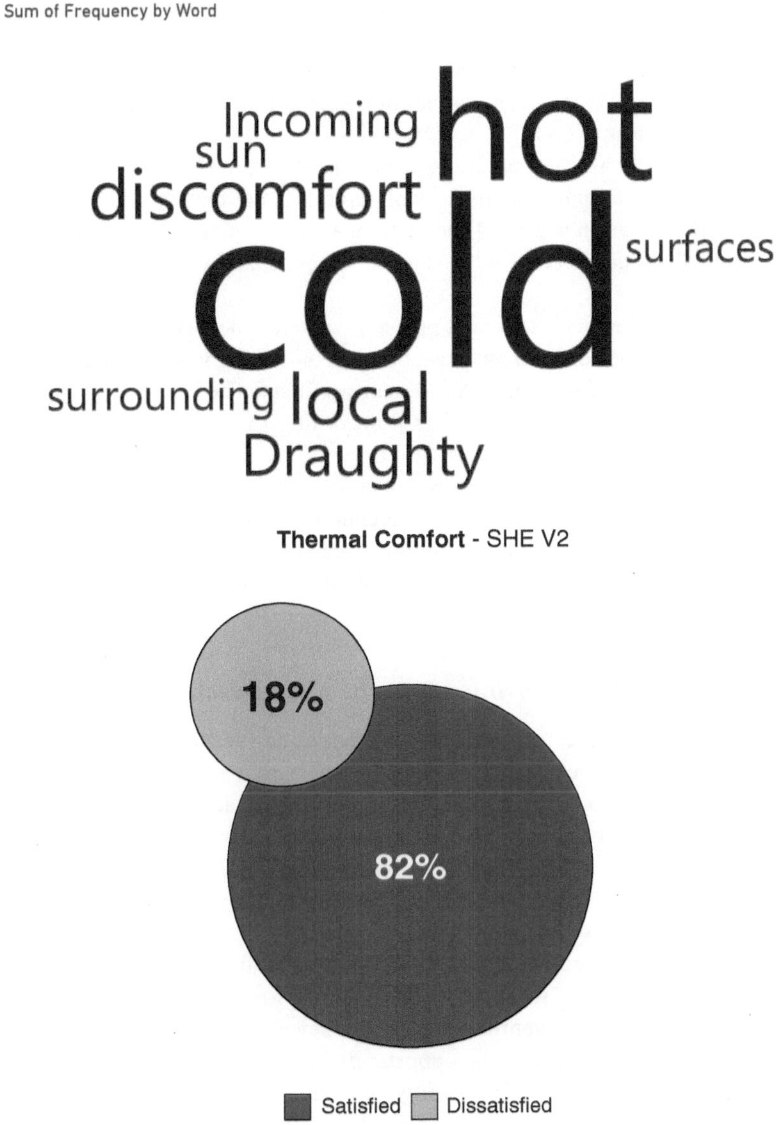

Figure 6.2 (a) Word cloud generated from the SHE POE dataset reporting dissatisfaction with thermal comfort and (b) Percentage of satisfied and dissatisfied workers with thermal comfort in the SHE POE dataset for all offices.

Source: SHE POE dataset, 2023

were more tolerant of, or adaptive to, the indoor thermal conditions when the building was in the natural ventilation mode of operation compared to the air-conditioning operational mode.

There are three main types of mixed-mode ventilation, which are elaborated as follows: The first type is that the natural ventilation system and the mechanical air-conditioning system operate alternately. When the outdoor condition permits, only natural ventilation is used, and the mechanical ventilation system is turned off; when the outdoor environment rises or falls to a certain limit, the natural ventilation system is turned off and the mechanical ventilation system is turned on, and there is no interference between the two. The key to this type of mixed-mode ventilation is to select appropriate control parameters so that the switching between the natural ventilation mode and the mechanical ventilation mode can meet the requirements of indoor thermal comfort and air quality with the least energy consumption.

The second type is fan-assisted natural ventilation. When the natural driving force is insufficient, the fan is turned on to maintain the flow of air and ensure the requirement of airflow rate. In other cases, natural ventilation is used. The key to this type of mixed-mode ventilation is to design an automatic control system to control the start and stop of fans according to changes in outdoor conditions.

The third type is air pressure– and heat pressure–assisted mechanical ventilation. Mechanical ventilation is the main method under various climatic conditions, while natural ventilation formed by wind pressure and thermal pressure is used as an auxiliary. The key to this type of mixed-mode ventilation is to control mechanical ventilation according to the changes in wind pressure and thermal pressure.

When designing a mixed ventilation system, other passive energy-saving techniques should be also incorporated, such as building shading technology, solar chimney, underpass pre-cooling technology, night ventilation, etc. Such technologies can effectively prolong the utilisation time of natural ventilation and improve the indoor thermal environment, especially for extreme outdoor temperatures.

Adaptive environments with natural ventilation

Natural ventilation can be used as a low-cost alternative to mechanical ventilation. It leverages the airflow from natural sources such as doors, windows and vents to create a more comfortable indoor environment. Therefore, when designing natural ventilation for office buildings, the following factors should be considered: location and orientation, building form, indoor partitions or obstacles and openings and urban layouts (Lawrence et al., 2020).

As indicated previously, studies in terms of thermal comfort revealed that the opportunities provided by the built environment could play a significant role in forming occupants' comfort expectations based on their preferences and needs (Luo et al., 2018). Therefore, the desire for comfort based on the occupants' wants can lead to comfort-related reactions to achieve their preferred thermal condition. Natural ventilation can offer several benefits in terms of thermal comfort and occupants' satisfaction. It creates the opportunities for greater control and adaptability based on individual preferences by offering a variety of options for controlling passive building systems (e.g., windows) and adjusting airflow. This flexibility is particularly beneficial in naturally ventilated workspaces, where each occupant may have different comfort requirements due to factors such as location within the workspace, outdoor conditions and personal sensitivities. A study conducted by Candido et al. (2010) showed the significant role of "thermal history on affecting occupants" and their thermal perception of their indoor environment. The findings demonstrated that opportunities of passive strategies can be welcomed by occupants and need to be exploited as much as possible.

Several studies have explored natural ventilation in workspaces, revealing positive findings regarding occupants' thermal comfort. Occupants in naturally ventilated buildings have exhibited higher overall comfort levels and satisfaction compared to those in air-conditioned spaces. By comparing a naturally ventilated building with an air-conditioned one, Wang et al. (2021)

concluded that occupants in the former building were more tolerant to temperatures that deviated from neutral than in the latter building. This accommodation of natural adaptability of occupants in the naturally ventilated building operation strategy has considerable positive impacts for energy efficiency (Kim et al., 2019). A study regarding the implementation of natural ventilation in office buildings revealed that implementation of naturally ventilated design strategies could bring about energy efficiency while maximising occupants' thermal comfort (Zoure & Genovese, 2023). Also, the ability to feel connected to the outside environment and experience natural airflow has been shown to contribute to a sense of well-being and improved thermal comfort in occupants. For instance, in the context of workplace semi-outdoor environments, Lyu et al. (2022) found that there was an association between thermal adaptive opportunity and restorative benefits in semi-outdoor spaces with dynamic thermal environmental conditions.

Different types of natural ventilation systems that can be employed to enhance occupants' thermal comfort. One approach is single-sided ventilation, where airflow occurs through openings on one side of the building, such as windows or vents. This type of ventilation benefits from prevailing winds and temperature differentials to promote airflow. Cross-ventilation, on the other hand, involves creating openings on opposite sides of the building to facilitate air movement across the space. This approach results in a higher level of natural airflow and can be effective in providing consistent thermal comfort inside buildings. In a thermal comfort study carried out in Brisbane, Australia (Omrani et al., 2017), it was found that cross-ventilation could provide thermal comfort on a typical hot summer day for most of the day (greater than 70% of the time), while, for single-sided ventilation, the thermal conditions of internal spaces was comfortable for only 1% of the time. Additionally, stack ventilation relies on the principle of warm air rising and escaping though openings at higher levels, while cooler air enters through lower openings, promoting natural ventilation. Each type of ventilation has its own advantages and considerations, and the choice depends on factors such as building design, climate conditions and occupant needs. Therefore, it is crucial to carefully design and manage natural ventilation systems to ensure optimal performance. Factors such as building orientation, window design, cross-ventilation opportunities and shading technologies play a significant role in maximising the benefits of natural ventilation while minimising potential drawbacks (Elaouzy & El Fadar, 2022), such as overheating or insufficient airflow during unfavourable weather conditions.

By implementing such design approaches, it can be possible to achieve thermal comfort while maintaining energy efficiency and providing individuals with great control over their indoor environment.

Achieving high-performance workplaces

An operational approach to carbon-zero buildings

Almost 40% of all energy-related greenhouse emissions come from buildings, and 28% come from the operations of buildings themselves, therefore reducing energy consumption in the whole life cycle of a building; in particular, the building operation phase is crucial while maintaining thermal comfort in workplaces. Operational carbon refers to all emissions produced when a building is in use. This includes the energy needed to heat, cool, light, power and ventilate a space.

Various approaches can be employed to reduce the operation energy demand of the buildings. Table 6.1 lists the energy efficiency measures (ECMs) for typical commercial buildings, which can be divided into non-HVAC-side measures and HVAC-side measures. The non-HVAC-side

Table 6.1 Energy efficiency measures (ECMs) for office buildings

Classifications	*Non-HVAC Measures*	*HVAC Measures*
ECMs	1. External wall insulation 2. Roof insulation 3. Shading 4. Window replacing 5. Trombe wall 6. PCM 7. BIPV 8. Lighting control	**AHU:** 1. minimum VAV airflow rate reset; 2. Discharge air temperature reset 3. Supply fan static pressure reset; 4. VAV box commissioning; 5. Sensor calibration. **FAN COIL UNITS:** 1. Supply air temperature reset; 2. Operation reschedule; 3. Unit commissioning. **CHILLER PLANT:** 1. Installed speed drives on the chilled water/ condenser water pumps; 2. Chilled water secondary loop pressure difference reset; 3. Condenser water temperature reset; 4. Chilled water supply temperature reset; 5. Stage up/down control. **BOILER PLANT:** 1. Installed variable speed drives on primary hot water pumps; 2. Supply hot water temperature reset; 3. Secondary loop differential pressure reset; 4. Primary hot water flow and secondary loop water flow matching.

measures mainly focus on reducing the thermal load of the buildings, e.g., optimising the insulation level for the exterior walls and roof to reduce the conduction heat loss/gain through the building envelope; using external shading to block the solar radiation when it is too strong; replacing single-layer clear windows with Low-E double-layer windows; using Trombe wall and PCM material to store solar heat in the daytime and release it at night; adopting BIPV to produce the energy needed for the building; and applying smart lighting control coupled with shading.

The HVAC-side measures include a series of intelligent control improvements on the air-handling units (AHUs), fan coil units (FCUs), chiller plant and boiler plant, e.g., dynamic reset on the VAV minimum airflow settings, discharge air temperature reset, supply water temperature reset, etc.

Personal control systems

Personalised ventilation (PV) is an individually controlled air-distribution system aimed at improving the quality of inhaled air and the thermal comfort of each occupant. In comparison with traditional mechanical ventilation systems, PV can improve occupants' health, inhaled air quality, thermal comfort and productivity.

A PV system can be divided into four categories according to different air-supply methods: PV from raised floor, PV from desktop, PV from partition wall and PV from false ceiling. The floor personalised air-supply system (Figure 6.3) is the most commonly used form of PV. The floor personalised air-supply system installs air diffusers on the raised floor near the occupants. The entire space under the raised floor is used as an air-supply channel, and a fan is installed under each air diffuser to blow the air to the work area. Occupants can adjust air-supply parameters, such as air-supply angle and air velocity, according to their own needs.

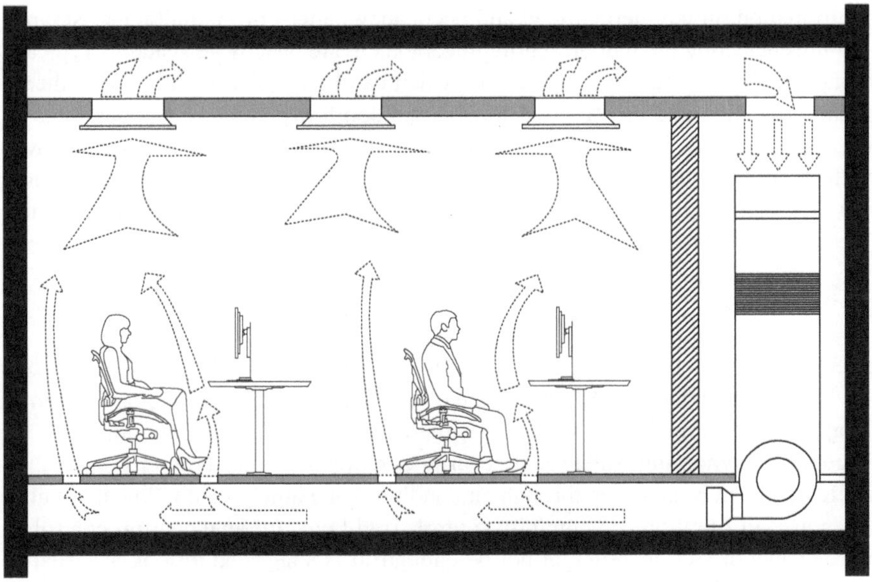

Figure 6.3 Personalised ventilation from raised floor.

Moving from a static to an adaptive HVAC system

As mentioned before, static indoor conditions provided by the HVAC system sometimes fail to satisfy the thermal comfort requirements for occupants. The HVAC industry therefore needed to define "comfort" in terms of the physical variables that could be controlled using the HVAC system (Nicol & Roaf, 2017). The PMV model only proved to be valid for a person in a steady-state environment (de Dear, 2004) because people generally do not just passively perceive the ambient environment. They continually adapt to the ambient environment in order to approach thermal comfort by physiological adaptation, psychological adaptation and behavioural adjustment (Roaf et al., 2010).

ASHRAE Standard 55 (2020) recommends that thermal comfort is associated with outdoor air temperature, indicating that the indoor operating temperature can increase with the outdoor air temperature. The thermal load of the building varies with the ambient weather conditions as well as the occupancy patterns, and the thermal comfort setpoint should be adaptive to the weather and personalised comfort condition. Accordingly, the HVAC system needs to operate to meet the thermal load of the building, thus adaptive control instead of static on the HVAC cold/heat source operation (Yan et al., 2008). Typical adaptive control strategies include supply air temperature reset of the AHU according to the outdoor air temperature; duct static pressure reset according to the thermal load of the building; supply chilled/hot water temperature reset according to outside air temperature and occupancy pattern; indoor air temperature reset according to outside air temperature and occupancy pattern, etc.

Sensing technology used to develop predictive models

With the development of sensing technology, thermal comfort in the workplace can be improved greatly by developing accurate predictive models. The adaptive control of the HVAC system requires information on the thermal load and occupancy pattern of the buildings. Smart lighting control requires detecting the indoor lighting level to activate/deactivate shading. Typical sensors therefore include the outdoor air temperature, which can be coupled with building thermal load data for load prediction and can be used for thermal comfort prediction and air/water temperature reset prediction, and air/water flow rate sensor to measure the supply air/water flow rate and couple with an air/water temperature sensor to calculate the AHU/chiller/boiler operation load. In addition, a CO_2 sensor can be installed at the return side of the AHU to determine the indoor air quality and can be used for personalised/demand control ventilation.

Considerations post-COVID

The outbreak of COVID-19 reminded us of the importance of the healthy building. According to the WELL Building Standard (IWBI, 2016), the ideal healthy building technology system consists of nine major elements, including ventilation, thermal comfort, air quality, noise, air filtration, humidity control, daylighting, safety and security and water quality (Lin et al., 2022). Among these, six elements can be achieved through air conditioning, namely ventilation, thermal comfort, air quality, noise, air filtration and humidity control. Traditional thermal comfort control based on temperature or indoor CO_2 level might not be enough. It is suggested to look at visual comfort, thermal comfort and air pollution control concurrently to ensure a comfortable and healthy indoor environment.

Large numbers of people have been working from home since the start of the pandemic, and when people are at home for long periods of time, thermal comfort and energy efficiency of homes become salient topics. Many existing homes were built before energy building standards came into effect, resulting in poor energy performance and uncomfortable thermal conditions. Research shows that two-thirds of homes were too cold for good health but that many householders were not aware of the risks (Ketchell, 2022). In EU countries (e.g., Germany, Switzerland) initiatives have been examined to retrofit thermally energy-inefficient residential buildings (Galvin, 2022; Streicher et al., 2018). The quality of housing in other countries, such as Poland, has been pointed out as an important factor affecting people's health (Sokołowski et al., 2023). In the UK, Zahiri and Elsharkawy (2018) pointed out the necessity of retrofitting to achieve more climate-resilient and energy-efficient residential buildings. In China thermal inefficient building design has hindered energy-saving goals due to occupants' higher air-conditioning preferences (Sun, 2013). Being too hot is also a significant problem for Australian homes, as climate change is leading to an increased frequency and severity of heat waves. Over the coming decades it is likely that mainland Australia will require more cooling than heating (Saman et al., 2013).

In recent years, numerous studies have focused on investigating the issue of energy poverty in different countries by using various conventional and new variables, combining socio-economic indicators with the energy performance of buildings (Castaño-Rosa et al., 2020; Sanchez-Guevara et al., 2019). Therefore, another issue occupants are tackling in their buildings is residential thermal comfort. In Australian residential buildings low-income households suffer from overheated or cold homes and experience problems associated with energy inefficiency and poor thermal comfort, which ultimately affect residents' quality of life, comfort, well-being and physical and mental health (Haddad et al., 2019). This thermally inefficient housing has also impacted vulnerable UK populations, such as elderly and unemployed people with disabilities within the low-income energy poverty group (Elsharkawy & Rutherford, 2018). These circumstances are the main drivers of a social challenge known as energy poverty (EP) when residents have difficulties in paying the electricity bills. A priority should be given to improve thermal comfort in low-income households as residents are exposed to serious environmental and health risks. Efforts should be intensified to promote programmes to improve the thermal performance of the low-income dwellings and programmes to supply energy at low prices to satisfy basic needs (Haddad et al., 2019).

Conclusion

Maintaining thermal comfort in indoor work environments is very critical to a worker's overall morale and work performance. There are two inherent problems with traditional HVAC systems in providing thermal comfort in modern office buildings. Firstly, unnecessary heating and cooling is provided even if only part of the space in the office area is occupied, resulting in a great waste of energy. Secondly, individual thermal comfort preferences cannot be accommodated. These two problems can be well resolved by using personalised ventilation and a mixed-mode ventilation system.

A high-performance checklist for delivering a thermally comfortable workplace includes reducing operational building energy consumption by using energy efficiency measures, applying personal HVAC control and mix-mode ventilation, making use of sensing technologies to develop more accurate predictive models and considering visual comfort, thermal comfort and air pollution control concurrently to ensure a comfortable and healthy indoor environment.

A "high-performance" checklist for thermal comfort is provided here:

Principle	*Description*
ENERGY CONSUMPTION Reducing operational building energy consumption	• Using energy efficiency measures • Applying personal HVAC control • Mixed-mode ventilation
MODELS Develop more accurate predictive models	• Making use of sensing technologies
IEQ Ensure a comfortable and healthy indoor environment	• Considering visual comfort, thermal comfort and air pollution control concurrently

References

ASHRAE. (2020). *ASHRAE standard 55–2020*. Thermal environmental conditions for human occupancy. American Society of Heating, Refrigerating and Air-Conditioning Engineers, Atlanta.

Candido, C., de Dear, R., Lamberts, R., & Bittencourt, L. (2010). Cooling exposure in hot humid climates: Are occupants 'addicted'? *Architectural Science Review*, *53*(1), 59–64. https://doi.org/10.3763/asre.2009.0100

Caroline, K., Stefano, S., & Edward, A. (2018). Percentage of commercial buildings showing at least 80% occupant satisfied with their thermal comfort. *Proceedings of 10th Windsor Conference*, *2018*, 1–7.

Castaño-Rosa, R., Solís-Guzmán, J., & Marrero, M. (2020). Energy poverty goes south? Understanding the costs of energy poverty with the index of vulnerable homes in Spain. *Energy Research & Social Science*, *60*, 101325. https://doi.org/10.1016/j.erss.2019.101325

Cheung, T., Schiavon, S., Parkinson, T., Li, P., & Brager, G. (2019). Analysis of the accuracy on PMV–PPD model using the ASHRAE Global Thermal Comfort Database II. *Building and Environment*, *153*, 205–217. https://doi.org/10.1016/j.buildenv.2019t.01.055

Cleary, M., Raeburn, T., West, S., & Childs, C. (2019). The environmental temperature of the residential care home: Role in thermal comfort and mental health? *Contemporary Nurse*, *55*(1), 38–46. https://doi.org/10.1080/10376178.2019.1583068

de Dear, R. (2004). Thermal comfort in practice. *Indoor Air*, *14*(s 7), 32–39.

de Dear, R. J., & Brager, G. S. (1998). Developing an adaptive model of thermal comfort and preference. *ASHRAE Transactions*, *104*(1), 145–167.

de Dear, R. J., Brager, G. S., Reardon, J., & Nicol, F. (1998). Developing an adaptive model of thermal comfort and preference/discussion. *ASHRAE transactions*, *104*, 145.

Deuble, M. P., & de Dear, R. J. (2012). Mixed-mode buildings: A double standard in occupants' comfort expectations. *Building and Environment*, *54*, 53–60. https://doi.org/10.1016/j.buildenv.2012.01.021

Du, H., Lian, Z., Lai, D., Duanmu, L., Zhai, Y., Cao, B., Zhang, Y., Zhou, Z., Wang, Z., Zhang, X., & Hou, Z. (2022). Evaluation of the accuracy of PMV and its several revised models using the Chinese thermal comfort Database. *Energy and Buildings*, *271*, 112334. https://doi.org/10.1016/j.enbuild.2022.112334

Elaouzy, Y., & El Fadar, A. (2022). Energy, economic and environmental benefits of integrating passive design strategies into buildings: A review. *Renewable and Sustainable Energy Reviews*, *167*, 112828. https://doi.org/10.1016/j.rser.2022.112828

Elsharkawy, H., & Rutherford, P. (2018). Energy-efficient retrofit of social housing in the UK: Lessons learned from a Community Energy Saving Programme (CESP) in Nottingham. *Energy and Buildings*, *172*, 295–306. https://doi.org/10.1016/j.enbuild.2018.04.067

Fanger, P. O. (1970). *Thermal comfort*. Danish Technical Press.

Galvin, R. (2022). Net-zero-energy buildings or zero-carbon energy systems? How best to decarbonize Germany's thermally inefficient 1950s-1970s-era apartments. *Journal of Building Engineering*, *54*, 104671. https://doi.org/10.1016/j.jobe.2022.104671

García, A., Olivieri, F., Larrumbide, E., & Ávila, P. (2019). Thermal comfort assessment in naturally ventilated offices located in a cold tropical climate, Bogotá. *Building and Environment*, *158*, 237–247. https://doi.org/10.1016/j.buildenv.2019.05.013

Haddad, S., Pignatta, G., Paolini, R., Synnefa, A., & Santamouris, M. (2019). An extensive study on the relationship between energy use, indoor thermal comfort, and health in social housing: The case of the New South Wales, Australia. *IOP Conference Series: Materials Science and Engineering*, *609*, 042067, https//doi.org/10.1088/1757-899X/609/4/042067

International WELL Building Institute (IWBI). (2016). *The WELL building standard-V2 pilot*, New York.

Kaushik, A., Arif, M., Tumula, P., & Ebohon, O. J. (2020). Effect of thermal comfort on occupant productivity in office buildings: Response surface analysis. *Building and Environment*, *180*, 107021.

Ketchell, M. (2022). https://theconversation.com/as-power-prices-soar-we-need-a-concerted-effort-to-tackle-energy-poverty-98764

Kiki, G., Kouchadé, C., Houngan, A., Zannou-Tchoko, S. J., & André, P. (2020). Evaluation of thermal comfort in an office building in the humid tropical climate of Benin. *Building and Environment*, *185*, 107277. https://doi.org/10.1016/j.buildenv.2020.107277

Kim, J., Tartarini, F., Parkinson, T., Cooper, P., & de Dear, R. (2019). Thermal comfort in a mixed-mode building: Are occupants more adaptive? *Energy and Buildings*, *203*, 109436.

Lamsal, P., Bajracharya, S. B., & Rijal, H. B. (2023). A review on adaptive thermal comfort of office building for energy-saving building design. *Energies*, *16*(3), 1524. https://doi.org/10.3390/en16031524

Lan, L., Wargocki, P., Wyon, D. P., & Lian, Z. (2011). Effects of thermal discomfort in an office on perceived air quality, SBS symptoms, physiological responses, and human performance. *Indoor Air*, *21*(5), 376–390. https://doi.org/10.1111/j.1600-0668.2011.00714.x

Lawrence, T., Darwich, A. K., & Means, J. K. (Eds.). (2020). *ASHRAE greenguide: Design, construction, and operation of sustainable buildings: Complete guidance on green building from planning to operation* (5th ed.). ASHRAE.

Li, Z., Yang, B., Jin, D., Li, X., Wang, F., & Li, A. (2022). The synergy effect of temporal and spatial alliesthesia on occupants' thermal comfort in air-conditioned temporarily occupied spaces (TOS). *Building and Environment*, *210*, 108699. https://doi.org/10.1016/j.buildenv.2021.108699

Lin, Y., Yuan, X., Yang, W., Hao, X., & Li, C. (2022). A review on research and development of healthy building in China. *Buildings*, *12*, 376. https://doi.org/10.3390/buildings12030376

Liu, Y., Xu, H., Zheng, P., Lin, B., Wu, H., Huang, Y., & Li, Z. (2021). Thermal preference prediction based on occupants' adaptive behavior in indoor environments-A study of an air-conditioned multi-occupancy office in China. *Building and Environment*, *206*, 108355. https://doi.org/10.1016/j.buildenv.2021.108355

Luo, M., Wang, Z., Brager, G., Cao, B., & Zhu, Y. (2018). Indoor climate experience, migration, and thermal comfort expectation in buildings. *Building and Environment*, *141*, 262–272. https://doi.org/10.1016/j.buildenv.2018.05.047

Lyu, K., de Dear, R., Brambilla, A., & Globa, A. (2022). Restorative benefits of semi-outdoor environments at the workplace: Does the thermal realm matter? *Building and Environment*, *222*, 109355. https://doi.org/10.1016/j.buildenv.2022.109355

Mamani, T., Herrera, R., Rivera, F. M., & Atencio, E. (2022). Variables that affect thermal comfort and its measuring instruments: A systematic review. *Sustainability, 14*(3), 1773. https://doi.org/10.3390/su14031773

Marzban, S., Candido, C., Brambilla, A., Gocer, O., Vijapur, D., & Jensen, C. (2022). Is 24.9° C too hot to think? A call to raise temperature setpoints in Australian offices. *Buildings, 12*(12), 2259. https://doi.org/10.3390/buildings12122259

Nicol, J. F., & Roaf, S. (2017). Rethinking thermal comfort. *Building Research & Information, 45*(7), 711–716. https//doi.org/10.1080/09613218.2017.1301698

Omidvar, A., & Kim, J. (2020). Modification of sweat evaporative heat loss in the PMV/PPD model to improve thermal comfort prediction in warm climates. *Building and Environment, 176*, 106868. https://doi.org/10.1016/j.buildenv.2020.106868

Omrani, S., Garcia-Hansen, V., Capra, B. R., & Drogemuller, R. (2017). Effect of natural ventilation mode on thermal comfort and ventilation performance: Full-scale measurement. *Energy and Buildings, 156*, 1–16. https://doi.org/10.1016/j.enbuild.2017.09.061

Pan, Y., Du, C., Fu, Z., & Fu, M. (2021). Re-thinking of engineering operation solutions to HVAC systems under the emerging COVID-19 pandemic. *Journal of Building Engineering, 43*, 102889. https://doi.org/10.1016/j.jobe.2021.102889

Parkinson, T., & de Dear, R. (2015). Thermal pleasure in built environments: Physiology of alliesthesia. *Building Research & Information, 43*(3), 288–301. https://doi.org/10.1080/09613218.2015.989662

Parkinson, T., & de Dear, R. (2017). Thermal pleasure in built environments: Spatial alliesthesia from air movement. *Building Research & Information, 45*(3), 320–335. https://doi.org/10.1080/09613218.2016.1140932

Parkinson, T., de Dear, R., & Brager, G. (2020). Nudging the adaptive thermal comfort model. *Energy and Buildings, 206*, 109559. https://doi.org/10.1016/j.enbuild.2019.109559

Parkinson, T., de Dear, R., & Candido, C. (2012, April). Perception of transient thermal environments: Pleasure and alliesthesia. In *Proceedings of 7th Windsor Conference: The changing context of comfort in an unpredictable world* (No. 56). Cumberland Lodge, Windsor.

Parkinson, T., de Dear, R., & Candido, C. (2016). Thermal pleasure in built environments: Alliesthesia in different thermoregulatory zones. *Building Research & Information, 44*(1), 20–33. https://doi.org/10.1080/09613218.2015.1059653

Residovic, C. (2017). The new NABERS indoor environment tool–the next frontier for Australian buildings. *Procedia Engineering, 180*, 303–310. https://doi.org/10.1016/j.proeng.2017.04.189

Roaf, S., Nicol, F., Humphreys, M., Tuohy, P., & Boerstra, A. (2010). Twentieth century standards for thermal comfort: Promoting high energy buildings. *Architectural Science Review, 53*(1), 65–77.

Rupp, R. F., Parkinson, T., Kim, J., Toftum, J., & de Dear, R. (2022). The impact of occupant's thermal sensitivity on adaptive thermal comfort model. *Building and Environment, 207*, 108517. https://doi.org/10.1016/j.buildenv.2021.108517

Saman, W., Boland, J., Pullen, S., de Dear, R., Soebarto, V., Miller, W., Pocock, B., Belusko, M., Bruno, F., Whaley, D., Pockett, J., Bennetts, H., Ridley, B., Palmer, J., Zuo, J., Ma, T., Chileshe, N., Skinner, N., Chapman, J., Vujinovic, N., Walsh, M., Candido, C., & Deuble, M. (2013). A framework for adaptation of Australian households to heat waves. In *National climate change adaptation research facility, Gold Coast* (p. 242). NCCARF Publication 87/13.

Sanchez-Guevara, C., Peiró, M. N., Taylor, J., Mavrogianni, A., & González, J. N. (2019). Assessing population vulnerability towards summer energy poverty: Case studies of Madrid and London. *Energy and Buildings, 190*, 132–143. https://doi.org/10.1016/j.enbuild.2019.02.024

Shahzad, S., & Rijal, H. B. (2022). Mixed mode is better than air-conditioned offices for resilient comfort: Adaptive behaviour and visual thermal landscaping. In *Routledge handbook of resilient thermal comfort* (pp. 329–346). Routledge.

Sharma, A., Kumar, A., & Kulkarni, K. S. (2021). Thermal comfort studies for the naturally ventilated built environments in Indian subcontinent: A review. *Journal of Building Engineering, 44*, 103242. https://doi.org/10.1016/j.jobe.2021.103242

SHE POE dataset. (2023). *Sustainable and healthy environments post-occupancy evaluation dataset*. SHE Lab (not published).

Sokołowski, J., Frankowski, J., & Lewandowski, P. (2023). Energy poverty, housing conditions, and self-assessed health: Evidence from Poland. *Housing Studies*, 1–30. https://doi.org/10.1080/02673037.2023.2176831

Son, Y. J., & Chun, C. (2018). Research on electroencephalogram to measure thermal pleasure in thermal alliesthesia in temperature step-change environment. *Indoor Air*, *28*(6), 916–923. https://doi.org/10.1111/ina.12491

Song, B., Bai, L., & Yang, L. (2022). Analysis of the long-term effects of solar radiation on the indoor thermal comfort in office buildings. *Energy*, *247*, 123499. https://doi.org/10.1016/j.energy.2022.123499

Streicher, K. N., Padey, P., Parra, D., Bürer, M. C., & Patel, M. K. (2018). Assessment of the current thermal performance level of the Swiss residential building stock: Statistical analysis of energy performance certificates. *Energy and Buildings*, *178*, 360–378. https://doi.org/10.1016/j.enbuild.2018.08.032

Sun, F. (2013). Achieving suitable thermal performance in residential buildings in different climatic regions of China. *Energy and Buildings*, *67*, 11–21. https://doi.org/10.1016/j.enbuild.2013.07.037

Tartarini, F., Schiavon, S., Quintana, M., & Miller, C. (2022). Personal comfort models based on a 6-month experiment using environmental parameters and data from wearables. *Indoor Air*, *32*(11), e13160. https://doi.org/10.1111/ina.13160

Thayer, J. F., Verkuil, B., Brosschotj, J. F., Kevin, K., West, A., Sterling, C., Christie, I. C., Abernethy, D. R., Sollers, J. J., Cizza, G., & Marques, A. H. (2010). Effects of the physical work environment on physiological measures of stress. *European Journal of Preventive Cardiology*, *17*(4), 431–439.

Vendor. (2020). https://www.hvacrnews.com.au/news/covid-19-forcing-a-rethink-on-ventilation/

Wang, X., Yang, L., Gao, S., Zhao, S., & Zhai, Y. (2021). Thermal comfort in naturally ventilated university classrooms: A seasonal field study in Xi'an, China. *Energy and Buildings*, *247*, 111126. https://doi.org/10.1016/j.enbuild.2021.111126

Wang, Z., Zhang, H., He, Y., Luo, M., Li, Z., Hong, T., & Lin, B. (2020). Revisiting individual and group differences in thermal comfort based on ASHRAE database. *Energy and Buildings*, *219*, 110017. https://doi.org/10.1016/j.enbuild.2020.110017

Wu, Y., Liu, H., Li, B., Kosonen, R., Kong, D., Zhou, S., & Yao, R. (2019b). Thermal adaptation of the elderly during summer in a hot humid area: Psychological, behavioral, and physiological responses. *Energy and Buildings*, *203*, 109450. https://doi.org/10.1016/j.enbuild.2019.109450

Wu, Z., Li, N., Wargocki, P., Peng, J., Li, J., & Cui, H. (2019a). Field study on thermal comfort and energy saving potential in 11 split air-conditioned office buildings in Changsha, China. *Energy*, *182*, 471–482. https://doi.org/10.1016/j.energy.2019.05.204

Yan, Y., Zhou, J., Lin, Y., Yang, W., Wang, P., & Zhang, G. (2008). Adaptive optimal control model for building cooling and heating sources. *Energy and Buildings*, *40*(8), 1394–1401. https://doi.org/10.1016/j.enbuild.2008.01.003

Yang, L., Gao, S., Zhao, S., Zhang, H., Arens, E., & Zhai, Y. (2020). Thermal comfort and physiological responses with standing and treadmill workstations in summer. *Building and Environment*, *185*, 107238. https://doi.org/10.1016/j.buildenv.2020.107238

Zahiri, S., & Elsharkawy, H. (2018). Towards energy-efficient retrofit of council housing in London: Assessing the impact of occupancy and energy-use patterns on building performance. *Energy and Buildings*, *174*, 672–681. https://doi.org/10.1016/j.enbuild.2018.07.010

Zhang, S., Cheng, Y., Oladokun, M. O., Wu, Y., & Lin, Z. (2020). Improving predicted mean vote with inversely determined metabolic rate. *Sustainable Cities and Society*, *53*, 101870.

Zheng, P., Wang, C., Liu, Y., Lin, B., Wu, H., Huang, Y., & Zhou, X. (2022). Thermal adaptive behavior and thermal comfort for occupants in multi-person offices with air-conditioning systems. *Building and Environment*, *207*, 108432. https://doi.org/10.1016/j.buildenv.2021.108432

Zoure, A. N., & Genovese, P. V. (2023). Implementing natural ventilation and daylighting strategies for thermal comfort and energy efficiency in office buildings in Burkina Faso. *Energy Reports*, *9*, 3319–3342. https://doi.org/10.1016/j.egyr.2023.02.017

7
INDOOR AIR QUALITY

Arianna Brambilla, Ozgur Gocer, and Christhina Candido

We need clean air just as much as we need clean water.

– Authors

Introduction

In recent years, the quality of the air we breathe has become a topic of increasing global interest, both in scientific research and in the community. Factors such as widespread bushfires in various countries and the emergence of a global pandemic have elevated the importance of air quality in public discussions about health and well-being. This has been particularly significant in evaluating the risks associated with returning to work after lockdowns. The million-dollar question that everyone is trying to answer is: are our offices equipped to provide us with fresh air and healthy indoors? And the truth is there is no binary, simple, and quick answer to this question.

In the field, Indoor Air Quality (IAQ) refers to the quality of the air inside buildings, and it relates to the presence and concentration of various pollutants that can affect the health, comfort, and well-being of the occupants. It is paramount when delivering healthy and safe spaces for people to work. As COVID-19 highlighted, building design and operation are intrinsically correlated to its capacity to maintain occupants' safety by determining the quality of the indoor air. However, it is not only in exceptional and extreme circumstances that IAQ impacts occupants, as the air pollutants that linger indoors go beyond bushfire by-products of viruses but comprise a broader number of chemical and biological compounds, including those determined by some humans' activities, such as CO_2 from respiration. With the increased reliance on airtight, fully air-conditioned buildings, the risk of not properly managing IAQ conditions comes with a significant price tag in terms of workers' health and productivity. Increased asthma, dry eyes, headaches, and irritated throat are the most common health symptoms related to poor IAQ in workplaces. Further, research has also linked poor IAQ to reduced productivity and performance over time in workplaces. Not surprisingly, IAQ has been on the radar of those designing, building, managing, and maintaining workplaces because of its known links to human health and well-being, satisfaction, and productivity. Data from the SHE POE dataset (Figure 7.1) shows stuffy and humid air, lack of air movement, and odors are among the main reasons for dissatisfaction with IAQ in workplaces (SHE POE dataset, 2023).

DOI: 10.1201/9781003328728-8

This chapter has been made available under a CC-BY-NC-ND 4.0 license.

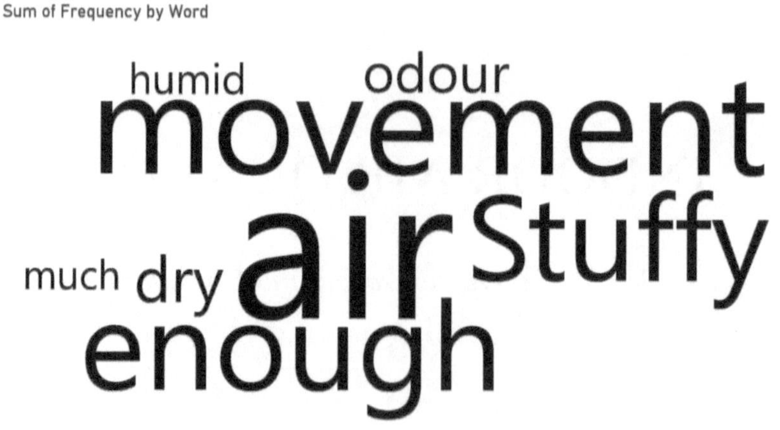

Figure 7.1 Word cloud generated from the SHE POE dataset reporting dissatisfaction with IAQ. (SHE POE dataset, 2023)

Understanding what the factors influencing IAQ are and what can be done to increase the quality of the indoor air is critical to ensure that high-performing workplaces foster health and well-being for their workers. This chapter provides an overview of the different types of indoor pollutants that can affect the air quality within a building, including biological pollutants like mold, bacteria, and viruses, as well as chemical pollutants like volatile organic compounds (VOCs), carbon monoxide, and radon. It delves into current trends and strategies for controlling and improving IAQ, such as the use of air filtration systems, ventilation systems, and indoor plants. It also discusses the role of building design and construction in ensuring healthy IAQ. Overall, this chapter provides an overview of indoor air pollutants and the importance of maintaining healthy IAQ. It highlights the different strategies and technologies available to improve IAQ and provides readers with valuable insights on how to create healthier indoor environments.

Indoor pollutants

IAQ is determined by various factors, including the interaction between chemically or biologically originated pollutants. Chemical pollutants refer to inorganic compounds present in the air, while biological pollutants include pollen, mold, mites, and other compounds. Both indoor and outdoor sources can contribute to air pollution, with outdoor sources typically being more immediate, such as particulate matter from traffic. However, indoor sources can also play a significant role, including the use of chemical cleaning products or consumer electronics, as well as building materials that may release gases like formaldehyde, organic chemicals, and inorganic chemicals. The specific requirements for IAQ may vary depending on factors such as location, building type, intended use, and exposure. Poor IAQ can lead to a range of health problems, such as headaches, fatigue, allergies, and respiratory issues (Wolkoff, 2018; Tran et al., 2020), but in the workplace can also have financial implications. Poor IAQ can reduce workers' satisfaction and productivity, increase absenteeism, and result in higher turnover rates (Kelly & Fussel, 2019). The extent of these implications can be higher than $1.6 billion a year, considered to be the economic loss in Australia due to lower respiratory infections derived from poor IAQ (Morawska et al., 2022).

Table 7. 1 Summary of the air pollutants commonly found in buildings, their source, and the recognized effects on humans (ABCB, 2018).

Contaminant	*Source*	*Hazard for Humans*
CARBON MONOXIDE (CO)	Incomplete combustion process of carbon	Reduction of oxygen-carrying capacity of blood due to the conversion of hemoglobin into carboxyhemoglobin. Reduced oxygenation leads to headache, nausea, dizziness, loss of brain function, loss of consciousness, and death.
CARBON DIOXIDE (CO2)	Human respiration	Loss of mental acuity, dizziness, and headache.
FORMALDEHYDE (HCHO)	Furniture and indoor materials, such as particleboard and carpet	Eye irritation, dermatitis, headache, nausea, cancer.
PARTICULATE MATTER (PM)	Airborne particles, such as dust, dirt, sand, smoke, and liquid droplets	Eye irritation, respiratory tract irritation, cough, bronchitis, asthma.
OZONE	Photocopiers, ultraviolet light sources, air cleaners, car exhaust	Respiratory disorder, reduced exercise capability.
MOLD AND MYCOTOXINS	Fungi	Allergic reactions, skin irritation, respiratory tract irritation, dizziness.
BACTERIA (LEGIONELLA PNEUMOPHILIA)	Waters containing bacteria, often air ducts	Fever, cough, pneumonia, death.
VIRUSES	Droplets form infected people (can linger in the air for 2 hours, depending on the virus)	Minor viral disease (influenza) to death.
ORGANIC SOLVENTS	Polyurethane, insulation materials, paints, cleaning liquids, smoke	Eye irritation, respiratory tract irritation, nausea.
OTHER COMBUSTION PRODUCTS, LESS COMMON: NITRIC OXIDE (NO), NITROGEN DIOXIDE (NO2), SULPHUR DIOXIDE (SO2)	Fuel burning and smoke	Respiratory disorder, lung damage, eye irritation.
OTHER BIOLOGICAL PRODUCTS (DANDERS, SCALES, HAIR, DUST MITES)	Animals, microspoci organisms, humans	Allergic reaction, asthma.
INSECTICIDES	Pest-control products	Nausea, headache, breathing difficulties, liver damage, convulsions, cancer.

Chemical pollutants

Chemical pollutants can be generated either inside the building or outside and then transported inside through ventilation systems, windows, or cracks in the building envelope. The level of risk associated with their presence depends on factors such as the concentration, density, and characteristics of the pollutants and their sources. In the case of outdoor pollutants, the distance from the source and the direction of the wind are important factors to consider. As an illustration, pollutants from road traffic can impact a building's IAQ up to a distance of 375 meters if the wind is blowing in that direction (Hitchins et al., 2000).

Among the chemical pollutants most found in offices, there are carbon dioxide (CO_2) and carbon monoxide (CO), particulate matters, and volatile organic compounds. CO_2 is a direct by-product of human respiration. The concentration of CO_2 in a space is a reliable indicator of human presence, activities, and ventilation. A high concentration of CO_2 can lead to symptoms such as headaches, dizziness, confusion, dyspnea, disorientation, hypertension, and even loss of consciousness. The American Society for Heating, Refrigerating, and Air Conditioning Engineers (ASHRAE) Standard 62.1 recommends a maximum CO_2 level of 1000 parts per million (ppm) (ASHRAE, 2019), and the National Construction Code of Australia goes further and recommends a limit of 850 ppm over an 8-hour period (ABCB, 2018).

CO is an odorless and colorless poisonous gas, a product of incomplete combustion processes. The outdoor concentration of CO is 0.2 ppm, but larger cities can reach significantly higher values. Milder symptoms of CO poisoning include headache, dizziness, weakness, nausea, vomiting, chest pain, and confusion, which can quickly escalate, causing loss of consciousness and death. CO can mix with hemoglobin and impede oxygen transportation in the blood vessels. This pollutant can be generated indoors by burning incense, oil or gas-fired heaters, and stoves. As such, it is of major concern within the residential sector. In offices, the major source of CO is outdoor polluted air infiltrating indoors. The outdoor sources can be volcanoes or bushfires, burning of fossil fuels for power generation, motor vehicle exhaust, or other manufacturing industries. CO, being a relatively unreactive gas under ambient air conditions, does not get absorbed by building materials or filters in ventilation systems. Consequently, in the absence of indoor CO sources, the concentration of CO in indoor air remains the same as that of outdoor air, which is either ventilated or infiltrating. Levels indicated by the Australian Building Code, consistent with those reported by the World Health Organization (WHO, 2021), are:

- 90 ppm averaged over 15 minutes,
- 25 ppm averaged over 1 hour,
- 10 ppm averaged over 8 hours.

Total volatile organic compounds (TVOC or VOC) are substances that evaporate easily at room temperature, a process usually referred to as off-gassing. VOCs are a mixture of different chemicals, such as benzene, formaldehyde, trichloroethylene (TCE), alkanes, aromatics, aldehydes, ketones, alcohols, and ethers. VOCs are responsible for photochemical smog pollution and may cause eye and upper respiratory irritation, nasal congestion, headache, and dizziness. The risk associated with VOCs is mainly due to the prolonged exposure time rather than high concentrations, as these compounds are emitted from most materials, whether they are synthetic or natural. The sources of VOCs are primarily new materials, such as office furniture, adhesives, paints, caulking, fillers, pressed wood products, carpets and underlays, stored supplies, printers, photocopiers, and electrical equipment. Generally, the newer the material, the greater the number of VOCs emitted, but solvents commonly used in adhesives, paints, fillers, and sealants have the potential for long-term slow release. The acceptable safe threshold for VOC concentration is generally considered to be approximately 500 mg/m^3 (ABCB, 2018). Amongst the general VOC, formaldehyde is the most commonly found indoors. It is generally produced through off-gassing of particleboard, fiberboard, and plywood, and it is strongly associated with allergies, asthma, and respiratory effects. Despite its adverse health effects, it is widely employed in construction materials due to its superior bonding properties and low cost. The specific threshold for formaldehyde is 0.1 mg/m^3 averaging over 30 minutes (ABCB, 2018).

Dust, dirt, sand, smoke, and liquid droplets with varying sizes and visibility, as well as all airborne particles, are grouped and referred to as particulate matters (PMs). It is possible to differentiate them based on their size, dividing between:

- coarse particles PM_{10}: diameter < 10 μm,
- fine particles $PM_{2.5}$: diameter < 2.5 μm,
- ultrafine particles: diameter < 0.1 μm.

These pollutants can be generated by either natural processes or human activities. Adverse health effects resulting from exposure to these pollutants include irritation of the eyes, nose, throat, and respiratory tract, as well as coughs, bronchitis, asthma, and other lung conditions. Additionally, they can cause respiratory and allergic responses, exacerbate existing respiratory and cardiopulmonary diseases, and even lead to lung cancer. The safe thresholds for these PM are, for PM_{10}, 50 $\mu m/m^3$ averaged over 24 hours or 25 $\mu m/m^3$ over 1 year, while for $PM_{2.5}$ are 25 $\mu m/m^3$ averaged over 24 hours and 8 over 1 year (ABCB, 2018).

Biological pollutants

Biological pollutants include bacteria, molds, viruses, dust mites, cockroaches, and pollen. These are the invisible threats that populate buildings, live and proliferate inside damp homes, and are a common catalyst for an unhealthy indoors. There are several health risks that can be associated with biological contaminants, which have been shown to affect the more general psychological well-being of the occupants. These effects can be mild, such as sense of fatigue and reduction of the capacity to concentrate, but they can escalate to severe cases of cognitive impairment (Gordon et al., 2004). In the workplace, these symptoms clearly impact overall efficiency and productivity (Finell & Nätti, 2021).

The main factor that causes biological contaminants to spread is dampness and high humidity levels. Mold germination and growth can be triggered by any condition resulting in excessive dampness (Brambilla & Sangiorgio, 2020). At present, rain leaks and plumbing defects that result in stagnant water within the building envelope or inaccessible areas are the most common sources of moisture that cause problems with mold. In Australia, recent research has shown that one in three buildings experience mold issues, primarily due to inadequate envelope performance and condensation problems, as well as uneven indoor temperatures and inadequate air circulation. In addition to construction and design deficiencies, excessive moisture can be caused by the use of mist humidifiers, unvented clothes dryers, overcrowding, and other human activities. Currently, there isn't an agreed threshold for limiting the presence of biological pollutants, rather most of the guidelines impose a limit value to optimal indoor humidity. The major building codes incorporate guidelines to avoid mold growth in the form of design criteria, prescriptive provisions and methods for the assessment of the risk, with different degrees of success. For example, Australia introduced explicit provisions only in 2019 that regulate the building envelope permeability, yet they apply only for certain building typologies and only for certain climate zones (ABCB, 2019).

Implementing best practices

Designing a building with good IAQ requires a holistic approach that considers various factors such as ventilation, filtration, and source control. IAQ must be incorporated into the design process from the early stages to ensure that the building's systems are designed to deliver clean and healthy indoor air. Fortunately, there are emerging trends in building design that are tackling IAQ from different aspects that, coupled with technological advancements, unlock high-performing spaces also in terms of IAQ.

Envelope, ventilation, and filtering strategies for IAQ

One of the most effective ways to improve IAQ is to prevent pollutants from entering the indoor environment in the first place. The building envelope is a critical component of building design that can have a significant impact on IAQ. It serves as a barrier between the indoor and outdoor environments and helps to regulate the pollutants into and out of the building. To promote healthy IAQ, two important factors to consider are material selection and air tightness. Firstly, it's crucial to choose building materials that have low levels of VOCs to minimize their release into the indoor air. Additionally, selecting materials that are resistant to moisture and mold growth can help prevent the spread of spores, which significantly lowers the risk of mold proliferation in the indoor environment. Secondly, airtightness can also play a role in reducing the exchange of indoor and outdoor air, minimizing the movement of pollutants between the two environments. However, pollutants may infiltrate indoors anyway, or be generated directly indoors. Adequate ventilation is critical for maintaining good IAQ. Buildings should be designed to provide sufficient ventilation to ensure that pollutants are diluted and removed from the indoor environment. This can be achieved through the use of natural ventilation, mechanical ventilation, or a combination of the two (hybrid ventilation). If natural ventilation has proved to be the preferred option for COVID-19 outbreak control, it is hardly found in high-performing workplaces, which usually rely on highly efficient HVAC systems. For this reason, filters are key to any IAQ strategy. However, the filters in standard HVAC systems are typically located in the return-air ducts and are only operational when the system is running. Consequently, during bushfire events, the HVAC system must remain constantly switched on while occupied to allow for adequate PM filtration, resulting in significant energy consumption (Brambilla et al., 2021). The efficiency of PM removal from the air by filters is expressed through their minimum efficiency reporting values (MERV), ranging from 1 to 16, with higher MERV ratings indicating greater filter efficiency. The literature reports contradicting findings on the efficiency of these filters. Chen et al. (2016) demonstrated that mechanical ventilation systems with MERV 7 filters can achieve a removal efficiency of 30% for particles with diameters smaller than 0.1 μm. Contrarily, some evidence shows that either fan-coil units equipped with high-grade filters or portable air cleaners may be effective in removing indoor PM.

Generally, the available studies indicate that filter efficiency is key in reducing the indoor concentrations of pollutants that originated outdoors, with different degrees of efficacy. However, there is still a lack of conclusive evidence and research regarding the comprehensive filtration of outdoor-generated air pollutants. This represents a significant gap that hinders the development of informed IAQ management strategies. Established filtration systems for the removal of air pollutants include high-efficiency particulate air (HEPA) and carbon filters. A HEPA filter is a type of air filter designed to trap and remove very small particles from the air, such as dust, pollen, mold spores, and bacteria. HEPA filters are made up of a mat of randomly arranged fibers that are typically made from fiberglass, and they are constructed in a way that maximizes their surface area and airflow. HEPA filters are very effective at removing particles from the air because they use a combination of mechanical and electrostatic methods to trap particles. As air flows through the filter, the fibers in the filter create a maze-like pathway that captures and traps particles of various sizes. The electrostatic charge on the fibers also attracts and traps particles that are too small to be captured by mechanical filtering. These filters are designed to trap larger particles, such as dust and pollen, and are often used in HVAC systems to improve IAQ. The choice of air filters used in an office will depend on a variety of factors, including the specific air-quality requirements of the workplace and the budget available for air filtration systems.

Leveraging sensing technologies for enhanced IAQ

Real-time monitoring and control systems are increasingly being used to help manage IAQ in buildings. These systems can be an effective tool for detecting and addressing IAQ issues as they arise and enabling prompt and bespoke strategies to address them. One example of real-time monitoring in IAQ is the use of sensors to measure CO_2 levels. Elevated levels of CO_2 can indicate inadequate ventilation, which can lead to poor IAQ and negatively impact occupant health and comfort. By monitoring CO_2 levels, building managers can take action to adjust the building's ventilation systems as needed to maintain healthy IAQ. In addition to CO_2 sensors, other types of sensors can be used to detect the presence of specific pollutants, such as radon or VOCs. Once detected, building managers can take appropriate steps to address the issue, such as increasing ventilation or using air purification systems. Control systems can also be used to automate IAQ management, such as by adjusting ventilation rates based on occupancy or outdoor air quality. These systems can help to ensure that the building is providing a healthy indoor environment while also optimizing energy efficiency. Real-time monitoring and control systems can provide valuable insights into IAQ in buildings and help to identify and address potential issues before they become serious problems. By incorporating these systems into building design and management practices, it is possible to create healthier and more comfortable indoor environments for building occupants.

Fit-out specifications

When selecting materials for workplace fit-out, it is crucial to choose low VOCs for walls and floors, such as hardwood flooring, ceramic or natural stone, and low-VOC paint. Easy maintenance and durability for finishes can help to promote good IAQ in the workplace. Avoiding excessive use (such as wall to wall) of carpets in workplaces could prevent asthma and allergy problems, since it is like a sink for particles, dust, and indoor air pollutants. Proper waste management for quick disposal of waste and regular maintenance can prevent the accumulation of pollutants in the indoor air. Incorporating IAQ frameworks and guidelines for fit-out specifications proposed by both WELL Building Standard (X06 VOC restrictions) and Green Star Rating Scheme (Office Interiors v1.1 IEQ 11 Volatile Organic Compounds), it is possible to create healthy IAQ in workplace environments.

Implementing biophilic design strategies

Biophilic design, which is the incorporation of natural elements and patterns into indoor environments, can be useful for improving IAQ in several ways. Increased ventilation and the use of natural materials and finishes can help to dilute indoor air pollutants and improve the overall IAQ. Biophilic design elements such as green plants/walls are effective at enhancing IAQ by purifying the air of pollutants, VOCs, and PM and producing oxygen through photosynthesis. Laboratory experiments conducted by Kulkarni and Dixit (2022) indicate that green wall plants substantially reduce the concentrations of PM_{10} and $PM_{2.5}$. Potted plants are also considered a simple and cost-effective technique for mitigating indoor air pollution. Gubb et al. (2022) investigated the effectiveness of 3 species of plants to remove in situ concentrations of NO_2 under various light and humidity levels. They estimate that 5 plants in a small office could remove approximately 3 ppb of NO_2 after 1 hour. Su and Lin (2015) concluded that the pot plant birds nest fern (Asplenium nidus Linn.) could be used for CO_2 and HCHO removal depending on the results of reduced CO_2 and HCHO concentration levels from 2000 ppm to 800 ppm and 2 ppm to 0.1 ppm, respectively. Torpy et al. (2017) research confirms the findings with equivalent results, indicating that a 5 m^2 green wall could balance the respiratory emissions of a full-time occupant. In addition, portable stands which include a self-contained ecosystem with its own active biofiltration system are useful to remove air pollutants like particles from bushfire smoke, dust, allergens, and VOCs.

Over the past two decades, a variety of active botanical biofiltration (ABB) systems have been developed to mitigate high concentrations of air pollutants associated with bushfires. These systems use a vertical plant growth substrate and foliage to filter air pollutants, and a mechanically generated active airflow passes contaminated air through the system, where the pollutants are removed by the substrate and root system (Pettit et al., 2017). According to a study by Pettit et al. (2020), a green wall biofilter with an active airflow drawing system can effectively filter NO_2 with greater efficiency than O_3 and $PM_{2.5}$. However, while the effectiveness of ABB systems has been evaluated from various perspectives, investigations in real indoor environments are required to obtain conclusive long-term results.

Post-occupancy evaluation

Although many aspects of IAQ can be physically measured, occupant satisfaction may or may not correlate with these measurements. To verify the design intent, identify IAQ problems, provide feedback from occupants, and identify opportunities for continuous improvement, post-occupancy evaluation (POE) could be used as an effective tool for assessing the performance of IAQ in workplace environments. The WELL Building Standard and Green Star rating tool recommend POE studies in buildings as a way to evaluate and improve the building's environmental performance and to ensure that it is meeting the objectives of the rating system. Both include a credit specifically for POE and ongoing performance monitoring. The credit requires building owners to conduct a POE study (within 12–36 months after the building is occupied) and to develop an action plan based on the findings of the study. By conducting POE, building owners and designers can ensure that IAQ is optimized for the health and well-being of building occupants.

Conclusion

The provision of IAQ is a complex task that involves time-dependent physical and chemical parameters. However, the significant impact of poor IAQ on workers' health and well-being has not yet been fully understood. Relying solely on natural ventilation or HVAC systems does not guarantee indoor air pollution control for a healthy workplace environment, as outside air may be polluted and filters may not be effective enough.

To provide an improved IAQ in workplaces, a "high-performance" checklist could include:

- Optimizing natural ventilation rates to control IAQ and passive cooling by using intelligent controls for an effective control strategy that integrates PM and CO_2 concentrations.
- Utilizing sensing technologies to measure PM and CO_2 concentrations in a space and a communication system that activates control modes to ensure improved IAQ conditions.
- Implementing sustainable building practices, such as green walls and ABB systems, to purify pollutants.
- Incorporating live walls, breath stands, and plants indoors to accelerate the removal of indoor air pollutants and improve workers' health and well-being.
- Including HEPA and carbon filters to reduce indoor concentrations of pollutants and providing regular maintenance to replace the filters.

In conclusion, ensuring good IAQ in office buildings is crucial for the health and well-being of the occupants. Poor IAQ can lead to various health issues, decreased productivity, and increased absenteeism. Designers and building professionals must take the necessary steps to provide improved IAQ in workplaces. With the ongoing pandemic, the importance of IAQ has become even more critical, as the virus can spread through the air. Therefore, it is imperative for designers and building professionals to consider IAQ in their designs and ensure that indoor spaces are healthy and safe for the occupants. By implementing these measures, designers and building professionals can create a healthier and more productive environment for office workers.

A "high-performance" checklist for IAQ is provided here:

Principle	*Strategies*
ENVELOPE, VENTILATION, AND AIR FILTERING	• Choose materials with low VOC levels. • Choose materials that are resistant to biological contaminations, especially in locations close to wet areas, high-humidity zones, and/or possible water ingress. • Increase the air tightness of the envelope. • Increase the air exchange rate, using natural or hybrid ventilation systems. • Use high-efficient filters with HVAC. • Regularly maintain HVAC and filters.
SENSING, MONITORING, AND CONTROLLING TECHNOLOGIES	• Use real-time monitoring systems to respond to and predict extreme events or failure.
FIT-OUT SPECIFICATIONS	
BIOPHILIC DESIGN STRATEGIES	• Integrate natural elements such as green walls to naturally clean indoor air. • Increase the use of potted plants. • Integrate portable stands: self-contained ecosystems with biofiltration. • Integrate active botanical biofiltration: vertical plant growth substrate and foliage to filter air pollutants, and a mechanically generated active airflow passes contaminated air through the system, where the pollutants are removed by the substrate and root system.
CLOSE THE LOOP	• Deploy POE protocol to analyze, assess, and refine the IAQ strategies.

References

ASHRAE. (2019). *ANSI/ASHRAE standard 62.1–2019: Ventilation for acceptable indoor air quality*. American Society of Heating, Refrigerating and Air-Conditioning Engineers, Inc.

Australian Building Code Board (ABCB). (2018). *Indoor air quality handbook*. Canberra Act.

Australian Building Code Board (ABCB). (2019). *National construction code of Australia* (vol. 1). ABCB.

Brambilla, A., Candido, C., Sangiorgio, M. F., Gocer, O., & Gocer, K. (2021). Can commercial buildings cope with Australian bushfires? An IAQ analysis. *Buildings and Cities*, *2*(1).

Brambilla, A., & Sangiorgio, A. (2020). Mould growth in energy efficient buildings: Causes, health implications and strategies to mitigate the risk. *Renewable and Sustainable Energy Reviews*, *132*, 110093.

Chen, A., Cao, Q., Zhou, J., Yang, B., Chang, V. W. C., & Nazaroff, W. W. (2016). Indoor and outdoor particles in an air-conditioned building during and after the 2013 haze in Singapore. *Building and Environment*, *99*, 73–81.

Finell, E., & Nätti, J. (2021). Self-reported mould and long-term sickness absences from work. *Scandinavian Journal of Public Health*, *49*(8), 914–920.

Gordon, W. A., Cantor, J. B., Johanning, E., Charatz, H. J., Ashman, T. A., Breeze, J. L., Haddad, L., & Abramowitz, S. (2004). Cognitive impairment associated with toxigenic fungal exposure: A replication and extension of previous findings. *Applied Neuropsychology*, *11*(2), 65–74.

Gubb, C., Blanusa, T., Griffiths, A., & Pfrang, C. (2022). Potted plants can remove the pollutant nitrogen dioxide indoors. *Air Quality, Atmosphere & Health*, *15*(3), 479–490.

Hitchins, J., Morawska, L., Wolff, R., & Gilbert, D. (2000). Concentrations of submicrometre particles from vehicle emissions near a major road. *Atmospheric Environment*, *34*(1), 51–59.

Kelly, F. J., & Fussell, J. C. (2019). Improving indoor air quality, health and performance within environments where people live, travel, learn and work. *Atmospheric Environment*, *200*, 90–109.

Kulkarni, R. S., & Dixit, S. A. (2022). Impact of green walls on indoor air quality in corporate offices. *ECS Transactions*, *107*(1), 3705.

Morawska, L., Marks, G. B., & Monty, J. (2022). Healthy indoor air is our fundamental need: The time to act is now. *The Medical Journal of Australia*, *217*(11), 578–581.

Pettit, T., Irga, P. J., Abdo, P., & Torpy, F. R. (2017). Do the plants in functional green walls contribute to their ability to filter particulate matter? *Building and Environment*, *125*, 299–307.

Pettit, T., Irga, P. J., & Torpy, F. R. (2020). The botanical biofiltration of elevated air pollution concentrations associated the Black Summer wildfire natural disaster. *Journal of Hazardous Materials Letters*, *1*, 100003.

SHE POE dataset. (2023). *Sustainable and healthy environments post-occupancy evaluation dataset*. SHE Lab (not published).

Su, Y. M., & Lin, C. H. (2015). Removal of indoor carbon dioxide and formaldehyde using green walls by bird nest fern. *The Horticulture Journal*, *84*(1), 69–76.

Torpy, F. R., Zavattaro, M., & Irga, P. J. (2017). Green wall technology for the phytoremediation of indoor air: A system for the reduction of high CO_2 concentrations. *Air Quality, Atmosphere & Health*, *10*(5), 575–585.

Tran, V. V., Park, D., & Lee, Y. C. (2020). Indoor air pollution, related human diseases, and recent trends in the control and improvement of indoor air quality. *International Journal of Environmental Research and Public Health*, *17*(8), 2927.

Wolkoff, P. (2018). Indoor air humidity, air quality, and health–An overview. *International Journal of Hygiene and Environmental Health*, *221*(3), 376–390.

World Health Organization (WHO). (2021). *Roadmap to improve and ensure good indoor ventilation in the context of COVID-19*. Retrieved March 03, 2024, from https://www.who.int/publications/i/item/10665-336265

8
VISUAL COMFORT

Wenye Hu

> Light has not just intensity, but also a vibration, which is capable of roughening a smooth material, of giving a three-dimensional quality to a flat surface.
>
> – *Renzo Piano*

Introduction

Lighting can enhance the aesthetic appeal of a space, create a sense of warmth and comfort, and positively impact the overall well-being and productivity of the occupants. A well-lit space can be more pleasant and comfortable for the occupants. However, 'well-lit' in this context does not only refer to adequate lighting. Although sufficient lighting is certainly important for the safe movement and navigation of people within a space, it is not the only factor to consider. A well-lit space is one that provides good visual comfort for the people using the space. Especially when it comes to performing day-to-day activities, visual comfort is paramount. For tasks that require fine detail work or prolonged periods of computer use, a visually comfortable lighting environment can reduce occupants' eye strain and improve their productivity.

Technically, visual comfort is defined as a subjective condition of well-being induced by the visual environment (European Standards, 2018). The workplace design always tries to maximise visual comfort since its influence on occupants' satisfaction, work productivity, and well-being has been proven in previous studies (Candido et al., 2021). Additionally, a recent qualitative study that interviewed experienced professionals in Australia recommended that visual comfort is a critical element in improving the sense of belonging in the workplace (Nanayakkara et al., 2021).

One way to improve visual comfort is to avoid factors that contribute to visual discomfort. Like thermal comfort, building occupants do not commonly notice visual comfort unless they experience visual discomfort. In other words, they are not extremely sensitive to the visual environment unless the lighting is in poor condition (Boubekri, 2008). For example, building occupants may complain about the lack of visual comfort when there are some glary light sources within their visual field or light reflection appears on their computer screens. On the other hand, they do not consciously notice the visual comfort when the lighting is appropriate in the space, although they are actually experiencing the visual comfort. Since visual comfort itself is difficult to define and quantify, it is commonly considered the absence of visual discomfort, which can be caused by a

DOI: 10.1201/9781003328728-9

This chapter has been made available under a CC-BY-NC-ND 4.0 license.

variety of factors, including glare, sharp shadows, the lack of outdoor views, etc. It is not surprising that both daylight and electric light contribute to visual comfort. However, in workplaces, the light from modern computer screens should also be considered since it has been shown to have strong non-image-forming effects on human circadian rhythms.

In this chapter, the factors that influence visual comfort will be first introduced and discussed. Some factors are impacted by the lighting environment, such as the amount of light and glare, while others are determined by the nature of a space and the architectural properties. The factors related to the physical environment are relatively easier to investigate, and an extensive body of research has been conducted to examine their effects on visual comfort and discomfort, especially in the context of workplaces. However, occupant-related factors, such as the use patterns of blinds or electric lighting systems are the most difficult to predict and evaluate. After understanding the influential factors in the following section, the positive influence of visual comfort and the negative consequences of visual discomfort on occupants will be discussed. Due to the complexity of visual comfort, it is difficult to develop a single metric that can be applied to all conditions. Different existing metrics and their limitations are briefly introduced and discussed later in the chapter. It is not surprising that new technologies will continue to advance and improve the visual comfort of architectural spaces in the near future. The final section discusses some innovative technologies and state-of-the-art solutions to create a dynamic visual environment in workplaces.

Influential factors of visual comfort

Shafavi et al. (2020) reviewed 58 field studies and lab experiments published from 2012 to 2020 and summarised the influential factors of visual (dis)comfort into three categories: lighting-related parameters, architectural properties, and occupant-related parameters.

Lighting-related parameters

Lighting-related parameters usually can be physically measured and mathematically expressed. For example, they can be discomfort glare, the amount of light (illuminance/luminance, etc.), the colour quality of light, and flicker. Also, a group of metrics can describe the non-uniformity in the occupants' visual fields, including brightness contrast, luminance ratios, etc. Data from the Sustainable and Healthy Environments (SHE) survey (SHE POE, 2023) show that glare, sunlight, bright screens, and reflections are the main issues in workplaces (Figure 8.1a). However, the data indicated that 91% of the participants were satisfied with the visual comfort and lighting of the space (Figure 8.1b).

Glare, probably the most studied factor, is the term used to describe unpleasant sensations that are caused by an excessively bright light source within the visual field. Part of the reason that it has been most studied is that it is possible to quantify the extent of glare by measuring the photometric quantities of the lighting environment and the occupants' physiological responses, such as pupil size. Therefore, a variety of metrics have been developed to evaluate and predict discomfort glare, which will be discussed later in this chapter. Additionally, the relationship between glare and visual discomfort has been well established. Extensive existing research has proven that the absence of glare leads to better visual comfort. For example, in one study, when subjects were instructed to rate the perceived glare level and the visual comfort of their workspace in questionnaires, their answers to these two questions showed a strong correlation (Suk et al., 2016). Strictly speaking, glare can be classified into two types: disability glare and discomfort glare. Disability glare is usually caused by light scattering within the eye, which reduces the contrast of the image. It impairs

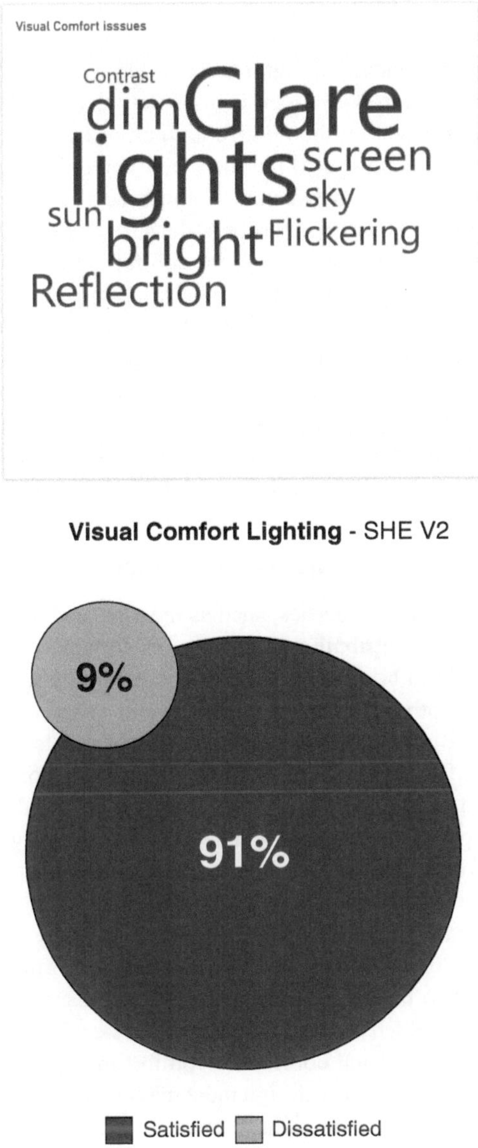

Figure 8.1 (a) Word cloud generated from the SHE POE dataset reporting dissatisfaction with visual comfort and (b) percentage of satisfied and dissatisfied workers with visual comfort in the SHE POE dataset.

Source: SHE POE dataset, 2023

vision but does not necessarily induce visual discomfort. Discomfort glare produces visual discomfort and induces the occupants' instinctive desire to look away from the glare source. The mechanisms for discomfort glare are still not fully understood, as there is no single known physiological cause. These two types of glare can (and often do) co-occur, but they can also arise separately.

Illuminance and luminance, two photometric quantities, are heavily tied to contrast, which impacts the presence or absence of glare. The glare caused by a glary light source in the visual field can be reduced by either reducing the luminance of the light source or increasing the luminance or illuminance of the background. Glare is not solely determined by the absolute amount of light in the space; it is dependent on the relative amount of light, i.e. the contrast. Luminance ratio is a contrast describing the luminance differences between objects, usually a target object and its background. For example, the ratio between the luminance of a piece of paper where an occupant is writing and the luminance of its background, the surface of the desk where the paper sits (Dilaura et al., 2011). Brightness contrast refers to the contrast between task and ambient lighting. The ratio/contrast-related metrics have a common characteristic: there is an optimised range for better visual comfort. If the ratio/contrast is too low – for example, all surfaces in a room are lit to the same brightness or objects are lit similarly to their background – then the visual environment lacks sufficient visual interest, and visual systems would be tried to search for the visual interest. An experienced lighting designer would usually deliberately vary the lighting intensity to create a rhythm of light in a space. If the ratio/contrast is too high, such as direct sunlight from a window upon entering a dim room or a glary lamp in the visual field, discomfort glare can be the result.

Architectural properties

There is no doubt that architectural properties, such as the sizes and locations of windows and the colour and texture of walls, also contribute to a visually comfortable environment. Although, technically speaking, it is possible to bring in daylight without windows, windows are still the most frequently used approach to introduce daylight into interior spaces. Therefore, they are crucial elements for visual comfort. Building codes and standards worldwide require a minimum window size in the percentage of the floor area of the room. In Australia, according to National Construction Code, Part F4 Light and ventilation, natural light must be provided in Class 2, 3, 4, 9a, and 9c buildings. One common approach is to design windows with an aggregate light-transmitting area measured at more than 10% of the floor area of the room (Australian Building Codes Board, 2019).

Windows can maximise the use of daylight and significantly reduce the energy consumed by electric light. They also create an important connection with the exterior environment, which improves the occupants' visual comfort and satisfaction. Unfortunately, excessive daylight through windows is believed to be the main cause of thermal discomfort and visual discomfort. The configurations of windows, such as window orientation, size, height, area, etc., were reported to have a strong correlation with visual comfort/discomfort in daylit spaces (Kong et al., 2018; Shafavi et al., 2020). A successful window design must maximise daylight levels in interior spaces while minimising the glare created by daylight to create a visually comfortable environment for occupants.

Data from the SHE POE dataset shows a weak but statistically significant correlation between the proximity to external windows and occupants' sleep quality, ρ_s (747) = -0.116, $p = 0.002$. When occupants' distances to external windows were less than 3 metres, they reported a higher quality of sleep and higher satisfaction with the lighting environment, ρ_s (747) = -0.231, $p < 0.001$ (SHE POE dataset).

A view of the outside is another criterion for a visually comfortable environment. It is not surprising that window views impact the occupants' subjective impression of glare, especially the glare caused by daylight (Chauvel et al., 1982; Hirning et al., 2014). On a sunny day, people sitting under the shade of a café umbrella actually experience a sharp brightness transition, but those outdoor seats are usually the most popular ones, as the street view is pleasant. Due to the psychological difference, the same brightness contrast in an open-plan office without any nice view is probably considered visual discomfort. It has been proven independently in multiple studies that a window with a high-quality view increases the users' tolerance to high luminance from windows (Hirning et al., 2014).

Light, either daylight or electric light, falls on surfaces and objects in a space and then reflects off them and enters human eyes. A strong positive correlation, $\rho_s\,(752) = 0.598, p < 0.001$ between the lighting environment and satisfaction with indoor visual aesthetics was found in the SHE POE dataset.

Earlier studies reported that the effect of the colour of the light (expressed as correlated colour temperature) on visual discomfort was subtle in terms of either the subjective rating or the physiological measurements (e.g. pupil size, eyeball movement speed, electrooculography responses) (Lin et al., 2015). However, colours and reflectance of room surfaces have a stronger impact on human perception of visual comfort. Many studies have been published on the subjects that explore the effects of surface colours in architectural spaces on occupants' mood, visual comfort, performance, etc. For example, a study investigated how to use interior wood panels with different colours (e.g. oak, Cape Cod grey, and dark walnut coatings) to create a visually comfortable environment (Jafarian et al., 2018). A computational simulation was conducted to investigate how surface reflectance influences the Unified Glare Rating (UGR), which is an index of discomfort glare caused by electric lighting systems. Surfaces with higher reflectance (i.e. 80% for walls, 90% for ceilings, and 40% for floors) resulted in less glare, while lower reflectance (i.e. 50% for walls, 70% for ceilings, and 20% for floors) led to more glare (Makaremi et al., 2019). However, few conclusive results on the influence of surface colours were commonly accepted due to the lack of systematic research and demographic complexity. Since the surface reflectance and transmittance in real-world spaces can be complicated, instead, to simplify the problem, luminance ratio is sometimes used as a convenient metric (Dilaura et al., 2011).

The design of the office layout – which determines the occupants' sitting orientation, distances to windows, access to outdoor views, etc. – also contributes to the visual comfort in office spaces. From the interview conducted in the eight Australian design and consultant firms, it is believed that in the future office designs will increasingly focus on occupants' physical and psychological well-being (Nanayakkara et al., 2021). A few rules of thumb provide interior designers with some general recommendations, such as arranging the desks about 1 metre away from the window, using high reflectance and light colour surfaces adjacent to windows, choosing vertical or horizontal blinds according to the different window orientations, etc.

Biophilic office design, which brings the outdoors into the interior workplace and enhances occupants' connection with nature, has been proven to reduce occupants' stress and improve their productivity (Nanayakkara et al., 2021). Greenery, daylight, and access to outdoor views are the main elements of biophilic offices. Gray and Birrell interpreted biophilic office design in the Australian context. In a retrofit project, five plants were selected and potted in recycled materials such as used wood pallets and milk crates. Results from the qualitative interviews showed that occupants perceived the renovated biophilic office as more spacious. They further commented that their collaboration increased and workplace relations improved, which may lead to higher productivity (Gray & Birrell, 2014). In the new Sydney office completed in 2019, Arup successfully demonstrated the biophilic design principles. Plants and some green furniture were used to increase the quality of indoor air and create a connection between occupants and nature. The type of light sources and background contexts also impact the occupants' perception of visual comfort. Multiple studies independently discovered that people are more sensitive to the glare from electric lighting than the glare caused by daylight (Hirning et al., 2014).

Occupant-related parameters

Among all parameters, the occupant-related ones (e.g. the use pattern of blinds or electric lighting controlled by occupants) are the most difficult to predict and evaluate. Consequently, they are the least studied. Most visual comfort studies deliberately exclude the impact of the occupants' use patterns from the research. Either no curtains or blinds were used during the studies, or they were set to fully open to bring in the maximum amount of daylight (Shafavi et al., 2020). This is reasonable given that user behaviour patterns vary significantly and are difficult to predict. Hence, occupants' use patterns should be treated as a controlled variable during research. However, the exclusion of occupant-related variables limits the possibility of applying research outcomes directly to real applications.

Impact of visual (dis)comfort on occupants

One of the direct consequences of visual discomfort on occupants is visual fatigue. As early as 1974, when video display units were increasingly popular in work environments, researchers had already established the correlation between glare, screen reflections, and visual discomfort symptoms, such as eye focusing problems, dry eyes, and tired eyes (Glimne et al., 2012). Discomfort glare was proven to be the cause of orbicularis muscle contraction and excessive stress associated with asthenopia (Glimne et al., 2012). Although pupil size constriction is largely impacted by the background lighting, researchers revealed that, even after subjects adapted to the background illumination, their pupils constricted further when they were exposed to glare sources. To compromise the discomfort glare, pupils constricted to reduce the amount of light that entered the eyes, which affected the trigeminal nerve as well as the constrictor muscles and consequently led to visual fatigue (Lin et al., 2015). Eye movements and spontaneous blink rate may also be indicators of visual discomfort, though further research is needed (Hamedani et al., 2020). By using electrooculography to record eye movements, Lin's team measured the average eyeball movement speed (AEMS) and relative pupil size (RPS). Results revealed that these two physiological responses correlated well with subjective ratings of discomfort. The physiological responses also provided a possible explanation of visual fatigue and eyestrain under long-term exposure to discomfort glare (Lin et al., 2015). Scientists understand the urgency of optimising the lighting environment for better visual comfort. Although much effort has been made by scientists, this topic has not been fully understood (Hamedani et al., 2020).

Another negative impact of visual discomfort is the reduction in visual performance. The reaction time and accuracy of completing required tasks, which are two indicators commonly used to evaluate visual performance, were examined under three different lighting conditions, which presented, respectively, high, medium, and low discomfort glare levels (Hamedani et al., 2020). The Daylight Glare Probability (DGP) calculated for low glare conditions was less than 35, with average vertical illuminance at eye levels of 2100 lx, while DGP for high glare conditions was greater than 40, with average vertical illuminance of 4800 lx. Medium glare conditions have a DGP in between. A score combining the accuracy and reaction time was lowest under the lighting conditions with high discomfort glare. No statistical difference was found between the low and medium glare groups (Hamedani et al., 2020).

It is not surprising that there is a positive correlation between visual comfort and occupants' productivity. A study conducted in nine offices in Australia showed that occupants in offices with better spatial comfort, visual comfort, and connection to the outdoor environment also reported higher perceived productivity (Candido et al., 2021). Among all these factors, light-related visual comfort or discomfort strongly impacts occupants' productivity, health, and well-being. Light has both visual effects, which are contributed by the light perceived by rods and cones, and non-visual biological effects, also known as 'non-image-forming' (NIF) effects, on human circadian rhythms. In 2002, a special type of photoreceptor – intrinsically photosensitive retinal ganglion cells (ipRGCs) – was discovered and characterised by Berson (2003). Unlike the other photoreceptors, ipRGCs send signals directly to the brain to synchronise circadian rhythms with the day–night cycle, according to the light and dark alternation (Berson, 2003). They can trigger the pineal gland to suppress or secrete a hormone called melatonin that controls our sleeping and waking cycles. As the ipRGCs are most sensitive to light with short wavelengths (in the blue light region) and less sensitive to longer wavelengths (red light region), the colour appearance of light is no longer just an element for visual aesthetics. It holds the power to boost alertness, reduce fatigue and sleepiness, and consequently improve occupants' cognitive performance and productivity in workplaces. However, light's influence is complex and not fully understood, or at least, it is not quantified yet. After reviewing 59 articles, Siraji et al. (2022) summarised that the circadian effects of light depend on multiple factors, including the intensity and spectral composition of light, time of day, duration of light exposure, and homeostatic sleep drive, as well as the complexity of tasks. For instance, the influence of light on alertness is stronger than its effects on higher cognitive functions. Time of day is also a key factor. For simple tasks, such as testing reaction time, light with rich short-wavelength components has a greater beneficial influence on task performance in the afternoon compared to in the morning (Siraji et al., 2022). Although research on this topic is still ongoing, existing findings urge more innovative design strategies to create a dynamic visual environment in workplaces. Some state-of-the-art solutions will be discussed in the final section of this chapter.

Indices to evaluate visual comfort

While the influential factors can be easily identified through observation, quantitatively predicting and evaluating visual (dis)comfort is extremely challenging. There is still a lack of reliable metrics and evaluation models. This is not suggesting that no effort has been made. In fact, during the past half-century, numerous attempts have been made by researchers globally to quantify visual comfort, and they significantly contributed to the existing literature. Carlucci et al. (2015) summarised 34 indices and concluded that 50% of them assess visual comfort (actually visual discomfort) by the extent of glare, 26% predict visual comfort according to the amount of light, and 20% are devoted to evaluating the colour-rendering quality of light. Only one index assesses the uniformity of light in a space. However, due to the variations in the occupants' ages, genders, cultural backgrounds, activities, alertness, visual preferences, etc., results could hardly be generalised to different contexts (Shafavi et al., 2020). Shafavi et al. (2020) further suggested that just one global glare metric for various conditions seems to be impossible due to the complexity of visual comfort. It is important to consider the specific conditions and needs of a space when evaluating visual comfort and to use the appropriate metric.

Many existing indices are defined by evaluating the perceived intensity of glare, such as the Daylight Glare Index (DGI), DGP, Unified Glare Rating (UGR), CIE Glare Index (CGI), and Visual Comfort Probability (VCP). Discomfort glare can be mathematically assessed by reporting the average luminance at typical viewing angles, or the maximum luminous intensity, independent of applications or task types (Dilaura et al., 2011). Some indices (e.g. DGI, DGP) focus on daylight, and some evaluate electric light (e.g. UGR).

The discomfort glare caused by daylight is more difficult to assess than the discomfort glare caused by electric lighting, because the intensity, colour, and direction of daylight vary over the day and from season to season. The use of daylight should provide sufficient light for the occupants' visual performance but also limit glare to create a comfortable and pleasing workspace. Identifying the trade-off can be challenging especially when reliable tools and evaluation systems are currently limited.

To better predict glare perception, the metric DGP, which showed a strong correlation with the occupants' subjective responses, was proposed by Wienold and Christoffersen (2006). This metric is popular because designers can calculate results using software. However, Hirning's team reported large variances in subjective responses to glare when this metric was evaluated in real workspaces. Their conclusion was based on a large-scale investigation of discomfort glare conducted in five green buildings in Brisbane, Australia, in 2013, with 493 surveys collected from full-time employees who worked in those buildings under everyday lighting conditions (Hirning et al., 2014). Another research team further noticed that the DGP did not predict glare well when the sun is behind the window shades and within the occupants' visual field. They proposed a new equation with modified DGP coefficients for this situation, which happens almost every day in the real world (Konstantzos & Tzempelikos, 2017).

Suk et al. (2016) defined the absolute glare factor based on absolute luminance values and the relative glare factor based on the contrast ratios between the luminance of glare sources and background luminance. Luminance threshold values were also proposed according to different types of tasks performed by the occupants. For example, luminance below 1920 cd/m^2 is considered imperceptible when occupants perform typical typing tasks, while this threshold recedes to 1696 cd/m^2 when occupants perform typical writing tasks on the horizontal plane. Their research further proved that the type of task is a critical variable in visual comfort. However, to simplify the problem, glare from electric lighting was excluded from their model and the participants were a small group of experienced people, instead of a large group of naive participants.

The impact of electric lighting on visual comfort can be calculated using UGR or VCP. UGR, which is defined by Commission Internati onale de l'E´ clairage (CIE), is commonly used to assess the discomfort glare caused directly by luminaires in an indoor space (CIE, 1995). Some large lighting manufacturers also contribute to the improvement of visual comfort through innovative products. For instance, the inner part of the luminaire shown in Figure 8.2 distributes the light from the vertically mounted LED modules through a curved waveguide. This creates a uniform mixing chamber. The outer shell is composed of a micro-pyramidal optic at the bottom and longitudinal prisms on the sides. This secondary optic balances the light distribution on the task area, vertical walls, and ceilings and reduces glare.

There is no doubt that the perception of visual comfort/discomfort is also a subjective evaluation, which can be affected by individual sensitivity, cultural background, and physiological differences. For example, it has been observed that people who usually wear sunglasses are more sensitive to a high level of glare (Hamedani et al., 2020).

Advanced technologies and strategies to improve visual comfort, productivity, and well-being

Smart windows and shading systems are increasingly popular as they can balance the urgency of reducing energy consumption and the need for maintaining appropriate thermal and visual comfort. Smart windows utilise a type of emerging glazing technology that controls the transmission properties of glass. They can block some or all light, and only allow light with certain wavelengths to

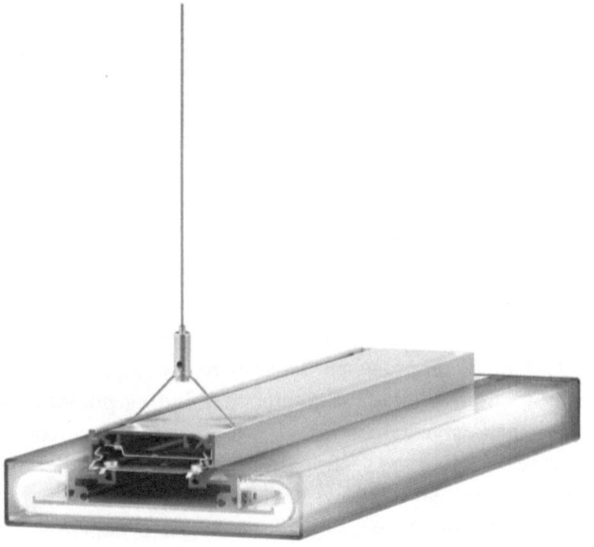

Figure 8.2 Cross-section of an office luminaire from Zumtobel Group. The optical package of this luminaire is designed to minimise glare, while efficiently distributing light into the space. (Courtesy of Zumtobel Group)

pass through. Glass can adjust transmission properties in response to a change in electricity, radiation (usually ultraviolet radiation), or heat, and they are named electrochromic glass, photochromic glass, and thermochromic glass, respectively. One challenge for smart windows is durability. They must withstand difficult climatic and solar conditions and are expected to be used for decades. It is not uncommon that they are sometimes combined with clear glass in real applications.

To maximise the use of daylight, minimise electricity consumption, and optimise the visual environments, smart windows and shading systems should be integrated into dimmable electric lighting systems. However, this requires more advanced lighting control systems and reliable control algorithms. As early as 2003, researchers addressed that for large-scale buildings, prediction algorithms need to be developed to create more reliable automated controls. The research on this topic is increasingly popular recently. The development of reliable optimisation algorithms becomes more urgent with the desire for integrating electric lighting systems and daylight control into smart building systems. Machine learning has gained more attention recently because the output can be predicted based on historical data, without explicating the underlying relationship between input and output. This is extremely useful when human behaviour is involved in a study.

As a probably over-simplified example, if a large dataset shows that, for better visual comfort, most occupants tend to dim the electric light and adjust the shading system to a specific position/angle at a certain time or in a particular weather condition, then the computer programme trains itself to provide a similar environment for that time or weather condition. Prediction models can be developed without truly understanding the reason for the occupants' behaviour. Historical data can be either computational simulation or real-world measurement. This can be extremely helpful given that, as mentioned earlier, most visual comfort studies deliberately exclude the impact of user behaviour patterns, as they greatly vary and are difficult to predict.

A control approach using machine learning techniques based on real measurement was proposed to predict daylight–electric light and achieve better visual comfort and thermal comfort

(Sanjeev Kumar et al., 2020). They used the irradiance obtained from a pyranometer, the temperature measured by a sensor in the room, and daylight on the window collected by light sensors to predict the position of the window blind and dimming level of luminaires, to optimise the energy consumption and visual comfort. In another study (Bian & Hu, 2023), *Radiance* software was used to generate training data representing the lighting environment and then a genetic algorithm was used to predict the optimal dimming level of each electric light. The trained model provided real-time optimal dimming levels to the lighting control system to minimise energy consumption without negatively impacting occupants' visual comfort.

Using sophisticated products without sufficient consideration of the design may not always grant visual comfort. Sometimes simple design strategies can effectively improve the occupants' visual comfort. A field study conducted in an open-plan office in downtown Milwaukee, Wisconsin, has proven the effectiveness of simple approaches. This office is equipped with an automatic Mecho-shade system controlled by outdoor solar radiometers and indoor photometric sensors. However, users still complained about their negative visual experience. The research team applied some simple strategies, such as rearranging the seating orientation to be parallel to windows, increasing the spacing between workstations and windows, using Mecho-shades with lower openness factors (2– 3%), using more flexible furniture, etc. To understand the occupants' visual comfort and satisfaction in the renovated environment, researchers measured lighting parameters, simulated the lighting environment, and conducted interviews and questionnaires. Results comparing the visual experience before and after the renovation show that the renovated design strategies improved the occupants' visual comfort (Kong et al., 2018).

Data from field measurements show that light from modern computer screens has a surprisingly high impact on human circadian rhythms (Hu & Davis, 2021). When typical office tasks, such as word processing and reading and writing emails, are undertaken, the circadian effect of light from computer screens can even exceed the effect of overhead electric lighting (Hu & Davis, 2021). While this does benefit alertness levels and productivity, it could also lead to delayed sleep phases and poor sleep quality for people who regularly work late. To optimally support occupants' productivity and well-being, electric lighting systems, shading systems, and even computer displays need to be connected. It is possible to adjust electric lighting and/or daylight automatically using a smart system when users perform computer tasks in which the circadian effect of the light from the display is high. Modern LED technology and sophisticated lighting control systems also equip designers with the power to tune the spectrum or colour of the light. As shown in Figure 8.3, after installation, colour-tuneable lighting systems can still change the colour appearance of light. Such a dynamic visual environment is crucial to optimise both occupants' visual needs and NIF needs. It is evident that in the near future, new technologies will push the transitional boundary and take visual comfort environments to new heights.

Conclusion

Visual comfort is a complex concept that is influenced by a variety of factors, including the lighting conditions, the nature of the space, and the task being performed, as well as the occupants' behaviours, ages, genders, cultural backgrounds, etc. It is challenging, even impossible, to develop a single metric to accurately quantify visual comfort. However, visual comfort is an important aspect of building design that should not be overlooked since it significantly benefits the building occupants in terms of improving their well-being and productivity. Therefore, despite the challenges, scientists and researchers have made significant progress in understanding visual comfort and developing various methods for evaluating it. By better understanding how visual comfort is

Figure 8.3 Tunable White LED lighting system. Left (warm-white light), middle (neutral-white light), and right (cool-white light). (Courtesy of Zumtobel Group)

influenced, architects, designers, and facility managers can make informed decisions about the design and maintenance of lighting environments.

In recent years, there have been advances in technologies that have the potential to improve visual comfort in buildings. For example, the integration of electric lighting and daylighting can help to create a more dynamic and comfortable environment, and the use of automation systems, such as smart windows and shading systems, allows for the optimisation of visual comfort and energy efficiency. By considering the specific needs and conditions of a space and using the appropriate technologies, architects and designers can improve visual comfort for building occupants.

A 'high-performance' checklist for visual comfort is provided here:

Principle	*Description*
ANALYSE SPACE PROPERTIES & OCCUPANT NEEDS	• Evaluate physical properties of the space • Analyse potential visual tasks performed by occupants. • Determine appropriate light levels based on tasks. Information about recommended illuminance can usually be found in national lighting standards.
CREATE A WELL-BALANCED LIGHTING ENVIRONMENT	• Use combination of natural and electrical light. • Choose light sources with suitable correlated colour temperature (CCT) and high colour rendering index (CRI). • Choose luminaires with excellent optical design. • Assess glare in the space with computer simulation software, such as DIALux or AGi32, then on-site after installations. • Using high reflectance and light-coloured surfaces, especially in the areas adjacent to windows.
CONSIDER USING NEW TECHNOLOGIES	• Implement lighting control systems for task-based adjustments. • Use connected systems to integrate electric lighting, daylight, and computer display light.

References

Australian Building Codes Board. (2019). *National Construction Code (NCC): Volume one amendment 1.* https://ncc.abcb.gov.au/

Berson, D. (2003). Strange vision: Ganglion cells as circadian photoreceptors. *Trends in Neurosciences, 26*(6), 314–320. https://doi.org/10.1016/S0166-2236(03)00130-9

Bian, W., & Hu, W. (2023). A machine-learning-aided approach to improve occupancy-based lighting control systems. In *CIE Australia lighting research conference 2023.* CIE Australia.

Boubekri, M. (2008). *Daylighting, architecture, and health: Building design strategies* (1st ed.). Elsevier Architectural Press.

Candido, C., Marzban, S., Haddad, S., Mackey, M., & Loder, A. (2021). Designing healthy workspaces: Results from Australian certified open-plan offices. *Facilities, 39*(5–6), 411–433. https://doi.org/10.1108/F-02-2020-0018

Carlucci, S., Causone, F., De Rosa, F., & Pagliano, L. (2015). A review of indices for assessing visual comfort with a view to their use in optimization processes to support building integrated design. *Renewable and Sustainable Energy Reviews, 47*, 1016–1033. https://doi.org/10.1016/j.rser.2015.03.062

Chauvel, P., Collins, J. B., Dogniaux, R., & Longmore, J. (1982). Glare from windows: Current views of the problem. *Lighting Research & Technology, 14*(1), 31–46. https://doi.org/10.1177/096032718201400103

CIE. (1995). *CIE 117–1995: Discomfort glare in interior lighting.* International Commission on Illumination (CIE).

Dilaura, D. L., Houser, K. W., Mistrick, R. G., & Steffy, G. R. (2011). *The lighting handbook reference and application.* Illuminating Engineering Society of North America (IES).

European Standards. (2018). *EN 12665: Light and lighting – Basic terms and criteria for specifying lighting requirements.* European Committee for Standardization (CEN).

Glimne, S., Seimyr, G. Ö., Ygge, J., Nylén, P., & Brautaset, R. L. (2012). Measuring glare induced visual fatigue by fixation disparity variation. *Work, 45*(4).

Gray, T., & Birrell, C. (2014). Are biophilic-designed site office buildings linked to health benefits and high performing occupants? *International Journal of Environmental Research and Public Health, 11*(12), Article 12. https://doi.org/10.3390/ijerph111212204

Hamedani, Z., Solgi, E., Hine, T., Skates, H., Isoardi, G., & Fernando, R. (2020). Lighting for work: A study of the relationships among discomfort glare, physiological responses and visual performance. *Building and Environment, 167*, 106478. https://doi.org/10.1016/j.buildenv.2019.106478

Hirning, M. B., Isoardi, G. L., & Cowling, I. (2014). Discomfort glare in open plan green buildings. *Energy and Buildings, 70*, 427–440. https://doi.org/10.1016/j.enbuild.2013.11.053

Hu, W., & Davis, W. (2021). Toward a connected system – Understanding the contribution of light from different sources on occupants' circadian rhythms. *Applied Sciences, 11*(21), 9939. https://doi.org/10.3390/app11219939

Jafarian, H., Demers, C. M. H., Blanchet, P., & Laundry, V. (2018). Effects of interior wood finishes on the lighting ambiance and materiality of architectural spaces. *Indoor and Built Environment, 27*(6), 786–804. https://doi.org/10.1177/1420326X17690911

Kong, Z., Utzinger, D. M., Freihoefer, K., & Steege, T. (2018). The impact of interior design on visual discomfort reduction: A field study integrating lighting environments with POE survey. *Building and Environment, 138*, 135–148. https://doi.org/10.1016/j.buildenv.2018.04.025

Konstantzos, I., & Tzempelikos, A. (2017). Daylight glare evaluation with the sun in the field of view through window shades. *Building and Environment, 113*, 65–77. https://doi.org/10.1016/j.buildenv.2016.09.009

Lin, Y., Fotios, S., Wei, M., Liu, Y., Guo, W., & Sun, Y. (2015). Eye movement and pupil size constriction under discomfort glare. *Investigative Ophthalmology & Visual Science, 56*(3), 1649–1656. https://doi.org/10.1167/iovs.14-15963

Makaremi, N., Schiavoni, S., Pisello, A. L., & Cotana, F. (2019). Effects of surface reflectance and lighting design strategies on energy consumption and visual comfort. *Indoor and Built Environment, 28*(4), 552–563. https://doi.org/10.1177/1420326X18793170

Nanayakkara, K. T., Wilkinson, S. J., & Ghosh, S. (2021). Future office layouts for large organisations: Workplace specialist and design firms' perspective. *Journal of Corporate Real Estate, 23*(2), 69–86. https://doi.org/10.1108/JCRE-02-2020-0012

Sanjeev Kumar, T., Kurian, C., & Shetty, S. (2020). A data-driven approach for the control of a daylight–artificial light integrated scheme. *Lighting Research & Technology, 52*(2), 292–313. https://doi.org/10.1177/1477153519841104

Shafavi, N. S., Zomorodian, Z. S., Tahsildoost, M., & Javadi, M. (2020). Occupants visual comfort assessments: A review of field studies and lab experiments. *Solar Energy*, *208*, 249–274. https://doi.org/10.1016/j.solener.2020.07.058

SHE POE dataset. (2023). *Sustainable and healthy environments post-occupancy evaluation dataset*. SHE Lab (not published).

Siraji, M. A., Kalavally, V., Schaefer, A., & Haque, S. (2022). Effects of daytime electric light exposure on human alertness and higher cognitive functions: A systematic review. *Frontiers in Psychology*, *12*, 765750. https://doi.org/10.3389/fpsyg.2021.765750

Suk, J. Y., Schiler, M., & Kensek, K. (2016). Absolute glare factor and relative glare factor based metric: Predicting and quantifying levels of daylight glare in office space. *Energy and Buildings*, *130*, 8–19. https://doi.org/10.1016/j.enbuild.2016.08.021

Wienold, J., & Christoffersen, J. (2006). Evaluation methods and development of a new glare prediction model for daylight environments with the use of CCD cameras. *Energy and Buildings*, *38*(7), 743–757. https://doi.org/10.1016/j.enbuild.2006.03.017

9

ACOUSTIC PRIVACY

Manuj Yadav and Densil Cabrera

> After 50 years of studies in offices of various designs, one thing is clear: intelligible speech has consistently been reported as the main source of distraction and annoyance by employees.
>
> – *Authors*

Introduction

Throughout the history of the open-plan design – from the lofty ambitions enshrined within the seed concepts of *Bürolanschaft* and the *Action Office* iterations in the 1960s, to the love–hate relationship with cubicles in the 1980s–90s, and all the way to newer embodiments in *activity-based* workplaces and similar concepts – acoustic issues have held a special notoriety (Haapakangas et al., 2017; Kaufmann-Buhler, 2016; Saval, 2014; Yadav et al., 2021a). In this chapter, the open-plan design/office/workplace refers to any office floorplan with more than three workstations not separated by walls on at least one side. The focus is on medium-to-large-sized floor plans, and/or subsets thereof.

The terms *noise*, *background noise*, and *noise environment* have broad meanings in OPOs and are variously used to refer to the entire *sound environment*, unwanted sounds, etc. In this chapter, *background noise* refers exclusively to the relatively steady-state noise in unoccupied offices, which may include contributions from HVAC (heating, ventilation, and air-conditioning) operation, other building services and environmental sounds, and electroacoustic sound-masking systems. *Beneficial* sound environment for occupants may consist of a mix of various sounds, including background noise, which, in good circumstances, can mask distractions. A *detrimental* sound environment refers to unwanted sound/noise that has the potential to distract and hence affect task performance and/or lead to annoyance. *Acoustic privacy* at OPO workstations can then be defined as (a) the possibility to concentrate on a task when needed and/or (b) speech privacy, i.e., the ability to have private conversations without excessive influence of detrimental sounds (more in the section 'Acoustic Privacy in OPOs: An Overview').

The rest of the chapter is organised as follows. The next three sections provide a broad overview of the acoustic privacy issues in open-plan offices (OPOs), the latest metrics to characterise the acoustics of open-plan workplaces, and suggestions for implementing acoustic privacy at workplaces based on traditional and novel acoustic solutions, respectively. The last section

DOI: 10.1201/9781003328728-10

This chapter has been made available under a CC-BY-NC-ND 4.0 license.

summarises the main aspect of acoustic privacy in high-performance workplaces. Most of the data used here comes from a long-term study of OPOs in Australia from 2016 to 2019, including room acoustic measurements on 36 office floors (Yadav et al., 2019) using the latest international standard (ISO 3382–3, 2022), sound measurements during occupied hours (43 office floors) (Yadav et al., 2021a), along with an occupant survey of 426 participants (Yadav et al., 2021b).

Sounds and acoustic privacy in open-plan offices

Sound sources in open-plan offices: speech is special

Sound environment in OPOs broadly comprises various non-speech sources (e.g., telephone rings, footfall, workstation sounds including typing, etc.) and speech. The latter can include partly or wholly *intelligible/meaningful speech*, referring to task-irrelevant multi-talker speech usually from nearby workstations and/or speech that is barely intelligible but is clearly perceived as speech, which is referred to as *unintelligible speech* in the following. Figure 9.1 shows how the Australian OPO occupants rated the relevant sound groups in order of how distracting they were (Yadav et al., 2021b). From this figure, and from over 50 years of studies in offices of various designs, one thing is clear: *intelligible speech has consistently been reported as the main source of distraction and annoyance* by employees (Yadav et al., 2021a). That speech holds special potency in terms of distraction and annoyance should not be surprising. However, what will be developed further in this chapter is that attenuating intelligible speech from nearby workstations is not a trivial task, which explains in part the widespread severity of the speech problem in OPOs.

Speech is a very redundant signal, which can retain intelligibility to a certain degree even after substantial deterioration (Bronkhorst, 2015). For humans, slow amplitude fluctuations (< 20 Hz) in sounds over time are especially distracting, with peak sensitivity at around 4 Hz fluctuations, which is close to syllable rate in speech – known as 'fluctuation strength' in psychoacoustics (Zwicker & Fastl, 1999). The *babble*-like condition, where multiple voices combine to resemble steady-state sound stream to provide beneficial masking/background noise is rarely achieved for

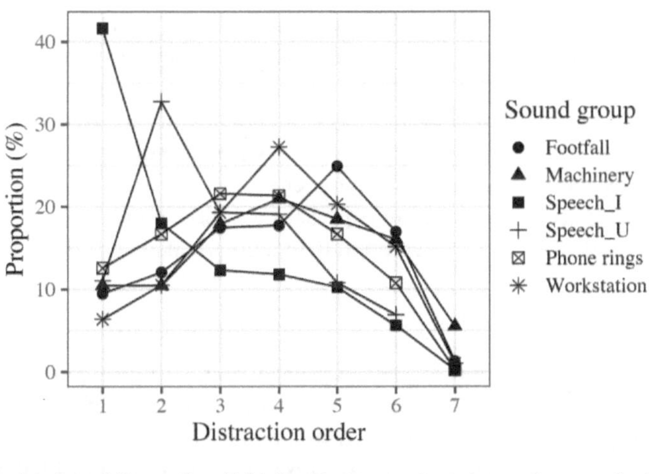

Figure 9.1 Reported order of distraction (1 highest) among selected sound groups by OPO occupants surveyed in Australia. The 'speech_I' group refers to intelligible speech and the 'speech_U' group refers to unintelligible speech.

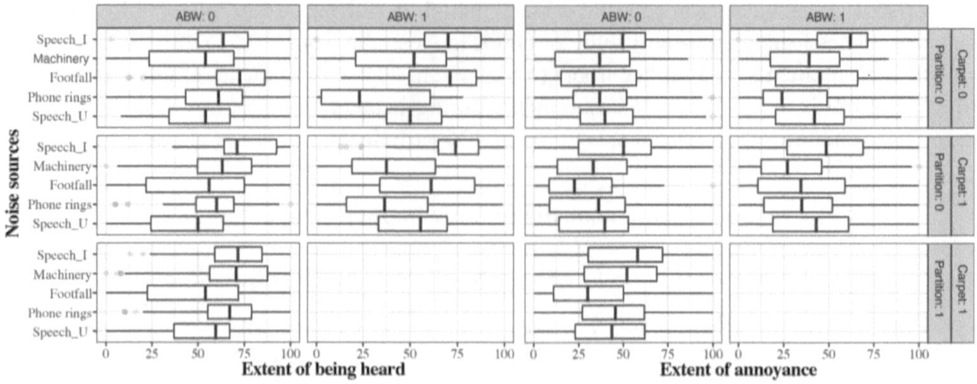

Figure 9.2 The x-axis for the two columns on the left denotes the extent to which each sound source was heard from the workstation, and that for the right two columns denotes the extent of annoyance by these noise sources, as reported by office occupants on a 0–100 scale each. 0 and 1 refer to Yes and No, respectively. ABW: Offices based around activity-based working. Carpet:0 and Partition:0 refer to no carpeting, and no partition/screen between workstations, respectively. Carpet:1 and Partition:1 refer to any kind of carpeting (usually fabric) and any type of partition (cubicle, single partition, etc.), respectively. Speech_I and Speech_U refer to intelligible and unintelligible speech, respectively.

nearby talkers. Both intelligible (i.e., meaningful) and unintelligible (even foreign) speech can be distracting due to changing-state spectro-temporal signal fluctuations, which is linked to decline in short-term memory performance (Hughes, 2014). Moreover, meaningful speech can negatively impact typical office tasks (short summary in Keus van de Poll et al., [2015]).

Further, under certain conditions, non-speech sounds that exhibit changing-state characteristics can have deleterious effects (Schlittmeier & Liebl, 2015). This is noted in Figure 9.2 (two columns on the left) where, in conditions with no carpeting and partitions between desks (signifying insufficient sound absorption) – which is common in some newer office designs – footfall and certain machinery sounds can be heard more often or as frequently as intelligible speech. Other examples where non-speech sounds could be problematic include idiosyncrasies such as faulty HVAC systems and proximity to certain areas such as kitchens. Individual sensitivity to sounds can further exacerbate such conditions.

To summarise, sound environment in OPOs is a complex mix of spatially spread speech and non-speech sound sources and relatively diffuse background noise, which can be perceived in a variable manner by the occupants and provide either beneficial sound masking or distraction. However, the role of speech with meaning is perhaps the most important, while other speech and non-speech sounds with slow spectro-temporal fluctuations can also be detrimental.

Acoustic privacy in open-plan offices: an overview

Acoustic privacy, as defined here (i.e., speech privacy and ability to concentrate), is but one of many such Indoor Environmental Quality (IEQ) factors that are relevant in OPOs. Figure 9.3 shows that out of several key IEQ factors in Australian OPOs, occupants were least satisfied with speech privacy, or the ability to have private conversations. Satisfaction with the ability to concentrate was also one of the least rated IEQ factors. Hence, the two acoustic privacy factors are some of the lowest-rated IEQ factors in Australian OPOs. This finding is consistent in general with those

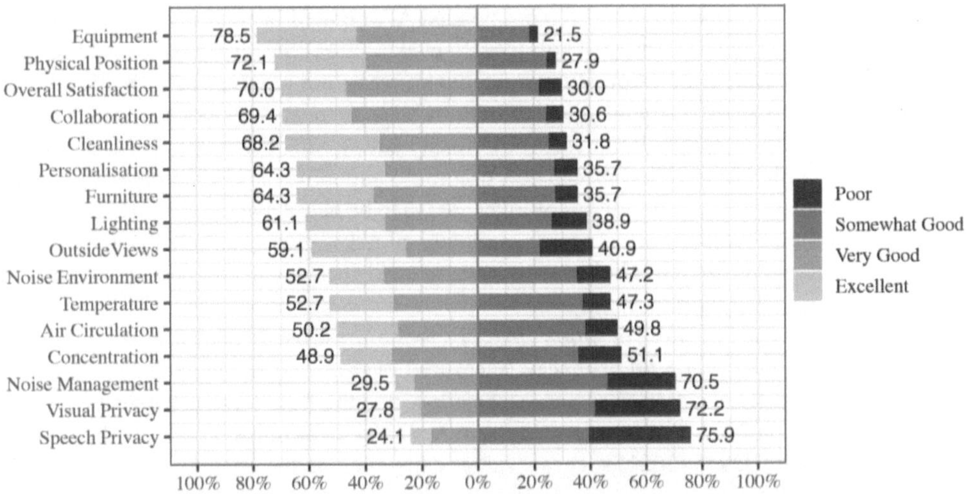

Figure 9.3 Rated satisfaction with several indoor environmental quality factors, as experienced at or near occupants' workstations. Sum of categories (in percentage) on either side of 0% is listed. The categories are based on a quartile split on the original ratings (0–100 scale).

from similarly extensive surveys in Finnish (Haapakangas et al., 2017) and French (Pierrette et al., 2015) OPOs, where sound/noise-based disturbance is a major issue.

The next-worst-performing IEQ factor after speech privacy was visual privacy, which denotes the satisfaction with the possibility to not be seen by others. There is high correlation between speech and visual privacy here. However, since the data doesn't allow categorical differentiation between these factors, visual privacy is not considered extensively or as part of acoustic privacy. Noise management, which can mean several things that may or may not involve acoustic solutions (e.g., headphones, negotiations with colleagues), was the next-worst-performing IEQ factor. However, to avoid ambiguity, and to focus on aspects that are related to acoustic solutions, it is not included as an acoustic privacy aspect, although it will be considered here at various points.

Figure 9.2 (two columns on the right) presents a more detailed overview of relevant sound groups. Intelligible speech was reported as the most annoying in general, even when intelligible speech was not the most commonly heard sound in some offices. When asked about specific aspects affected by intelligible speech, some of the responses included: 'all aspects/work', 'work requiring concentration/solving complex problems/critical thinking', 'phone conversations', and 'motivation', amongst others. This underlines again the special role of intelligible speech in terms of distraction and annoyance in OPO. However, other sources, such as unintelligible speech, intermittent machinery sounds, etc., also contributed towards annoyance.

Acoustic indicators of quality in open-plan offices

Overview

Acoustic issues in OPOs are multifaceted, hence several metrics are used in combination based on recent standards (ISO 3382–3, 2022; ISO 22955, 2021). Adequate *background noise* is desirable in OPOs for beneficial sound masking. Recommended A-weighted background noise SPL in an unoccupied but operational OPO is 40–45 dB (Veitch et al., 2002). ISO 22955 uses sound levels in *occupied* offices as a quality indicator, with target maximum values ranging from 48 dBA (limited collaborative work) to 55 dBA (frequent collaborations between nearest workstations or receiving public). In lively multi-talker environments (notoriously eating establishments, but potentially in busy offices with little absorption), speech can become competitive as people raise their voices (based on the Lombard effect; Brumm & Zollinger, 2011) to be heard over the babble. While SPLs in occupied OPOs rarely reach values posing audiological risks, high 'perceived' sound levels at workstations are common, which is linked to lowered acoustic privacy in OPO environments (Perrin Jegen & Chevret, 2016; Yadav et al., 2021b).

In architectural acoustics, *reverberation time* (T) is the most used room acoustics indicator, quantifying the time taken for a 60 dB decay (measured over a smaller range and extrapolated). The T of OPOs is not always easy to assess, especially when the floor plate is extensive, limiting its usefulness. AS/NZS 2107 (2016) recommends minimising T for noise control, with an indicative value of 0.4 s. ISO 22955 (2021) suggests values depending on the office type: ≤0.5 s for most circumstances, but ≤0.8 s when the office involves receiving the public. ISO 3382–3 (2022) makes no reverberation time recommendation, instead focusing on metrics that more directly affect occupants, described later.

Given the importance of speech, conditions quantifying speech transmission, including its spatial decay, are used as acoustic quality indicators in both ISO 3382–3 and ISO 22955. For a comfortable OPO, a high value of spatial decay rate of A-weighted speech ($D_{2,S}$) is desired: ISO 22955 requires a minimum value of 7 dB generally, or a minimum of 8 dB for offices in which the activity mainly involves collaboration between people at the nearest workstation (also indicated by ISO 3382–3, 2022). The speech SPL from a single talker is also assessed. $L_{p,A,S,4m}$ is the SPL 4 m from a simulated talker; and comfort distance r_C is the distance at which the SPL is 45 dB (i.e., equal to the upper design recommended limit for masking noise). A short comfort distance is desirable (<5 m), as well as a low speech SPL at 4 m (<48 dBA) (ISO 3382–3, 2022).

A more holistic measure of conditions for speech, and an indicator of speech intelligibility, is provided by the speech transmission index (STI; 0–1 range), which assesses how the temporal and spectral envelope of speech is affected by background noise, absolute SPL, and reverberation, and considers speech 'rhythms', auditory masking, and audibility. *Distraction distance* (r_D) is the distance at which STI is equal to 0.5 (in unoccupied conditions), a short distance (<5 m) being desirable for OPO acoustic quality (ISO 3382–3, 2022); r_D is considered to be an important predictor of acoustic/noise disturbance in OPOs (Haapakangas et al., 2017), although more studies are needed in this regard (Yadav et al., 2021b).

An obvious question is why we need both speech level and STI-based metrics. The speech level metrics do not take background noise into account, whereas the STI-based distraction distance does, and there are associated advantages and disadvantages. For example, acoustic improvements might be attempted by replacing hard screens with sound-absorptive screens – which may improve speech level–based metrics (r_C, etc.) – but distraction distance can become greater if the added sound absorption also reduces the office's background noise (although not always [Hongisto et al., 2016]). Another reason for the seeming proliferation of metrics is the need to cater for both simple and sophisticated approaches to assessment. Our recommendation is to follow the standards as closely as possible. While ISO 3382–3 allows planning/modelling and evaluation of room acoustic treatment, ISO 22955 goes a step further by including more detailed considerations for acoustic treatment in relation to office types and occupied levels.

Acoustic quality indicators of OPOs in Australia

As seen in Figure 9.4, none of the offices in the Australian sample were in the 'good' category for both $L_{p,A,S,4\,m}$ (SPL-based speech decay metric) and r_D (STI-based speech decay metric) with most offices in the 'bad' category for the former. Four offices that were in the 'not-so-good' but 'not-so-bad' categories for both the metrics (offices in the middle bounded by two solid and two broken lines) were generally well-rated and had some partitions/screens between workstations. The occupied SPLs in the Australian sample had an average value of around 54 dBA, with a roughly 48–59 dBA range, indicating that most of these OPOs would not meet the ISO 22955 target for working conditions with limited collaborations and communication.

On the one hand, it is clear from Figure 9.4 and the previous discussion that more than one metric is required to understand the effect of acoustics on occupants' perceptions. Yet, it is also clear that these metrics (from ISO 3382–3 and ISO 22955) may not be completely indicative of occupants' perception in all cases. More detailed analyses are possible based on the type of work activity, workstation density, etc., but lead overall to the same message – the use of room acoustic metrics to indicate acoustic privacy aspects is necessary from a design perspective, but more than just the metrics are needed for understanding occupants' perception of acoustic privacy.

Solutions

Overview

In terms of solutions to lack of acoustic privacy, the most obvious (and least likely/practical) one would be private offices with adequate sound insulation for most people. Barring this, presumably the next best solution could be to approximate an acoustic environment that has sufficient sound

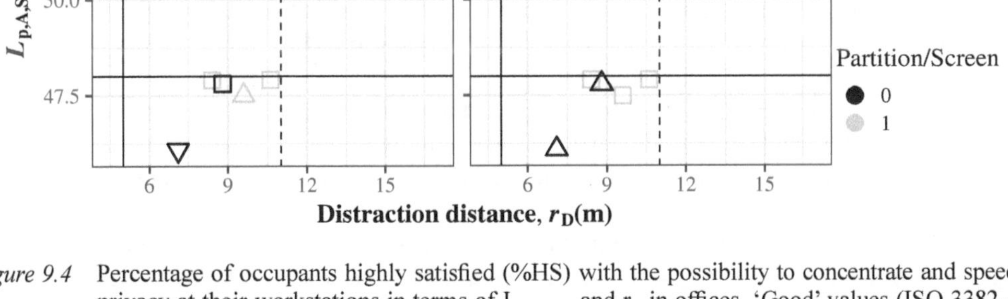

Figure 9.4 Percentage of occupants highly satisfied (%HS) with the possibility to concentrate and speech privacy at their workstations in terms of $L_{p,A,S,4m}$ and r_D in offices. 'Good' values (ISO 3382–3, 2022) for $L_{p,A,S,4m}$ and r_D shown below the horizontal solid lines and to the left of the vertical solid lines, respectively. 'Bad' values (ISO 3382–3, 2022) for $L_{p,A,S,4m}$ and r_D shown above the horizontal broken lines and to the right of the vertical broken lines, respectively. 0: No, 1: Yes.

absorption, screens/partitions (also for visual privacy), and sound masking to attenuate and mask sounds between workstations (details later). However, this may not be a practical or even desired solution from several perspectives. First, the amount of traditional sound absorption required to achieve very quiet offices, and to especially minimise sound transmission between neighbouring workstations, is exorbitant (Haapakangas et al., 2017; Yadav et al., 2021a). Speech privacy in particular may be beyond most open-plan designs and designated private rooms for conversations might be a preferred solution. Second, very quiet offices can be counterproductive in many cases where the sound environment may otherwise either provide beneficial sound masking and/or 'lively' ambiance (Yadav et al., 2021a; Yadav et al., 2021b). Interaction with psychological factors may mean that relatively quiet offices may be perceived negatively through processes that are not completely understood yet (Acun & Yilmazer, 2018; Yadav et al., 2021b). Third, recent trends in open-plan designs include more 'open' OPOs with limited use of partitions/screens and in many cases limited carpeting and ceiling absorption. This means considering solutions that are consistent with such design philosophies while integrating sensible acoustic design principles. Personal solutions such as noise blocking/cancelling devices are becoming popular as a coping strategy, including playing music over such devices (Yadav et al., 2021b). Yet the science behind their efficacy is not very promising (Schlittmeier & Hellbrück, 2009). Playing music over headphones over long periods may also present audiological hazards. Finally, the role of 'acoustic' furniture, such as pods, providing more localised acoustic privacy is also a developing field (Hongisto et al., 2020).

Overall, the solutions suggested here will cater for a variety of cases, from enclosed cubicles to completely open offices with limited acoustic treatment. For a practitioner, acoustic privacy planning may include predictions based on room acoustic theory (non-trivial due to non-diffuse acoustic conditions), access to physical acoustic measurements, room acoustic simulations, site inspections and consultations, etc. These modelling and prediction methods are mainly implied here and are not discussed extensively. The main strategies to address acoustic privacy issues may include sound absorption and sound masking, and more alternative interventions. The goal is to present these main strategies, which can be combined based on the overall design, activities, and the stage of intervention (e.g., new design or refurbishment).

Sound absorption

The traditional way to vary the physical acoustic performance of OPOs has been the use of sound absorption both vertically and horizontally along the floor plan. An excessively sound absorptive office is neither the aim nor a practical solution. For acoustic privacy, however, an appropriately high spatial decay of sounds and especially speech between workstations is crucial, and designers can model or measure the effect of various sound absorption profiles using methods presented in the previous section.

In basic terms, carpeted floors minimise impact-borne sound from walking, dropped and moving items, etc., and highly sound-absorbent carpets may be important when sound absorption is low otherwise. Ceiling absorption provides one of the most unobtrusive and effective locations for sound absorption (Keränen et al., 2020). Along the horizontal plane, options include absorptive treatment along the walls, which may sometimes be limited due to logistical and spatial constraints (e.g., glazed surfaces). However, some absorptive/diffusive treatment on walls can at least avoid flutter echoes in cuboid offices, even those with absorptive floors and ceilings.

Partitions/screens represent the conventional approach to attenuate direct sound transmission and to implement sound absorption and visual privacy (blocking direct line of sight) between workstations. Some degree of acoustic/visual barriers may be essential for privacy, which is moreover augmented with adequate and adaptive sound masking (see later) for a variety of OPOs. Simple guidelines for planning partition/screen placements can be accessed from many sources (Long, 2005), and speech level reduction from workstation furniture ensembles can be calculated using standardised methods (Hongisto et al., 2020; ISO 23351–1, 2020). Substantial attenuation of speech (up to 15 dB) between adjacent workstations has been reported by using highly sound absorptive ceilings and (high) partitions (Virjonen et al., 2007). Given the directional nature of human speech (Chu & Warnock, 2002), strategic workstation placements could achieve maximal directivity-dependent SPL attenuation around 90° angular separation either side of a talker. However, given that talkers move their heads during conversations, predicting the effect of such angular separation may be hard.

Recommendations to achieve the most rapid spatial decay of speech include high sound absorption for ceilings, walls, furniture, and partitions, with partition heights of at least 1.7 m (Keränen et al., 2020). In such conditions, speech/sound attenuation across large distances can be substantial (Keränen et al., 2020). However, it is important to note that sound absorption, especially if used excessively relative to requirements, would also attenuate beneficial masking sounds, including background noise, which can appreciably affect metrics such as distraction distance (Rindel, 2018). Hence, sufficient acoustic privacy may not be achieved (Haapakangas et al., 2017; Virjonen et al., 2007; Yadav et al., 2017; Yadav et al., 2021b) especially from speech/sounds from nearby workstations without balancing sound absorption with additional measures such as electroacoustic sound masking (Haapakangas et al., 2017; Virjonen et al., 2009). Further, customised design based on occupants' activities within various working zones (see 'Alternative Criteria/Solutions') can be appropriate in many cases instead of a uniform sound absorption profile across the floor plan, although the latter represents a much simpler implementation in principle.

A primary limitation/reservation about sound absorptive treatment is that once implemented, modifications are generally difficult. While fixed sound absorption may not always be a deterrent, it can lead to several behavioural responses, including some negative aspects usually associated with cubicle-like designs (Saval, 2014). This brings us to the juncture where physical acoustic recommendations and actual OPO design practice may (and generally do) become incompatible. This is evidenced by recent trends of eschewing sound absorption in many workplaces, especially the use of partitions/screens. Around a quarter of workplaces in the Australian sample, especially activity-based workplaces, had little or no partitions between workstations except for computer screens and many with no carpeting leading to footfall sound issues (Yadav et al., 2021a). From one perspective, screens/partitions in open-plan areas could be avoided when the occupants can relocate to other work areas as required. However, this can still be problematic, as respondents in our survey reported lack of acoustic privacy irrespective of availability of multiple working areas, besides the general paucity of such alternative working areas, which is highlighted in other studies/countries as well (Haapakangas et al., 2018).

The main message here is that the singular role of passive sound absorption, including partitions/screens, in achieving acoustic privacy, and to an extent visual privacy, is undeniable. However, careful design to alleviate negative associations is key. Combined with active control of the sound environment via adequate sound masking, sound absorption represents the main tool for achieving acoustic privacy for most OPO designs. What remains a bigger question, however, for all OPO stakeholders is the all-important willingness and/or the extent of sound absorption implementation.

Sound masking

Compared to the generally fixed/passive role of sound absorption, electroacoustic sound masking represents a more dynamic mode to vary acoustic privacy. Sound masking can be useful with/without adequate sound absorption (Chanaud, 2007), especially for *active* control of acoustic privacy between adjacent workstations (Virjonen et al., 2007). For the latter, even exorbitant sound absorption (sometimes potentially counterproductive) can be ineffective (Haapakangas et al., 2017; Virjonen et al., 2007). Even when acoustic privacy between adjacent workstations is not required (e.g., conversations with neighbours are essential), sound masking can be used to mitigate the effect of irrelevant background sounds over longer distances. Moreover, most modern HVAC systems have become quieter over the years (Yadav et al., 2021a), and natural ventilation can be challenging as a source of uncontrolled noise from the external environment and adjacent spaces. Hence, electroacoustic masking systems have a critical role in many scenarios in providing a stable diffuse noise source. None of the offices in our sample had electroacoustic masking despite relatively low background noise (mean: 42 dBA) in several offices. Potentially, many Australian OPOs would benefit from sound masking, especially with lower occupation and associated SPLs predicted in post-pandemic conditions.

The general idea with electroacoustic masking systems is to augment either insufficient background noise (unoccupied L_{Aeq}) or insufficient background sounds during occupation (usually calculated as L_{A90}: 90th percentile A-weighted SPL) to reach a SPL and a spectrum considered acceptable for masking unwanted sounds to varying degrees (ASTM, 2018; Chanaud, 2007). Hence, key factors include the SPL and spectral characteristics of masking sounds, and whether these factors are static or adaptive, besides ensuring spatial diffuseness. The latter, which is dependent on spatial implementation of masking systems (e.g., loudspeaker placement) (Chanaud, 2007) is beyond the scope here; relevant standards can be accessed for guidelines (ASTM, 2018, 2022). Instead, the focus is on characteristics of masking sounds and their effect on acoustic privacy. Since speech is most detrimental, the desired outcome is effectively reducing intelligibility of task-irrelevant speech with increased masking (reducing STI and hence distraction distance), which is expected to address both aspects of acoustic privacy (i.e., speech privacy and ability to concentrate). Utmost care is required to ensure that masking sounds are perceived (if at all) as unobtrusive and benign by the occupants, i.e., necessary for acoustic privacy and not a nuisance, which is a rather involved consideration, and an active area of research (Chanaud, 2007; Francis, 2022; Haapakangas et al., 2011; Hongisto et al., 2017; Lenne et al., 2020). However, customised calibration per OPO is possible and recommended along with occupants' assessments.

A common masking sound recommendation in OPOs refers to pink noise filtered to have a spectral slope of -5 dB/octave (Blazier, 1997) presented at around 45 dBA but not exceeding 48 dBA (Veitch et al., 2002). There is limited research and real-world evidence, however, validating this recommendation, with even 45 dBA reported as too loud in a recent long-term field study (Lenne et al., 2020). The quality of this noise is an important consideration: more sound is needed at lower frequencies, as in -5 dB/octave spectral slope or similar (ANSI S12.2, 2008; Beranek, 1989; Blazier, 1997), and steeper slopes around -7 dB/octave have been suggested too (Hongisto et al., 2015); the noise must not have distinct tonal components (e.g., whistling or humming; [Jeon et al., 2011]); and steady rather than fluctuating noise (Liebl et al., 2016). Alternatives include water-based sounds (Haapakangas et al., 2011; Hongisto et al., 2017), speech-shaped noise/babble (Haapakangas et al., 2011; Keus van de Poll et al., 2015; Liebl et al., 2016), pink noise with various slopes (Hongisto et al., 2015) and/or with finer 1/3rd octave-band equalization (Chanaud, 2007), etc. The findings regarding masking sound efficacy are sometimes inconsistent across studies, generally attributed to methodological differences, settings (e.g., laboratory vs. real-world, office activities), and study durations (Hongisto et al., 2017). Further, it is unknown whether occupants would in general accept out-of-context sounds, i.e., not present naturally in OPOs, including water sounds, which may be perceived negatively (Acun & Yilmazer, 2018).

Overall, the jury is still out with respect to the ideal, and importantly context-appropriate, masking sound(s), with most recent studies suggesting longer-term and repeatable in-situ research (Hongisto et al., 2017; Lenne et al., 2020). Moreover, none of the studies have adequately addressed the Lombard effect, which is likely to be relevant around recommended masking SPLs. Despite the seeming lack of a silver bullet, OPO designers can benefit substantially from the many available possibilities and active nature of sound masking. Adaptive sounds and zone-based masking are now implemented in several commercial systems (Chanaud, 2007; Lenne et al., 2020), which is a welcome advancement if it keeps up with latest research findings.

Benign masking sounds with an appropriate spectrum (pink or similar) and mostly uniform spatial distribution at 40–45 dBA (potentially even lower) SPL along with appropriate sound absorption, represent an acoustically and psychoacoustically logical solution for high-performance acoustic privacy, with fine-tuning possible with future research findings.

Alternative criteria/solutions

Despite the advocacy of acoustic indicators of quality given earlier and some solutions to meet targets, a thorny question remains: Are the metrics included in the standards sufficient to achieve acoustic privacy in all types of OPOs? The two main studies in this regard, one from Finland (Haapakangas et al., 2017) and the other using the current sample of Australian OPOs (Yadav et al., 2021b), present contradictory findings: it is not clear if room acoustic improvements always lead to an increase in acoustic privacy (Yadav et al., 2021b).

The Australian study (Yadav et al., 2021b), and another from the UK with a smaller sample (Park et al., 2020), did indicate that metrics based on occupied sound environment (e.g., L_{Aeq}) were more consistent with expectations, with higher values (e.g., louder offices) leading to a decrease in acoustic privacy aspects; the Finnish study did not include measurements during occupation. Hence, a simple answer to the earlier question is that there is limited research validating the methods in the standards. Perhaps non-acoustic considerations during occupation, such as the office type, activities, etc. may be quite important while planning for acoustic privacy. This, however, does not mean that improvements to room acoustics and sound masking are not important. Instead, it is more likely that the application of these tools is perhaps not optimised for a wide range of OPOs yet (Rindel, 2018), and inclusion of behavioural and organisational aspects needs further work.

With that in mind, the following considers some relevant design criteria and suggestions that may seem straightforward/common-sense but are overlooked at times. In most cases, these considerations buttress the improvements based on relevant standards (ISO 3382–3, 2022; ISO 22955, 2021) and include:

- *Zoning*: Strategic divisions of the office into separate/non-contiguous zones based on teams, activities, and acoustic profile can be crucial. Some of these strategies are part of most workplaces, based on the floor plan and/or organisational structure, and be implemented during the floor-plan design and/or at later stages. Effective zoning includes spatial considerations to prioritise solutions when acoustic privacy is compromised between zones. While this may seem obvious, occupants often reported disregard of careful zoning in the Australian sample (e.g., a busy kitchen next to workstations). Another common complaint included occupants disregarding quiet areas. Hence, workplaces can benefit from regular correspondence between building managers, planners, and occupants about zoning.

- *Office etiquette*: Perhaps the most obvious and arguably underused aspect of acoustic privacy includes occupants being considerate towards each other. Most office etiquettes address speech and telephone usage and a general appreciation of the fact that ability to cope with sounds/ noise varies drastically among individuals. Annex C of ISO 22955 lists several 'rules' for co-working, which can constitute part of a work charter. Examples of proper etiquette include speaking quietly and avoiding long discussions especially in/around quiet zones and intensive work areas, using sound-insulated rooms for meetings, avoiding ringtones, and taking long calls away for workstations if possible, etc. Such measures can sometimes provide the most respite from issues regarding acoustic privacy and nurture a workplace based on mutual respect. On the other hand, not maintaining etiquette has the potential to undo any/most acoustic measures, which underlines its potency.
- *Special furniture*: OPOs have lately seen proliferation of partially/fully enclosed furniture such as pods, booths, high-back chairs, etc. The principle behind such furniture (see examples in [Hongisto et al., 2016]) is similar to a workstation with some degree of enclosure using screens/ partitions. However, the consideration here is the use of such furniture away from main workstation areas, which, in a way, represents local islands with some (usually greater) degree of acoustic/visual privacy suitable for activities such as conversations, performing group/individual work, etc. In some workplaces, such furniture may be the only places with some acoustic privacy, including being part of the overall design strategy where the workstation areas have limited sound absorption. Such a situation was typical of several offices supporting activity-based working in our Australian sample, and it is unclear how effective such a solution was, based on survey responses. Yet, with careful planning, a good compromise may be achieved between workstation areas with adequate degree of traditional acoustic solutions and special furniture for higher degree of acoustic (and/or visual) privacy, besides closed rooms. However, important considerations include the degree of acoustic privacy provided by such furniture, which are sometimes marketed with an 'acoustic' function, although seldom with any measurement data and/or are used indiscriminately. For instance, many such pieces of 'acoustic furniture' during our site visits were either badly designed or badly located (e.g., next to busy lobbies) from an acoustic perspective. It is strongly recommended that the acoustic benefits from such furniture and workstations in general are quantified more regularly by manufacturers using ISO 23351–1 (2020) and their use in OPOs critically evaluated by designers and practitioners. While the main use of special furniture is to provide acoustic isolation from the rest of the office, more experimental scenarios include using open-ceiling meeting rooms (Yu et al., 2016), high-back chairs (Cabrera et al., 2017), and retroreflective surfaces/ceilings (Cabrera et al., 2018). However, despite their promising prospects, proving long-term efficacy in OPOs is ongoing work.

Conclusions

Most OPOs are not designed for acoustic privacy, which is one of the major sources of occupants' dissatisfaction with OPOs. Intelligible speech is the main acoustic issue in OPOs, although non-speech sounds can be detrimental in certain contexts, especially when acoustic design is ignored. ISO 3382–3 and ISO 22955 can help guide the acoustic design, with the latter providing suggestions based on predominant office activities. Even with the best solutions, acoustic privacy between closest workstations may be difficult to achieve. Hence, it is critical to combine acoustic measurement methods with occupants' perception of acoustic privacy, while being inclusive of individual sensitivities towards sound/noise, and variable degrees of privacy and concentrated work. It is recommended that this is an iterative and continual process.

A 'high-performance' checklist for acoustic privacy is provided here:

Principle	*Description*
ZONING OF WORKPLACE	• Sensible zoning of work areas and workstations based on activities. • Separate rooms (proportional to occupant count) recommended for private conversations, long meetings, and concentrated work. • Special furniture, such as pods, can be useful as local zones of acoustic privacy. Their acoustic performance should be measured using ISO 23351–1 rather than marketing claims. • Office etiquettes may be indispensable besides the acoustic solutions.
SPACIAL DECAY OF SPEECH	• Using adequate sound absorption. Carpeting and ceiling absorption can be unobtrusive and quite effective. However, some absorptive partitions/screens may be essential for strategic acoustic and visual privacy and for crucially blocking direct sound transmission. • Using adaptive and spatially diffuse electroacoustic sound masking, especially when background noise is below (approximately) 40–45 dBA. This may be vital during lower occupancy, including post-pandemic measures. • Using *both* sound absorption and sound masking to avoid offices that are either too quiet or too lively.
ACOUSTIC PRIVACY	• To alleviate acoustic privacy issues in such cases, and in general, separate rooms (proportional to occupant count) are recommended for private conversations, long meetings, and concentrated work.

References

Acun, V., & Yilmazer, S. (2018). A grounded theory approach to investigate the perceived soundscape of open-plan offices. *Applied Acoustics*, *131*, 28–37.

ANSI S12.2. (2008). *American national standard – Criteria for evaluating room noise*. Acoustical Society of America.

AS/NZS 2107. (2016). *Acoustics – Recommended design sound levels and reverberation times for building interiors*. Standards Australia.

ASTM E1374–18e1. (2018). *Standard guide for office acoustics and applicable ASTM standards*. American Society of Testing and Materials.

ASTM E1573–22. (2022). *Standard test method for measurement and reporting of masking sound levels using a-weighted and one-third-octave-band sound pressure levels*. American Society of Testing and Materials.

Beranek, L. L. (1989). Balanced noise-criterion (NCB) curves. *The Journal of the Acoustical Society of America*, *86*(2), 650–664.

Blazier, W. E. (1997). RC Mark II; a refined procedure for rating the noise of heating, ventilating and air-conditioning (HVAC) systems in building. *Noise Control Engineering Journal*, *45*(6), 243–250.

Bronkhorst, A. W. (2015). The cocktail-party problem revisited: Early processing and selection of multi-talker speech. *Attention, Perception, & Psychophysics*, *77*(5), 1465–1487.

Brumm, H., & Zollinger, A. (2011). The evolution of the Lombard effect: 100 years of psychoacoustic research. *Behaviour*, *148*(11), 1173.

Cabrera, D., Yadav, M., & Ciccarello, B. (2017). Quantifying the local acoustic effects of high-backed chairs. *Applied Acoustics*, *119*, 39–49.

Cabrera, D., Yadav, M., Reinhardt, D., Holmes, J., Ciccarello, B., Caldwell, H., & Hannouch, A. (2018). Experiments with high-back chairs and retroreflective surfaces for increasing the support of one's own voice over short conversational distances. *The Journal of the Acoustical Society of America, 143*(3), 1725–1725.

Chanaud, R. C. (2007). Progress in sound masking. *Acoustics Today, 3*(4), 21.

Chu, W. T., & Warnock, A. C. C. (2002). *Detailed directivity of sound fields around human talkers* (IRC-RR-104). National Research Council Canada.

Francis, A. L. (2022). Adding noise is a confounded nuisance. *The Journal of the Acoustical Society of America, 152*(3), 1375–1388.

Haapakangas, A., Hongisto, V., Eerola, M., & Kuusisto, T. (2017). Distraction distance and perceived disturbance by noise – An analysis of 21 open-plan offices. *The Journal of the Acoustical Society of America, 141*(1), 127–136.

Haapakangas, A., Hongisto, V., Varjo, J., & Lahtinen, M. (2018). Benefits of quiet workspaces in open-plan offices – Evidence from two office relocations. *Journal of Environmental Psychology, 56*, 63–75.

Haapakangas, A., Kankkunen, E., Hongisto, V., Virjonen, P., Oliva, D., & Keskinen, E. (2011). Effects of five speech masking sounds on performance and acoustic satisfaction. Implications for open-plan offices. *Acta Acustica United with Acustica, 97*(4), 641–655.

Hongisto, V., Haapakangas, A., Varjo, J., Helenius, R., & Koskela, H. (2016). Refurbishment of an open-plan office – Environmental and job satisfaction. *Journal of Environmental Psychology, 45*, 176–191.

Hongisto, V., Keränen, J., & Hakala, J. (2020). Accuracy experiment of ISO DIS 23351-1 – speech level reduction of furniture ensembles and enclosures. *Applied Acoustics, 164*, 107249.

Hongisto, V., Oliva, D., & Rekola, L. (2015). Subjective and objective rating of spectrally different pseudorandom noises? Implications for speech masking design. *The Journal of the Acoustical Society of America, 137*(3), 1344–1355.

Hongisto, V., Varjo, J., Oliva, D., Haapakangas, A., & Benway, E. (2017). Perception of water-based masking sounds – Long-term experiment in an open-plan office. *Frontiers in Psychology, 8*.

Hughes, R. W. (2014). Auditory distraction: A duplex-mechanism account: Duplex-mechanism account of auditory distraction. *PsyCh Journal, 3*(1), 30–41.

ISO 22955. (2021). *ISO 22955 Acoustics – Acoustic quality of open office spaces*. International Organization for Standardization.

ISO 23351-1. (2020). *ISO 23351-1 Acoustics – Measurement of speech level reduction of furniture ensembles and enclosures – Part 1: Laboratory method*. International Organization for Standardization.

ISO 3382-3. (2022). *ISO 3382-3:2022. Measurement of room acoustic parameters. Part 3: Open plan offices*. International Organization for Standardization.

Jeon, J. Y., You, J., Jeong, C. I., Kim, S. Y., & Jho, M. J. (2011). Varying the spectral envelope of air-conditioning sounds to enhance indoor acoustic comfort. *Building and Environment, 46*(3), 739–746.

Kaufmann-Buhler, J. (2016). Progressive partitions: The promises and problems of the American open plan office. *Design and Culture, 8*(2), 205–233.

Keränen, J., Hakala, J., & Hongisto, V. (2020). Effect of sound absorption and screen height on spatial decay of speech – Experimental study in an open-plan office. *Applied Acoustics, 166*, 107340.

Keus van de Poll, M., Carlsson, J., Marsh, J. E., Ljung, R., Odelius, J., Schlittmeier, S. J., Sundin, G., & Sörqvist, P. (2015). Unmasking the effects of masking on performance: The potential of multiple-voice masking in the office environment. *The Journal of the Acoustical Society of America, 138*(2), 807–816.

Lenne, L., Chevret, P., & Marchand, J. (2020). Long-term effects of the use of a sound masking system in open-plan offices: A field study. *Applied Acoustics, 158*, 107049.

Liebl, A., Assfalg, A., & Schlittmeier, S. J. (2016). The effects of speech intelligibility and temporal–spectral variability on performance and annoyance ratings. *Applied Acoustics, 110*, 170–175.

Long, M. (2005). *Architectural acoustics*. Elsevier.

Park, S. H., Lee, P. J., Lee, B. K., Roskams, M., & Haynes, B. P. (2020). Associations between job satisfaction, job characteristics, and acoustic environment in open-plan offices. *Applied Acoustics, 168*, 107425.

Perrin Jegen, N., & Chevret, P. (2016). Effect of noise on comfort in open-plan offices: Application of an assessment questionnaire. *Ergonomics*, 1–12.

Pierrette, M., Parizet, E., Chevret, P., & Chatillon, J. (2015). Noise effect on comfort in open-space offices: Development of an assessment questionnaire. *Ergonomics, 58*(1), 96–106.

Rindel, J. H. (2018). Open plan office acoustics–a multidimensional optimization problem. In *Proceedings of DAGA2018, Munich.*

Saval, N. (2014). *Cubed: A secret history of the workplace*. Doubleday.

Schlittmeier, S. J., & Hellbrück, J. (2009). Background music as noise abatement in open-plan offices: A laboratory study on performance effects and subjective preferences. *Applied Cognitive Psychology*, *23*(5), 684–697.

Schlittmeier, S. J., & Liebl, A. (2015). The effects of intelligible irrelevant background speech in offices – cognitive disturbance, annoyance, and solutions. *Facilities*, *33*(1/2), 61–75.

Veitch, J. A., Bradley, J. S., Legault, L. M., Norcross, S., & Svec, J. M. (2002). *Masking speech in open-plan offices with simulated ventilation noise: Noise level and spectral composition effects on acoustic satisfaction*. Institute for Research in Construction, Internal Report IRC-IR-846.

Virjonen, P., Keränen, J., Helenius, R., Hakala, J., & Hongisto, O. V. (2007). Speech privacy between neighboring workstations in an open office-a laboratory study. *Acta Acustica United with Acustica*, *93*(5), 771–782.

Virjonen, P., Keränen, J., & Hongisto, V. (2009). Determination of acoustical conditions in open-plan offices: Proposal for new measurement method and target values. *Acta Acustica United with Acustica*, *95*(2), 279–290.

Yadav, M., Cabrera, D., Kim, J., Fels, J., & de Dear, R. (2021a). Sound in occupied open-plan offices: Objective metrics with a review of historical perspectives. *Applied Acoustics*, *177*, 107943.

Yadav, M., Cabrera, D., Kim, J., Love, J., Holmes, J., Fels, J., & de Dear, R. (2021b). Investigating noise disturbance in open-plan offices using measurements of the room acoustics, and of the sound environment during occupancy. In *Proceedings of Euronoise 2021, Euronoise 2021, Madeira, Portugal*. Euronoise.

Yadav, M., Cabrera, D., Love, J., Kim, J., Holmes, J., Caldwell, H., & de Dear, R. (2019). Reliability and repeatability of ISO 3382–3 metrics based on repeated acoustic measurements in open-plan offices. *Applied Acoustics*, *150*, 138–146.

Yadav, M., Kim, J., Cabrera, D., & de Dear, R. (2017). Auditory distraction in open-plan office environments: The effect of multi-talker acoustics. *Applied Acoustics*, *126*, 68–80.

Yu, J., Wang, S., Qiu, X., Shaid, A., & Wang, L. (2016). Contributions of various transmission paths to speech privacy of open ceiling meeting rooms in open-plan offices. *Applied Acoustics*, *112*, 59–69.

Zwicker, E., & Fastl, H. (1999). *Psychoacoustics: Facts and models* (2nd ed.). Springer-Verlag.

10
COLLABORATIVE TECHNOLOGY

Dian Tjondronegoro and Christhina Candido

If all you need is a laptop and wifi to do your work, what is the office for?

– *Authors*

Introduction

Technology-enabled advances change where and how people work. Computers, cloud-based systems, Wi-Fi access, and collaborative technology allowed workers to become mobile, supporting the rapid uptake of Scrum and Agile work methodologies. From a physical environment perspective, this mobility untethered workers from their desks, allowing them to move around the office and work from zones that best support their task at hand, enabling the uptake of activity-based working (ABW) at scale. Online and digital technologies have changed how we connect, collaborate, work, and socialize. Thanks to Internet connectivity, online presence, and digital business tools, many businesses have seamlessly managed the shift to flexible work. COVID was a catalyst for the acceleration and uptake of collaborative technology at a large scale, allowing workers to be untethered from offices while enabling them to work from anywhere in synchronous and asynchronous ways. There is little doubt that the quality of the digital infrastructure ecosystem made available to workers is central to delivering a high-performance workplace environment allowing for seamless collaboration and the flow of information needed for people to perform their work anywhere.

From the workers' perspective, technological changes also made work pervasive. Office and productivity apps on smartphones enable work and communication at any time. However, always-on culture entrenched in workplaces could lead to stress and burn-out, compromising workers' ability to perform their work well and significantly negatively affecting physical and mental health. The right to disconnect came as a response to this significant issue, being recently proposed as a human right not to engage with work communications outside work hours. Further, the constant engagement with collaborative tools and the increased uptake of distributed teams means that people may spend more time bound to their screens. If not properly balanced, this reduced reliance on face-to-face interactions poses challenges to workers' health from the cognitive load of engaging with colleagues on screens, the increased time they spend seated, and other potentially harmful consequences of ways of working. Rapid development of artificial intelligence (AI) technologies,

DOI: 10.1201/9781003328728-11
This chapter has been made available under a CC-BY-NC-ND 4.0 license.

particularly generative AI models, promotes the use of AI-enabled tech as collaborative tools by rapidly analyzing and synthesizing data and large amounts of information to assist workers in making decisions and using data effectively for work.

From an environmental, social, and governance (ESG) perspective, technological changes are also important to organizational capabilities and sustainability. For example, cloud-based services like Office365 have become the standard approach for supporting scalable computing, including managing, processing, and securing data. Cloud computing has been recognized as having a larger carbon footprint than air travel, raising significant concerns about its environmental costs. In parallel, the rise of the Internet of Things (IoT) enabled building owners to sprinkle assets with miniaturized devices to capture building and Indoor Environmental Quality (IEQ) performance, space utilization, and occupancy at scale as well as a plethora of other types of data. This means that AI-enabled data analysis and sometimes "big data" can be harnessed for fine-tuning buildings to achieve high-performance targets regarding energy consumption (and carbon) and health.

Smart offices make use of technologies to transform workspaces through effective integration of human–computer interfaces, cloud, and embedded computing capabilities. We are still in the progress of solving the gaps in technology use for productivity. The smarter our environment is, embedded with intelligent sensing and computation, the more people must harness it. Hence, we will introduce smart offices and how technology (integrated and intelligent systems) enables people to work more efficiently through autonomous sensing and rapid analysis of humans and the physical environment. To understand how technologies can support work, we will explore the relationship between IoT, AI, machine learning (ML), and robotics. Through a multidisciplinary perspective, this chapter will also discuss how we can address key challenges in harnessing technologies, including data privacy and security risks, sensing and AI limits, and the challenges in initiating and managing the positive adoption of technologies for productivity. We are surrounded by a deluge of data generated by increasing autonomous technologies (tech), but we need to utilize tech or harness the rich data available. The chapter will conclude by identifying the critical steps for addressing that gap through digital transformation and skilling up the workforce to use technology optimally for improving productivity and work–life balance.

Technologies at the workplace: from smart offices to pervasive work

This section will focus on the incorporation of technology in offices or "IoT and other smart office/office sensing fundamentals and its relation to workers health and productivity" and how tech becomes prevalent and relevant to office and workplaces. The section also discusses how AI and big data support high-performing workspaces and concludes with the need for the ethical use of AI and tech at work.

The rise and pervasiveness of the technology as the fundamentals of smart offices

Smart offices are rapidly becoming pervasive in a world where everything is connected, mobile, and utilizing the IoT and cloud computing–enabled innovative products and services previously thought impractical or impossible for lightweight devices. AI has become so prevalent in our interactions with technology that we often become unaware of when and how AI is used within everyday activities: live, work, and play. Intelligent systems can integrate and analyze 1) *hard data* from smart sensors – mobile devices, wearable/embedded sensors, robots, drones, etc., and 2) *soft-sensing data* from social media, crowd-sourced knowledge, and interaction patterns. Effective fusion of hard and soft-sensing data analytics can empower intelligent systems with contextual information, such as geospatial location, environmental characteristics, personal biometrics, and shared social interest data. This will consequently enrich human–machine interactions and data flow, giving humans unprecedented control over the surroundings and shaping how people will interact with each other and the environment. Pervasive and augmented computing user interfaces, such as Microsoft HoloLens and Apple Vision Pro, bring this type of natural interface to the next level, augmenting the information directly to the objects that people see, which means that people can look at information without losing awareness at the same time as performing the tasks. Nowadays, these interfaces are embedded into our day-to-day devices, such as smartphones, tablets, and wearables, forming intelligent systems that blur the line between work and life activities and increase productivity, health, and well-being.

A simple yet profound example is how virtual concierge or smart assistant services like Microsoft's Cortana and Apple's Siri can support intuitive speech-based conversational human–computer interactions to complete tasks, such as composing emails and documents and obtaining recommendations and answers to questions based on the Web's large-scale knowledge base, which includes contextual and crowd-sourced information. These smart assistants also use sensor data to understand the environmental and surrounding data, including location awareness, such as weather forecasts, to further tailor recommendations and solutions based on user preferences and their needs within the current situation. Within the context of smart offices, these technologies will support IEQ, as the smart virtual assistants can automatically adjust workspaces for optimal lighting, thermal comfort, and ergonomic desks while providing recommendations to physical activity management, opportunities to stay active at work, making recommendations to maintain privacy within cloud-computing environments, and manage the balance of personal and focused work time with the need to socialize.

AI and high-performing workspaces: harnessing intelligence for work productivity

To fully appreciate how interconnected sensing and intelligent systems underpinned by rapidly advancing AI technologies are augmenting human intelligence and promoting work productivity, it is important to learn more about their technologies and anticipate their growth locally and globally (Tjondronegoro, D., 2019). AI can be defined as a computer's ability to 1) process data into useful information; 2) analyze extracted information to support decision-making and augment human knowledge; 3) develop cognition and perception abilities, including seeing and listening, which would enable it to ultimately 4) become autonomous and act according to logic, context, rules, and laws; as well as 5) predict and anticipate emerging contexts or events. AI is, therefore, often mentioned in the same breath as big data and the IoT. AI is a computer's central core processing unit that enables it to think and act. Just like how a human's brain grows its intelligence and ability to make decisions, AI needs to be trained (by big data), connected to the source of knowledge (produced by the IoT), and governed by laws and rules (becoming responsibly autonomous).

Deep learning algorithms (LeCun et al., 2015) enable AI and autonomous systems to self-learn and continuously improve their knowledge to augment human intelligence and decision-making ability. This rapid development of AI implementations change how computers can support cognitive tasks (seeing, listening, talking, driving, interpreting human emotions, etc.) and making decisions and predictions. Deep learning enables machines to automatically extract useful features from any data and identify patterns that can be used to make decisions. The more data AI can leverage, the more accurate and useful it can become, which is why the term "big data" was coined to signify both the requirement and the capacity of today's computers to produce and process data and information at high volume, velocity, variety, and veracity. High-performance workspaces are enabled by AI and deep learning through rapid analysis of big data in a way that was humanly impossible to rapidly make sense of and extract meaningful information from a massive amount of unstructured data continuously and in a short time.

The IoT is the Internet-enabled interconnected network of computing devices embedded in everyday objects so that they can communicate via data with or without human intervention. When everything in the world is connected, we will witness a sharp increase in data volume generated by users' daily life experiences, businesses (i.e., transactional records), and social interactions. Big data generated by the IoT can be scaled and managed effortlessly using cloud storage, along with the ever-increasing number of new devices and data types. As millions of connected things generate big data, it will support AI's deep learning. IoT-generated big data is crucial to computationally reveal useful patterns, trends, and associations to learn and interpret behavior and interactions between humans, machines, and the environment.

AI and pervasive intelligent systems are transforming work and productivity, and it is now virtually possible to replace many jobs with computers. However, Kai-Fu Lee's book on AI superpowers (Lee, 2019) posited that humans choose to do a job because it gives them meaning in life via satisfaction and happiness from how other people appreciate them for what they contribute to daily living. Humans probably would never let AI rule the world, even if the technology were so advanced in the next decades. Humans are still the best at providing genuine caring and meaningful empathy during interactions with other people, which machines can never replace, even if AI could one day precisely compute emotions. The future of work and professions will shift due to AI advancements, but there will always be a requirement to apply humanistic characteristics. Human–computer interaction will shift the role of the computer from being a mere automation tool into an enabler for future knowledge workers to solve complex problems. Today this concept is even more prevalent, as scientists are developing AI applications to support humans' ability to perform tasks and improve their quality of life. Just as AI is already helping us to have an active and healthy lifestyle, it will continue to help us do our jobs better, making better decisions dynamically based on real-time data and predictive analysis.

Ethical and responsible AI adoption

There still needs to be a significant gap between expectations and the successful adoption of AI to innovate and improve businesses. AI adoption is complex, as it often incorporates big data and the IoT, affecting data privacy. Existing frameworks have identified the need to focus on human-centered design, combining technical and business/organizational perspectives. However, trust remains a critical issue that needs to be designed from the beginning (Tjondronegoro et al., 2022). AI relies on sufficiently representative and diverse data to effectively train the models for making reliable and unbiased decisions.

Transparent and *Explainable AI* aims to apply new processes, technologies, and layers to existing AI systems to make AI models understandable to users and programmers. The human-in-the-loop concept denotes human involvement in the design and evaluation processes to maintain a supervisory role over autonomous systems. The supervisory process ensures that AI aligns with human rights, social norms, and privacy practices and oversees automation biases.

Privacy and processing of personal data are an essential part of an individual's freedom and fundamental rights, as well as society's democracy. Europe's General Data Protection Regulation (GDPR) is widely considered the most cutting-edge world regulation on personal data protection

(Inverardi, 2019). Given the scope and amount of data used by AI, ethical privacy practices need to be embedded into the design specifications of technologies, business practices, and physical infrastructures. In addition, a growing number of emerging privacy-preserving measures must be applied to the hardware, software, and datasets.

Beyond privacy, ethical issues are the hardest to manage due to the potential conflict between users' and communities' ethical principles for an autonomous system's decisions. The challenge is to balance the freedom of individuals to make responsible decisions and the freedom and safety of others. Therefore, the challenge is whether AI should ethically support individuals to exercise their freedom of choice or enforce the law by autonomously intervening in the decisions and taking actions for the benefit and safety of others and society. Another challenge is whether AI should be ethically required to provide all data and information for law enforcement officers to make a fair decision or whether AI should maintain an individual's privacy rights and wait for consent before disclosing. Fairness is another major issue since the data fed into its ML algorithms largely determines AI's ability to analyze information and make decisions. An issue is that the data may be biased, reflecting the AI's algorithms and outcomes. The rapid adoption of deep learning has shifted the development of AI capability from intellectual engineering to data-driven engineering. Therefore, there is a general expectation that AI is biased in contexts where the data is collected.

The gaps in the high-performance environment using tech

The challenge for business leaders to fully implement flexible work is maintaining the traditional layers of workforce management: place, time, role, and leave (Meta5, 2020). However, the sudden large-scale shift to flexible working has allowed business leaders and managers to transform toward a more sustainable work environment. Productivity and well-being considerations for incorporating digitized workspaces have become a part of the new normal for flexible work, combined with ABW and WFH (working from home). Data from the Sustainable and Healthy Environments (SHE) Post-Occupancy Evaluation survey (SHE POE dataset, 2023) showed that 94% of the participants were satisfied with their access to technology in their workplaces (Figure 10.1). Drawing from the lessons learned during the COVID-19 lockdown, the following will explore: 1) the opportunities from the digitized workspace and 2) the challenges in managing flexible work that supports productivity and well-being. These will inform and empower business leaders to develop a strategy for implementing productive yet flexible work environments for a more sustainable future of work.

The opportunities for digitized workspaces

Digital capability is the term we use to describe the skills and attitudes that individuals and organizations need to thrive in today's technological world. At an individual level, we define digital capabilities as equipping someone to live, learn, and work in a digital society. Businesses adopting digital technologies to maintain productivity must use various techniques appropriately and effectively in different contexts.

Online presence through a website and social media has become the primary requirement for conducting business, interacting with and supporting the end users, and managing sales and transactions. For critical services, such as healthcare and social assistance, an online presence was essential to continue supporting public health and well-being during the COVID-19 pandemic. In addition, an online presence was essential for some sectors like education, training, arts, hospitality, and tourism to sustain business activities during the lockdown. For the internal operation

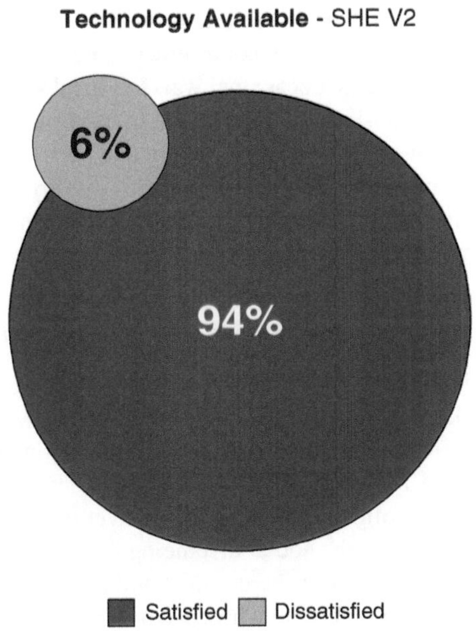

Figure 10.1 Percentage of satisfied and dissatisfied workers with accessibility of technology in their workdays according to the SHE POE dataset.

Source: SHE POE dataset, 2023

of businesses, workers can use the Internet to access *digital business tools* from anywhere for communication, collaboration, and management (of projects, finance, human resource, stock and inventory, supply chain and logistics, and customer relationships). Before the pandemic, some businesses were still reluctant to rely entirely on these tools for digitizing the workspace due to cybersecurity concerns, digital literacy, and the difficulties in providing online tech support for the staff. However, the large-scale lockdown has pushed businesses to immediately shift toward digitized workspaces and innovate their product and service offerings.

Online meeting tools, such as Zoom and Microsoft Teams, have seen the highest increase in usage and exposure during the lockdown. Suddenly most people and businesses realized that they were more connected than ever with others around the globe. People suddenly became more accessible, as they did not need to spend hours, or even days in some cases, to travel to connect and collaborate with colleagues. Asynchronous communication gives people more agency about when/where to work. For the health sectors, these online meeting tools have helped deliver care to broader and distant communities and reduce contagion risks. The combination of digital business tools, asynchronous communications, and a backbone office has enabled workers to maintain productivity during the pandemic, albeit the challenges associated with the sudden shift to WFH and ABW. People suddenly realized that they could adapt to the tools fast enough while at the same time develop their digital capability to become more future-ready.

The shift toward online and digitalized business was generally seen as inevitable, but the COVID-19 pandemic helped speed up the journey by at least ten years. People have somehow leapfrogged their fear and skepticism from the uncertainties over risks and challenges if their business and work were shifted fully online. The new normal will undoubtedly benefit from the digitized workspace to promote efficiency and provide opportunities for a more inclusive workforce.

By saving time from traveling to and from the office, working parents can use the extra time gained to better juggle between home and work commitments. For some people, WFH has allowed them to enjoy more home-cooked meals, occasional walks to local shops, walking their dogs, and exercising more regularly at their leisure, all of which help to promote their well-being. WFH is impossible for others due to a non-conducive environment and personal circumstances. Therefore, managers factored WFH challenges into a common productivity variation for most of 2020. In the new normal, ABW-based design of office spaces is influenced by the newly acquired confidence to use digital business tools to work in different settings.

Challenges in managing productivity and well-being of digitized workspaces

Learning from the lessons of flexible working arrangements during the COVID-19 lockdown will help managers and workers find mutually suitable solutions. For example, there has been an increase in reported psychological stress and divorce filings (Commonwealth Media Release, 2020). This phenomenon could be primarily caused by the increased pressure from juggling work and childminding, homeschooling, and the concerns over health and socioeconomic uncertainties. On the other hand, even after the social distancing restrictions were eased, some people preferred to continue WFH to benefit from the comfort and privacy of the home office and still use the office space to connect and collaborate with co-workers and clients. Hence, the "new normal" post-pandemic for flexible work should incorporate effective use of technology and smart offices, combining WFH, ABW, and physical and digitized workspaces effectively to promote productivity and well-being. The challenge is how to find the right combination and manage work–life balance through effective implementation of technologies for smart offices and collaborative tools.

The first challenge is managing based on trust, which means that workers can decide the place and time to perform tasks and achieve outcomes based on their assigned role and take the responsibility to manage their leave. The notion of "leader as a coach" (Ibarra, H., Scoular, A., 2019), which is becoming more widely adopted in large organizations, promotes the concept of shared decision-making when it comes to managing the nature of work if the job is completed and achieving the outcomes.

One of the critical ingredients for leading a productive team is to focus on the team's dynamics instead of the mechanics in leading high-performing teams. For example, suppose a team shares a vision and purpose and agrees on the required performance and deadlines. In that case, everyone should be trusted to have the flexibility to manage the work and be accountable for the delivery quality and timeline. Project and organization managers can adopt many existing project management and collaboration functionalities to help lead teams and work. Therefore, it is crucial for business managers and project leaders to continually learn the latest tools and tailor them to their team's dynamics and mechanics.

The second challenge is promoting a distributed work–life balance to maintain productivity and well-being. Workers need to understand that they need to take breaks and look after themselves. If trust is established in performing and achieving the tasks within the required timeline, each person should propose the best opportunities for taking leave. The manager's role should be that of a coach, seeing the big picture and helping to synergize individual plans and ensure that the common goal is achieved. Strategies like job sharing, staggered start-finish, travel while working, compressed week, and time-in-lieu should be explored to find the right balance for the individuals and the team. Managers may adopt cloud-based file sharing, asynchronous chats, and online meetings to support flexible work arrangements that would work for the team's work–life balance. The most glaring risk of digitized workspaces is the need for observing availability so that people can be fully "signed-off" and "away" from work and not "on-call."

The role of managers as coaches is crucial to ensure staff are not at overcapacity and to promote flexible work arrangements. Home and parenting duties should no longer be associated with a particular gender, and likewise, workers with school-age children should not be disadvantaged. Moreover, people should not feel pressured to work beyond capacity over a prolonged period, making their productivity and well-being unsustainable. In short, it is time to move away from a traditional 9–5 presence-based workplace and embrace a blended approach that is more inclusive and better for the environment and people. AI is now embedded in calendar tools such as Microsoft Outlook to make suggestions for breaks and focus work by blocking times and automatically suggesting people, places, and documents for meetings, socializing, and exercise.

The third and most emerging challenge is using AI and intelligent systems for automation and augmenting work. Smart offices that use embedded intelligent systems to improve IEQ and support data-driven decisions and productivity tools will need to be managed properly to enhance trust. People will become wary when data is appropriately misused, privacy is at risk, or when autonomous decisions and analysis are not accurate, reliable, or explainable. Moreover, the rise of generative AI models enable machines to create content, including writing paragraphs, visualizing information into graphs, and synthesizing documents into tables, summaries, and other creative forms, like scripts and PowerPoint notes. Therefore, the key challenge is to establish a trusted use of AI as collaborative assistants to support human intelligence and responsibly using the AI-generated content.

To promote "trust-by-design," business implementation of AI should involve all stakeholders from the beginning while considering the strategy and policy within the institutions and practices to overcome anxiety and understand their preferred use of technologies. To embrace AI's benefits and fully reimagine the future of work and decision-making, a comprehensive synthesis of the complementarity of humans and AI in organizational processes, including decision-making, will help foster a deeper understanding of how AI can help to augment, not replace, human contributions. Next-generation managers and leaders must consider AI's performance and impact on economic productivity to weigh the trade-offs of various policy approaches for AI adoption in businesses. The future of work and professions will shift due to AI advancements, and there will always be a requirement to apply humanistic characteristics. Tech will continue dominating the AI-dominated digital economy, driving an industrial revolution and the technological disruptions that shape the behavior of the global society toward a new way of work, productivity, and digitalized workspaces.

Conclusion

Technology advancement creates new opportunities to transform work, promoting productivity and well-being. Smart offices and AI-enabled intelligent systems will challenge the traditional way of working and require managers to shift their thinking for embracing technologies in a responsible and ethical manner. We are still in the process of solving the gaps in technology use, and we need to rise and get better at it by transforming the people, infrastructure, organizational process, and governance of cyber-physical systems toward the future of productivity based on digitalized workspaces and intelligent systems. Our environment will continuously become smarter, increasingly embedded with intelligent sensing and real-time AI computation. Hence, people must harness it to improve work–life balance and quality of life. People's key concerns with AI are the future of work and jobs lost due to automation. These concerns are often inflated due to a lack of understanding or bloated expectations from AI and the lack of trust in these systems and the use of personal data. Security and privacy issues are becoming more prevalent due to the rapid growth of technology, business/organizational transformation, and increasing dependency on the digitalized workspace interconnected with embedded AI. Everyone has a role in embracing tech, such as AI, for the future of work. Next-generation applications increasingly need to consider long-term impacts through multi-perspectives and strategic themes. Tech and AI maturity must start with lifelong learning, transformational education, and skills for community awareness, human resources, tech literacy and competency, and tech development leadership. The capstone of tech maturity focuses on community impact, including responsible development, deployment, and scaling of AI innovations that maintain the sovereignty of human intellectual capacity and prepare the next generation of workers that can work collaboratively with AI within the digitalized workplace. Flexible work arrangements and tech-enabled, smarter ways of working should be the key themes to enhance our future productivity and well-being at work.

A "high-performance" checklist for technology is provided here:

Principle	*Description*
SECURITY and PRIVACY	• Secure, privacy-preserving use of big data, which needs a digital management system to ensure ethical and responsible automation works for organizations.
PRODUCTIVITY	• Strategic allocation of tasks to AI and have more time for creative tasks by workers.
DIGITALIZATION: AI and INTELLIGENT SENSING	• Utilization and optimization of data and resources' benefits for improving productivity and decision-making. • AI-enabled smart offices and intelligent systems to promote sustainability and benefits of work.
WORK–LIFE BALANCE (ENABLING WORK ELSEWHERE)	• Seamless tech and applications to allow hybrid, fully virtual and face-to-face collaboration. • Online presence through a website and social media. • Flexible work through integration of smart offices and digitalized work for accomplishing life tasks, from day-to-day to the most complex tasks.

References

Commonwealth Media Release. (2020). *Family Court of Australia and Federal Circuit Court of Australia launch COVID-19 list to deal with urgent parenting disputes*. Retrieved June 26, 2020, from http://www.familycourt.gov.au/wps/wcm/connect/fcoaweb/about/news/mr260420

Ibarra, H., & Scoular, A. (2019). The leader as coach. *Harvard Business Review*. Retrieved June 26, 2020, from https://hbr.org/2019/11/the-leader-as-coach

Inverardi, P. (2019). The European perspective on responsible computing. *Communications of the ACM*, 62(4), 64. https//doi.org/10.1145/3311783

LeCun, Y., Bengio, Y., & Hinton, G. (2015). Deep learning. *Nature*, *521*(7553), 436.

Lee, K. (2019). *AI superpowers*. https://aisuperpowers.com/

Meta5. (2020). *The post-COVID-19 workspace: What will it look like, and how can companies make it a success?* Retrieved June 26, 2020, from https://www.meta5group.com/the-post-covid-19-workspace-what-will-it-look-like-and-how-can-companies-make-it-a-success

SHE POE dataset. (2023). *Sustainable and healthy environments post-occupancy evaluation dataset*. SHE Lab (not published).

Tjondronegoro, D. (2019). *The next AI superpower: Why Australia's regional positioning and global outlook are important to the future of industry*. Regional Outlook Paper No. 63, 2019. Griffith University Publication. Working paper. https://www.griffith.edu.au/__data/assets/pdf_file/0024/912651/RO63-Tjondronegoro-web.pdf

Tjondronegoro, D., Yuwono, E., Richards, B., Green, D., & Hatakka, S. (2022). Responsible AI implementation: A human-centered framework for accelerating the innovation process. arXiv preprint arXiv:2209.07076. https://arxiv.org/pdf/2209.07076

PART II

Human factors

DOI: 10.1201/9781003328728-12
This chapter has been made available under a CC-BY-NC-ND 4.0 license.

11
GENDER AND AGE

Fan Zhang and Maryam Khoshbakht

To create a work environment that appeals to both genders and all generations in the workforce, organisations must embrace flexible set-ups rather than a one-size-fits-all approach.

– *Authors*

Introduction

The physical environments have a direct impact on office workers, as they spend most of their time inside buildings. Physical environmental factors such as ergonomics, noise, air quality, temperature, lighting, colours, plants, and interior plans are known to influence overall satisfaction, work performance, and occupant health (Candido et al., 2021; Zhang et al., 2019; Wang et al., 2021). However, gender and age differences in workplace environment perceptions and preferences have not yet been adequately documented. Previous research has shown that demographic factors have an impact on how people of all ages and genders perceive workplace environments. In fact, young and old and men and women are as different in their professional lives as in their personal lives. These distinctions have an impact on how successful businesses are, and a desirable and satisfying work environment helps retain talent and lower costs associated with turnover, worker's compensation, and medical claims.

There has been an on-going discussion for equality in the workplace for many decades. From the lens of workspace design, it is crucial that the building design is "inclusive" to embed responsiveness to diversity and promote equitable mental well-being, social cohesion, and enjoyment. In this process, it is essential to consider both workers' different demographic needs and preferences to achieve employee satisfaction and create productive and healthy workplace environments. It is equally important to consider differences in terms of space design and performance and address the needs of a gender diverse and aging workforce. The pandemic and forced work from home (WFH) arrangements during lockdowns have changed the way people work and the way organizations operate. Although limited in numbers, previous studies on the effect of WFH orders on different genders and age groups have revealed that WFH can be both a blessing and a curse (Krivkovich et al., 2022). Examining what WFH has meant for different gender and age groups and figuring out how to get the most out of it are essential, given that the degree of WFH is predicted to be significantly higher than it was before the pandemic (The Productivity Commission,

DOI: 10.1201/9781003328728-13

This chapter has been made available under a CC-BY-NC-ND 4.0 license.

2021). This chapter examines the existing research evidence focusing on differences in satisfaction, perceived productivity, and perceived health observed in the contemporary gender- and age-diverse workforce, including lessons during WFH orders, with the aim of providing a road map for organizations to achieve a high-performance workplace.

Gender and age differences in workplaces

In terms of individual differences, gender and age are the most studied demographical factors. In workplace research studies, demographical influences are mostly investigated by post-occupancy evaluation (POE) surveys using either or both subjective and objective methods. Previous studies generally reveal that demographical differences in the workforce such as gender and age significantly affect how workers perceive and evaluate their physical working environment (Haynes, 2011; Rothe et al., 2012; Kim et al., 2013). Next, we will discuss how gender and age mediate the impacts of physical workplaces on occupant satisfaction, perceived productivity, and health.

Occupant satisfaction

Interior design

Interior design is the comprehensive, professional activity of addressing, safeguarding, and meeting human needs in interior spaces. It combines method and strategy, a mandate for well-being, safety, and health, with well-informed judgements regarding style and aesthetics (IIDA, n.d.). Layout, furniture, plants, materials and coating, coverings, colours, finishes, and other elements are included. When it comes to our emotional state and how it affects our satisfaction in work environments, interior design can have a significant impact (Candido et al., 2016). Perceptions of interior design may vary between gender and age groups. Khoshbakht et al. (2021) discovered that while satisfaction was similar for both men and women in private offices and offices shared by no more than four co-workers, women felt less satisfied than men in large, open-plan offices shared by five or more people. Men view brightly coloured interiors more favourably than women do (Yildirim et al., 2011). Men tend to be noticeably more satisfied with concentration spaces, how their workstyle is supported by office layout, and their ability to engage in physical activity, according to POE surveys that Marzban et al. (2021) conducted across five open-plan offices. Contrarily, women valued access to nature more than men did (see Figure 11.1).

It seems that various generations have diverse tastes in workplace design. According to Pullen (2014), there are notable differences in how different age groups view flexible workplaces with no designated spaces versus private offices. Younger employees (those under 31) preferred flexible offices over private offices, and as respondents became older, their perceptions of flexible workplaces seemed to become more negative. Rasila and Rothe (2012) investigated Generation Y's (or millennials, born 1980–1994) perceptions of privacy, density and crowding, loss of concentration, social situations, low efficiency and increased workload, and environmental conditions in open-plan offices and reported that although they recognized the drawbacks of open-plan layouts, they saw them as a fair trade-off for the benefits of having interesting things going on around them and being able to sit next to their friends. Similarly, Marzban et al. (2021) reported that when compared to Generation Y, Generation X (born 1965–1979) seemed to be more content with workplaces that provide people with zones for concentrated work, connection to the outdoor environment, and the capacity to be physically active. The youngest respondents born between 1995 and 2012 (Generation Z) displayed higher satisfaction in all aforementioned categories than Generations X and Y.

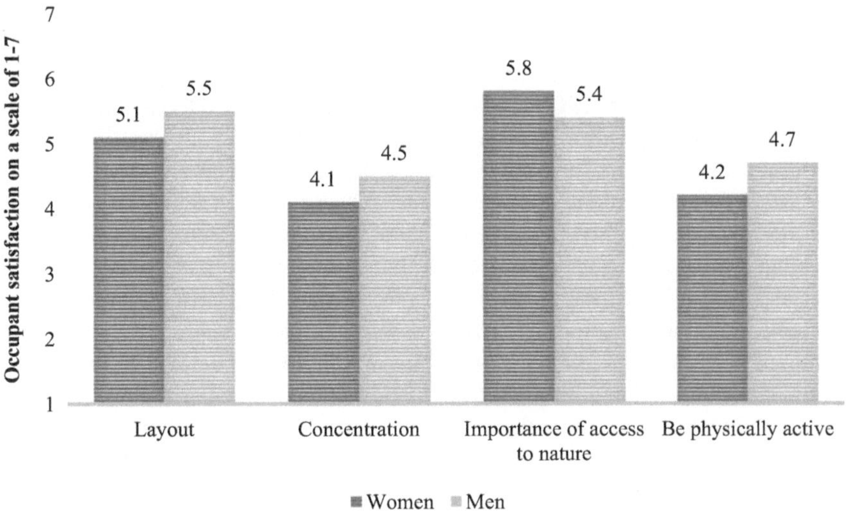

Figure 11.1 Comparison of occupant satisfaction of different genders, redrawn from Marzban et al. (2021).

Rothe et al. (2012) discovered both similarities and differences in the preferences of different age groups in the workplace. Preferences in personal services, restaurant offerings, and collaboration spaces showed significant differences between age groups, whereas privacy, concentration, and the virtual environment did not (Rothe et al., 2012). According to research by Joy and Haynes (2011), younger generations of office workers favoured informal meeting spaces to support knowledge work as opposed to their older counterparts, who preferred formal meeting spaces for this type of work. All generations recognize the advantages of being close to one another, or co-presence, in knowledge transfer and the facilitation of tacit knowledge through "creative eavesdropping" (Haynes, 2011), and there have been no findings of generational differences in team-based working environments (Appel-Meulenbroek, 2010).

To create workplaces that can accommodate the needs of people with different genders and ages, organizations and architects should adhere to the *universal design* principles. If the workplace is designed well, it can help increase the employment participation of all walks of life. This topic is discussed in detail in Chapter 2.

Indoor environmental quality (IEQ)

The term "Indoor Environmental Quality" (IEQ) refers to the quality of an indoor space, and it depends on a number of variables (see Chapters 4–9 for more details on IEQ). There have been research interests in how IEQ affects office workers' overall satisfaction for a long time (e.g., Kim et al., 2013; Bae et al., 2020). Building occupants respond to and prefer IEQ conditions differently, and numerous researchers have previously tried to categorize these preferences based on demographic differences (e.g., Indraganti & Humphreys, 2021).

According to Kim et al.'s (2013) analysis of the POE survey database, which included over 38,000 satisfaction votes gathered by the University of California, Berkeley, women consistently rated their satisfaction with all surveyed IEQ parameters – including temperature, IAQ (indoor air quality), amount of light, visual comfort, noise level, sound privacy, building cleanliness, workspace cleanliness, and building maintenance – lower than that of their male counterparts. Women were more likely than men, regardless of age or job characteristics, to express dissatisfaction with IEQ, particularly with thermal, IAQ, and sound issues. These findings suggest that women may be more sensitive to IEQ factors, particularly those related to heating, ventilation, and air-conditioning (HVAC) systems.

Gender differences in thermal comfort is one of the most studied and debated topics in the workplace, known as the "battle of the thermostat" (Chang & Kajackaite, 2019). A plethora of studies have revealed that women perceive the same thermal environment as being cooler than men (Karjalainen, 2012; Zhang & de Dear, 2019; Indraganti & Humphreys, 2021). According to Parkinson et al. (2021), regardless of the season, women are less satisfied with office temperatures. The conventional justifications in thermal comfort literature claim that differences in thermoregulation and thermal perception are caused by morphological differences between genders, such as larger surface-to-volume ratios, different body compositions, and lower metabolic rates in women, which invariably attribute the causes of issues to women rather than the excessively low thermostat setpoint temperature in workplaces. Although this may be true, it is the current air-conditioning practice – widespread overcooling in offices – and lack of individual control that has led to the thermal dissatisfaction of women, so the space fit-out and cooling approach need to move away from this conservative, old-fashioned, "average male wearing suits"–centric approach. To improve this, workplaces need to expand the opportunities for people to find spaces that suit their thermal preferences (see Chapter 1 – Interior Design), to use personal control systems, and to adjust their clothing to adapt to their surroundings (see Chapter 6 – Thermal Comfort).

Prior studies also revealed intergenerational differences in terms of perceptions of IEQ. A nine-year longitudinal POE study (Bae et al., 2020) revealed that, in comparison to workers between 18 and 34 years old and above 55 years old, the medium age group (35–54 years old) was less satisfied with the majority of the IEQ factors. However, Jowkar et al. (2020) found no statistically significant difference between the thermal comfort of the various age groups. To be more inclusive, workplaces need to allow for adjustability of IEQ to suit different user needs (Noell-Waggoner, 2017). Rothe et al. (2012) provided evidence that being able to adjust the indoor climate is more important for older generations than for the younger groups.

Significant gender, age, and individual differences can be seen in the occupants' perceptions of and preferences for IEQ. As a result, there isn't a single indoor environmental control method that works for everyone. Individual control over the immediate working environment can be a useful tool for enhancing the IEQ satisfaction of employees (Kim et al., 2013). In addition to saving energy, implementing higher indoor temperatures in offices that adhere to international thermal comfort standards can enhance the comfort and satisfaction of female employees (Zhang et al., 2017). This environmental solution may help people of both genders experience greater comfort and satisfaction in their workspaces when used in conjunction with personal cooling systems, such as desk fans or cooling chairs, if additional cooling is required.

Perceived productivity

Despite numerous studies, there is little agreement regarding how workplace environments affect employees' productivity. Haynes et al. (2017) conducted a POE survey with 220 UAE office workers asking them to rate how different aspects of the office environment have affected their perceived productivity. The results show that although both genders viewed interaction (work interaction, social interaction, closeness to manager, proximity to colleagues and privacy) to have a favourable overall influence on their perceived productivity, women reported it to be more positive than men.

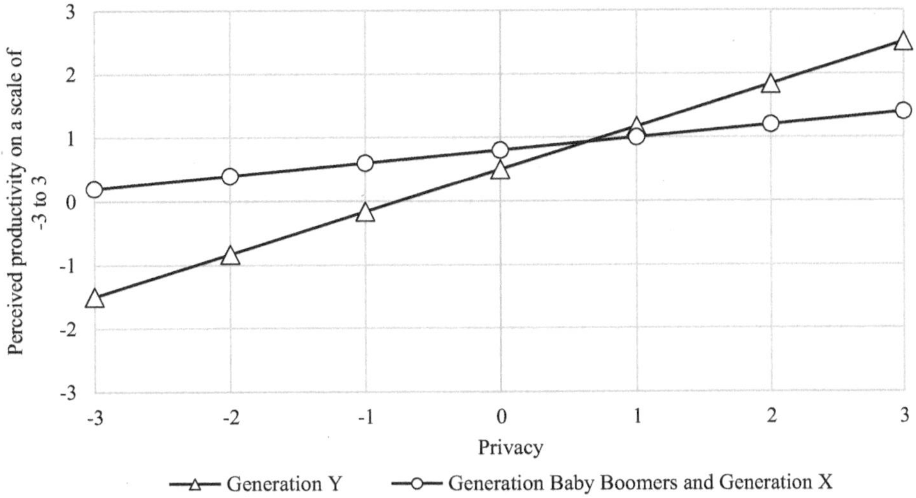

Figure 11.2 Comparison of the impact of privacy on perceived productivity between different generations, redrawn from (Yunus & Ernawati, 2018).

This result has contradicted the previous findings (Kim et al., 2013; Indraganti & Humphreys, 2021). Meanwhile, Haynes et al. (2017) stressed that women perceive distraction to have more negative effects on their productivity than their male counterparts, which is in line with previous studies.

There has been no consistent finding on younger and older generations' perceptions towards how their physical working environment affects their perceived productivity. In alignment with Rasila and Rothe (2012), Marzban et al. (2021) and Khoshbakht et al. (2021) reported that younger office workers under 30 years old had higher perceived productivity when sharing offices with multiple workers, while workers with 30 years or more preferred private offices to maximize their productivity. As illustrated in Figure 11.2, Yunus and Ernawati (2018) also revealed similar findings that the relationship between the capacity to regulate interruption or distraction (privacy) and productivity was stronger in the younger generation (Gen Y) than the older generation (baby boomers and Gen X). However, Haynes et al. (2017) reported completely opposite results, where older workers were more positive about the influence of the open-plan workplaces on their perceived productivity than younger workers. Although the precise link between the workplace environment and employee productivity is still debated, there is no doubt that happier building occupants generally translate into better outcomes for the companies. To make occupants happy and satisfied, organizations need to incorporate the needs of different genders and generations in workspace design.

Health

According to research, elements of office design that promote physical activity, privacy, the availability of daylight, and access to greenery have a favourable link with both physical and mental health (Colenberg et al., 2021). The term "sick building syndrome" (SBS) describes circumstances in which building occupants have acute health and comfort consequences that seem to be connected to time spent in a building, but no specific ailment or cause can be established (EPA, 1991).

In this regard, gender and age differences tend to have an influence on the frequency and intensity of SBS and other perceived physical and mental health issues.

By comparing physical health among gender groups, Kim et al. (2013) indicated that women were more likely than men to experience SBS symptoms such as tiredness; headaches; irritated or dry eyes, noses, and throats; as well as skin symptoms. In terms of mental health, women tend to have lower psychological well-being and more health issues than men (Gómez-Baya et al., 2018). Women who work in offices that are constructed with male ergonomics may experience injuries and discomfort due to the differences in morphologies.

According to Suzuki et al. (2021), younger workers are more likely to experience SBS symptoms than older workers, and Brasche et al. (2001) found that risks are higher for younger male workers. One study by Haghighat and Donnini (1999) found that while fatigue and sleepiness decreased with age, sore throat incidences increased. But what is evident is that the more climate control occupants have over their workstations, the fewer symptoms of SBS are reported (Marmot et al., 2006).

To support the health and well-being of different genders and generations, the design of furniture, technology, and equipment in offices needs to consider the physical ergonomics of all demographics, e.g., providing sit-stand desks, adjustable chairs, and foot support and footrests to accommodate different physical needs. Older generations' psycho-social requirements should also be accommodated. Providing individual control over workstations not only boosts IEQ satisfaction, but also reduces workers' SBS symptoms.

Work from home (WFH) influences

Although limited in numbers, there are already studies on how WFH affects different genders. WGEA found that gender equality was improved via flexible work (WGEA, 2021). Women particularly like the ability to work remotely. The reasons are beyond flexibility; they report encountering fewer microaggressions and have a stronger sense of psychological safety (Krivkovich et al., 2022). Employers who support flexible work arrangements for all workers and at all organizational levels can help staff members support better integration of personal and professional obligations and encourage higher career advancement for women. Additionally, flexible work schedules might encourage increased gender diversity in leadership positions (WGEA, 2021). Widespread flexible work schedules can also diversify their talent pipelines while reducing gendered occupational and industrial segregation.

Few studies have looked at the age differences in the perceptions of WFH. An online survey of 3,600 US workers across industries (The Conference Board, 2021) revealed that 43% of respondents questioned the need to return to offices after the pandemic. Across different generations, more millennials (55%) questioned the wisdom of returning to the workplace, compared to Gen X (45%) and baby boomers (36%). Millennials are also the generation that expressed the greatest concern towards mental health, stress, and burnout (70% of millennials versus 59% of Gen X and 42% of baby boomers). There have only been a few studies on the effect of WFH on productivity, and the findings are far from definitive. Morikawa (2022) compared studies of Etheridge et al. (2020), Barrero et al. (2021), and Morikawa (2020), which were all based on self-perceived WFH productivity. The two former studies both reported equal or higher productivity while WFH, whereas the latter one reported reduced WFH productivity. There is a lack of study on how WFH affects different genders' productivity. Xiao et al. (2021) found a link between WFH and poor physical health outcomes like increased musculoskeletal pain, weight gain, and exhaustion. More often than men, women reported having two or more new physical health problems. Although women prefer the option of flexible working, their experience has been harmed because they are more likely than men to experience mental stress while WFH.

Another drawback of WFH is the possibility that there will be favouritism towards those who work on-site, while those who work remotely will feel stigmatized for doing so (Cox, n.d.). Working mothers and millennials may be the groups most impacted by this. To avoid penalizing WFH staff, employers should evaluate employee performance based on the quality of the completed task rather than how long it takes them to complete it. Additionally, they must guarantee that WFH employees receive equal opportunities for promotion. Employers also should be more aware of and supportive of employees' mental health in remote and hybrid work environments.

Conclusion

It is essential to design workplace environments that cater to all types of preferences of workers from all walks of life with different work styles, needs, and preferences. To create a work environment that appeals to the needs of a diverse workforce, organizations must embrace flexible set-ups rather than a one-size-fits-all approach.

A "high-performance" checklist for diversity is provided here:

Principle	*Description*
OFFICE TYPES Avoid allocating space according to hierarchy and rank.	• Balancing the dual needs of egalitarian and hierarchical structures.
INDOOR ENVIRONMENTAL QUALITY Ensure a desirable indoor environment and provide individual control for different demographics.	• Workplaces must provide more opportunities for employees to find spaces that suit their thermal preferences. • Provide workers with individual control over their own thermal environment (van Hoof, 2008). • Designing for a diverse range of workers' psycho-social requirements in vision, hearing, physical ergonomics, and wayfinding (Haynes, 2011). • Providing furniture that can be adjusted to suit various physical needs from different demographics.
WORK FROM HOME Employers should ensure gender and age equality while WFH.	• Evaluating employee performance based on the quality of the completed task. • Equal opportunities for employee promotion. • Respecting the boundaries between work and personal time (WGEA, 2021). • Additional support for employees' mental health while WFH.

References

Appel-Meulenbroek, R. (2010). Knowledge sharing through co-presence: Added value of facilities. *Facilities*, *28*(3), 189–205.

Bae, S., Asojo, A. O., & Martin, C. S. (2020). Impact of occupants' demographics on indoor environmental quality satisfaction in the workplace. *Building Research & Information*, *48*(3), 301–315.

Barrero, J. M., Bloom, N., & Davis, S. J. (2021). Why working from home will stick. In *NBER Working Paper No. 28731*.

Brasche, S., Bullinger, M., Morfeld, M., Gebhardt, H. J., & Bischof, W. (2001). Why do women suffer from sick building syndrome more often than men? Subjective higher sensitivity versus objective causes. *Indoor Air*, *11*(4), 217–222.

Candido, C., Gocer, O., Marzban, S., Gocer, K., Thomas, L., Zhang, F., Gou, Z., Mackey, M., Engelen, L., & Tjondronegoro, D. (2021). Occupants' satisfaction and perceived productivity in open-plan offices designed to support activity-based working: Findings from different industry sectors. *Journal of Corporate Real Estate*, *23*(2), 106–129.

Candido, C., Zhang, J., Kim, J., de Dear, R., Thomas, L., Strapasson, P., & Joko, C. (2016). Impact of workspace layout on occupant satisfaction, perceived health and productivity. In F. Nicol, S. Roaf, L. Brotas, & M. A. Humphreys (Eds.), *Proceedings – 9th International Windsor Conference 2016: Making Comfort Relevant* (pp. 1214–1225). NCEUB.

Chang, T. Y., & Kajackaite, A. (2019). Battle for the thermostat: Gender and the effect of temperature on cognitive performance. *PLoS One*, *14*(5), e0216362.

Colenberg, S., Jylhä, T., & Arkesteijn, M. (2021). The relationship between interior office space and employee health and well-being–a literature review. *Building Research and Information*, *49*(3), 352–366.

The Conference Board. (2021, July). *Survey: Amid higher productivity, 43 percent of US workers question need to return to workplace*. Retrieved December 4, 2022, from https://www.conference-board.org/press/Return-to-Work-Survey-June2021

Cox, J. (n.d.). *More than just #FOMO: How hybrid workplace models exacerbate gender inequality*. Forbes. Retrieved December 4, 2022, from www.forbes.com/sites/josiecox/2021/06/04/more-than-just-fomo-how-hybrid-workplace-models-exacerbate-gender-inequality/?sh=14dcfbc35d1a.

Environmental Protection Agency. (1991). *Indoor air facts no. 4 sick building syndrome*. United States Environmental Protection Agency.

Etheridge, B., Tang, L., & Wang, Y. (2020). Worker productivity during lockdown and working from home: Evidence from self-reports. *Covid Economics*, *52*, 118–151.

Gómez-Baya, D., Lucia-Casademunt, A. M., & Salinas-Pérez, J. A. (2018). Gender differences in psychological well-being and health problems among European health professionals: Analysis of psychological basic needs and job satisfaction. *International Journal of Environmental Research and Public Health*, *15*(7), 1474.

Haghighat, F., & Donnini, G. (1999). Impact of psycho-social factors on perception of the indoor air environment studies in 12 office buildings. *Building and Environment*, *34*(4), 479–503.

Haynes, B., Suckley, L., & Nunnington, N. (2017). Workplace productivity and office type: An evaluation of office occupier differences based on age and gender. *Journal of Corporate Real Estate*, *19*(2), 111–138.

Haynes, B. P. (2011). The impact of generational differences on the workplace. *Journal of Corporate Real Estate*, *13*(2), 98–108.

IIDA. (n.d.). *What is interior design?* Retrieved November 30, 2022, from https://iida.org/about/what-is-interior-design

Indraganti, M., & Humphreys, M. A. (2021). A comparative study of gender differences in thermal comfort and environmental satisfaction in air-conditioned offices in Qatar, India, and Japan. *Building and Environment*, *206*, 108297.

Jowkar, M., Rijal, H. B., Montazami, A., Brusey, J., & Temeljotov-Salaj, A. (2020). The influence of acclimatization, age and gender-related differences on thermal perception in university buildings: Case studies in Scotland and England. *Building and Environment*, *179*, 106933.

Joy, A., & Haynes, B. P. (2011). Office design for the multi-generational knowledge workforce. *Journal of Corporate Real Estate*, *13*(4), 216–232.

Karjalainen, S. (2012). Thermal comfort and gender: A literature review. *Indoor Air*, *22*(2), 96–109.

Khoshbakht, M., Baird, G., & Rasheed, E. O. (2021). The influence of work group size and space sharing on the perceived productivity, overall comfort and health of occupants in commercial and academic buildings. *Indoor and Built Environment*, *30*(5), 692–710.

Kim, J., de Dear, R., Cândido, C., Zhang, H., & Arens, E. (2013). Gender differences in office occupant perception of indoor environmental quality (IEQ). *Building and Environment*, *70*, 245–256.

Krivkovich, A., Yee, L., Liu, W., Rambachan, I., Robinson, N., Nguyen, H., & Williams, M. (2022). *Women in the workplace 2022*. Retrieved November 30, 2022, from https://www.mckinsey.com/featured-insights/diversity-and-inclusion/women-in-the-workplace

Marmot, A. F., Eley, J., Stafford, M., Stansfeld, S. A., Warwick, E., & Marmot, M. G. (2006). Building health: An epidemiological study of "sick building syndrome" in the Whitehall II study. *Occupational and environmental medicine*, *63*(4), 283–289.

Marzban, S., Candido, C., & Gocer, O. (2021). Satisfaction with open plan offices: Personality, age and gender as human factors. In *The proceedings of the 20th EuroFM research symposium 2021*. European Facility Management Network, online conference.

Morikawa, M. (2020). Productivity of working from home during the COVID-19 pandemic: Evidence from an employee survey. *Covid Economics*, *49*, 123–147.

Morikawa, M. (2022). *Are you more productive working from home? This study looks for answers*. World Economic Forum. Retrieved November 30, 2022, from https://cepr.org/voxeu/columns/productivity-dynamics-working-home

Noell-Waggoner, E. (2017). Lighting and the elderly. In R. Karlicek, C. C. Sun, G. Zissis, & R. Ma (Eds.), *Handbook of advanced lighting technology* (pp. 847–863). Springer International Publishing.

Parkinson, T., Schiavon, S., de Dear, R., & Brager, G. (2021). Overcooling of offices reveals gender inequity in thermal comfort. *Scientific Reports*, *11*(1), 23684.

The Productivity Commission. (2021). *Working from home: Research paper*. Retrieved December 4, 2022, from https://www.pc.gov.au/research/completed/working-from-home/working-from-home.pdf

Pullen. (2014, September 4). Age, office type, job satisfaction and performance. *Work and Place*, 18–22. Retrieved December 4, 2022, from https://workandplace.com/amp/age-office-type-job-satisfaction-and-performance/

Rasila, H., & Rothe, P. (2012). A problem is a problem is a benefit? Generation Y perceptions of open-plan offices. *Property Management*, *30*(4), 362–375.

Rothe, P., Lindholm, A., Hyvönen, A., & Nenonen, S. (2012). Work environment preferencesdoes age make a difference? *Facilities*, *30*(1), 78–95.

Suzuki, N., Nakayama, Y., Nakaoka, H., Takaguchi, K., Tsumura, K., Hanazato, M., Hayashi, T., & Mori, C. (2021). Risk factors for the onset of sick building syndrome: A cross-sectional survey of housing and health in Japan. *Building and Environment*, *202*(2021), 107976.

van Hoof, J. (2008). Forty years of Fanger's model of thermal comfort: Comfort for all? *Indoor Air*, *18*(3), 182–201.

Wang, C., Zhang, F., Wang, J., Doyle, J. K., Hancock, P. A., Mak, C. M., & Liu, S. (2021, April 15). How indoor environment quality affects occupants' cognitive functions: A systematic review. *Building and Environment*, *193*, 107647.

Workplace Gender Equality Agency. (2021, December 8). *Flexible work post-COVID*. Retrieved December 4, 2022, from https://www.wgea.gov.au/publications/flexible-work-post-covid

Xiao, Y., Becerik-Gerber, B., Lucas, G., & Roll, S. C. (2021). Impacts of working from home during COVID-19 pandemic on physical and mental well-being of office workstation users. *Journal of Occupational and Environmental Medicine*, *63*(3), 181–190.

Yildirim, K., Hidayetoglu, M. L., & Capanoglu, A. (2011). Effects of interior colors on mood and preference: Comparisons of two living rooms. *Perceptual and Motor Skills*, *112*(2), 509–524.

Yunus, E. N., & Ernawati, E. (2018). Productivity paradox? The impact of office redesign on employee productivity. *International Journal of Productivity and Performance Management*, *67*(9), 1918–1939.

Zhang, F., & de Dear, R. (2019). Impacts of demographic, contextual and interaction effects on thermal sensation – Evidence from a global database. *Building and Environment*, *162*, 106286.

Zhang, F., de Dear, R., & Hancock, P. (2019, February 15). Effects of moderate thermal environments on cognitive performance: A multidisciplinary review. *Applied Energy*, *236*, 760–777.

Zhang, F., Haddad, S., Nakisa, B., Rastgoo, M. N., Candido, C., Tjondronegoro, D., & de Dear, R. (2017). The effects of higher temperature setpoints during summer on office workers' cognitive load and thermal comfort. *Building and Environment*, *123*, 176–188.

12
PERSONALITY

Samin Marzban and Christhina Candido

Our personality makes us unique and defines our preferences, choices, needs and expectations from a physical environment and influences how we perceive it.

– *Authors*

Introduction

Personality is described as 'patterns of emotion, thought and behaviour that represent stable and lasting differences between individuals' and form and individuals' distinctive character (Perkins, 2016). Our personality makes us unique and defines our preferences, choices, needs and expectations from a physical environment and influences how we perceive it. In the workplace research, personality is known to affect people's perception of their work environment and either boost or hinder workers' productivity, health and satisfaction. While providing a healthy and productivity-promoting workplace is a complicated task on its own, the fact that various individual variables affect people's perception of the environment further adds to this complication.

Although the research evidence sound promising to accentuate the importance of personality as an indicator for user satisfaction, productivity, and health in the workplace, not much has been done in terms of design within the industry. This seems problematic considering the crucial role of workers' overall satisfaction on their productivity, the acknowledged synergy between people and workplace in the production of high-quality work and the dependability of existence of businesses on people's productivity (Needle & Mallia, 2021). In addition, with little knowledge and awareness around the strength of each personality trait, there has been a tendency to praise specific personality traits such as extroversion. For example, the term 'Extrovert Ideal' by Susan Cain (2013) describes the dominant cultural preference for extroversion, a phenomenon so widespread that most people are unaware of it. Thus, businesses favour the personality traits such as extraversion in their organizations and leadership, and leaders make decisions impacting office environments. In this context, the strength of other personality traits, such as introversion or agreeableness, is devaluated, and the fact that granting people with the autonomy and flexibility to choose between different work options can help them thrive has been underrated.

Soon after the appearance of COVID-19 in 2020, the isolation and obligatory work from home (WFH) arrangement brought productivity and mental/physical health discussions to the surface

DOI: 10.1201/9781003328728-14
This chapter has been made available under a CC-BY-NC-ND 4.0 license.

within the industry. The fact that getting accustomed to the new situation was easier for people with certain personality traits such as introversion and agreeableness and more problematic for people with other personality traits such as extraversion and neuroticism raised concerns about people's satisfaction and health in WFH arrangements and how it might affect their productivity and business's profit as a consequence. However, these discussions faded quickly as businesses started to push people back to the office just before they realized that flexible working is now hardwired in workers' minds and that the pandemic has changed the synergy between people, organizations, and workplaces forever.

This chapter commences by briefly looking at the definition of personality and the well-respected method of Big Five to measure personality traits in the workplace research. It continues by digging into the relationship between five personality traits and workers' satisfaction, perceived productivity and health in the workplace. This chapter also looks at how individuals with different needs and preferences might perceive the environment differently based on their personality traits. Finally, drawing upon the strands of research into personality and the workplace, this chapter makes a case for how WFH arrangements after the onset of the COVID-19 pandemic has highlighted the need for granting workers with the flexibility and autonomy to choose how, where and when they want to work.

Personality and how to measure it

As personality can be seen as an underlying behavioural and emotional description of how an individual feels, acts and performs in the workplace (or any other environment), understanding various traits can significantly add to workers' productivity, therefore increasing the business's profits. Researchers have incorporated various methods, such as the Thematic Apperception Test (TAT), Millon Clinical Multiaxial Inventory (MCMI), NEO Personality Inventory (NEO-PI), and Big Five, to measure and investigate personality traits. Some of these methods have oversimplified the complex nature of the human being by trying to break people into types; however, psychological approaches suggest personality traits as a more competent approach. Among all psychological methods, the Big Five personality traits are by far the most research-backed, scientifically based model that is well acknowledged by workplace researchers as a method to understand the relationship between workers' personalities and workplace design. Each trait in this model occurs along a spectrum from low to high, and traits are independent of one another, making for an infinite composition of human personalities in individuals. This model comprises five factors of neuroticism, extroversion, openness to experience, agreeableness and conscientiousness (John & Srivastava, 1999).

In general, as described by Goldberg (1990), high scores of neuroticism are linked with negative emotions, and it may indicate a higher propensity toward burnout, as those individuals might have a tougher time managing their emotions. On the other side of the neuroticism scale, high emotional stability might be linked to higher job satisfaction, better handling of workplace demands and lower stress levels (Garbarino et al., 2014; Hlatywayo et al., 2013). Extraversion is associated with impulsiveness and socializing, and extroverts are more comfortable with taking charge of situations (Judge et al., 1997; Laney, 2002; Luong et al., 2022). People with high levels of openness are more curious and adaptable with changes in the environment, and they are eager to learn and experience new things (Matzler et al., 2008). High levels of agreeableness are linked with trustworthiness and a higher tendency to follow rules. People who are more agreeable are kind, and their behaviour is often counterproductive within the workplace environment (Goldberg, 1990). Finally, conscientiousness is associated with vigilance, thoughtfulness and goal-directed behaviours.

Personality was once thought to be stable in a person's lifespan, but evidence is accumulating that personality can change in adulthood. For example, consumption of a specific drug is reported to permanently increase the openness traits in people (Erritzoe et al., 2019), or several studies have reported that traumatic events lead to persisting personality change characterized by increased neuroticism (Mathews et al., 2008; Chung et al., 2006; Hyer et al., 1994). Personality also seems to change, slowly but naturally, over the course of a person's life. As people age, they become more extroverted, less neurotic, more agreeable and more conscientious. A study also found that emotional stability is the primary trait domain showing changes as a result of therapy, followed by extraversion (Roberts et al., 2017).

Satisfaction, productivity and health

Personality has been linked to a wide range of life outcomes, including satisfaction, health and performance (Gerlitz & Hülsbeck, 2023). Although much research has been done on many of these domains, the real relationship between personality and perception of the environment is under-investigated. In the context of workplace design, the associations between the Big Five personality trait (Goldberg, 1993) variables (neuroticism, extraversion, openness, agreeableness and conscientiousness) and satisfaction, productivity and health variables, such as IEQ (Indoor Environmental Quality), interior design, job performance and mental and physical health, are well investigated. However, contradictory results have been reported to date. Some studies (Seddigh et al., 2016; Sugino et al., 2019) reported high correlation between personality traits and various aspects of the workplaces, while others (Hartog et al., 2018; Marzban et al., 2021) showed that differences between personalities do not appear to have a high impact on user satisfaction, productivity or health. Hence, there sounds to be sufficient evidence to highlight the relationship between personality and the workplace; however, the extent and attributes of this relationship is unclear and needs to be further investigated.

Satisfaction

Satisfaction is used as a broad term in the area of workplace research. Studies have looked at various aspects of satisfaction related to physical environment, including IEQ, interior design and privacy. Satisfaction with the physical environment and personality traits are reported to have significant associations, with workers with higher levels of specific personality types such as extraversion, agreeableness and openness to experience to be in general more satisfied with the physical environment of their workplaces. However, key sources of dissatisfaction with the workplace are consistent for people with various personality traits. This means the general issues with workplaces, such as noise, distraction and insufficient spaces for concentration/collaboration/conversations, seem to dissatisfy all respondents with different personality traits (Marzban et al., 2021). In a study by Marzban et al. (2021), the three key sources of dissatisfaction related to the general layout of the workplace included lack of spaces assigned for concentration and insufficient meeting rooms and spaces for private conversations (Figure 12.1).

Among all personality traits, introversion-extraversion has received significant attention. As extroverts naturally have lower psychophysiological arousal (Geen, 1984) and lower reactivity to sensory stimulation compared to introverts (Stelmack, 1990), they perceive the physical environment differently. Several studies have indicated that introverts show higher levels of satisfaction and productivity under very low levels of background noise and distraction (Sugino et al., 2019), and they may be more critical about the interior layout, privacy and IEQ of their workplace

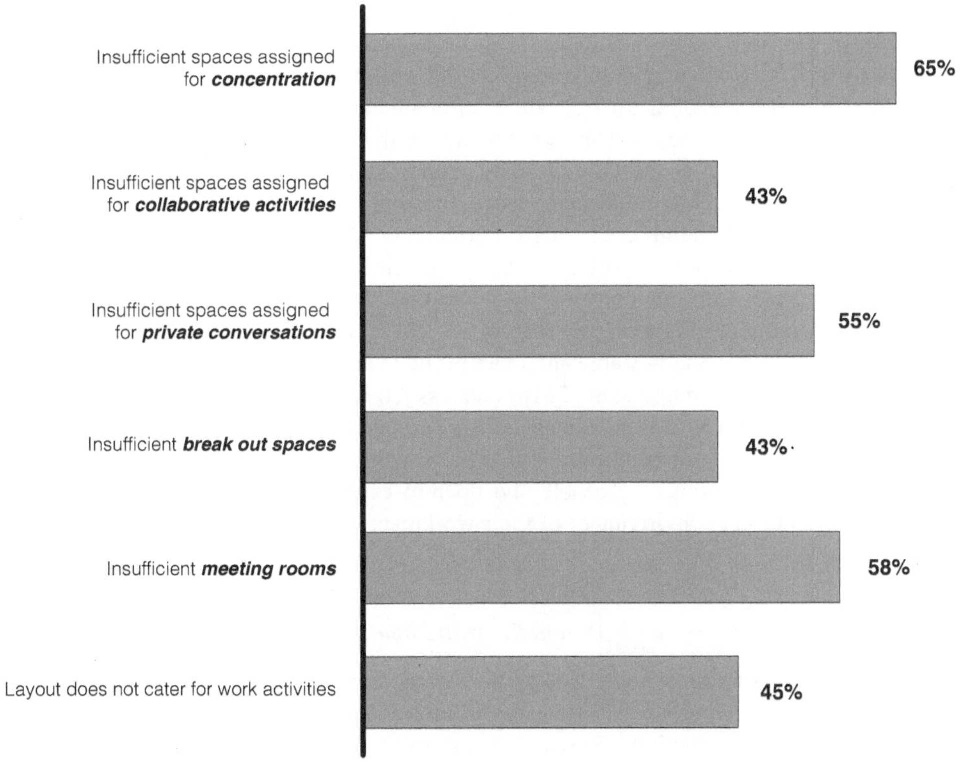

Figure 12.1 Key sources of dissatisfaction raised by respondents regarding office layout.
Source: Marzban et al., 2021

(Hartog et al., 2018). In contrast, extroverts prefer noisier environments to reach their optimal level of productivity (Belojevic et al., 2001; Dobbs et al., 2011; Oseland & Hodsman, 2018). They also benefit more from work settings such as open bench seating, as it is more beneficial for their happiness and memory focus (Lindberg et al., 2021). Interestingly, people with high levels of extroversion are likely to be stressed by insufficient environmental quality or to be more sensitive to environmental factors when under stress (Kallio et al., 2020).

Workers who are more open to new experiences are in general more satisfied with the physical characteristics of their work environment, as their curiosity is higher compared to other personality traits (Matzler et al., 2008). As expected, these workers prefer to meet in non-traditional spaces (e.g. bar or lounge room) (Oseland & Hodsman, 2018), and they also prefer a work environment which is adaptable (Hartog et al., 2018). Both positive and negative relationships between this personality trait and distraction are reported in open-plan settings. Higher levels of distraction in the office environment are reported by studies such as Seddigh et al. (2014), while negative correlations between openness to experience and distraction are reported by Sugino et al. (2019). People who are open to new experiences are imaginative and curious, which might be the reason for focusing on external stimuli and higher levels of distraction in open-plan settings.

People with high levels of agreeableness are sympathetic, warm and considerate, and they seek cooperation rather than competition (Liao & Chuang, 2004). Agreeable workers, similar to workers with high levels of openness, are more satisfied with the overall physical environment

(Reichherzer et al., 2022; Hartog et al., 2018) and the IEQ of their workplace. Agreeableness is also positively correlated with satisfaction with workspaces (whether fixed or flexible) and the general facilities/services available to workers in the workplace (Hartog et al., 2018). Agreeable workers show higher levels of distraction with environmental factors in open-plan settings (Sugino et al., 2019; Seddigh et al., 2016). This could be due to their tendency not to prioritize their own needs and less eagerness to assert themselves by expressing their needs (Seddigh et al., 2016).

Conscientiousness people are described as responsible and self-disciplined people who have higher job satisfaction (Seddigh et al., 2016; Furnham et al., 2009) and higher tendency to personalize the workplace (Wells & Thelen, 2002). It is remarkable that there are no defined relations reported between conscientiousness and user satisfaction with physical characteristics of the workplace (Hartog et al., 2018; Marzban et al., 2021). Finally, people with higher levels of neuroticism are less emotionally stable and more prone to anxiety and depression. These workers show higher distraction (Seddigh et al., 2016) and less job satisfaction.

In general people who have higher levels of life and job satisfaction have higher levels of satisfaction with the physical environment and IEQ in the work environment and vice versa (Cheung et al., 2022). As conscientious, agreeable and open-to-experiences people are in general more satisfied with the physical environment of their workplace, they might show higher job and life satisfaction too.

Productivity and health

Productivity as a measure of how efficiently a person can finish a work task is rated and measured with various terms, including job performance and career success, and it is related to terms such as creativity and creative productivity. Research has shown that personality traits can affect productivity, but the relationship between these two is complex.

Conscientiousness is known to have a positive relationship with productivity variables. Conscientious workers are more goal oriented and vigilant and have higher levels of job performance (Chiu & Chen, 2012) and intrinsic and extrinsic career success (Zakaria & Yusof, 2021). High openness or perseverance and passion might increase productivity levels in workers (Kawakubo & Arata, 2022), and higher levels of emotional stability, which indicates lower levels of neuroticism, are known as reasons for higher productivity and outstanding performance among workers (Kawakubo & Arata, 2022; Eshet & Harpaz, 2021). In addition, high extroversion is reported as a positive predictor of outstanding performance (Eshet & Harpaz, 2021), while lower extraversion is associated with excessive overtime work (Uchida et al., 2014). Agreeableness is known as a positive predictor of normative employees' performance (Eshet & Harpaz, 2021).

If we consider productivity as a variable related to the ability of a worker to concentrate on a work task, distraction plays a prominent role in it. The modern open-plan setting is more beneficial to memory focus for employees high in extroversion, while detrimental for those high in neuroticism (Lindberg et al., 2021). More emotionally stable and less neurotic workers reported lower distraction, while workers who are agreeable and open to experience showed higher levels of distraction as a result of the workplace's physical environment (Seddigh et al., 2016; Sugino et al., 2019). Negative correlations were also observed among extraversion or openness to experience and distraction.

Creativity and creative productivity as crucial measures specifically in creative industries are positively and negatively correlated with extraversion, agreeableness and negative emotionality, meaning that people who are more extroverted, more agreeable and less neurotic rate themselves higher in creativity (Marzban et al., 2021). Although only introverts tend to yearn for solitude to complete certain creative tasks, an open-plan office which is not designed well may indeed undermine creative productivity, not just among introverts but others as well (Needle & Mallia, 2021).

Regarding health, personality has been shown to affect exposure to stressors, influencing the nature and severity of stressor experiences (Bolger & Zuckerman, 1995); however, not much has been done in the context of the workplace. Extroversion was found to be positively correlated with stress, which suggests that more extroverted people are more likely to be more sensitive to environmental factors when under stress (Kallio et al., 2020). Introverts have lower levels of well-being compared to extroverts, and this may be because of their lack of person–environment fit (Merone & Whitehead, 2021).

For each personality trait, there are preferences and needs in terms of the physical environment of a workplace (Roskams & Haynes, 2020; Schweiker et al., 2016). A combination of design elements is reported to affect self-rated productivity and health (Poursafar et al., 2019). Each individual should have the flexibility and autonomy to set their needs and preferences for the task at hand. These preferences and needs might also differ for each work task.

Personality traits and work from home arrangements

The individuals with different personality traits played a distinct role in workplace adjustments to the COVID-19 pandemic, with some personality traits adapting to flexible working more easily (Kniffin et al., 2021; Gubler et al., 2021). People who tend towards introversion are often seen as fit candidates in the WFH setting, because they can thrive in quiet environments. But WFH can also limit the option for these workers to showcase their tremendous value and adversely affect their career success. Research showed introverted workers are significantly more likely to use words such as anxiety, fear and cautious when compared to more extroverted personalities (The Myers-Bridge Company, 2020). Whether the WFH arrangement has pushed introverted workers to their solitude more than ever is of concern, but it needs more research. Extroverts, on the other hand, might be more affected by WFH arrangements and social distancing policies, with higher concerns about finding outlets to socialize (The Myers-Bridge Company, 2020). The new work arrangements have sent many extroverts into total disarray, with more probability to use words around being confined and constrained (The Myers-Bridge Company, 2020). The advantage that being outgoing and talkative has brought to extroverts seems to have been lost in the WFH setting, and people with this personality type have been struggling with sustaining a community through WFH and social distancing.

Neuroticism is linked to negative emotions and anxiety; however, both positive and negative results are reported considering people with high levels of neuroticism in non-traditional work settings such as remote working. As one might expect, the deleterious effects of remote working on mental health are greater with higher levels of neuroticism, and less with higher levels of emotional stability (Wilmot et al., 2019). Emotionally stable workers are more capable of establishing good interpersonal relationships and capitalizing on positive emotions. However, people with high levels of neuroticism are also reported to have positive attitudes towards remote working (Clark et al., 2012), as they might find the management of their relationship more effortless (Michinov et al., 2022).

Conscientious personality trait is a two-edged sword giving the worker the personalization options they need in WFH arrangements but pressuring them with work responsibilities at the same time. These people are more inclined to develop well-being issues, but they are better applauded for their performance. Agreeableness and openness to experience appear to be positively related to remote working acceptability and employees' well-being in this work setting (Michinov et al.,

2022). Although agreeable people, due to higher levels of sympathy and trustfulness, are more inclined to work from the office rather than from home (Gavoille & Hazans, 2022), they also adjusted to the new work setting effortlessly and have shown the capability to communicate effectively in WFH arrangements. Openness to experience is positively associated with a higher productivity from home, as they are known for the curiosity and eagerness for new experiences.

When the COVID-19 pandemic hit the workplace, organizations worldwide rapidly created new working norms acknowledging that flexible work is no longer a temporary pandemic response but an enduring aspect of the new working world. Individuals with certain personality types adapted to the new work arrangements quicker than others and/or they enjoyed it more than other workers. However, if individuals are given the choice, flexibility and autonomy to choose how, when and where to work, they will adjust their work preferences based on their needs. An introvert might find one day per week at the office sufficient to build the social network for their career success, while an extrovert might find a four-day-per-week schedule well suited for their nature.

Conclusion

Several studies have looked at the relationships between personality traits and satisfaction, health and productivity in the workplace. Sufficient evidence suggests that a relationship does exist between these factors, with results agreeing or disagreeing on the positivity/negativity of this relationship. Studies also suggested that people's social behaviour, preferences, needs and performance might be predictable in the workplace to some extent. Having a deeper understanding of these aspects can help leaders create trust and cultivate a stronger workplace culture. From a workplace design perspective, creating a workplace that can cater to all individual needs is crucial. In addition, giving the workers the autonomy and flexibility to make the decision about how, where and when to work cannot be ignored specifically in the post-pandemic world.

A 'high-performance' checklist for diversity is provided here:

Principle	*Description*
PHYSICAL ENVIRONMENT	• Considering the needs and preferences of people with various personality traits in the workplace. • Considering zones with lower levels of noise and distraction for introverts, and zones with higher levels of background noise for extroverts. • Giving workers the option to adapt their work environment specifically for workers with high levels of openness to new experiences. • Considering non-traditional work settings, such as bar or lounge meetings, specifically for workers with high levels of openness to new experiences. • Granting workers the option to control and personalize their workplace specifically for conscientiousness workers.
AUTONOMY AND FLEXIBILITY	• Granting workers the autonomy and flexibility to make the decision about how, where and when they work. • Giving workers the opportunity to choose when and where they work from (office and elsewhere).

References

Belojevic, G., Slepcevic, V., & Jakovljevic, B. (2001). Mental performance in noise: The role of introversion. *Journal of Environmental Psychology*, *21*(2), 209–213.

Bolger, N., & Zuckerman, A. (1995). A framework for studying personality in the stress process. *Journal of Personality and Social Psychology*, *69*(5), 890.

Cain, S. (2013). *Quiet: The power of introverts in a world that can't stop talking*. Crown.

Cheung, T., Graham, L. T., & Schiavon, S. (2022). Impacts of life satisfaction, job satisfaction and the Big Five personality traits on satisfaction with the indoor environment. *Building and Environment*, *212*, 108783. https//doi.org/10.1016/j.buildenv.2022.108783

Chiu, K.-H., & Chen, T. (2012). Leadership as situational factor on personality-performance relationship: An empirical study of the Taiwan's office machinery sales force [Other Journal Article]. *International Journal of Business and Management Science*, *5*(1), 1–17. https://search.informit.org/doi/10.3316/informit.142153493743684

Chung, M. C., Berger, Z., Jones, R., & Rudd, H. (2006). Posttraumatic stress disorder and general health problems following myocardial infarction (Post-MI PTSD) among older patients: The role of personality. *International Journal of Geriatric Psychiatry*, *21*(12), 1163–1174. https://doi.org/10.1002/gps.1624

Clark, L. A., Karau, S. J., & Michalisin, M. D. (2012). Telecommuting attitudes and the 'Big Five' personality dimensions. *Journal of Management Policy and Practice*, *13*, 31–46.

Dobbs, S., Furnham, A., & McClelland, A. (2011). The effect of background music and noise on the cognitive test performance of introverts and extraverts. *Applied Cognitive Psychology*, *25*(2), 307–313.

Erritzoe, D., Smith, J., Fisher, P. M., Carhart-Harris, R., Frokjaer, V. G., & Knudsen, G. M. (2019). Recreational use of psychedelics is associated with elevated personality trait openness: Exploration of associations with brain serotonin markers. *Journal of Psychopharmacology*, *33*(9), 1068–1075. https://doi.org/10.1177/0269881119827891

Eshet, Y., & Harpaz, I. (2021). Personality traits' predictors of outstanding performance in the public sector. *Public Performance & Management Review*, *44*(6), 1367–1394. https://doi.org/10.1080/15309576.2021.1980064

Furnham, A., Eracleous, A., & Chamorro-Premuzic, T. (2009). Personality, motivation and job satisfaction: Hertzberg meets the Big Five. *Journal of Managerial Psychology*, *24*(8), 765–779.

Garbarino, S., Chiorri, C., & Magnavita, N. I. C. O. L. A. (2014). Personality traits of the Five-Factor Model are associated with work-related stress in special force police officers. *International Archives of Occupational and Environmental Health*, *87*, 295–306.

Gavoille, N., & Hazans, M. (2022, September 29). Personality traits, remote work and productivity. *Remote Work and Productivity*. https://papers.ssrn.com/sol3/papers.cfm?abstract_id=4233436

Geen, R. G. (1984). Preferred stimulation levels in introverts and extroverts: Effects on arousal and performance. *Journal of Personality and Social Psychology*, *46*(6), 1303.

Gerlitz, A., & Hülsbeck, M. (2023). The productivity tax of new office concepts: A comparative review of open-plan offices, activity-based working, and single-office concepts. *Management Review Quarterly*, 1–31.

Goldberg, L. R. (1990). An alternative "description of personality": The big-five factor structure. *Journal of Personality and Social Psychology*, *59*(6), 1216.

Goldberg, L. R. (1993). The structure of phenotypic personality traits. *American Psychologist*, *48*, 26–34.

Gubler, D. A., Makowski, L. M., Troche, S. J., & Schlegel, K. (2021). Loneliness and well-being during the Covid-19 pandemic: Associations with personality and emotion regulation. *Journal of Happiness Studies*, *22*(5), 2323–2342.

Hartog, L., Weijs-Perrée, M., & Appel-Meulenbroek, R. (2018). The influence of personality on user satisfaction: Multi-tenant offices. *Building Research & Information*, *46*(4), 402–416.

Hlatywayo, C. K., Mhlanga, T. S., & Zingwe, T. (2013). Neuroticism as a determinant of job satisfaction among bank employees. *Mediterranean Journal of Social Sciences*, *4*(13), 549.

Hyer, L., Braswell, L., Albrecht, B., Boyd, S., Boudewyns, P., & Talbert, S. (1994). Relationship of NEO-PI to personality styles and severity of trauma in chronic PTSD victims. *Journal of Clinical Psychology*, *50*(5), 699–707.

John, O. P., & Srivastava, S. (1999). The Big-Five trait taxonomy: History, measurement, and theoretical perspectives. In *Handbook of personality: Theory and research* (vol. 2). Guilford Press.

Judge, T. A., Martocchio, J. J., & Thoresen, C. J. (1997). Five-factor model of personality and employee absence. *Journal of Applied Psychology*, *82*(5), 745.

Kallio, J., Vildjiounaite, E., Koivusaari, J., Räsänen, P., Similä, H., Kyllönen, V., Muuraiskangas, S., Ronkainen, J., Rehu, J., & Vehmas, K. (2020). Assessment of perceived indoor environmental quality, stress and productivity based on environmental sensor data and personality categorization. *Building and Environment, 175*, 106787.

Kawakubo, S., & Arata, S. (2022). Study on residential environment and workers' personality traits on productivity while working from home. *Building and Environment, 212*, 108787.

Kniffin, K. M., Narayanan, J., Anseel, F., Antonakis, J., Ashford, S. P., Bakker, A. B., . . . & Vugt, M. V. (2021). COVID-19 and the workplace: Implications, issues, and insights for future research and action. *American Psychologist, 76*(1), 63.

Laney, M. O. (2002). *The introvert advantage: How quiet people can thrive in an extrovert world.* Workman Publishing.

Liao, H., & Chuang, A. (2004). A multilevel investigation of factors influencing employee service performance and customer outcomes. *Academy of Management Journal, 47*(1), 41–58.

Lindberg, C., Baranski, E., Gilligan, B., Fisher, J., Heerwagen, J., Kampschroer, K., Sternberg, E., & Mehl, M. R. (2021). Personality and workstation type predict task focus and happiness in the workplace. https://doi.org/10.31234/osf.io/nqbh9

Luong, V., Shields, C., Petrie, A., & Neumann, K. (2022). Does personality matter? Perceptions and experiences of introverts and extraverts as general surgeons. *Teaching and Learning in Medicine, 34*(3), 255–265.

Marzban, S., Candido, C., & Gocer, O. (2021). Satisfaction with open plan offices: Personality, age and gender as human factors. In *Proceedings 20th European Facility Management Network* (pp. 40–50). EuroFM.

Mathews, C. A., Kaur, N., & Stein, M. B. (2008). Childhood trauma and obsessive-compulsive symptoms. *Depression and Anxiety, 25*(9), 742–751.

Matzler, K., Renzl, B., Müller, J., Herting, S., & Mooradian, T. A. (2008). Personality traits and knowledge sharing. *Journal of Economic Psychology, 29*(3), 301–313.

Merone, L., & Whitehead, O. (2021). COVID-19 and working within health care systems: The future is flexible. *Asia Pacific Journal of Health Management, 16*(1), 28–32.

Michinov, E., Ruiller, C., Chedotel, F., Dodeler, V., & Michinov, N. (2022). Work-from-home during COVID-19 lockdown: When employees' well-being and creativity depend on their psychological profiles. *Frontiers in Psychology, 13*.

The Myers-Bridge Company. (2020). *The COVID-19 crisis: Personality and perception.* Retrieved March 3, 2023, from https://www.themyersbriggs.com/-/media/Myers-Briggs/Files/Resources-Hub-Files/Research/Covid-Perceptions-Survey-3-v1.pdf?la=en-US

Needle, R., & Mallia, K. (2021). Creatives in the office: Personality and the environmental effects of workspace. *Journal of Current Issues & Research in Advertising, 42*(3), 277–293.

Oseland, N., & Hodsman, P. (2018). A psychoacoustical approach to resolving office noise distraction. *Journal of Corporate Real Estate, 20*(4), 260–280.

Perkins, A. (2016). *The welfare trait: How state benefits affect personality*. Springer.

Poursafar, Z., Rodrigues, L. L., & Sriram, K. (2019). Architectural design model for office interior to suit personality types and to enhance productivity. *International Journal of Recent Technology and Engineering, 8*(2), 1916–1921.

Reichherzer, A., Wargocki, P., Mayer, F., Norrefeldt, V., & Herbig, B. (2022). Increased self-reported sensitivity to environmental stimuli and its effects on perception of air quality and well-being. *International Journal of Hygiene and Environmental Health, 246*, 114045.

Roberts, B. W., Luo, J., Briley, D. A., Chow, P. I., Su, R., & Hill, P. L. (2017). A systematic review of personality trait change through intervention. *Psychological Bulletin, 143*(2), 117.

Roskams, M., & Haynes, B. (2020). Employee-workplace alignment: Employee characteristics and perceived workplace requirements. *Facilities, 38*(3/4), 282–297.

Schweiker, M., Hawighorst, M., & Wagner, A. (2016). The influence of personality traits on occupant behavioural patterns. *Energy and Buildings, 131*, 63–75.

Seddigh, A., Berntson, E., Danielson, C. B., & Westerlund, H. (2014). Concentration requirements modify the effect of office type on indicators of health and performance. *Journal of Environmental Psychology, 38*, 167–174.

Seddigh, A., Berntson, E., Platts, L. G., & Westerlund, H. (2016). Does personality have a different impact on self-rated distraction, job satisfaction, and job performance in different office types? *PLoS One, 11*(5), e0155295.

SHE POE dataset. (2023). *Sustainable and healthy environments post-occupancy evaluation dataset*. SHE Lab (not published).

Stelmack, R. M. (1990). Biological basis of extraversion: Psychophysiological evidence. *Journal of Personality*, *58*, 293–311.

Sugino, R., Tanabe, S.-I., Takahashi, M., Tokumura, T., Wada, K., Kuroki, T., Nakagawa, J., Shinoda, J., & Shinoyama, T. (2019). Relationship between attributes of individual workers and concentration at work. In *E3S web of conferences*, 111.

Uchida, M., Kaneko, M., & Kawa, S. (2014). Effects of personality on overtime work: A cross-sectional pilot study among Japanese white-collar workers. *BMC Research Notes*, *7*, 1–9.

Wells, M., & Thelen, L. (2002). What does your workspace say about you? The influence of personality, status, and workspace on personalization. *Environment and Behavior*, *34*(3), 300–321.

Wilmot, M. P., Wanberg, C. R., Kammeyer-Mueller, J. D., & Ones, D. S. (2019). Extraversion advantages at work: A quantitative review and synthesis of the meta-analytic evidence. *Journal of Applied Psychology*, *104*(12), 1447.

Zakaria, N., & Yusof, H. M. (2021). Relationship Between the 'Big Five' personality and career success. *Journal of Advanced Research in Business and Management Studies*, *24*(1), 69–76.

13
NEURODIVERSITY

Kirsten Day and Andrew Martel

> It is about enabling choice within environments, in which both joy and calm can be found, and enabling the ingredients that contribute to a mind-friendly environment to be orchestrated into the most elegant of architecture, urban realms, and landscapes.
>
> – *Maslin Designing Mind-Friendly Environments*

Introduction

All spaces – all the time – are composed of the aggregated stimuli from all senses at varying levels of intensity. For most people those levels will fall within an envelope or range that is comfortable, or at least not uncomfortable and stress inducing. However, for a percentage of the workforce those levels will be above a comfort level (hypersensitivity – an atypically high response) or below a comfort level (hyposensitivity – an atypically low response). Workplace stress for neurodiverse people is most associated with an excess of – or lack of – environmental stimuli that might emanate from sound noise, visual noise, spatial layouts, or unwanted sensory feedback through smell, touch, taste, or temperature.

Neurodiversity describes the variation in human neurocognition (HOK Group, 2019a), capturing a range of diagnoses and dispositions of how people perceive and experience the world (Kenny et al., 2016). The challenge when designing the built environment and in particular workspaces is that each person who interacts with that location will experience it in a different way – whether identifying as neurotypical or neurodiverse (see Figure 13.1). This has a profound impact on the designer's consideration.

Normative processes frame how we view neurodivergence and its myriad variations (Boys, 2022). Boys provides three key tools to challenging ableist biases from disability studies.

1. Developing alternative terminologies beyond the binary of disability and ability. These simplistic divisions do not capture the fluid nature of stressors, temporary disability through to permanent, thereby misfitting people with an environment. We need to move beyond the view that disability/other is a difficulty to negotiate. As Boys challenges the designer – "this is not because neurodivergence or disability is the problem, but that architects tend to assume a 'normal' use; and then only add on the 'abnormal' – such as a space for a wheelchair user – requirements at the end of the design process, as merely a technical and legalistic issue" (2014).

DOI: 10.1201/9781003328728-15
This chapter has been made available under a CC-BY-NC-ND 4.0 license.

2. Centring disability-led and disability-oriented participatory processes. ensuring that there is a collaborative approach. "The obvious way to find out what disabled people want is to ask. In practice, the perspectives of disabled people (i.e., 'end users' in the engineering world) about technology are solicited and deemed valuable, though often late in the design process" (Goering & Klein, 2020, p. 616).
3. Disability positivity. Crucially this recognition of the complexity and nuances in relation to personal positioning – "being born with a disability, for example, compared to developing one in later life; social context, that is, how particular impairments are framed by society; and the considerable heterogeneity in experiences across and between different non-normative neurologies" (Boys, 2022, p. 45).

This chapter explores the importance of accommodating neurodiversity in the workplace and overviews the different methods that serve as guides to design for neurodiversity and the specifics of neurodivergent conditions. Contemporary office design draws focus on compliance with standards and codes for efficiency, constructability, durability, or accessibility, with little exploration of the psychosocial impact of the constructed environment. As we understand more about how the mind works, the definition of what is neurotypical and what is neurodiverse will broaden – and with it designers' understanding of how people move through, experience, and interpret space.

What is neurodiversity?

'Neurodiversity' describes a spectrum of neurocognitive profiles. Seeing this as a spectrum acknowledges the different ways by which people interpret information, respond, behave, and communicate. When we use the term neurodiversity, it includes not only people with autism but the spectrum between those with neurological difficulties, such as autism through to those with severe impairment, including dementia.

From a neurotypical perspective the concern is that neurodiversity isn't an 'over there' problem but a spectrum including the aging mind – not a condition that can be fixed, but one that can be accommodated. While we can view people with autism as an expert user group when assessing appropriate workplace design – neurodiversity as a term captures a range of characteristics that can change over time, including neurodegenerative disorders. While there are commonalities between neurodiverse people – including differences in communication, social interaction, sensory reception, and interests – these are a "constellation of characteristics that blends together for each individual" (IBCCES, 2018). With an aging workforce, and the addition of an increase in diagnoses of people with neurodiversity, it is important that workplace design responds to this challenge and opportunity.

Rate of diagnosis

The terms used in Table 13.1 describe 'neurotypical' as the majority. However, neurodiversity is the fastest growing diagnosed developmental disability globally, and there is an expanding awareness of neurodiversity and the impact of workplace design on the participation rate of neurodiverse people in the economy. The World Health Organization suggests that approximately 1 in 100 children has autism. This includes those who can live independently through to those who require lifelong care and support (World Health Organization, 2022). One theory for this significant increase in autism diagnosis rates is the increased awareness and diagnosis. The Centers for Disease Control and Prevention in the USA suggests that the rate of ASD (autism spectrum disorder) in 2018 was 1 in 44 (World Population Review, 2023).

Table 13.1 Neurodiversity as a spectrum. Neurodivergent and neurodegenerative are defined as neurodiverse. Neurotypical is considered 'the majority', although with increased diagnosis, this majority is being greatly reduced.

Neurotypical	*Neurodivergent*	*Neurodegenerative*
The majority	Autism ADHD Dyslexia	Sensory processing differences, typically age-related conditions – ie. dementia, Parkinson's

Given these numbers the design of public spaces in the future, including workspaces, needs be reconsidered. Just as all workplaces need to be safe and accessible, all workplaces should be designed to ensure that people can work effectively and efficiently without being disabled (or further disabled) by the environment they work in. Workplace design needs to accommodate neurological difference, and that is a critical challenge for employers (HOK Group, 2019b). HOK Group identifies four trends relative to neurodiversity that will impact the workplace:

1. Technological developments
2. Demographic developments
3. Focus on mental health and well-being
4. The fast pace of change and organizational business models

With increased diagnosis and greater understanding of causes and triggers that cause discomfort and distress in neurodiverse people, interventions can be made to better design the workplace – ensuring appropriate occupational health and safety of people who use the workplace, and a place of increased productivity.

Sensory design theory standards and guidelines

Design guidelines for people with a neurological condition like autism generally focus on sensory sensitivity and social exchange. There is an emphasis on the prevention of overstimulation and the provision of retreat spaces when people are overwhelmed. Sinclair warns that while this is the case for some people on the autism spectrum, we need to acknowledge that there is no uniform experience.

> It is possible, for example, for someone to be easily overwhelmed by auditory stimuli but to seek out intense visual stimulation, or to be extremely tactile defensive but crave (and also create) a lot of loud sounds, or to avoid some types or ranges of visual, auditory, tactile, olfactory, or gustatory stimuli while seeking out other types or ranges of stimuli, or any number of other combinations of sensory defensiveness and sensation-seeking within the same person.
>
> (Sinclair, 2022, p. 104)

At the heart of designing for neurodiversity is person-centred design – expanding Pallasmaa's holistic architecture (2012) and exploration of the senses is the acknowledgement that this experience has sensorial impact that is different to our own experience or intention. Manipulation of the environments to the benefit of the autistic user (Mostafa, 2014, p. 145) and to the neurodivergent

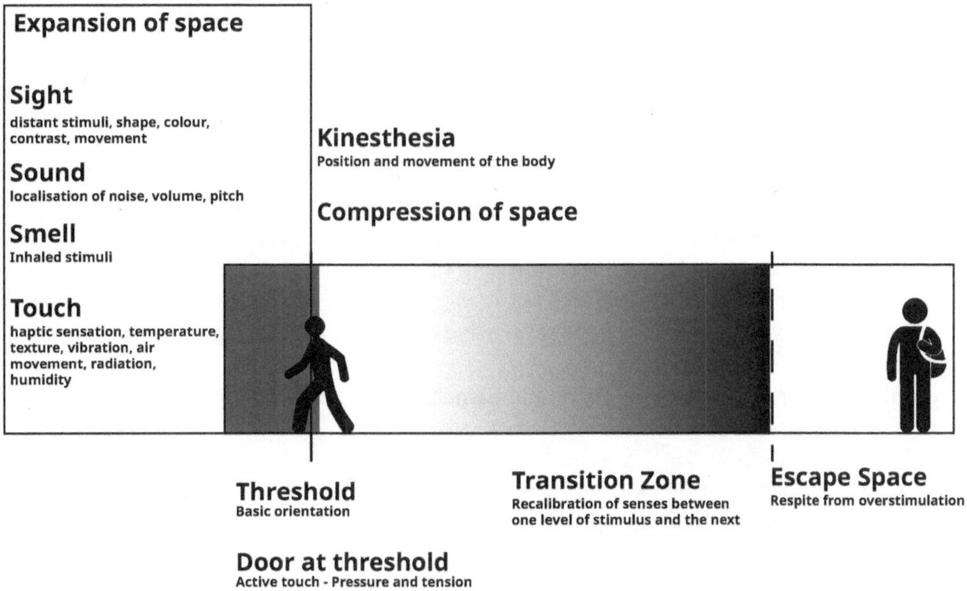

Figure 13.1 Sensory considerations – designing environments for mind-friendly spaces.

community and incorporating Mostafa's ASPECTSS™ provides a comprehensive overview of how the body might interact with the built environment. Many of these are captured in the sensory design elements of the standards and guidelines around neurodiversity. The sensorial concerns are addressed not only in how neurodiverse people respond to sensory stimuli but is also of key concern in regard to healthy buildings (Allen, 2017).

Figure 13.1 Sensory Considerations adapted from Malnar Vodvarka *Ranges of the Senses*

There are several standards and guides for the design of space for neurodiverse people. What can be achieved in the built environment can be broadly seen as addressing sensory stimulus. Magda Mostafa was one of the first designers to identify and codify key issues of the sensory environment and its relations to autistic behaviour in schools (Mostafa, 2014). Working with sensory design issues, Mostafa's empirical and evidence-based research led to her development of ASPECTSS™. The acronym stands for **A**coustics, **Sp**atial Sequencing, **E**scape Space, **C**ompartmentalization, **T**ransition Zones, **S**ensory Zoning, and **S**afety. Mostafa writes of her experience trying to identify any design code or guidelines for the design of favourable architectural environments and being told they did not exist (Mostafa, 2014, p. 143).

The Autism Planning and Design Standards from the Knowlton School of Architecture, at Ohio State University articulate a framework for designers to work towards that considers six 'feelings' the building should promote in their uses:

1. *Feel connected* – because they are easily reached, entered, and/or lead to destinations.
2. *Feel free* – because they offer relative autonomy and the desired spectrum of independence.
3. *Feel clear* – because they make sense and do not confuse.
4. *Feel private* – because they offer boundaries and provide retreat.
5. *Feel safe* – because they diminish the risk of being injured.

6. *Feel calm* – because they mitigate physical sensory issues associated with autism (Saltzman, 2018).

Neurodiversity design standards

The British Standard – PAS 6463:2022 *Design for the mind – Neurodiversity and the built environment* – is the world's first standard to be released for sensory and neurological needs. Aimed to provide guidance for the design of buildings and external spaces for public and commercial use. While it doesn't address specific issues that might be provided for in specialist care accommodations or educational facilities (as seen in the work of Ahrentzen or Mostafa respectively) – it does provide broad principles supportive of sensory processing and mental well-being in buildings.

Technical author of the Publicly Available Standard (PAS) and Senior Inclusive Design Consultant, Jean Hewitt states:

> I believe at least 20% of the population are negatively impacted by elements that could so easily be adjusted or eliminated during design without any cost implications. This PAS is an opportunity to ask designers to carefully consider this normal neurological diversity of humans rather than just meeting basic regulatory demands. Places should be comfortable to visit and use without encountering emotional distress or difficulty and I'm very excited to be involved in developing some guidance to help make this the case for many more people.
>
> (British Standards Institution, 2021)

The standard draws on a wide range of existing guides for working with disability, design for dementia, planning for children, and biophilic design. Factors addressed in PAS 6463:2022 are discussed in the next section.

The neurodiverse workplace

The aim of neurodiversity-aware design is to provide good, sensory-inclusive environments. British Standard BS8300 part 2 (2018) provides the following definition of an inclusive environment as one that:

1. Creates buildings, places and spaces that can be used easily, safely and with dignity by everybody.
2. Provides choice, is convenient and avoids unnecessary effort, separation or segregation.
3. Goes beyond meeting minimum standards or legislative requirements.
4. Recognises that everyone benefits from improved accessibility, including disabled people, older people and families with children, carers, and people who do not consider themselves to be disabled (BS 8300-2:2018, p. 8).

There are three principal design responses that promote the design of an inclusive workplace environment for neurodiverse people:

1. **Personal Control:** The ability to change or moderate the immediate environmental stimuli in order to shift it into a more comfortable zone.

2. **Wayfinding:** Transition spaces between areas of significantly different levels of stimuli need to be carefully considered. This includes ease of wayfinding and the provision of space (and time) to 'prepare' to enter a new space or 'repair' by reducing stimuli after exiting a space.
3. **Safety and Recovery:** Quiet rooms – spaces to go to reset and recover after an over (or under) stimulated environmental experience that has caused stress.

Personal control

Environmental stimuli and our neurological responses to them are necessary feedback mechanisms that allow us to understand and regulate our immediate environment. For example, the reflexive response to touching something hot by pulling away is an involuntary but useful evolutionary development. Other involuntary responses to certain stimuli can be uncomfortable and stressful, like the reaction to the sound of fingernails being scraped on a chalkboard. Maslin (2022) uses the analogy of bandwidth for digital data to explain sensory overload, likening it to trying to stream a lot of data on a narrow bandwidth, which causes everything to slow down. Some people have to narrow a bandwidth for certain sensory perceptions or that sensory processing causes so much data that the person struggles to perform with the bandwidth they have left (Maslin, 2022, p. 102).

Modern office workplaces contain numerous supportive technologies (air-conditioning, lighting, lifts, photocopiers, etc.) that support a productive working environment for the majority of workers. However, neurodiverse workers may have adverse reactions to stimuli that fall within a comfort envelope of other workers – and so thought must go into the ability to change or moderate stressful environments.

Air quality and conditioning

There are two main areas to consider when thinking about air quality and conditioning (see also Chapter 7). Firstly the quality of the air, which is a mixture of smells, movement, and temperature. Smell may be pleasant, from internal plants or gardens, or the kitchen around lunchtime, or unpleasant in the case of toilets, strong cleaning products, or rubbish bins. Careful consideration of zoning and adjacencies of space is necessary to control the effect of smell in the office. Similarly, sensitivity to temperature difference is a widely known phenomenon in offices (and not just for people who are neurodiverse), so zoning and the ability to individualize control as much as possible is also important here.

The other consideration concerns the side effects of the systems used to condition the air. HVAC equipment will always produce a background noise (a humming) that may not impact comfort levels for most workers but may be very distracting and painful to someone with hypersensitivity. Zoning and the positioning of vents and exhausts in relation to workspaces are important considerations here. The switches and controls that are provided for people to moderate their environment must be simple and intuitive to use as what is 'common sense' to one person might not be to another. See Reference: PAS 6463:2022 Section 9: Mechanical, Electrical, and Plumbing (British Standards Institution, 2021).

Acoustics and noise management

As noted earlier in relation to air-conditioning, noise may be generated actively by people talking, typing on keyboards, or answering the phone, or in the background by HVAC units, lifts, or internal lights. These repetitive background noises (also known as pervasive sound) can be particularly discomforting to people with hypersensitivity. A key consideration here is acoustic layout and zoning. Acknowledging what spaces are likely to be noise producing, such as meeting rooms and staff kitchens, and what spaces are likely to require a quiet working environment is important is designing office layouts. The adjacency of loud/quiet spaces needs to be considered along with the transition spaces between those zones.

Along with whole-of-floor acoustic design, individual rooms' and workstations' acoustic profiles need to be considered. Activity-based assessment of different rooms can be accompanied by material selection and layout to ensure that noise levels are appropriate to the intended use of the room. Specific quiet rooms intended to de-intensify stimuli caused by noise (or other stress inducers) should be provided. Similar to the recommendations around control of air-conditioning units, controls to plant systems (A/C, fans, lights) must be simple and intuitive to operate. See Reference: PAS 6463:2022 Section 10: Acoustics and Noise Management (British Standards Institution, 2021).

Light, lighting, and reflection

Light and light noise may emanate from many areas of a workplace. It is known that light, and light levels, directly affect the brain and brain function (Maslin, p. 127). Natural light is an essential element of well-being for all people, including those who are neurodiverse, but its provision into a workplace must be considered in relation to glare, flicker, shadows, temperature, and movement. Natural variation across the day and differing weather conditions mean that natural light has significant variation compared to artificial lighting. Much of this is beneficial to humans, but the ability to control natural light when it causes discomfort is necessary through screens, blinds, or the use of natural features such as deciduous trees.

Artificial light is necessary to complement natural light in workplaces and is used to provide a consistency of illumination levels. Along with the issues of glare, flicker, and shadows, artificial light needs consideration around the quality of the light and its colour temperature. Again, an activity-based assessment of individual spaces is required to determine the profile of the light required, along with an understanding of adjacency of light and dark spaces and the transition spaces between them.

Lighting levels are also an important factor in wayfinding (see the Wayfinding section of this chapter), and moderating the level of natural and artificial light in transitioning areas between indoor and outdoor spaces is important. See Reference: PAS 6463:2022 Section 11: Light, Lighting, and Reflection (British Standards Institution, 2021).

Surface finishings

Surface finishings have a wide impact not just on workers who are neurodiverse, but also people with vision and hearing impairment. Finishes may be considered in terms of their colour and texture/tactility. Colour considerations include the use of colour in wayfinding and spatial differentiation, and visual contrast in particular between vertical and horizontal surfaces. Care must be taken to avoid visual 'noise' and discomfort. The use of patterns on wall or floor surfaces must be carefully considered, as these are a frequent source of discomfort, disorientation, and sensory overload. Patterned surfaces on walls and floors should never be the same.

The tactility or texture of a surface (wall, floor, or workspace) can have an impact across several domains. The hardness or softness of a surface contributes to noise control, the reflection of light or glare, and, for floors, potential slip hazards. Texture may also play a role in the reduction of stress and anxiety through the touch of smooth, cold, or fuzzy surfaces as people move around a workplace, so a variety of different textures is recommended. See PAS 6463:2022 Section 12: Surface Finishings (British Standards Institution, 2021).

Fixtures, fittings, and furniture

When considering fixtures, fittings, and furniture in the workplace the key concerns are familiarity, intuitive use, and positioning. Many people who are neurodiverse find patterns and repetition calming, so the positioning of light switches, power-points, door handles, and air-conditioning controls should be consistent throughout the workplace and be intuitive to use. An example of intuitive use is having a push plate on one side of a door and a handle on the other rather than handles on both (these are also known as 'Norman doors' after Don Norman and his book *The Design of Everyday Things*). These principles also apply to the positioning of fixtures and furniture in a room – symmetry and order are often calming factors for people who are experiencing sensory overload. Quiet rooms or spaces should be designed with symmetry and balance in mind.

Fixtures and controls should also be designed to allow for acoustic control, and any technology in the workplace, such as screens, should avoid causing visual noise and discomfort through stimulus overload. See PAS 6463:2022 Section 13: Fixtures, Fittings, and Furniture (British Standards Institution, 2021).

Wayfinding

Supporting wayfinding is a critical element of workplace design and is based on the principle of making it simple, easy, and intuitive for people to negotiate moving from one place to another. People who are unfamiliar with a workplace, have a disability or impairment that makes moving through space difficult, or people who are susceptible to over or under sensory stimulus can find wayfinding stressful and are less likely to feel comfortable moving around their workplace. Best-practice wayfinding will utilize at least two senses, either visual, acoustic, or tactile to allow individuals to negotiate pathways in the most appropriate manner for themselves.

Making wayfinding simple and intuitive can be achieved using several complementary techniques, including preview information, wayfinding nodes and landmarks, and colour and contrast. Preview assistance allows people to anticipate their journey beforehand and may make use of layout maps near entrances or lift cores, or website-based maps to locations. The use of nodes and landmarks (as opposed to a list of instructions) is an intuitive and human-centred method of giving directions ('go down this corridor and then turn left at the big pot plant with the red leaves'). The use of different colours and contrasts is also effective in conveying non-verbal or written information, but care needs to be taken to not overload sensory perceptions.

Signage is important but should be used in conjunction with other sensory directions. A progression of signs should ideally complement each other by first directing, then confirming, and finally identifying the required destination. Signs should also be easy and clear to interpret. Along with signage, sensory clues, including touch, sound, and smell can assist people who have vision impairment or are hyper- (or hypo-) sensitive to particular stimuli. See Reference PAS 6463:2022 Section 6: Wayfinding (British Standards Institution, 2021).

Internal layouts

In addition to moving between different spaces using wayfinding, the ability to move with ease and clarity within a particular office space is affected by the internal layout of a space. Consideration around the size of spaces, the furniture layout, and consequent visual balance or order are important as calming factors for neurodiverse workers, as well as the relationships between workspaces and the position of key facilities such as toilets, kitchen lunch spaces, or meeting rooms. A balance is required between proximity and clear visual sightlines (preview) and the zoning of noise, smells, and visual over-stimulation.

Apart from the provision of recovery and quiet spaces, consideration of transition spaces between areas or zones of significantly differing sensory stimulation are among the most critical design decisions for a neurotypical-inclusive workspace. Transition spaces provide an opportunity to either prepare to enter a space of increased sensory stimuli or to repair after leaving a space that has been discomforting. These transition spaces should provide a level on contrast in sound, lighting, smell, or texture, from adjacent spaces to enable a re-balancing of emotional intensity. They should perform a similar role to recovery and quiet spaces without requiring total seclusion on the part of the discomforted worker.

Finally, many people find long and narrow corridors to be distressing and discomforting spaces. Views out of windows or atrium spaces that break up the feeling of enclosure and entrapment are recommended, as well as having sufficiently wide spaces that allow for easy wheelchair or mobility access but also allow traffic of multiple people without discomfortable encroachment on personal space for workers. See PAS 6463:2022 Section 8: Internal Layouts (British Standards Institution, 2021).

Safety and recovery

The provision of recovery and quiet spaces in the workforce is the most radical change to traditional office space design recommended in making workplaces equitable for neurodiverse workers. Over-stimulus (or under-stimulus) of the senses and the resulting discomfort and anxiety is a common experience for neurodiverse people and must be managed as part of the workplace experience. The provision of safe and quiet spaces was a key recommendation in the first-ever design guidelines for schools with neurodiverse students (Mostafa, 2014 – it is the E [Escape Space] in ASPECTSS™) and is a key design principle in neurodiverse-informed housing design as well. More generally, the impact of sensory overload (or underload) common with neurodiverse people needs to be considered in relation to workplace safety conditions, including escalators, lifts, trip hazards, and emergency evacuation procedures.

Safety, recovery, and quiet spaces

Recovery and quiet spaces are ones that engage with all of the senses in a calming way. Acoustics, temperature, and lighting are important with quiet, cool, and darker spaces beneficial for people with over-stimulated-related stress, while more stimulatory-activated spaces are appropriate for people who have hyposensitivity issues. Touch and texture is a critical feature of restorative spaces, so the surfaces of walls, floors, and furnishings should be considered to allow for touch, rubbing, and comfort. Some people find being closer to the ground relaxing, so design should allow for a variety of seating or lying down positions, such as floor cushions and rugs. All quiet rooms should have a clearly visible (and intuitive) signal that the room is occupied.

As part of the general provision of safety and support in the workplace, quiet rooms should ideally be in areas that can be monitored or where support is nearby. Neurodiverse workers may require additional support during emergency evacuation procedures due to the potential sensory overload caused by alarms, sirens, and the movement of large groups of people. See PAS 6463:2022 Section 14: Safety, Recovery and Quiet spaces (British Standards Institution, 2021).

Conclusion

> Like a canary in a coal mine alerted miners in a bygone era, the neurological experiences of people with accentuated neurological experience teach us to pay attention to the stressful aspects of environments around us – to the benefit of us all.
>
> (Maslin, 2022)

As Maslin notes in the previous quote, although the recommendations in this chapter are intended to promote workplace design that is inclusive and suitable for neurodiverse people, careful consideration and control of sensory stimuli that is appropriate for expected work tasks and reduces stress factors will help all workers. The key approaches required are the enabling of personal control over the many sensory stimuli that workers are exposed to in their daily activities, a considered and thoughtful wayfinding strategy that is consistent and intuitive, and the provision of safe and recovery-based spaces for workers to access. Activity-based assessment of the stimuli required and produced in different spaces of work (quiet reflection, team meetings, social spaces) enables a zoning strategy that separates areas of different stimuli to be employed, along with the design of the transition spaces between them that allow people to prepare or repair as they enter or exit specific zones. In addition, individual controls to levels of stimuli such as light switches, air-conditioning controls, or shading devices need to be clear, simple to use, intuitive, and have obvious feedback loops (this switch is off). Wayfinding should employ lighting and spatial strategies, including nodes and landmarks, that allow a prequel or early appreciation of the path ahead, with signs following a directing, confirming, and then identifying pattern logic. Quiet rooms should be placed to allow for discreet passive monitoring for health and safety while their fit-out should encompass all the senses but with a particular focus on touch and texture to allow other senses like sight and hearing to be relaxed. Far from being 'special' considerations, these design methodologies should be embedded in all high-performance workplace design approaches to reduce neurological stress in workers.

A 'high-performance' checklist for diversity is provided here:

Principle	*Description*
LIVING WORKPLACE The never finished and ever-evolving workplace that adjusts with its occupant organization and enables the business to change over time.	• Design (both spatial and non-spatial) that allows change and adjustment over time • Ability to tweak and change the workplace to suit the changing needs of occupants • Fluid functionality, i.e., the function of space can change without necessitating (major) spatial changes • Activity-based assessments of the sensory intensity of spaces allows for sensory zoning to occur • The experience of transition spaces between different sensory zones • Requires ongoing management and servicing

(*Continued*)

(Continued)

Principle	*Description*
CO-CREATION/CO-DESIGN A model of collaboration whereby creative solutions are generated and developed with clients, often working side-by-side.	• Client and designer working together to develop design solutions • Ideas are explored and interrogated together • Can be uncomfortable and messy, as it involves working through incomplete thoughts and ideas • Considerations of neurodiversity, hyposensitivity, and hypersensitivity can provide insights into comfort control that might be missed by neurotypical workers with a wider comfort envelope • Requires trust and respect between client and designer
WORKPLACE PILOT Testing new ways of working and new spatial solutions, typically at a small scale.	• Programme to test and trial new ways of working, new workplace designs, and new workplace systems • Provision of quiet, recovery and restorative spaces within the office for individual use in times of stress

References

Allen, J. G. (2017). The 9 foundations of Healthy Buildings. *Forhealth.Org*, 1–35.

Boys, J. (2014). *Doing disability differently: An alternative handbook on architecture, dis/ability and designing for everyday life* (1st ed.). Routledge. https://doi.org/10.4324/9781315777559

Boys, J. (2022). Disability studies, neurodivergence and architecture. In *Developments in neuroethics and bioethics* (Vol. 5, pp. 39–67). Elsevier. https://doi.org/10.1016/bs.dnb.2022.08.012

British Standards Institution. (2018). *BS 8300-2:2018 design of an accessible and inclusive built environment. Buildings – Code of practice*. British Standards Institution. www.bsi-global.com/

British Standards Institution. (2021). *PAS 6463:2021 design for the mind – Neurodiversity and the built environment – Guide*. British Standards Institution.

Goering, S., & Klein, E. (2020). Neurotechnologies and justice by, with, and for disabled people. In A. Cureton & D. T. Wasserman (Eds.), *The Oxford handbook of philosophy and disability* (pp. 615–632). Oxford University Press. https://doi.org/10.1093/oxfordhb/9780190622879.013.33

HOK Group. (2019a). *Designing a neurodiverse workplace*. https://www.hok.com/ideas/publications/trends-affecting-neurodiversity-toward-2030/

HOK Group. (2019b). *Trends affecting neurodiversity toward 2030*. https://www.hok.com/ideas/publications/trends-affecting-neurodiversity-toward-2030/

IBCCES. (2018, March 23). *Interview with Dr. Stephen Shore: Autism advocate & on the spectrum*. International Board of Credentialing and Continuing Education Standards. https://ibcces.org/blog/2018/03/23/12748/

Kenny, L., Hattersley, C., Molins, B., Buckley, C., Povey, C., & Pellicano, E. (2016). Which terms should be used to describe autism? Perspectives from the UK autism community. *Autism*, *20*(4), 442–462. https://doi.org/10.1177/1362361315588200

Maslin, S. (2022). *Designing mind-friendly environments: Design and architecture for everyone*. Jessica Kingsley Publishers.

Mostafa, M. (2014). Architecture for autism: Autism ASPECTSS™ in school design. *International Journal of Architectural Research*, *8*(1), 143–158.

Pallasmaa, J. (2012). *The eyes of the skin: Architecture and the senses* (3rd ed.). Wiley.

Saltzman, A. (2018). *Autism planning and design guidelines 1.0*. Knowlton School of Architecture, The Ohio State University. https://www.firstplaceaz.org/wp-content/uploads/Autism-P-and-D-Standards_reduced.pdf

Sinclair, J. (2022). Cultural commentary: Being autistic together. In *Developments in Neuroethics and Bioethics* (Vol. 5, pp. 99–128). Elsevier. https://doi.org/10.1016/bs.dnb.2022.08.002
World Health Organization. (2022, March 30). *Autism: Key facts*. World Health Organization. https://www.who.int/news-room/fact-sheets/detail/autism-spectrum-disorders
World Population Review. (2023). *Autism rates by country 2023*. World Population Review. https://worldpopulationreview.com/country-rankings/autism-rates-by-country

PART III

Organisational environment considerations

DOI: 10.1201/9781003328728-16
This chapter has been made available under a CC-BY-NC-ND 4.0 license.

14
LEADERSHIP AND CULTURE

Peter Gahan

The high-involvement model of human resource management (HRM) is seen as offering major benefits to organisations, employees and societies through enhancing motivation, enabling people to reach more of their potential, and producing better quality and innovation. However, it would be a mistake to imagine that we can stimulate more of it by simply 'turning up the volume' on its virtues.

– *Boxall & Hou, 2022*

Introduction

It is a generally accepted proposition among scholars in the field of human resource management (HRM) that targeted bundles of HR practices (HRPs) can be implemented to yield superior performance and, ultimately, provide an underlying source of sustainable competitive advantage for an organisation. Often referred to as 'high-performance' or 'high-involvement' work systems (HPWS), these bundles of HRPs have been the subject of focused empirical inquiry for almost half a century – drawing on an even older tradition of scholarship in management and labour relations seeking to identify the critical inputs required to create harmonious and more productive workplaces. Notwithstanding the voluminous research on the topic – and acceptance of the link to performance – an active debate concerning why such practices are not more widely deployed, why they often appear to be difficult to maintain or sustain, as well as how to go about implementing them effectively, remains contentious.

This chapter first provides an overview of the HPWS literature in HRM: its origins and key findings, the underlying theoretical foundations that have informed our understanding of the patterns it appears to have uncovered, and the current state of play in this field of study. In the context of the other chapters contained in this volume, it is useful to conceive of HRPs as one type of intangible affordance that exists alongside the physical infrastructure and design of the work environment that is intended to shape management and employee behaviour, support productive and rewarding work relationships, and ensure the interests of employees and the organisation remain aligned. In reflecting on these findings, the chapter addresses a core paradox that has remained at the heart of this body of work: if high-performance work systems yield performance benefits, why are they not more widely adopted and why are they often unstable? Several factors contribute to

DOI: 10.1201/9781003328728-17

This chapter has been made available under a CC-BY-NC-ND 4.0 license.

resolving this apparent paradox, but at the heart of them is an understanding of the employment relationship as ultimately one structured around conflicting interests and trade-offs.

The HPWS literature, which expanded rapidly since the early 1990s, originates from a longer-standing interest in identifying managerial and organisational antecedents to performance, as well as the more specific concerns prominent throughout the late nineteenth and twentieth centuries with what was often referred to as the 'labour problem' – that of assuring industrial harmony between management and organised labour and establishing productive working relationships in the workplace.

The chapter then examines the HPWS concept: the core theoretical framework that explains *how HRPs* might be configured to generate performance effects and an overview of key findings from the empirical literature. Here, we draw on a well-established taxonomy of social mechanisms to identify the different pathways through HRM practices found to influence performance. Having established that the HRM–performance relationship has many pathways, the following section addresses diffusion and sustainability paradoxes associated with high-performance work systems and then, the penultimate section addresses the challenge of translating insights from research into actionable managerial knowledge.

Origins

For as long as the modern organisational form has existed, concern over how management could most effectively elicit discretionary effort from employees in ways that contributed to higher productivity and improved efficiency has been a core concern among scholars and management practitioners. 'Modern' work organisation in fact has its origins in the late nineteenth and early twentieth centuries, when two key institutional innovations occurred at roughly the same time: the creation of the joint stock company in which shareholders invested and relied upon professional managers to run the business and manage people; and the emergence of the 'employment relationship', in which workers were engaged through continuous, open-ended work contracts under the authority of a manger, as the preferred model to organise work and complete tasks required to produce goods and services (Marsden, 1999). Despite the enormous changes in technology and the economy that have taken place over more than a century since, this form of organising work and production still dominates the organisation of contemporary economic activity – including in private, public, and the not-for-profit sectors of most economies (McDonnell & Bodie, 2021). Similarly, while different employment arrangements have proliferated over time, the employment relationship remains the central model for hiring workers (Aloisi & De Stefano, 2020).

The open-ended, continuous employment relationship has proved so resilient for several reasons; however, the main benefit generally associated with this form of engaging workers lies in the fact that it accommodates competing preferences of both employees and employers and is explicitly designed to address mutual concerns over opportunism (exploitation) and risk-sharing. By creating an open-ended relationship in which workers agree to submit to the direction of the employer ('management'), it also reduces the costs of continually re-negotiating the terms of engagement as production needs change (flexibility) and, at the same, assuring employees of ongoing employment (security).

However, the employment relationship also brought new challenges for both workers and employers. These challenges reflect two unique aspects of the employment relation as an economic exchange relationship. First and foremost, unlike other economic exchanges (for example, buying a car), the employment relationship involves a two-staged exchange relation: 'hiring' workers with the *capacity to work* (as opposed to their actual work effort or outputs); and, then, the stage in which management faces the task of eliciting discretionary effort from employees in the day-to-day process of undertaking work – that is, transforming the capacity to work into actual work effort.

The second unique feature of the employment relationship is the embedded 'human factor', not present in most other economic exchanges. Unlike purchasing other goods or services, the seller of labour (the worker) is inseparable, with the object of exchange (their capacity to work). Inevitably, where humans are involved, feelings and emotions become part of the challenge for management realising the value of opting for an open-ended exchange relationship. And principal among these feelings and emotions are perceptions of fairness (Bingham, 2016). Similarly, management is inevitably facing constraints – legal and other social constraints – on how workers can be treated in the pursuit of productivity.

In this context, it is unsurprising that the question of how best to manage employees remains contentious and subject to ongoing debate – both among scholars and in practice. There have been many different claims about 'the one best way' to manage work effectively over the course of the last 150 years. From Fredrick Winslow Taylor's early 'time and motion studies', through to the Hawthorn experiments and the rise of socio-technical approaches, and the more recent focus on uncovering management practices that elicit high levels of employee engagement at work. Across these different approaches has been the question of what mix of supervision and direction ('sticks') or motivation ('carrots') yields higher productivity. Over the last forty years of management research on this question, the concept of the HPWS has come to dominate.

The 'high-performance work system' concept – theoretical foundations

As one of the most important perspectives among these many different approaches, 'high-performance work systems' (sometimes referred to as 'high-involvement work systems) can be dated to a series of studies completed by industrial relations and HR researchers in the 1990s. Largely restricted to US manufacturing operations, these early studies relied upon employee and management surveys, linked to firm-level financial and productivity data, to identify statistical correlations between the presence of 'bundles' of HRPs and workplace performance (Appelbaum & Batt, 1994; Arthur, 1994). This first wave of HPWS studies complemented related research published in economics and industrial psychology, suggesting employee voice in the form of union representation and collective bargaining (Freeman & Medoff, 1984) and 'mutual gains' approaches to employee relations (Angle & Perry, 1986) motivated employee commitment and higher productivity.

These early findings motivated a number of subsequent studies testing this core proposition across many different firm, industry, market, and institutional contexts – often with limited attempt to uncover the underlying mechanisms that explain the connection between HRPs and organisational performance or other outcomes. Consolidation of scholarly understanding of what constitutes a HPWS and its consequences for employees and organisational outcomes has been hampered by a number of factors, including: a lack of a generally accepted definition of the HPWS concept; how best to measure the presence and application of HRPs, as well as how to design robust studies that isolate HPWS effects controlling for other confounding factors, or to identify how these effects are likely to be shaped by contextual factors.

Although some scholars have questioned the strength or explanatory foundation for the proposition that HPWS can be linked to higher productivity, improved efficiency, and other organisational outcomes (e.g., Kaufman, 2010), after more than forty years of continued research, it is now widely accepted among management and HR scholars (and practitioners) that HPWS have positive effects on organisational performance, as a series of meta-analytic analyses and reviews of the literature have concluded (e.g., Combs et al., 2006; Delery, 1998; Jiang et al., 2012a; Jiang & Messersmith, 2018). In general terms, a 'high-performance work system' is widely understood to be constituted by a coherent and complementary bundle of HRPs – 'coherent and complementary' in the sense that these different individual HRPs are mutually reinforcing in ways that enhance employees' skills, motivation to work effectively, and ability to participate in decisions about work production outcomes (Jiang & Messersmith, 2018).

Since the first wave of studies deploying the HPWS term, considerable effort has been devoted to isolating the underlying mechanism that links HRPs to organisational outcomes and establishing a more general theoretical framework for further refining our understanding of how HPWS work in different settings. Drawing on earlier frameworks devoted to human motivation at work, the Ability-Motivation-Opportunity (AMO) framework (Bailey, 1993) has found wide application in the field of HRM to explain how HRPs can contribute to employee performance, graphically summarised in Figure 14.1. This representation of the AMO framework highlights the core elements required for a coherent and complementary bundle of HRPs; namely, a bundle of practices that enhance employee knowledge, skills, and abilities (A); employee motivation (M); and practices that create opportunities (O) for employees to exercise discretion, deploy their skills and expertise, and to be involved in decisions affecting work. Across several studies (e.g., Gahan et al., 2012) researchers have demonstrated that whilst *individual* HR practices may yield a performance effect, the strength of these effects is magnified where they co-exist as a bundle of mutual reinforcing practices. From a practice perspective, it is also important to note that this research does not prescribe precisely what individual practices should be adopted (Jiang et al., 2012b). For many reasons, the specific configuration of performance-enhancing practices is likely to be expressed in different ways in different workplace contexts. For example, HRPs in smaller workplaces tend to operate in more informal or less structured ways than in larger organisational settings, yet ensuring a distribution of mutually reinforcing practices in these settings have also been found to have significant effects on performance (Arthur et al., 2021).

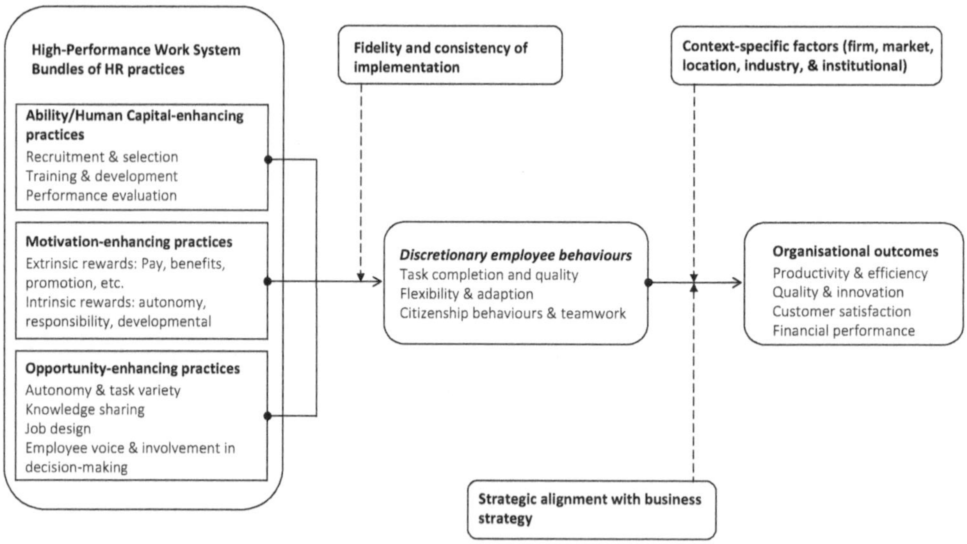

Figure 14.1 The AMO model of high-performance work systems.

One concern (for researchers and practitioners alike) has been the lack of clarity in specifying the underlying mechanisms through which these effects are created. The AMO framework described in Figure 14.1 suggests the key mechanism through which HRPs have influenced organisational performance is through their influence on discretionary employee behaviour. In other words, HPWS proffer one efficient solution to the core challenge faced in ensuring the capacity to work is transformed into actual work effort. However, as many researchers have noted, this specification remains imprecise in terms of the underlying mechanisms (processes) and the different expressions that constitute 'discretionary behaviour'. Not surprisingly, there has been a proliferation of alternative specifications of *how* HPWS shape employee behaviour.

Table 14.1 offers one approach to classifying these different pathways, the underlying psychological processes associated with them, and the different types of discretionary behaviours they may induce. This framework for classifying mechanisms (see Gross, 2009) highlights three distinctive processes that come into play and the discretionary behaviours with which each is associated. At the *intra-personal level*, HRPs may operate to influence an individual's cognitive-affective habits – that is, how they make sense of, and respond to, their work environment, generating clear routines and habits at the individual or team level that are conducive to productive work outcomes. Indeed, HR researchers have been especially keen to argue that these cognitive-affective responses

Table 14.1 Social mechanisms linking HPWS and employee behaviour.

Type of Mechanism	*Examples*	*Behavioural Effects*	*Representative Studies*
Cognitive-affective	• Job satisfaction, organisational commitment, work engagement • Psychological safety • Procedural justice	• Promotes trust and reciprocity. • Protects exchange by reducing the level of required monitoring of employee behaviour. • Willingness to share information and cooperate.	• Appelbaum et al. (2000) • Becker and Huselid (2006) • Kehoe and Wright (2010) • Liao et al. (2009) • Wu and Chaturvedi (2009)
Behavioural	• Work routines • Organisational citizenship behaviours	• Decreased cost of monitoring performance (for management) increases cost of shirking (for employees). • Higher effort levels. • Cooperation and coordination of work tasks.	• Arthur et al. (2021) • Han et al. (2019) • Harley et al. (2010) • Li et al. (2018) • Sun et al. (2007)
Collective (organisational)	• Organisational climate • Flexibility and adaptability • Informational flows • Relational coordination	• Reduces monitoring costs, increases transparency and accountability. • Enables responsiveness to external environment and institutional imperatives. • Improved coordination and enhanced decision-making. • Improved communication and task integration.	• Collins and Kehoe (2017) • Collins and Kehoe (2017) • Fu et al. (2015) • Gahan et al. (2021) • Han et al. (2019) • Kehoe (2022) • Patel et al. (2013) • Zhong et al. (2016)

are highly malleable and afford managerial influence over employee discretionary behaviours through well-designed HPWS (e.g., Liao et al., 2009; Jiang et al., 2012b), highlighting the role of commitment and engagement as critical cognitive-affective mechanisms that promote a sense of mutual reciprocity and trust, requiring less employee monitoring, and by facilitating cooperation and coordination among team members.

Although fewer in number, other studies highlight *inter-personal* processes that generate behavioural mechanisms. For example, Sun et al. (2007) tested a model that conceived of HPWS as proffering employees a clear signal of their employer's willingness to make a long-term investment in their development, in turn inducing a felt sense of obligation to cooperate and go the extra mile in the form of citizenship behaviours intended to support team performance. HPWS may, as we have already suggested, offer a number of different, more-specific signals – for example, in signalling the behavioural routines expected for efficient workplace or team functioning (Harley et al., 2010), or rewarding behaviours that contribute to quality or innovation outcomes (e.g., Li et al., 2018). At a collective level HPWS may also work to generate a strong and consistent culture or climate that supports high trust management, enables organisations to respond flexibly to external pressures and ensure that information flows between individuals and work teams and team members are able to coordinate interdependent work processes efficiently.

Finally, Figure 14.1 also highlights three important factors likely to moderate the linkages between HRP bundles and employee behaviours, and also between employee discretionary behaviours and organisational outcomes. These moderating factors again highlight the context-contingent nature of a high-performance bundle of HRPs, making clear prescriptive guidance for practitioners highly problematic. The first of these moderating factors relates to the extent to which HPWS bundles of HRPs are consistently and systematically implemented. In one of the most important theoretical contributions to understanding how HRPs shape behaviour and performance, Bowen and Ostroff (2004) conceive of HR practices as operating as a set of signals that guide both employee and managerial perceptions and behaviours. However, where the signal offered by different HRPs are inconsistent, or not widely practised or implemented, then the signal that HRPs offer as a *system* may be rendered imperfect, ambiguous, or contradictory, undermining their intended purposes. Similarly, other studies show that where HPWS bundles are inconsistently implemented across teams or work units within the same workplace or organisation, the strength of any effects are likely to be weakened or difficult to sustain over time (e.g., Chadwick, 2007).

In that context, HRPs designed to illicit strong behaviours, depending on the context in which these practices are implemented, may under certain conditions have weak, or sometimes contradictory, effects – for example, where desired behaviours themselves have limited consequence for organisation performance. Consider incentive pay schemes, which researchers have found can illicit strong employee psychological responses (e.g., commitment to the organisation), which in turn may drive more work effort and higher productivity (Larkin et al., 2012). However, these effects may prove weak – or even counterproductive – where other factors (e.g., an unexpected market shock, design biases perceived as unfair or arbitrary) intervene between an employee's efforts to improve productivity and incentive pay. In exploring various elements of the AMO model set out in Figure 14.1, researchers have also explored moderators influencing the strength of the relationship between employee behaviours and performance. In the case of HPWS, a host of firm, industry, market, and other factors have been shown to moderate the strength of the relationship between HPWS practices and performance, independent of their effects on employee behaviour (Han et al., 2019). Similarly, as noted earlier, HPWS have stronger effects where a specific bundle of HRPs include practices across the AMO range, and where they provide a degree of alignment between individual practices and the types of behaviours that support different forms of performance. One way to consider this problem is to view HPWS as yielding two related effects – the first is a *general* impact on employee motivation and behaviours, and the second effect are the consequence of *particular* practices intended to elicit *specific* employee behaviours. One context in which researchers have more recently explored these linkages related to innovation behaviours. Collins and Kehoe (2017), for example, demonstrate that the effects of HPWS on innovation may in fact be weak unless they incorporate specific practices that align with innovation as a strategic objective.

The dark side of HPWS

From the discussion so far, a casual reader would be forgiven for thinking that there was not only broad consensus about the positive effects of HPWS on organisational performance, but that HPWS were universally accepted among most scholars and practitioners as the 'right way' to effectively manage work and employees – and perhaps also that these benefits were realised with few, if any, downsides.

Although several early studies concluded that HPWS generally had positive consequences for employee perceptions about work (Troth & Guest, 2020), the broader evidence suggested a more complex set of outcomes (Boxall & Macky, 2014). Some researchers (e.g., Frick et al., 2013; Kaufman, 2010; Godard, 2001) have taken a highly critical view of the effects of HPWS on employee outcomes, highlighting that high-performance cultures may induce stress and burnout through the potential effects on role overload and the disciplines associated with highly pressured work environments. High-performance work environments may indeed be toxic workplaces.

Several recent studies find support for this conclusion. Although now somewhat dated, the most recent systemic review on the health and well-being effects of HPWS (Van Der Voorde et al., 2012) reported that, in general, employees report positive experiences working under HPWS regimes – however, those studies focused on physical and psychological health consistently report that HPWS practices have significant negative consequences for employees. Other studies have likewise suggested that HPWS may pose significant workplace safety concerns where little is done to counter excessive performance expectations or where employees have little input into decision making (e.g., Jensen et al., 2013). As we noted in relation to the strength of HPWS effects on organisational outcomes, an interaction with the quality of leadership may prove significant in countering some of these negative consequences. Recent studies of the negative consequences of HPWS for employees (Peláez-León et al., 2023; Xi et al., 2022), find that where HPWS induces higher levels of leader anxiety and, consequently, a climate for abusive supervision.

Implications for practitioners

The HPWS research presents a difficult challenge for practitioners to navigate. To begin with, this literature has become increasingly sophisticated in study design, seeking to isolate the true effects of HRPs on employee behaviour and organisational outcomes, avoid concerns about confounding factors, and identify multi-level interaction effects at the individual, team, and organisational levels. To accommodate these concerns, studies have drawn on increasingly sophisticated theoretical models and statistical analysis that, for non-experts, can be challenging to navigate or interpret. All that aside, the evidence presents a complex answer to what seemed a simple question: do HPWS matter for organisational outcomes? The answer of course is: 'it depends' – making it harder for the practitioner to know what they can reasonably draw from the academic research.

In highlighting the range of potential moderators shaping the strength of the linkages that underpin the HPWS model, the HPWS research suggests both researchers and practitioners should avoiding searching for the elusive 'secret' of high-performance. This implies a more immediate challenge for practitioners in drawing on the HPWS findings: namely, the challenge of identifying and agreeing on what specific practices to implement as part of a HPWS bundle. As the emerging view out of this research suggests, the high-performance paradigm offers a set of *guiding principles*, not a prescriptive formula, for identifying bundles of practices that are internally coherent (sometimes referred to 'horizontal alignment' or 'fit') and aligned with both the external environment in which they are intended to work as signals for both managers and employees and the business strategy, designed to create a source of competitive advantage within a particular market environment (i.e., 'vertical fit') (Kehoe, 2022). Indeed, there may be multiple pathways to achieve high-performance, and these pathways can vary in their impact and resilience to external shocks and changing conditions.

This insight has, in fact, led to an alternative (albeit, complementary) perspective for understanding how to design HPWS. Known as the 'resource-based view of the firm' (Gerhart & Feng, 2021), researchers within this tradition suggest that a core function of HR systems are to generate individual-, team-, and organisational-level capabilities to make decisions and take actions that support a firm's strategic objectives and, ultimately, to adapt in an increasingly dynamic environment. Within this tradition, in a recent study of a large representative sample of Australian organisations, Gahan et al. (2021) show that strength of HPWS effects on innovation and performance outcomes is likely to vary over time as firms experience varying conditions of environmental turbulence and uncertainty. They conclude that in more turbulent environments, HPWS retained weak effects, whereas competent leadership was more consequential for organisational outcomes. In contrast, in more predictable environments, HPWS proved more important for driving innovation performance than leadership.

Perhaps more concerning for practitioners seeking to draw lessons from the academic research on HPWS are the conclusions drawn in a recently published study co-authored by a mixed academic and practitioner team (Jewell et al., 2022). In reviewing the academic literature, Jewell et al. highlight the extensive practitioner-academic gap in the way HPWS are conceptualised, and how the challenges of system design, implementation, and change are understood. They concluded that this gap makes it virtually impossible for practitioners to leverage HPWS research findings. In particular, they conclude that academic researchers have "a superficial appreciation for the HPWS implementation process and practically none for the difficulties of deep organizational change" (p. 8). This may help explain the significant lag between discovery and diffusion in practice. This view is consistent with the observation that, despite the consistent finding that HPWS have largely positive effects on performance, the principles associated with HPWS are not widely practised.

There may indeed be several reasons beyond the context-contingent nature of specific HRPs, or practitioner-academic gap highlighted that contribute to explaining this paradox. Firstly, because HPWS are associated with high skill and high wages, it is not always the case that higher productivity and efficiency will translate into higher profitability (Gahan et al., 2012) – perhaps a stronger motivator for business organisations to invest in organisational innovation than efficiency. Moreover, in more dynamic environments, the returns are likewise dynamic, such that the returns on any investment in HPWS (even where productivity and efficiency gains are identifiable) are difficult to estimate with certainty. Finally, because the costs associated with implementation are typically included 'up front' while the potential benefits are uncertain and lagged over time, many organisations pursue partial, less effective versions of HPWS reform, undermining the multiplier effects associated with complementary bundles of HRPs.

Notwithstanding these significant caveats, there are several important implications for the practitioner that can be drawn from this research. First and foremost, the evidence shows unambiguously that there is no single solution – that is to say, no single 'best practice set' of HRPs that practitioners should adopt. However, there are guiding principles which, in design and implementation, require consideration of the context in which such practices are to be implemented. Second, the findings suggest a partial solution may yield some positive benefits, but the most significant effects derive from the whole-of-system effects associated with achieving horizontal and vertical fit. And similarly, as indicated by the opening quote to this chapter from Boxall and Hou (2022) indicated, the relationship between HPWS practices and performance is nonlinear, meaning that simply intensifying their deployment and or use is unlikely to result in a proportional improvement in productivity or efficiency. Third, effective HR systems are difficult to design and implement without extensive involvement of employees and other stakeholders in the process. While this makes the process of design and implementation of HPWS more challenging, the evidence also shows it yields a more resilient and sustainable system. Frustratingly, it also suggests that building and maintaining a high-performance work culture is likely to be an incremental and ongoing process (Olivas-Luján & Rousseau, 2010). Finally, I would contend that the emerging picture on the impact of external shocks (economic shocks, pandemics, etc.) on the lack of resilience in HPWS would indicate that their effectiveness is also dependent on taking a continuous improvement approach to their deployment – updating elements associated with the system on an ongoing basis to ensure they remain relevant and aligned with external conditions and strategic priorities.

Conclusion

This chapter has sought to provide an introduction to what is now a mature research literature on HPWS – defined here as complementary bundles of HRPs that serve to generate positive effects on employee motivations to exert discretionary effort towards improving productivity, efficiency, innovation, or other desirable organisational outcomes. Reflecting a long-standing concern about identifying a clear formula for doing so, the answer has in many respects proved elusive – although, as the chapter explains, the number of studies contributing to our understanding has grown significantly. One key conclusion that can be drawn is that the search for such a formula is misplaced. While there is no specific mix of HRPs that is likely to optimise the impact of HRPs on performance, the research has uncovered some general principles to guide practice (see previous checklist).

These principles are founded on three critical theoretical insights that this research has consolidated over several decades. First, the AMO framework, from which several insights around ensuring bundles of HRPs yield a multiplier effect. This effect is driven by the connections between investments in skills and ability, factors that motivate employee effort, and the need to ensure employees can direct their effort in productive ways and through which they have input into production decisions. The second theoretical insight is drawn from the notion of strategic HRM, which posits the need not only for the horizontal alignment between practices suggested by the AMO framework, but also a vertical alignment between the specific behaviours that any bundle of HRPs signal as important for achieving the organisation's business or operational strategy. Finally, the significant theoretical underpinning is drawn from the resource-based view of the firm, which highlights the complex, often ambiguous social processes through which formal policies and practices are implemented and (re-)negotiated on a day-to-day basis, and through which the knowledge, skills, and abilities of employees are combined collectively, and with other resources at the firm's disposal (physical, intellectual, etc.) to create organisational capabilities to execute strategic intent.

This chapter has also sought to caution against a mechanistic approach to design and implementation of HPWS, as well as the ongoing question of their efficacy under all operation environments and in increasingly volatile, uncertain, ambiguous, and complex times. In short, practitioner beware!

A 'high-performance' checklist for design and implementation of HPWS is provided here:

Principle	*Description*
PRINCIPLE #1: HORIZONTAL ALIGNMENT HR systems have stronger performance effects when they work as a 'bundle' of practices and policies.	HRM systems need to be designed as a complementary and mutually reinforcing bundle that aligns: a) the knowledge, skills, and abilities required to perform work (Ability); b) the extrinsic and intrinsic incentives to exert effort (Motivation); and c) opportunities for employees to voice preferences and empowers them to be involved in decisions affecting their work (Opportunity).
PRINCIPLE #2: VERTICAL ALIGNMENT HR systems have stronger performance effects where they support an organisation's business strategy.	HR systems are an important mechanism through which organisations create unique capabilities required to execute strategy and mobilise resources for sustainable competitive advantage.
PRINCIPLE #3: ACCOUNT FOR CONTEXT There is no 'one best way' to design or implement a HPWS – the bundle of practices will need to reflect a number of contextual factors.	There is no best practice model of HRPs that maximises performance – rather the design of a HPWS (i.e., the specific HRPS used) needs to reflect a number of different contextual factors (industry, size, union presence, quality of employer–employee relations, etc.). The specific bundle of practices needs to be negotiated with stakeholders.
PRINCIPLE #4: HPWS AS 'UNFINISHED PROTOTYPE' HPWS must operate in a VUCA environment and must therefore adapt and change to circumstances.	HRPs must operate in a volatile, uncertain, complex, and ambiguous world. To sustain performance effects they must therefore adapt to maintain horizontal and vertical fit, as well as evidence-based improvement. This will inevitably involve experimentation, renegotiation, and adaptation over time.

References

Aloisi, A., & De Stefano, V. (2020). Regulation and the future of work: The employment relationship as an innovation facilitator. *International Labour Review*, *159*(1), 47–69.

Angle, H. L., & Perry, J. L. (1986). Dual commitment and labor–management relationship climates. *Academy of Management Journal*, *29*(1), 31–50.

Appelbaum, E., Bailey, T., Berg, P., & Kalleberg, A. (2000). Manufacturing advantage: Why high-performance work systems pay off. *Academy of Management Review*, *26*(3). https://doi.org/10.2307/259189

Appelbaum, E., & Batt, R. L. (1994). *The new American workplace: Transforming work systems in the United States*. Cornell University Press.

Arthur, J. B. (1994). Effects of human resource systems on manufacturing performance and turnover. *Academy of Management Journal*, *37*(3), 670–687.

Arthur, J. B., Herdman, A. O., & Yang, J. (2021). Which way to high-performance? Comparing performance effects of high-performance work system components in small-to medium-sized establishments. *ILR Review*, *74*(2), 352–387.

Bailey, T. (1993). Discretionary effort and the organization of work: Employee participation and work reform since Hawthorne. In *Teachers college and conservation of human resources*. Columbia University (Sloan Foundation).

Becker, B., & Huselid, M. (2006). Strategic human resources management: Where do we go from here? *Journal of Management, 32*. https://doi.org/10.1177/0149206306293668

Bingham, C. (2016). *Employment relations: Fairness and trust in the workplace*. Sage.

Bowen, D., & Ostroff, C. (2004). Understanding HRM-performance linkages: The role of strength of the HRM system. *Academy of Management Review*, *29*, 203–221.

Boxall, P., & Hou, M. (2022). Fostering the high-invoolvement model of human resource management: What have we learnt and what challenges do we face? *Asia Pacific Journal of Human Resources*, *60*, 41–61. https://doi.org/10.1111/1744-7941.12305

Boxall, P., & Macky, K. (2014). High-involvement work processes, work intensification and employee well-being. *Work, Employment and Society*, *28*(6), 847–1047.

Chadwick, C. (2007). Examining non-linear relationships between human resource practices and manufacturing performance. *ILR Review*, *60*(4), 499–521.

Collins, C., & Kehoe, R. (2017). Examining strategic fit and misfit in the management of knowledge workers. *Industrial and Labor Relations Review, 70*(2), 308–335.

Combs, J., Liu, Y., Hall, A., & Ketchen, D. (2006). How much do high-performance work practices matter? A meta-analysis of their effects on organizational performance. *Personnel Psychology*, *59*(3), 501–528.

Delery, J. E. (1998). Issues of fit in strategic human resource management: Implications for research. *Human Resource Management Review*, *8*(3), 289–309.

Freeman, R., & Medoff, J. (1984). *What do unions do?* Basic Books.

Frick, B. J., Goetzen, U., & Simmons, R. (2013). The hidden costs of high-performance work practices: Evidence from a large German steel company. *Industrial & Labor Relations Review*, *66*(1), 198–224.

Fu, N., Flood, P. C., Bosak, J., Morris, T., & O'Regan, P. (2015). How do high-performance work systems influence organizational innovation in professional service firms? *Employee Relations*, *37*(2), 209–231.

Gahan, P., Michelotti, M., & Standing, G. (2012). The diffusion of HR practices in Chinese workplaces and organizational outcomes. *ILR Review*, *65*(3), 651–685.

Gahan, P., Theilacker, M., Adamovic, M., Choi, D., Harley, B., Healy, J., & Olsen, J. E. (2021). Between fit and flexibility? The benefits of high-performance work practices and leadership capability for innovation outcomes. *Human Resource Management Journal*, *31*(2), 414–437.

Gerhart, B., & Feng, J. (2021). The resource-based view of the firm, human resources, and human capital: Progress and prospects. *Journal of Management*, *47*(7), 1796–1819. https://doi.org/10.1177/0149206320978799

Godard, J. (2001). High-performance and the transformation of work? The implications of alternative work practices for the experience and outcomes of work. *Industrial and Labor Relations Review*, *54*, 776–805.

Gross, N. (2009). A pragmatist theory of social mechanisms. *American Sociological Review*, *74*, 358–379.

Han, J. H., Kang, S., Oh, I. S., Kehoe, R. R., & Lepak, D. P. (2019). The goldilocks effect of strategic human resource management? Optimizing the benefits of a high-performance work system through the dual alignment of vertical and horizontal fit. *Academy of Management Journal*, *62*(5), 1388–1412.

Harley, B., Sargent, L., & Allen, B. (2010). Employee responses to 'high-performance work system' practices: An empirical test of the disciplined worker thesis. *Work Employment and Society*, *24*(4), 740–760.

Jensen, J. M., Patel, P. C., & Messersmith, J. G. (2013). High-performance work systems and job control: Consequences for anxiety, role overload, and turnover intentions. *Journal of Management*, *39*, 1699–1724.

Jewell, D. O., Jewell, S. F., & Kaufman, B. E. (2022). Designing and implementing high-performance work systems: Insights from consulting practice for academic researchers. *Human Resource Management Review*, *32*(1), 100749. https://doi.org/10.1016/j.hrmr.2020.100749

Jiang, K., Lepak, D. P., Han, K., Hong, Y., Kim, A., & Winkler, A. L. (2012b). Clarifying the construct of human resource systems: Relating human resource management to employee performance. *Human Resource Management Review*, *22*(2), 73–85.

Jiang, K., Lepak, D. P., Hu, J., & Baer, J. C. (2012a). How does human resource management influence organizational outcomes? A meta-analytic investigation of mediating mechanisms. *Academy of Management Journal*, *55*(6), 1264–1294.

Jiang, K., & Messersmith, J. (2018). On the shoulders of giants: A meta-review of strategic human resource management. *The International Journal of Human Resource Management*, *29*(1), 6–33.

Kaufman, B. (2010). SHRM theory in the post-Huselid era: Why it is fundamentally misspecified. *Industrial Relations*, *49*(2), 286–313.

Kehoe, R. (2022). Revisiting the concepts of vertical and horizontal fit in HRM: What we know, what we don't know, and where we might go. *Academy of Management Perspectives*, *35*(2), 175–180.

Kehoe, R. R, & Wright, P. M. (2010). The impact of high-performance human resource practices on employees' attitudes and behaviors. *Journal of Management*, *39*(2), 366–391.

Larkin, I., Pierce, L., & Gino, F. (2012). The psychological costs of pay-for-performance: Implications for the strategic compensation of employees. *Strategic Management Journal*, *33*(10), 1194–1214.

Li, Y., Wang, M., van Jaarsveld, D. D., Lee, G. K., & Ma, D. G. (2018). From employee-experienced high-involvement work system to innovation: An emergence-based human resource management framework. *Academy of Management Journal*, *45*(9), 1437–1450.

Liao, H., Toya, K., Lepak, D. P., & Hong, Y. (2009). Do they see eye to eye? Management and employee perspectives of high-performance work systems and influence processes on service quality. *Journal of Applied Psychology*, *94*(2), 371–391. https://doi.org/10.1037/a0013504

Marsden, D. (1999). *A theory of employment systems: Microfoundations of societal diversity*. Oxford University Press.

McDonnell, B. H., & Bodie, M. T. (2021). From Mandates to governance: Restructuring the employment relationship. *Maryland Law Review*, *81*, 887.

Olivas-Luján, M. R., & Rousseau, D. M. (2010). Can the evidence-based management movement help e-HRM bridge the research-practice gap? *Evidence-based e-HRM? On the Way to Rigorous and Relevant Research*, *3*.

Patel, P. C., Messersmith, J. G., & Lepak, D. P. (2013). Walking the tightrope: An assessment of the relationship between high-performance work systems and organizational ambidexterity. *Academy of Management Journal*, *56*(5), 1420–1442.

Peláez-León, J. D., Salas-Arbeláez, L., & García-Solarte, M. (2023). Organizational culture and performance-based compensation in family firms: Does family involvement in management matter? *Revista Brasileira de Gestão de Negócios*, *25*(1), 33–51. https://doi.org/10.7819/rbgn.v25i1.4214

Sun, L. Y., Aryee, S., & Law, K. S. (2007). High-performance human resource practices, citizenship behavior, and organizational performance: A relational perspective. *Academy of Management Journal*, *50*(3), 558–577.

Troth, A. C., & Guest, D. E. (2020). The case for psychology in human resource management research. *Human Resource Management Journal*, *30*(1), 34–48.

Van De Voorde, K., Paauwe, J., & Van Veldhoven, M. (2012). Employee well-being and the HRM–organizational performance relationship: A review of quantitative studies. *International Journal of Management Reviews*, *14*(4), 391–407.

Wu, P.-C., & Chaturvedi, S. (2009). The role of procedural justice and power distance in the relationship between high-performance work systems and employee attitudes: A multilevel perspective. *Journal of Management*, *35*(5), 1228–1247. https://doi.org/10.1177/0149206308331097

Xi, M., He, W., Fehr, R., & Zhao, S. (2022). Feeling anxious and abusing low performers: A multilevel model of high-performance work systems and abusive supervision. *Journal of Organizational Behavior*, *43*(1), 91–111.

Zhong, L., Wayne, S. J., & Liden, R. C. (2016). Job engagement, perceived organizational support, high-performance human resource practices, and cultural value orientations: A cross-level investigation. *Journal of Organizational Behavior*, *37*(6), 823–844.

15
DIVERSITY AND PARTICIPATION

Victor Sojo

It is time for parents to teach young people early on that in diversity there is beauty and there is strength.

– *Maya Angelou*

Introduction

Over the last couple of decades, we have observed an intensified focus on how human resources and people management practices can impact organisational performance (Orlitzky & Frenkel, 2005). Studies on high-performance work systems have focused on human resources processes, such as professionalised selection and training, behaviour-based assessment criteria and processes, and reward systems that compensate for knowledge and incentivise commitment to organisational goals, as the key predictors of organisational outcomes. The most common outcome measures of high-performance observed in the literature encompass individual-, team-, and firm-level markers of work quality, productivity, costs, profits, and market value (Becker & Huselid, 1998).

Productivity at multiple organisational levels is important for the survival of any business. However, productivity alone does not tell us the full story of any high-performance organisation. A high-performance workplace is an environment where workers can belong, function, and thrive, where organisational goals are efficiently met with a net positive impact on the community. This chapter goes beyond classic research on high-performance workplaces to present an expanded understanding of high-performance outcomes by focusing on team- and firm-level performance. It includes innovation, firm governance, occupational well-being, and impact on the broader community where the firm operates. These outcomes present a more comprehensive picture of organisational functioning by incorporating human, social, operational, and governance dimensions, as well as considering internal and external impacts. Most of the research on high-performance work systems has focused on human resources management practices as the primary predictor of organisational outcomes. However, this chapter specifically emphasises workplace diversity as a distinct aspect of human resources and organisational behaviour that can have direct and indirect impacts on organisational functioning.

DOI: 10.1201/9781003328728-18

This chapter has been made available under a CC-BY-NC-ND 4.0 license.

Workplace diversity

Organisational diversity has attracted increased academic interest since the 1960s, and its pace accelerated in the late 1990s, when workforce diversity became a prominent topic (Roberson, 2019). Earlier discussions about diversity at work focused on demographic factors, whereas more contemporary accounts tend to differentiate between demographic factors (e.g., sex, race, nationality) and functional factors (e.g., experience, occupation) in relation to workforce diversity (van Knippenberg & Schippers, 2007). In organisational research, diversity is understood as a property of social groups that encompasses both subjective and objective *differences between the individuals* in groups (Harrison & Klein, 2007).

The overwhelming majority of the research about diversity is concerned with gender, ethnic, and task-capability diversity. More recently, there has been increasing interest in studying diversity in relation to disability, age, and LGBTQIA+ diversity. In general, studies of diversity focus on the levels of representation of various demographic groups within workplaces, occupations, economic sectors, and leadership roles. More specifically, there are at least three broad traditions of research on workplace diversity. First, there are descriptions of disparities in representation between different groups, which examine where these disparities exist and what they look like. Second, there are studies that aim to understand the reasons behind disparities in representation. These studies explain the disparities in terms of internal attributes of members of social groups, social and structural factors within organisations and the community, or interactions between these factors. Third, there is research on the impact of workplace diversity on individual, team, and organisational outcomes, as well as social and economic outcomes for families and communities. The focus of this chapter is on the review and analysis of research within this later area of work.

Kinds of workplace diversities

The research on the impact of diversity on organisational outcomes has led to disparate findings which can be attributed to how diversity has been conceptualised, the outcomes selected and measured, and the moderating factors accounted for (van Knippenberg & Schippers, 2007). Harrison and Klein (2007) proposed a classification of forms of organisational diversity that goes beyond demographic or functional dimensions. The authors identified three forms of diversity in group attributes, namely, separation, variety, and disparity.

Separation refers to horizontal differences among group members, such as variations in values, beliefs, attitudes, and other individual differences (e.g., differences in cultural values among team members). Variety relates to differences among group members in the type or source of knowledge or experience they possess so that individual members end up with unique or distinctive information (e.g., differences in professional background in a multidisciplinary team). Disparity relates to differences among group members in access to or ownership of socially valuable assets and resources (e.g., differences in the distribution of salaries or development opportunities across an organisation) (Harrison & Klein, 2007).

Research on workplace diversity has predominantly focused on investigating the association between the distribution of demographic attributes and dimensions of separation and variety, and disparity within organisational groupings. Similarly, research aimed at understanding the impacts of diversity in teams of leaders on occupational well-being, innovation, firm performance, governance, and organisational impacts on the community has utilised differences between social groups in values and interests (i.e., separation), experiences and functional background (i.e., variety), and relative power within organisations (i.e., disparity) to explain the variations in decisions and outcomes associated with different levels of diversity.

Theorising the relationship between diversity and high-performance workplace

There are two broad theoretical perspectives used to explain how workplace diversity is associated with relevant organisational outcomes: social categorisation theories (Byrne, 1971; Tajfel & Turner, 1986); and the information processing perspective on diversity (Cox & Blake, 1991; Williams & O'Reilly, 1998). The central argument of the *social categorisation and self-categorisation perspectives* is that humans use salient attributes of individuals as heuristics when forming impressions about others. This heuristic process both leads to the categorisation of individuals into groups and facilitates the development of attitudes towards those groups. Social identity theory posits that individuals' identity is attached to the groups they perceive they belong to. In efforts to maintain a positive self-concept, individuals engage in social comparisons between the groups they belong to versus those they see as out-groups. This can lead to favouritism towards the in-group and derogation of out-groups (Tajfel & Turner, 1986). Both demographic and functional diversity can lead to emotional conflict within teams and entire organisations. The individual identification with a specific social group at work and the derogation of those who are perceived as outsiders can contribute to tensions within diverse teams and across teams where there are relationships between different demographic attributes and functional roles (e.g., marketing team dominated by women interacting with a manufacturing team dominated by men). When members of work teams perceive themselves as belonging to different social groups, diversity has the potential to result in negative organisational outcomes, particularly when one group has more power than the other.

The *information processing perspective* on diversity assumes that demographic and functional diversity are associated with experiences and access to resources. In turn, the access to these experiences and resources can help groups develop different values, knowledge, and skills (van Knippenberg & Schippers, 2007). Therefore, when individuals from different backgrounds are brought together, their collective wealth of ideas can enhance the team's capacity to solve complex problems (Cox & Blake, 1991; Williams & O'Reilly, 1998). The diversity of ideas, values, and problem-solving skills that people bring to work teams can best be utilised when people engage in information elaboration processes that facilitate the constructive expression, processing, and integration of those diverse ideas in problem-solving. The task-related discussions that occur when individuals from different backgrounds work on a problem and explore the most effective ways to solve the problem can promote greater learning and enhance team performance. However, research suggests that differences in values within a team can also lead to increased task conflict and lower performance (Jehn & Mannix, 2001). Therefore, achieving team-level information elaboration without causing task conflict can be considered the "sweet spot" to realise the value of diversity and to enhance organisational performance.

Current research on the impact of diversity on relevant organisational outcomes often incorporates elements of the social categorisation and the information processing perspective as explanatory frameworks. In essence, the argument is that for the relatively small differences in knowledge, skills, and perspective that arise from diversity to contribute to high-performance organisational outcomes, an information processing mechanism that allows for the expression and integration of those different views, within a psychologically safe environment, has to be in place (Dollard & Bakker, 2010). This describes a triple interaction of the level of diversity, the

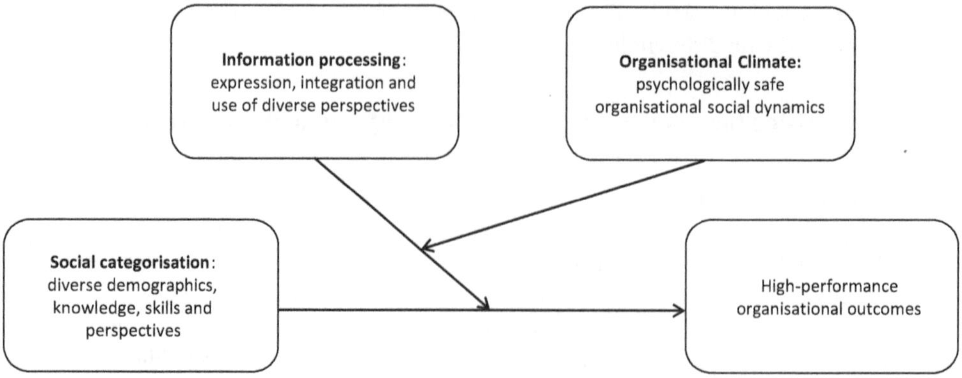

Figure 15.1 Interaction between diversity levels, information processing, and organisational climate on high-performance outcomes.

information elaboration, and the psychosocial climate impacting performance (See Figure 15.1). With the social categorisation and information processing perspectives as a foundation, we will now delve into the evidence regarding the relationship between workplace diversity and relevant organisational outcomes.

Workplace diversity and high-performance indicators

This chapter investigates the impact of workplace diversity and diversity management practices on several key outcomes, including team performance, firm financial performance, occupational well-being, governance, and community impacts.

Team performance

Team performance is a widely explored outcome in the context of workplace diversity, with a significant focus on differences in backgrounds and perspectives (Bunderson & Van der Vegt, 2018). Current evidence indicates that there is a small and non-significant association between demographic diversity (i.e., age, ethnicity, gender, nationality, and education level) and team performance (e.g., in-role performance or innovation). Furthermore, there is substantial variability in the effect sizes observed across studies. Many studies have used subjective measures of team performance, such as observers' or group members' rating of team performance. In those cases, a negative, significant, yet very small, association has been observed between age, ethnicity, gender, and educational diversity and team performance. However, these forms of diversity were not related to objective performance (e.g., financial performance, correct answers; van Dijk et al., 2012). In contrast, research indicated that diversity in functional background has a positive but small impact on both subjective and objective performance indicators, particularly in the context of innovation, compared to in-role performance. These results highlight the need for nuanced interpretations when discussing the relationships between diversity and team performance. It is important to note that functional diversity could be a driver for innovation, while the psychosocial climate of the work environment might need to be considered to prevent negative impacts of demographic diversity on subjective assessments of team performance.

Firm financial performance

The diversity–firm performance relationship is very complex, among other factors as a result of multiple indicators that have been explored in previous research, such as market share, revenue, productivity, sales growth, relative profits, and innovation (Bunderson & Van der Vegt, 2018; Fine et al., 2020). Some studies have found linear positive relationships between gender diversity in management teams and sale and profits (Herring, 2009), accounting and financial performance (Hoobler et al., 2018). On the other hand, some studies have found an inverted U-shape relationship between gender diversity and productivity (Ali et al., 2009), indicating that moderately gender diverse firms tend to achieve the most favourable outcomes. In other studies, gender diversity has predicted some positive firm outcomes, such as accounting returns, yet not market performance (Post & Byron, 2015). Given these mixed findings, researchers have shifted their focus towards understanding conditions under which diversity in teams and leadership can lead to improved organisational performance. These studies have found that demographic and functional diversity are better predictors of firm performance when firms operate in complex and changing environments (Carpenter, 2002; Eesley et al., 2014), particularly when team members are collocated and engage in substantive and frequent information exchange (Cannella et al., 2008) and information elaboration (Ruiz-Jiménez et al., 2016). Greater diversity may contribute to a wider variety of understanding and problem-solving skills which are crucial for effectively navigating complex situations (Bunderson & Van der Vegt, 2018), whereas frequent high-quality interactions among team members facilitate information elaboration and promote the development of trust.

Employees' well-being

This chapter examines two dimensions of well-being in the workplace: the quality of interpersonal relations in the workplace, and work attitudes as proximal outcomes, and physical and mental health as distal outcomes of workplace diversity (Dollard & Bakker, 2010; Sojo et al., 2016a). In relation to organisational interpersonal relations, there is consistent evidence about lack of ethnic and gender diversity. Traditionally male-dominated occupations have been characterised by hyper-masculine values, such as showing no weakness and hyper-competition, male superiority, and sexual bravado (Berdahl et al., 2018). These cultural attributes could be detrimental to the well-being and performance of all employees (Fine & Sojo, 2019). For example, such cultural norms may increase the likelihood of men engaging in physical risks at work (Stergiou-Kita et al., 2016). The prevalence of sexual harassment is higher in male-dominated work environments and sectors compared to more gender-diverse workplaces (Ilies et al., 2003). Also, women are more likely to experience gender-based discrimination and sexist events in male-dominated work environments compared to more gender-diverse settings or female-dominated areas (Gardiner & Tiggemann, 1999; Settles et al., 2006). Similarly, highly racialised organisations, in which practices and policies reinforce and perpetuate racial hierarchies (e.g., specific ethnic groups remain in the numerical minority, are considered to have lower status and be outsiders), there is a higher probability of interpersonal abuse and workplace discrimination towards ethnic minorities (Ray, 2019). Lack of demographic diversity in workplaces can contribute to the development of a set of values and a sense of entitlement among the dominant groups. This can lead to difficulties for minority groups to enter, fully participate, remain healthy, and thrive within the organisation.

The evidence about the impact of diversity in management teams on team climate is more mixed (Bunderson & Van der Vegt, 2018). While some authors have found a negative effect of tenure and functional diversity on the quality of communication between team members (e.g.,

Bunderson & Sutcliffe, 2002), other researchers have found no significant effect of functional diversity on team dynamics (e.g., Qian et al., 2013). These findings suggest that factors such as information elaboration and earlier psychosocial climate could potentially moderate the effects of diversity on well-being.

Looking at well-being outcomes, there is evidence indicating that lack of gender diversity, and particularly when women are numerically dominant in an industry, is associated with lower job satisfaction, organisational commitment, and intentions to stay in the job among men (Leonard & Levine, 2006; Mor Barak et al., 2016). In top management teams, research has identified negative effects of age and tenure diversity on turnover (Wiersema & Bird, 1993). Similarly, classic studies by Kanter (1977) about women and by Niemann and Dovidio (1998) about ethnic minority groups showed that the distinctiveness of being members of a numerical minority group had a detrimental impact on the employees' occupational well-being. Overall, these studies show the lack of demographic diversity could lead to negative outcomes for underrepresented groups, whether through experiences of discrimination and mistreatment or through status and minority anxiety.

Corporate governance

Corporate governance encompasses several processes, norms, policies, and laws related to how a firm is directed, administered, and controlled, including its relationship with stakeholders (Broni & Velentzas, 2012). The evidence about the impact of diversity on corporate governance is complex, with a significant focus on the study of women in top management teams (Fine et al., 2020). For instance, studies have found that gender diversity on boards was only associated with firm performance for organisations with weak governance, with the effect attributed to the monitoring efforts of more gender-diverse boards, with women more likely to have roles in nominating, audit, and corporate governance committees, all key firm monitoring roles (Adams & Ferreira, 2009). Research also indicated that in more transparent regulatory environments, where board directors are more readily held accountable, having more women on boards leads to better firm accounting returns (Post & Byron, 2015). The impact of diversity on governance appears contingent on contextual factors and the extent to which diversity dimensions contribute to improved monitoring activities.

Community impacts

Ethical decision making and corporate social responsibilities are two crucial aspects of corporations' relationship with communities and the environment. Previous research has shown, albeit with weak effect sizes, that women are more likely to favour ethical business practices (Kish-Gephart et al., 2010). Additionally, organisations with more gender-diverse boards have been found to be less inclined to engage in business practices that could degrade the environment or negatively impact communities and customers (Boulouta, 2012). Ethnic minority public servants are more likely to advocate for the interests of communities they belong to, as highlighted in the research by Fernandez, Malatesta, and Smith (2013). Additionally, research has shown that female and ethnic minority employees and clients place high importance on whether firms are fulfilling their corporate social responsibilities (Smith et al., 2001). These findings indicate that more diverse decision makers can help prioritise a positive impact on the community.

The workforce mutuality literature is particularly useful to understand the impact of workplace diversity on firms' community impacts. Workforce mutuality refers to the degree of alignment between the diversity within a firm and the diversity of the surrounding community (HealthWest

Partnership, 2020; Sojo & Ainsworth, 2020). Mutuality is an effective approach to reduce the obstacles that members of the community might face when accessing the services provided by organisations. In organisations with more workforce mutuality, services are more responsive to the needs of the community, promoting access and positive outcomes (Cohen et al., 2002; Spevick, 2003). Higher workforce mutuality also means that firms are providing employment opportunities to a diverse range of community members. This can have a direct positive impact on economic equality, standards of living, and the overall health outcomes within the community.

Managing diversity to enhance high-performance outcomes

The principles of social categorisation theories (Byrne, 1971; Tajfel & Turner, 1986) and the information processing perspective on diversity (Cox & Blake, 1991; Williams & O'Reilly, 1998) can be applied to identify critical areas of action to enhance the positive impact of diversity on firm performance. Specifically, the evidence from social categorisation emphasises the importance of fostering understanding and respect among employees from diverse backgrounds to facilitate effective collaboration in achieving organisational goals. The initial step in this process involves leaders setting the tone for the type of inclusive culture they are expecting from all employees. Table 15.1 outlines actions that leaders can take in this regard.

Planning and rewarding are other important leadership behaviours to reduce ingroup favouritism in workplaces. Leaders should plan the distribution of projects and resources in a way that is equitable and that does not disadvantage already marginalised members of their workforce. The allocation of projects and resources should not only serve as a mechanism for rewarding good performance, but also as a strategy to develop the entire workforce. Finally, the type of behaviour that leaders reward is critical for the social climate of the team. Leaders must ensure they observe citizenship behaviours of support and collegiality among employees, incorporating these behaviours into their analysis of the team members' performance. Such behaviours can be rewarded through public commendations and decisions about promotions and bonuses. Similarly, it is important to clarify a set of values employees are expected to uphold and to ensure workers who engage in harassment or discrimination towards colleagues or members of the community are not promoted. This will help communicate to all workers the expected standard of behaviour.

The information processing perspective (Cox & Blake, 1991; Williams & O'Reilly, 1998) will lead us to pay attention to the way we gather, elaborate, and use knowledge, skills, and networks from diverse teams. Specifically, organisations wanting to leverage the full potential of their diverse workforce need to put in place mechanisms that facilitate employee voice and information sharing. Direct consultations or organising meetings in a manner that encourages the participation of all team members are just two ways to ensure diverse voices are heard before decision-making. Similarly, it is crucial to invite diverse voices to the decision-making table. This process helps ensure that minority opinions are not overlooked when final decisions are made. Of course, for individuals to feel empowered to use their voices, it is essential that the appropriate psychosocial climate has been established (Dollard & Bakker, 2010), as outlined earlier.

In a more programmatic approach, organisations aiming to maximise the potentials of their diverse workforce need to start by ensuring they have a diverse workforce. In this regard, equal opportunity, supply-side, and demand-side strategies play a crucial role in ensuring that diverse voices exist within the organisation (Cooney-O'Donoghue et al., 2022; Sojo et al., 2016b). First, organisations need to ensure the equal rights and employment opportunities of all members of the communities where they operate. In particular, open, transparent, and unbiased recruitment, selection, evaluations, and promotion decisions are crucial. Second, to ensure diverse backgrounds and range of qualified workers, organisations can go upstream and start supporting schools in disadvantaged communities and creating pathways for employment. For employees already within their workforce, organisations can focus on targeted development and mentoring and sponsorships as strategies for equitable employee development. Finally, on the demand-side, organisations must have robust data and reporting in place to track diversity across recruitment, selection, performance evaluation, and promotions at various levels and functional units. This data will provide a clear understanding of the current situation and guide the implementation of diversity management strategies.

Organisations can utilise the principles and areas of intervention outlined earlier to engage in a programme of work that targets all human resources management processes, establish clear expectations regarding the standard of inclusive behaviour, and implement the information elaboration mechanisms needed to ensure diverse voices are heard and their insights are effectively incorporated in the decision-making process.

Conclusions

The relationship between diversity and high-performance workplace outcomes is complex and influenced by social and information elaboration processes. Additionally, the specific environmental demands can play an important role in whether having a diverse workforce can lead to improved team and firm performance, a healthier culture and outcomes, better governance, and a net positive impact on the community. For organisational stakeholders aiming to leverage diversity as a tool to achieve positive organisational outcomes, there are multiple pathways. First, it is crucial to establish an inclusive psychosocial climate that fosters a sense of belonging and contribution for individuals from diverse demographic and functional backgrounds. Second, it is essential to implement mechanisms to incentivise sharing and utilisation of ideas from different stakeholders in decision-making and problem solving. Lastly, maintaining operations that facilitate the recruitment, selection, development, and promotion of diverse workers, using equal opportunity, supply-side and demand-side strategies.

A "high-performance" checklist for diversity is provided here:

Principle	*Description*
SOCIAL CATEGORISATION	Leaders: • demonstrate the value of equity and inclusion via active listening, consultation, respectful responses, and well-being checks on all employees; • plan for and distribute developmental projects, opportunities, and resources equitably; and • reward respectful and inclusive behaviour among their employees.
INFORMATION ELABORATION	Organisations: • put in place processes and mechanisms to facilitate employee voice (e.g., employee fora, leaders' open-door policies, and round robins during meetings); • implement practices to invite diverse voices to important decisions (e.g., budget allocations, employee recruitment, and promotions); and • use tools and spaces to facilitate the exchange, elaboration, and use of diverse ideas in decision-making.

(*Continued*)

(Continued)

Principle	*Description*
HUMAN RESOURCES OPERATIONS	Human resources partners and leaders: • design, implement, and audit open, transparent, and unbiased recruitment, selection, evaluations, and promotion processes; • identify under-represented groups in the organisation and actively attract and develop these employees; and • collect reliable data, report on current status, and set goals around the representation of diverse groups.

References

Adams, R. B., & Ferreira, D. (2009). Women in the boardroom and their impact on governance and performance. *Journal of Financial Economics*, *94*, 291–309. https://doi.org/10.1016/j.jfineco.2008.10.007

Ali, M., Kulik, C. T., & Metz, I. (2009). The impact of gender diversity on performance in services and manufacturing organizations. *Academy of Management Proceedings*, *2009*(1), 1–6. https//doi.org/10.5465/AMBPP.2009.44243048

Becker, B. E., & Huselid, M. A. (1998). High-performance work systems and firm performance: A synthesis of research and managerial implications. *Research in Personnel and Human Resources Management*, *16*, 53–101.

Berdahl, J. L., Glick, P., & Cooper, M. (2018, November 2). How masculinity contests undermine organisations, and what to do about it. *Harvard Business Review*. Retrieved March 1, 2023, from hbr.org

Boulouta, I. (2012). Hidden connections: The link between board gender diversity and corporate social performance. *Journal of Business Ethics*, *113*, 185–197. https://doi.org/10.1007/s10551-012-1293-7

Broni, G., & Velentzas, J. (2012). Corporate governance, control and individualism as a definition of business success. The idea of a "Post – Heroic" Leadership. *Procedia Economics and Finance*, *1*, 61–70. https//doi.org/10.1016/S2212-5671(12)00009-3

Bunderson, J. S., & Sutcliffe, K. M. (2002). Comparing alternative conceptualizations of functional diversity in management teams: Process and performance effects. *The Academy of Management Journal*, *45*(5), 875–893. https://doi.org/10.2307/3069319

Bunderson, J. S., & Van der Vegt, G. S. (2018). Diversity and inequality in management teams: A review and integration of research on vertical and horizontal member differences. *Annual Review of Organizational Psychology and Organizational Behavior*, *5*(1), 47–73. https://doi.org/10.1146/annurev-orgpsych-032117-104500

Byrne, D. (1971). *The attraction paradigm*. Academic.

Cannella, A. A., Park, J. H., & Lee, H. U. (2008). Top management team functional background diversity and firm performance: Examining the roles of team member colocation and environmental uncertainty. *Academy of Management Journal*, *51*(4), 768–784. https://doi.org/10.5465/AMJ.2008.33665310

Carpenter, M. A. (2002). The implications of strategy and social context for the relationship between top management team heterogeneity and firm performance. *Strategic Management Journal*, *23*(3), 275–284. https://doi.org/10.1002/smj.226

Cohen, J. J., Gabriel, B. A., & Terrell, C. (2002). The case for diversity in the health care workforce. *Health Affairs (Project Hope)*, *21*(5), 90–102. https://doi.org/10.1377/hlthaff.21.5.90

Cooney-O'Donoghue, D., Adamovic, M., & Sojo, V. (2022). Exploring the impacts of the COVID-19 crisis for the employment prospects of refugees and people seeking asylum in Australia. *Australian Journal of Social Issues*, *57*, 88–110. https://doi.org/10.1002/ajs4.177

Cox, T. H., & Blake, S. (1991). Managing cultural diversity: Implications for organizational competitiveness. *The Executive*, *5*(3), 45–56. http://www.jstor.org/stable/4165021

Dollard, M. F., & Bakker, A. B. (2010). Psychosocial safety climate as a precursor to conducive work environments, psychological health problems, and employee engagement. *Journal of Occupational and Organizational Psychology*, *83*, 579–599. https://doi.org/10.1348/096317909X470690

Eesley, C. E., Hsu, D. H., & Roberts, E. B. (2014). The contingent effects of top management teams on venture performance: Aligning founding team composition with innovation strategy and commercialization environment. *Strategic Management Journal*, *35*(12), 1798–1817. https://doi.org/10.1002/smj.2183

Fernandez, S., Malatesta, D., & Smith, C. R. (2013). Race, gender, and government contracting: Different explanations or new prospects for theory? *Public Administration Review*, *73*(1), 109–120. https//doi.org/10.1111/j.1540-6210.2012.02684.x

Fine, C., & Sojo, V. (2019). Do women add value? Beyond the business case for diversity and inclusion. *The Lancet*, *393*(10171), 515–516. https//doi.org/10.1016/S0140-6736(19)30165-5

Fine, C., Sojo, V., & Lawford-Smith, H. (2020). Why does workplace gender diversity matter? Justice, organizational benefits, and policy. *Social Issues and Policy Review*, *14*, 36–72. https//doi.org/10.1111/sipr.12064

Gardiner, M., & Tiggemann, M. (1999). Gender differences in leadership style, job stress and mental health in male-and female-dominated industries. *Journal of Occupational and Organizational Psychology*, *72*(3), 301–315. https://doi.org/10.1348/096317999166699

Harrison, D. A., & Klein, K. J. (2007). What's the difference? diversity constructs as separation, variety, or disparity in organizations. *Academy of Management Review*, *32*(4), 1199–1228. https://doi-org.ezp.lib.unimelb.edu.au/10.5465/AMR.2007.26586096

HealthWest Partnership. (2020). *Workforce mutuality toolkit. Standards for workforce mutuality*. HealthWest Partnership.

Herring, C. (2009). Does diversity pay? Race, gender, and the business case for diversity. *American Sociological Review*, *74*(2), 208–224. https://doi.org/10.1177/000312240907400203

Hoobler, J. M., Masterson, C. R., Nkomo, S. M., & Michel, E. J. (2018). The business case for women leaders: Meta-analysis, research critique, and path forward. *Journal of Management*, *44*(6), 2473–2499. https://doi.org/10.1177/0149206316628643

Ilies, R., Hauserman, N., Schwochau, S., & Stibal, J. (2003). Reported incidence rates of work-related sexual harassment in the United States: Using meta-analysis to explain reported rate disparities. *Personnel Psychology*, *56*, 607–631. https//doi.org/10.1111/j.1744-6570.2003.tb00752.x

Jehn, K. A., & Mannix, E. A. (2001). The dynamic structure of conflict: A longitudinal study of intragroup conflict and group performance. *Academy of Management Journal*, *44*, 238–251. https://doi.org/10.5465/3069453

Kanter, R. M. (1977). Some effects of proportions on group life: Skewed sex ratios and responses to token women. *American Journal of Sociology*, *82*(5), 965–990. http://www.jstor.org/stable/2777808

Kish-Gephart, J. J., Harrison, D. A., & Treviño, L. K. (2010). Bad apples, bad cases, and bad barrels: Meta-analytic evidence about sources of unethical decisions at work. *Journal of Applied Psychology*, *95*, 1–31. https//doi.org/10.1037/a0017103

Leonard, J. S., & Levine, D. I. (2006). The effect of diversity on turnover: A large case study. *ILR Review*, *59*(4), 547–572. https://doi.org/10.1177/001979390605900402

Mor Barak, M. E., Lizano, E. L., Kim, A., Duan, L., Rhee, M. K., Hsiao, H. Y., & Brimhall, K. C. (2016). The promise of diversity management for climate of inclusion: A state-of-the-art review and meta-analysis. *Human Service Organizations: Management, Leadership & Governance*, *40*(4), 305–333.

Niemann, Y. F., & Dovidio, J. F. (1998). Relationship of solo status, academic rank, and perceived distinctiveness to job satisfaction of racial/ethnic minorities. *Journal of Applied Psychology*, *83*(1), 55–71. https://doi.org/10.1037/0021-9010.83.1.55

Orlitzky, M., & Frenkel, S. J. (2005). Alternative pathways to high-performance workplaces. *The International Journal of Human Resource Management*, *16*(8), 1325–1348. https://doi.org/10.1080/09585190500220176

Post, C., & Byron, K. (2015). Women on boards and firm financial performance: A meta-analysis. *Academy of Management Journal*, *58*(5), 1546–1571. https://doi.org/10.5465/amj.2013.0319

Qian, C., Cao, Q., & Takeuchi, R. (2013). Top management team functional diversity and organizational innovation in China: The moderating effects of environment. *Strategic Management Journal*, *34*(1), 110–120. http://www.jstor.org/stable/23362651

Ray, V. (2019). A theory of racialized organizations. *American Sociological Review*, *84*(1), 26–53. https://doi.org/10.1177/0003122418822335

Roberson, Q. M. (2019). Diversity in the workplace: A review, synthesis, and future research agenda. *Annual Review of Organizational Psychology and Organizational Behavior*, *6*, 69–88. https//doi.org/10.1146/annurev-orgpsych-012218-015243

Ruiz-Jiménez, J. M., del Mar Fuentes-Fuentes, M., & Ruiz-Arroyo, M. (2016). Knowledge combination capability and innovation: The effects of gender diversity on top management teams in technology-based firms. *Journal of Business Ethics*, *135*(3), 503–515. https//doi.org/10.1007/s10551-014-2462-7

Settles, I. H., Cortina, L. M., Malley, J., & Stewart, A. J. (2006). The climate for women in academic science: The good, the bad, and the changeable. *Psychology of Women Quarterly*, *30*, 47–58. https//doi.org/10.1111/j.1471-6402.2006.00261.x

Smith, W. J., Wokutch, R. E., Harrington, K. V., & Dennis, B. S. (2001). An examination of the influence of diversity and stakeholder role on corporate social orientation. *Business & Society*, *40*(3), 266–294. https://doi.org/10.1177/000765030104000303

Sojo, V., & Ainsworth, S. (2020). More women in workplace leadership could make the difference post-Covid. In *Essays on equality* (Vol. 2). Global Institute of Women's Leadership, King's College London.

Sojo, V., Wood, R., & Genat, A. (2016a). Harmful workplace experiences and women's occupational well-being: A meta-analysis. *Psychology of Women Quarterly*, *40*, 10–40. https//doi.org/10.1177/0361684315599346

Sojo, V., Wood, R., Wood, S., & Wheeler, M. (2016b). Reporting requirements, targets, and quotas for women in leadership. *The Leadership Quarterly*, *27*, 519–536. https://doi.org/10.1016/j.leaqua.2015.12.003

Spevick, J. (2003). The case for racial concordance between patients and physicians. *AMA Journal of Ethics*, *5*(6), 163–165. https//doi.org/10.1001/virtualmentor.2003.5.6.jdsc2-0306

Stergiou-Kita, M., Mansfield, E., Colantonio, A., Moody, J., & Mantis, S. (2016). What's gender got to do with it? Examining masculinities, health and safety and return to work in male dominated skilled trades. *Work*, *54*(3), 721–733. https//doi.org/10.3233/WOR-162322

Tajfel, H., &Turner, J. C. (1986). The social identity theory of intergroup behavior. In S. Worchel & W. G. Austin (Eds.), *The psychology of intergroup relations* (pp. 7–24). Nelson-Hall.

van Dijk, H., van Engen, M. L., & van Knippenberg, D. (2012). Defying conventional wisdom: A meta-analytical examination of the differences between demographic and job-related diversity relationships with performance. *Organizational Behavior and Human Decision Processes*, *119*, 38–53. https//doi.org/10.1016/j.obhdp.2012.06.003

van Knippenberg, D., & Schippers, M. C. (2007). Work group diversity. *Annual Review of Psychology*, *58*, 515–541. https//doi.org/10.1146/annurev.psych.58.110405.085546

Wiersema, M. F., & Bird, A. (1993). Organizational demography in Japanese firms: Group heterogeneity, individual dissimilarity, and top management team turnover. *The Academy of Management Journal*, *36*(5), 996–1025. https://doi.org/10.2307/256643

Williams, K., & O'Reilly, C. (1998). The complexity of diversity: A review of forty years of research. In D. Gruenfeld & M. Neale (Eds.), *Research on managing in groups and teams* (vol. 20, pp. 77–140). JAI Press.

16

SENSE OF BELONGING AND PROFESSIONAL IDENTITY

Iva Durakovic and Laurie Aznavoorian

I miss the beautiful office.

– Employee

Introduction

The COVID-19 pandemic inspired a stronger focus on employees' expectations in the workplace with an emphasis on work–life balance and purpose that will drive changes to workplace design and appearance. This evolution is likely to continue as emerging technology is deployed to support the integration of processes and people. New opportunities, capabilities and thinking about what intrinsically motivates humans will impact the way we interact, driving an altered dynamic. Workplace once considered a vehicle of organisational profit and productivity has evolved to become a moniker of brand, with COVID driving a redefinition of its purpose as an influencer of behaviour and interaction.

Existing research offers a starting point, but our current understanding of spatial influences of relationships and human behaviours is rudimentary at best. For the next evolution of workplace design, a greater overlap between human sciences and architecture will be necessary to appreciate emotional triggers, processes and mechanisms through which an expanded notion of workplace will be born. This will include physical space, the metaverse and other associated virtual reality (VR) and augmented reality (AR) environments that influence people. Reframing our notion of the workplace and incorporating what we have seen and experienced over the past two years suggests technology platforms will become the place where work is done, and the physical workplace will act as an enabling tool for other related activities. This view opens the door to the notion of workplace as a product that can be intentionally designed to act on humans' deep internal triggers and desires for reward, renewal and constant change. This shift will uncover avenues in how to motivate, delight and inspire users.

Place is critical to the success of a high-performing workplace and the human psychology that underpins its potential and value, namely, our innate condition for place attachment, need for belonging and evolving professional identities. Explained through the framework of self-determination theory, with evidence from Australian research, the potential of individual and

DOI: 10.1201/9781003328728-19
This chapter has been made available under a CC-BY-NC-ND 4.0 license.

organisational outcomes will be highlighted, followed by a discussion of the nuances, shifts and challenges that the pandemic presented for employees and organisations.

Identity, place and belonging – theory

Identity, or a person's sense of self, is informed by two key aspects critical to understand connection to the workplace. First is personal identity defined by our personal values, needs, attributes and desires. Second is social identity, defined by relations to other collectives like work, social groups, teams or the organisation and profession (Luong et al., 2020).

Social identity theory tells us identities are not fixed. They are evolving self-concepts that respond, adapt and are continuously shaped by interactions with people, places, our internal landscapes and external circumstances. These interactions call for various forms of expression which over time develop into symbols, meanings and behavioural norms that bind us together (Ogasawara, 2001).

Behavioural scientists call identity work the process of managing, filtering and censoring parts of ourselves to suit the personas our environments ask of us seeking the most meaningful, comfortable and secure fit within these environments (Carnevale & Hatak, 2020). This implies a constant relational learning; as multifaceted individuals with multiple identities, we evolve our behaviours and networks throughout the courses of our working lives.

> The significance of architecture is premised on . . . the conviction that it is architecture's task to render vivid to us who we might ideally be.
>
> (de Botton, 2006, p. 13)

Our identities are intrinsically linked to places, people and internal emotional landscapes and value systems; it is through alignment of these to our external socio-spatial contexts that attachments and connections form to foster a sense of belonging. Maslow's work tells us belonging is fundamental to human motivation, and self-determination theory posits all human behaviour is motivated by the fulfilment of three basic psychological needs – relatedness, autonomy and competence (Caligiuri & Cieri, 2021). The extent to which individuals using subjective experiences of fulfilment can satisfy these needs within a given context is what matters most.

A fundamental feature of belonging is a person's feeling of being valued, needed and important to other people, groups, objects, organisations and environments or spiritual dimensions. To belong, a person's experiences should fit with others in the group, through shared or complementary characteristics (Hagerty & Putasky, 1995). Physical workspaces can provide important cues to belonging that affect workers' motivation and organisational commitment (Fenwick, 2010). These are affected by stage in life and other contextual factors, such as emotions, that play a role in how workers navigate experiences and engage with the workplace through professional identities (Ayoko & Ashkanasy, 2020). Being at home in our identities implies we have infused ourselves with time, spaces (when, where, how) and values (organisational culture), finding meaning, comfort and security within them. This is a core part of the psychological ownership developed over our work, workplaces and organisational cultures that fuels motivation, performance and satisfaction (Pierce & Brown, 2020). Collective psychological ownership fosters organisational social capital, which keeps relational learning, building of networks, communities and reciprocal productive relationships between organisations and employees thriving.

Professional identity is a multidimensional phenomenon with subjective and objective experiences. Subjective experiences refer to perceptions and constructs of self within the work context. Objective experiences relate to the established norms of the role, professional field, organisation and parameters for evaluation of performance surrounding these, such as organisational KPIs (Key Performance Indicators). Professional identity manifests at three levels in the workplace: individual professional identity, collective or team identities, and the organisation's identity.

For the individual, work is not only a place and activity to spend and invest a large proportion of time, but also a critical facet of their professional selves and source of self-esteem; work provides a sense of purpose and meaning to one's existence (Luong et al., 2020). At the team level work communities and networks become powerful sources of identity, practice and knowledge that satisfy needs for recognition, competence, participation and meaning (Fenwick, 2010). Our subjective sense of knowledge in work is important, but it must also be valued and validated by our teams to support identity and belonging.

At an organisational level collective workplace identity is an anchor which facilitates the attachment of individuals to the workplace; at its best supporting positive outcomes such as learning, commitment, group identification and work values through positive influence (Sulphey, 2019). Patterns of interaction at this level define the culture of the organisation and infuse the corporation, its activities and products with meaning, shaping culture and facilitating identification at all three levels – my place of work, where we work and our building (Barclay & York, 2001).

The physical environment presents a critical organisational asset, and organisations must realise the responsibility they have to fulfil employees' needs if they are to retain talent and sustain human performance (Pierce & Brown, 2020). Person–environment fit (Appel-Meulenbroek et al., 2019; Caplan, 1983) resources demands models (Demerouti et al., 2001; Schaufeli & Taris, 2014), workplace self-space identity models (Luong et al., 2020; Csikszentmihalyi & Rochberg-Halton, 1981) and self-determination theory (Deci et al., 2017; Ryan & Deci, 2000) are human science frameworks used in human resources, management and organisational literature. They are increasingly applied to workplace design research to better understand how physical spaces can impact human behaviours and occupants' satisfaction, performance and well-being, creating high-performance workplace (HPW) environments.

HPW enablers of belonging and professional identity

The B:Hive study (Aznavoorian et al., 2020), conducted in late 2019 to March 2020, explored the phenomenology of a co-working environment in the creation of work communities, networks and sense of belonging amongst occupants. Findings illustrate how place can trigger a sense of comfort and how the design supports each layer of comfort: physical, functional and psychological. All are enablers of connection, belonging and professional identity supporting a sustainable model of motivation, productivity, satisfaction and well-being.

Longitudinal surveys (Durakovic et al., 2023a; Marzban et al., 2021) and workshops (Durakovic & Munao, 2022) were conducted during the extended Australian lockdowns of 2020/2021 with organisations, managers and employees across a range of sectors, capturing a snapshot of experiences, challenges and anecdotes from working at home. These studies gathered lessons learned from the early days of returning to the office and evolving hybrid workstyles. Questions compare experiences between working in the office and working elsewhere of collaboration, autonomy, team management, productivity, motivation, working hours, meetings and sense of belonging, value and community. Findings unanimously indicate the aspect of the office participants have missed most are the human connections it facilitates.

As organisations tackle the difficulties in attracting people back into the office whilst simultaneously navigating the cultural, physical and leadership challenges of hybrid working, Australian firm Mirvac has been testing, learning and experimenting with possible solutions through a pilot within their exiting office accommodation (see Chapter 21). Observations, surveys, utilisation studies and interview methods were used to gather feedback from occupants to better understand affective challenges of new ways of working in-office and elsewhere (Durakovic et al., 2023b). The study focused on spatial and workplace design solutions impacting the emotive dimensions of work and social capital, namely, a sense of togetherness, team connection and belonging.

These studies and the pandemic trajectory reinforce the value of work and place in professional belonging and identities, particularly in our evolving societal landscape. Through them, we can understand the mechanisms and ecosystem through which the workplace can support, trigger, nudge, nurture and motivate.

The critical role of comfort in HPW

If motivation is the lifeblood, environmental comfort is the conduit enabling the workplace to act as a powerful tool of work. Jaqueline Vischer's extensive work into the psychology of "workspaces" shows that an individual's experience (subjective and objective) of comfort in the workplace can be organised into three core components – physical, functional and psychological. In HPW these layers work together to build transformational behaviours, communities, positive cultures and outcomes, leading to long-term benefits of sustained human performance, satisfaction and talent attraction (Vischer, 2008). Figure 16.1 illustrates how HPWs leverage the mechanisms of comfort to activate natural conditions for place attachment, thereby nurturing professional identity, feelings of belonging, sense of ownership and control over the workspace.

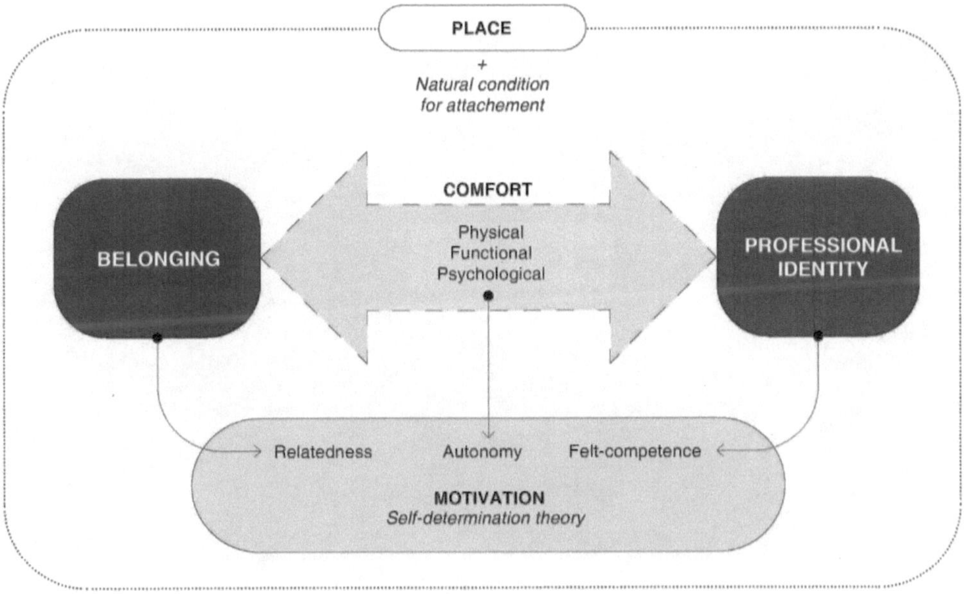

Figure 16.1 Leveraging comfort through experiences of environmental and place attachment.

The body of research discussed earlier illustrates how autonomy (sense of control and ownership) speaks to comfort. Autonomy is in direct causal relationship with experiences of competence and relatedness, dependent on a strong positive feedback loop with our work environments and professional identities. Akin to Maslow's hierarchy of human needs, employees cannot experience positive psychological comfort in the workplace without having their physical and functional comfort needs met first.

Physical and functional comfort

Physical comfort entails the basic conditions for safe occupancy in the workplace which are a given (Vischer et al., 2015). Appropriate choices of furniture, finishes, universal design principles and accessibility are well-researched influencers, as are aesthetics, ergonomics and Indoor Environment Quality (IEQ), which are explained in detail throughout Chapters 1–10. They are important baseline conditions for occupant behaviour and affective experience.

The B:Hive study found 77% of occupants felt comfortable in the space. When asked specifically what it was about the B:Hive that made them feel this way, responses indicated the décor, permission to adjust the space to fit their needs, the level of noise and distraction and the way other B:Hivers behaved. When asked about the impact of IEQ, 43% said the level of daylight made them feel happier about being at work and 26% felt more energised. The building has both natural and mechanical ventilation; consequently, responses relating to air quality also indicated occupants were happier and more energised (Aznavoorian et al., 2020).

Encompassing many dimensions of environmental conditions in the workplace, functional comfort ultimately is about choice and settings that support work. Spatial organisation supports the transitions and activities of the workday (Wohlers & Hertel, 2017). The environment supports "bump n spark" meetings of like-minded people and facilitates unexpected partnership through

Image 16.1 B:Hive – comfort and space chronology. (Architecture and interior design by BVN Architecture. Photography by John Gollings.)

sequencing, zoning and design of workspaces that dictate the user's journey, creating routine and opportunities for interaction.

Psychological comfort

Supported by the physical and functional, the psychological layer creates what many called vibe, making them feel part of something bigger and offering the opportunity to see and hear what's going on. The B:Hive was described as a whole package that was not just a workplace or brand but everything involved in the space, including the people who make the place; in turn, place dictates the people who office there, "if you get crappy people the workplace will be crap. You won't find crappy people in a building like this".

The B:Hive demonstrates the role environment plays in creating a community workers want to be a part of. This view is consistent with literature that suggests co-working offers the missing relational component of traditional office working, diminishing isolation, self-motivation and productivity problems independent professionals struggle with (Brown, 2017).

Places are meaningful, hold symbolism and support individuals' emotional needs for identity and belonging. The pandemic instigated disconnection from workplaces, but our surveys found workers sought professional and emotional support from the workplace delivered through proximity; hearing and seeing colleagues helped gain a sense of a community and understanding of what's happening, making workers feel secure and psychologically safe (Durakovic et al., 2023a).

At a functional level, psychological comfort builds trust. One of the biggest challenges we face in working remotely comes from lower levels of trust due to the inability to spontaneously connect with colleagues. This occurs because micro-expressions play a role in effective connections. Since

Image 16.2 B:Hive – creating community. (Architecture and interior design by BVN Architecture. Photography by John Gollings.)

these actions cannot be controlled, they are related to emotions, which hold clues to the authenticity of interactions that lead to trust (Iwasaki & Noguchi, 2016).

The work from home (WFH) experience reignited desire for human contact but also raised awareness of the lack of control in a typical open-plan office design. Psychological comfort relies on the ability to have control and a sense of empowerment. One of the greatest benefits of the WFH experiment was reduced unwanted interruptions and ability to not answer calls. Working remotely, we make the trade-off between connection and productivity.

In our surveys workers not only commented on the loss of delineation between work and life, but included more nuanced transitions such as mindset shifts in preparation for business that comes from the office's clear structure and routine. Similarly, exercising on breaks and movement between meetings were missed, as was the variety of environments and rituals married to locations, such as morning coffee (Durakovic et al., 2023a). Moving forward we might consider a time-based rather than task-based framework as we define the tools and spaces needed to support work post-pandemic.

The role of time in HPW: developing connection, meaning and workplace purpose

Kamp et al. (2011) talk about the changing qualities of time in post-industrial work, which they categorise as acceleration, compression, uncertainty and asynchrony. COVID brought new clues to this mix in the structure of work and the pros and cons of technology. Clearly technology cannot support serendipity or deep emotional connections, but it does offer opportunities for connection, particularly regarding the inclusion of introverts, neurodiverse workers and those outside of CBD (central business district) areas.

The notion of time to listen and understand patients' experiences and needs in healthcare offers insights as to why reattaining workspace in some capacity is beneficial. Space facilitates opportunities for uninterrupted face-to-face time, building deeper, authentic contacts and connections. Global studies found that through the extended WFH experience, people craved human connection prompting organisations to simplistically decide future offices should be for collaboration only with individual work happening elsewhere. This approach undermines the importance of social connections and time together in space to create connections. Just as space enables comfort through a chronology structure, and boundaries by which we navigate work and our professional and emotive needs, so does time.

Time manifests in the workplace in various ways:

Learning time

Collaboration and innovation can be done digitally, but disconnection from the office illuminated how much knowledge is created, shared and absorbed through physical proximity. This is particularly true for younger workers eager to learn and build professional and social networks. Spaces in-between, and the time and opportunity to see, hear and feel how others work, play a critical role in succession planning and career progression (Durakovic & Munao, 2022).

Relational time

Data consistently indicates employees are prioritising collaboration with their teams and social interaction as reasons to go into the office (Durakovic et al., 2020, 2023a; Marzban et al., 2021).

Image 16.3 B:Hive – taking time – spatial cues. (Architecture and interior design by BVN Architecture. Photography by John Gollings.)

The emotive connections and functional support of the physical workplace are evident, and these findings show that environment impacts employees over the time they work. Togetherness is expressed through yearning for interaction and companionship; it is demonstrated through time and space to banter, chat and see friends and colleagues daily. This delivers a feeling of belonging.

Place provides a venue for workers to relate to one another and is a catalyst to take the time that workers would not be taking when working from home divorced from spatial cues.

Quick time

A distinct emphasis on productive connections and the spatial elements that enable quick, impromptu and incidental problem solving and collaboration was noted in surveys (Durakovic et al., 2023a; Durakovic & Munao, 2022). The physical workplace plays a role in the rapid and efficient exchange of information that is not facilitated effectively through digital channels. It helps us focus on common targets, facilitating effectiveness and collective psychological ownership (Pierce & Brown, 2020).

Intentionality and alignment – motivation, meaning and purpose in the workplace

Motivation is born of belonging and alignment to values, purpose and authentic identity that are core self-concepts; we become a part of something bigger (Kamp et al., 2011).

COVID uncovered a misalignment and lack of authenticity in work masked behind pay cheques, promotions and other extrinsic forms of motivation. The pandemic offered a chance to hit the pause button to investigate (Cambon, 2021) problems with work itself. Employees crave authenticity in an organisation's values and goals and want them to marry to their own if they are to find work meaningful and rationalise giving up time with loved ones, reconnection to passions and community, which matter more now.

Removal of in-person presence removed the mechanisms through which design can, and in the best examples does, cultivate collective psychological ownership that employees identify with. Without teams and professional personas in our private spaces, other senses of our selves emerged, illuminating the discords that existed. Not being in the workplace highlighted parts of our personas that were more fundamental to motivation than previously understood.

Collective psychological ownership was lost when we were cut off and had no physical space to attach to, but a new sense of psychological ownership was gained over workspaces, workstyles and professional purpose. One survey respondent noted the benefits of newfound purpose as "independence and reinforcing self-motivation" (Durakovic et al., 2023a). The challenge ahead is marrying this with the evolving purpose and experience of workplace environments.

Boundaries

Ownership and territory are commonly expressed through personalisation and appropriation of space; users mark territory, constructing boundaries for social groups, to mask disruption, define ways of working and communication protocols and for environmental control: noise, privacy, décor, furniture arrangements, etc. (Sundstrom et al., 1982; Vischer, 2008).

Prior to the pandemic, open-plan, activity-based and agile offices designed to optimise productivity through flexibility and choice gave workers permission to control visual and auditory privacy and configure individual and team environments to suit workstyles and project demands. Choice enabled identities to be expressed through place, done on workers' terms but within the values of the wider organisation (Baldry & Barnes, 2012). Spatial boundaries have blurred to include remote offices, cafés, third-party places and home, but professional identities were still grounded in the transitions created by the workday hours, commute, physical location and impermeability of technology into our private realms (Kamp et al., 2011).

COVID took us out of work environments completely, we lost control we once had and were invited into the private lives of leaders and colleagues, seeing identities not previously shared in the workplace context (Kniffin et al., 2020). For some this created deeper connections with co-workers, but others felt disarmed.

Motivation

The self-environment relationship in workplace varies in meaning and nature depending on an employee's career stage and experience. Surveys indicate what people missed about working in the office highlights these differences (Image 16.4). Managers, whose role is to manage workflows, processes and outputs, place emphasis on face-to-face interaction and proximity. This supports efficacy in decision making, communication and monitoring of employees' well-being and workloads through reading body language. Environment also impacts the manager's sense of professional identity and competence. For employees, the social and emotive connections the workplace facilitates is at the forefront; all these elements impact a sense of relatedness, attachment and belonging (Durakovic et al., 2023a).

Mirvac's Adaptive Workplace Pilot (Durakovic et al., 2023b) set out to improve connection, collaboration and social capital in hybrid work styles. Occupants noted physical proximity had

Image 16.4 *(a)* Employees and (b) managers free text responses to "What do you miss most about working in the office". (Adapted from Durakovic et al., 2023a)

impact and is still an essential ingredient for motivation, productivity (of some tasks) and morale. However, what became clear is workers' sense of attachment to the organisation was primarily a manifestation of people they worked with and not the environment or the company. Workplace is beneficial for connection, learning and to bond with one's team.

> [T]he way that it was set out allowed us to connect in a much more reasonable and meaningful way for the activities that we were working on . . . the whole point for us to actually be in the office was to be there to talk to each other and share ideas . . . to find out something about us beyond just our work.
>
> Because that actually ended up helping us with what we were doing at work. . . . To understand a little bit more about how each other thought meant that we could then find the right space for us to connect.
>
> (Durakovic et al., 2023b)

Autonomy

Autonomy sits in a reciprocal relationship with relatedness and professional competence. A clear trend emerged through the surveys, indicating the experience of autonomy and control over time, environment and workstyle we gained stagnated as disconnection from teams and work communities increased (Durakovic & Munao, 2022). This suggests the wider social system of the workplace and social capital built through relational learning (Fang et al., 2017) is critical to perceptions of individual effectiveness and value to the organisation/system, inadvertently affecting motivation and a willingness to continue investing ourselves into that system/collective work outcomes.

Passion is increasingly becoming a requisite for professional success (Bartleby, 2023). Achieving harmonious passion, the genuine enjoyment of an activity, requires the right motivations,

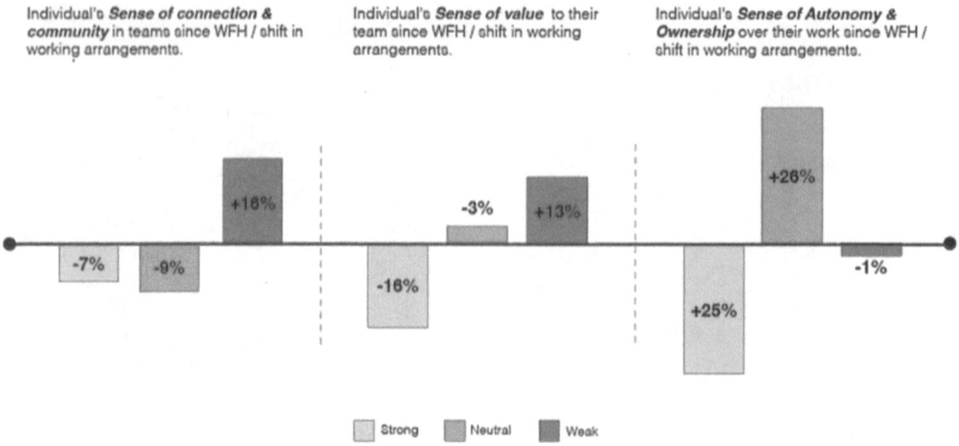

Figure 16.2 Percentage shifts in workers' experiences of (a) connection and community; (b) sense of value to their team; and (c) autonomy and ownership between 2020 and 2021. (Adapted from Durakovic & Munao, 2022)

which come from alignment of expectations and experiences of relatedness, autonomy and competence within the workplace and organisational culture. Moving forward, organisations must recognise there are different motivators and sentiments for returning to the physical workplace that need to be rationalised.

The path ahead for HPW

An American sitcom from the 1960s starring Eddie Albert and Eva Gabour called *Green Acres* is an apt starting point for a discussion on the future of work and the status of hybrid work. The show features a couple who moves from NYC to a country farm, taking with them a version of their past life that does not apply to country living. Oliver, once a successful lawyer, performs farm chores in a suit and drives a Lincoln convertible; his high-maintenance wife tosses the dishes out of the kitchen window rather than washing them.

There are parallels to what lies ahead for the future of the workplace. The current unsatisfactory status of hybrid work stems from applying an office pathology to homes without the deep thinking this problem deserves. In our haste to rapidly introduce hybrid work we forfeited thinking and planning; as a result, employees left the office and transported home what was broken, e.g., a culture of presenteeism, time wasting and unhealthy attitudes about effectiveness.

We now have the space and time. Microsoft recently found 66% of managers plan to redesign their office space for hybrid work (Microsoft, 2021), but how will this happen? Will the widespread dysfunction of remote and hybrid work continue, should we opt for always in or always out? More importantly, should the problem not include the physical places we work in as well as an examination of the role of work in our lives?

A problem predating but exacerbated by the pandemic is the erosion of institutions and social infrastructures that were places to connect, build a community, and identify with. This left work as the primary means of interaction, connection and comfort. The design of the contemporary office illustrates our attempt to fill the gap by including amenity spaces that make workers feel at home and part of the community. At the same time many continue to encourage unhealthy relationships with work and treat overworking as a badge of honour. This hypocrisy has not been lost on workers who are hungry for greater purpose and meaning.

Removing amenities from the workplace is likely to be undesirable, although an argument could be made that they are less relevant with flexible work schedules and greater choice. Assuming the current practice of blurring work, home and community continues; perhaps the answer lies in blurring lines further by designing workplaces that truly integrate the community, extending the hours of operations to breathe air into cities that have lost their vibrancy. By aligning place with the internal emotional landscapes and value systems that define people's identity, a sense of belonging will result.

Included in the calculus of the future of the workplace should be the dissatisfaction many have with work that made conditions ripe for "quiet quitting" and "The Great Resignation" (Allman, 2021; Geisler, 2021; Kaplan, 2021). The pandemic offered time and opportunity to reassess priorities, whilst employees realised their jobs were not fulfilling. Therefore, considering employees' motivations for working makes sense.

Perceptions have changed, giving rise to an activist workforce that holds business to account and prioritises well-being over career progression. There is an expectation that businesses address broader societal issues, presenting an opportunity to reinforce alignment in motivation and values, assuming it exists. Before leaping to solutions, an examination of work should occur that investigates what it means and should mean to us, what we expect and how personal motivations and company values can align. Only then should design be considered.

Conclusion

Recalibrate workplace

Research suggests 75% of the workforce would prefer to work from home one to five days per week. For many, flexibility is non-negotiable, 30% of employees working remotely said they would resign if their organisation removed the remote work option (Barrero et al., 2021). It is still too early to tell whether attitudes will change. Humans are social beings, and place attachment plays a role in identity; therefore, it is unlikely the office is dead, as some predict, but it is equally unlikely to return to pre-pandemic occupancy patterns.

Uncertainty about our future suggests workplaces must be far more flexible than they have been, given we do not know what is to come and have no precedent to follow. Not knowing means developing a hypothesis, testing, evaluating and changing environments as we learn (see Chapter 21). This degree of flexibility will not come from assembling the same elements differently, but through reimagining the workplace, starting with buildings services distribution. We need fluidity, which requires new means of accessing services that support user manipulation (see Chapter 20).

The pandemic busted many workplace myths, including those related to collaboration happening near water coolers and in hallways. Research already proved that was false, but it took offices being boarded up and workers sent home to prove connection and collaboration can occur online using digital platforms. Except for intense creative brainstorming, activities lumped under the umbrella term "collaboration", like coordinating, reviewing, editing and contributing to work, happen as effectively, if not more, without office distractions.

What cannot be duplicated online is being with colleagues. Work is a social affair; interactions are the essence of being human. Face-to-face connections and impromptu conversations in a non-formal setting nurture personal relationships through increased empathy and trust (Hopkins & Figaro, 2021), leading to improved employee relationships, higher productivity, creativity, innovation and commitment (Pentland, 2014).

Workers like working from home and they will not want to abandon that entirely, but they also now know which activities are best done in the office: connecting professionally and socially and tapping into company culture. Consequently, recalibration of the workplace to favour spaces dedicated to togetherness designed to facilitate social interaction, teamwork and special events seems to make sense.

Assuming the hypothesis is correct, and the primary utility of the office has changed to be the place where people come together, then where does the "real heads down work" happen? Obviously somewhere else, or in specially designed places within the environment for focus away from the noise and distraction of togetherness spaces.

Technological advancements provide a platform for diverse teams to work together spanning cities, cultures and continents. It has also made expansion of the labour pools possible, leading to greater inclusion of introverted employees and those with disabilities and neurodiversity. In contemplating the future of work, we must consider the reasons that past workplaces led to actual and psycho-emotional disablism (Reeve, 2019).

The role of technology cannot be underestimated. This is where work happens; it is the place, and the physical workplace is an enabler, expanding the future workplace problem to include the digital environment. This gives designers another element to deal with when they have not yet cracked the issue of digital inequity, let alone how digital space reinforces identity and belonging; nevertheless, it may be an easier road to toe given its freedom from bias and physical obstacles.

Conceiving of space as secondary allows a leap to occur. Co-working defined space as a service. Does it open doors to think of space as a product? Is it possible to borrow ideas from technology designers and Internet companies who used neuroscience to develop attachment, and can this merge with theories of place attachment and place identity to create future environments we want to be in?

Thomas Edison said, "I find out what the world needs. Then I go ahead and try to invent." We need solutions to cataclysmic problems of our times, the ones that keep the people who occupy the workplaces we design up at night. We have experienced a major disruption that allowed us to hit the pause button; can we move forward with the intention of doing more with the physical and digital environments to embed a deep sense of belonging and identity?

A "high-performance" checklist for fostering belonging and re-calibration is provided here:

Principle	*Description*
ENVIRONMENTAL COMFORT	• Thermal and visual comfort • Access to natural air, light and views • Use biophilia/biophilic design principles • Accessibility • Functional requirements meet spatial chronology and flow
FLEXIBILITY	• Choice must be available • Variety of places to work • User malleability supported by management/culture and design • Untethering from fixed services
CONNECTION	• Visual connectivity in the workplace • Digital equity • Design to encourage encounters, meetings and connection • Expression of organisational values and social responsibilities

(*Continued*)

(Continued)

Principle	*Description*
TECHNOLOGY The place of work	• Recalibrate thinking to consider the digital environment • Recognise continual evolution • Leverage technology for learning, identity and motivation • Seamless experience of connection
MOTIVATION	• Alignment of places and processes to employees' expectations and needs • Malleable design, leadership and purposeful environment • Autonomy and control to teams and individuals • Clarity of purpose
PLACE ATTACHMENT	• Togetherness places that support a collective • Concierge services and social event planning • Unique places that act as anchors
PLACE IDENTITY	• Physical and digital space to support learning, leading to commitment • Physical and digital space reinforces company values, building group identity

References

Allman, K. (2021). Career matters: 'The great resignation' sweeping workplaces around the world. *LSJ: Law Society of NSW Journal*, (81), 46–47.

Appel-Meulenbroek, R., Le Blanc, P., & de Kort, Y. (2019). Person–environment fit: Optimizing the physical work environment. In O. B. Ayoko & N. M. Ashkanasy (Eds.), *Organizational behaviour and the physical environment* (pp. 251–267). Routledge.

Ayoko, O. B., & Ashkanasy, N. M. (2020). Introduction: Organizational behaviour and the physical environment. In O. B. Ayoko & N. M. Ashkanasy (Eds.), *Organisational behaviour and the physical environment* (pp. 3–12). Routledge.

Aznavoorian, L., Grose, J., & Durakovic, I. (2020). *A study of the phenomenology of B: Hive in its totality*. Commissioned Research Report. Retrieved July 3, 2023, from http://handle.unsw.edu.au/1959.4/unsworks_83665

Baldry, C., & Barnes, A. (2012). The open-plan academy: Space, control and the undermining of professional identity. *Work, Employment and Society*, *26*(2), 228–245. https//doi.org/10.1177/0950017011432917

Barclay, L., & York, K. (2001). Space at work: Exercises in the art of understanding physical indicators of culture. *Journal of Management Education*, *25*(1), 54–69.

Barrero, J. M., Bloom, N. D., & Steven, J. (2021). *Let me work from home, or I will find another job*. University of Chicago, Becker Friedman Institute for Economics. Working Paper No. 2021–87. https//doi.org/10.2139/ssrn.3890988

Bartleby. (2023). The pitfalls of loving your job a little too much. *The Economist*. Retrieved March 26, 2023, from https://www.economist.com/business/2023/02/09/the-pitfalls-of-loving-your-job-a-little-too-much

Brown, J. (2017). Curating the "Third Place": Coworking and the mediation of creativity. *Geoforum*, *82*, 112–126.

Caligiuri, P. M., & De Cieri, H. (2021). Predictors of employees' preference for working from home post-pandemic. *Macrothink Institute Business and Economic Research*, *11*(2), 1–19. https://doi.org/10.5296/ber.v11i2.18411

Cambon, A. (2021). *The problem isn't remote working – It's clinging to office-based practices*. Retrieved November 26, 2022, from https://www.theguardian.com/commentisfree/2021/jun/21/remote-working-office-based-practices-offices-employers

Caplan, R. D. (1983). Person-environment fit: Past, present, and future. In C. L. Cooper (Ed.), *Stress research* (pp. 35–78). Wiley.

Carnevale, J. B., & Hatak, I. (2020). Employee adjustment and well-being in the era of COVID-19: Implications for human resource management. *Journal of Business Research*, *116*, 183–187. https://doi.org/10.1016/j.jbusres.2020.05.037

Csikszentmihalyi, M., & Rochberg-Halton, E. (1981). *The meaning of things: Domestic symbols and the self*. Cambridge University Press.
De Botton, A. (2006). *The architecture of happiness*. Hamish Hamilton.
Deci, E. L., Olafsen, A. H., & Ryan, R. M. (2017). Self-determination theory in work organizations: The state of a science. *Annual Review of Organizational Psychology and Organizational Behaviour*, *4*, 19–43. https://doi.org/10.146/annurev-orgpsych-032516-113108
Demerouti, E., Bakker, A. B., Nachreiner, F., & Schaufeli, W. B. (2001). The job demands-resources model of burnout. *Journal of Applied Psychology*, *86*(3), 499–512.
Durakovic, I., Aznavoorian, L., & Candido, C. (2023a). Togetherness and (work)Place: Insights from workers and managers during Australian COVID-induced lockdowns. *Sustainability*, *15*(1), 94. https://doi.org/10.3390/su15010094
Durakovic, I., Munao, L., & Finlayson, S. (2023b). *Supporting social-capital in an omni-channel workforce*. Swayn Open Research. Retrieved July 3, 2023, from https://alastairswaynfoundation.org/funded-research/supporting-social-capital-in-an-omni-channel-workforce/
Durakovic, I., Munao, L., & Marshall, K. (2020). *What is 2020 teaching us about the future of work*. Retrieved July 3, 2023, from https://www.indesignlive.com/ideas/what-is-2020-teaching-us-about-the-future-of-work
Durakovic, I., & Munao, M. (2022). *What is the future of work? Industry research report*. Retrieved November 29, 2022, from https://static1.squarespace.com/static/625e021c614ac44584dba54d/t/62cd1d0d833ce244d303c074/1657609509718/What-is-The-Future-of-Work-2022-Davenport-Campbell.pdf
Fang, R., McAllister, D. J., & Duffy, M. K. (2017). Down but not out: Newcomers can compensate for low vertical access with strong horizontal ties and favorable core self-evaluations. *Personnel Psychology*, *70*, 517–555, https://doi.org/10.1111/peps.12177
Fenwick, T. (2010). Trends in workplace learning research. In P. Peterson, E. Baker, & B. McGaw (Eds.), *International encyclopedia of education* (pp. 83–88). Elsevier. ISBN: 978-0-08-044894-7.
Geisler, J. (2021). The great resignation: Reality or myth? *Healthcare Financial Management Magazine*, *75*, 44–45.
Hagerty, B. M., & Putasky, K. (1995). Developing a measure of sense of belonging. *Nursing Research*, *44*(1), 9–13.
Hopkins, J. Y., & Figaro, K. (2021). The great resignation: An argument for hybrid leadership. *International Journal of Business and Management Research*, *9*(4), 393–400. http://doi.org/10.37391/IJBMR.090402
Iwasaki, M., & Noguchi, Y. (2016). Hiding true emotions: Micro-expressions in eyes retrospectively concealed by mouth movements. *Nature: Scientific Reports*, *6*(22049).
Kamp, A., Lund, H. L., & Hvid, H. S. (2011). Negotiating time, meaning and identity in boundaryless work. *Journal of Workplace Learning*, *23*(4), 229–242. https//doi.org/10.1108/13665621111128655
Kaplan, J. (2021). The psychologist who coined the phrase "great resignation" reveals how he saw it coming and where he sees it going. *Business Insider*, 14–17.
Kniffin, K. M., Narayanan, J., Anseel, F., Antonakis, J., Ashford, S. P., Bakker, A. B., Bamberger, P., Bapuji, H., Bhave, D. P., Choi, V. K., Creary, S. J., Demerouti, E., Flynn, F. J., Gelfand, M. J., Greer, L. L., Johns, G., Kesebir, S., Klein, P. G., Lee, S. Y., . . . Vugt, M. v. (2020). COVID-19 and the workplace: Implications, issues, and insights for future research and action. *American Psychologist*, *76*(1), 63–77. https://doi.org/10.1037/amp0000716
Luong, M., Peters, K., von Hippel, C., & Dat, M. (2020). Fitting into the workplace: The motivational implications of self-space identity compatibility at work. In O. B. Ayoko & N. M. Ashkanasy (Eds.), *Organisational behaviour and the physical environment* (pp. 113–127). Routledge.
Marzban, S., Durakovic, I., Candido, C., & Mackey, M. (2021). Learning to work from home: Experience of Australian workers and organisational representatives during the first Covid-19 lockdowns. *Journal of Corporate Real Estate*, *23*(3), 203–222. https//doi.org/10.1108/JCRE-10-2020-0049
Microsoft. (2021). *The next great disruption is hybrid work – Are we ready? Work trend index annual report*. Retrieved March 29, 2023, from The Next Great Disruption Is Hybrid Work – Are we ready? (microsoft.com).
Ogasawara, Y. (2001). Expression and interaction: Microfoundations of expressive forms. In N. J. Smelser & P. B. Baltes (Eds.), *International encyclopedia of the social & behavioral sciences* (pp. 5174–5180). Pergamon. https://doi.org/10.1016/B0-08-043076-7/04072-9
Pentland, A. (2014). *Social physics: How good ideas spread–the lessons from a new science*. The Penguin Press.

Pierce, J. L., & Brown, G. (2020). Psychological ownership and the physical environment in organizations. In O. B. Ayoko & N. M. Ashkanasy (Eds.), *Organisational behaviour and the physical environment* (pp. 67–95). Routledge.

Reeve, D. (2019). Psycho-emotional disablism, the missing link? In N. Watson, A. Roulstone, & C. Thomas (Eds.), *The Routledge handbook of disability studies*. Taylor & Francis, pages 15, eBook. ISBN: 9780429430817.

Ryan, R. M., & Deci, E. L. (2000). Self-determination theory and the facilitation of intrinsic motivation, social development, and well-being. *American Psychologist*, *55*, 68–78. https://doi.org/10.1037/0003-066X.55.1.68

Schaufeli, W. B., & Taris, T. W. (2014). A critical review of the job demands-resources model: Implications for improving work and health. In *bridging occupational, organizational and public health*. Springer. https://doi.org/10.1007/978-94-007-5640-3_4

Sulphey, S. S. (2019). The concept of workplace identity, its evolution, antecedents and development. *International Journal of Environment, Workplace and Employment*, *5*(2), 151–168. https://doi.org/10.1504/IJEWE.2019.103022

Sundstrom, E., Town, J., Brown, D., Forman, A., & McGee, C. (1982). Physical enclosure, type of job, and privacy in the office. *Environment and Behavior*, *14*(5), 543–559.

Vischer, J. C. (2008). Towards an environmental psychology of workspace: How people are affected by environments for work. *Architectural Science Review*, *51*(2), 97–108, https//doi.org/10.3763/asre.2008.5114

Vischer, J. C., Malkoski, K., & Schiavello, P. (2015). *The power of workspace for people & business*. Schiavello International.

Wohlers, C., & Hertel, G. (2017). Choosing where to work at work – Towards a theoretical model of benefits and risks of activity-based flexible offices. *Ergonomics*, *60*(4), 467–486, https//doi.org/10.1080/00140139.2016.1188220

PART IV

Case studies

DOI: 10.1201/9781003328728-20
This chapter has been made available under a CC-BY-NC-ND 4.0 license.

17
CASE STUDY
Arup – Melbourne, Australia

Evodia Alaterou

> Our offices should be used as a tool by which we can highlight to architects, interior designers, developers and project managers the progressive and ingenuitive nature of our design work.
>
> – *Arup employee*

Introduction

Arup is a global firm of engineers, designers, and consultants across the built environment. Their purpose is to improve the world we live in and do so in a humane and sustainable way. As expert engineers in commercial and workplace buildings, they are well-known thought leaders in the global workplace community. As an organisation they are owned by their people and strive above all to be human-centric and socially conscious. Culturally they thrive on relationships and generosity of spirit. But, generally speaking, their own workplaces, while of good standard, could, 10 years ago, have done more to express their expertise, brand, values, and personality.

This case study tells the story of how Arup transformed their workplace in Melbourne.

The process of imagining, designing, and delivering its new workplace was, in itself, a catalyst for organisational transformation, enabled by three key elements, which will be discussed.

Firstly, that the workplace is a live organism. As an organisation that believes the status quo can always be improved, Arup started thinking about new workplace ideas long before the designers got involved and throughout the time of creating the new workplace. Today, several years after the move into the space, the workplace is still tended to as one would a growing organism, with time, attention, and resources.

Secondly, just as Arup started realising that its way of working was shifting away from traditional consulting to co-creative consulting with clients, so too did they approach the delivery of their own workplace. Co-creating the new workplace with the design team was a non-negotiable requirement of the process for this project.

Which neatly dovetails into the third element, which is the relationship of trust and respect between client and designer. Co-design can be an uncomfortable and messy process at times, involving showing others your half-baked thoughts and allowing them to comment and add their views (i.e., criticise). Traditionally, this has not been the way consultants work. This project gave

DOI: 10.1201/9781003328728-21

This chapter has been made available under a CC-BY-NC-ND 4.0 license.

Arup and their designers, Hassell, the opportunity to work differently, but they had to trust each other, hear each other out, and respect every point of view.

For simplicity, this case study is structured in three parts:

1. The why – which explores the organisational context and why Arup was ready to take a transformational leap in its workplace design.
2. The how – which looks at the workplace vision and how it could be enabled through design, and
3. The what – which focuses on the spatial and non-spatial design and how the workplace is kept alive and relevant day to day.

Part 1 – The why: organisational context

Timing is everything

To understand Arup's workplace, it is important to understand the story behind it. After about 50 years in Australia, a few vital elements came together that set the organisation up for transformation.

In 2010 the world experienced another year of disruption following the global financial crisis and Arup's global strategy, set by Arup's Group Board, was formulated within this context. The Board considered four drivers that would impact the business over the decade ahead: the global economy and shifts of power and productivity, demographics and people's expectations of life and work, climate change and its impact on business, and technology and communications advancements that will significantly change the way we work.

The strategy focused on four pillars:

1. Design: amplify and develop Arup's leadership in design and foster its creative and joined-up thinking.
2. Investment: clarity on the markets, practices, and locations it would focus on and balancing new pursuits with commercial outcomes.
3. Talent: attracting and retaining the right talent and providing a working environment that supports the rich diversity of people, skillsets, and experiences needed for success.
4. Operations: a robust operational platform to ensure the business is both secure and flexible enough to respond to change.

(Arup, 2010a, 2010b)

Around this time a seemingly small, but culturally significant, change was brewing in Arup's Melbourne office.

A handful of employees identified the need for change in their workplace environment. They looked at what was essential to their work (teams, communication, and collaboration) and realised that the setup (people tethered to desks and keeping to themselves) was not aligned. They needed mobility and to collaborate in fluid ways.

This small group of employees was the forerunner of new ways of working at Arup. They successfully made a case for running a simple workplace pilot in which 34 volunteers participated. Volunteers were given laptops and the freedom to work at unassigned desks and in areas designated for quiet work and collaborative work specifically.

The outcome was an increase in collaboration and concentration in the workplace for all participants. Being able to sit with people you are working with at any given time delivered huge benefits, and freedom to choose a space based on something as personal as your mood was a bonus. On the flipside the pilot also highlighted some of the concerns with a flexible way of working, so they could be addressed.

When Hassell and Arup partnered up in 2013, the implementation of the new business strategy had begun, and the success of the workplace pilot had been heard, meaning that the workplace strategists and designers joined an organisational environment that was ready for change – a critical element of any transformation.

Trust and bravery

The process of briefing for a high-performance workplace is as important as the physical workplace itself. At the very start of this process, before project managers determine programmes and before designers start visualising ideas, a beautiful moment exists for the remarkable to happen. This is the moment when all possibilities can be explored, when organisations can be at their bravest to try new things, at their most innovative to do things differently. This is the moment to explore and set the direction for the type of workplace that will enable people to deliver the strategy.

The relationship of trust between the Arup and Hassell teams allowed for genuinely open, explorative, and non-directional enquiry. This was assisted by leaders being open about what was working in their business and culture and, critically, what wasn't, as well as employees sharing

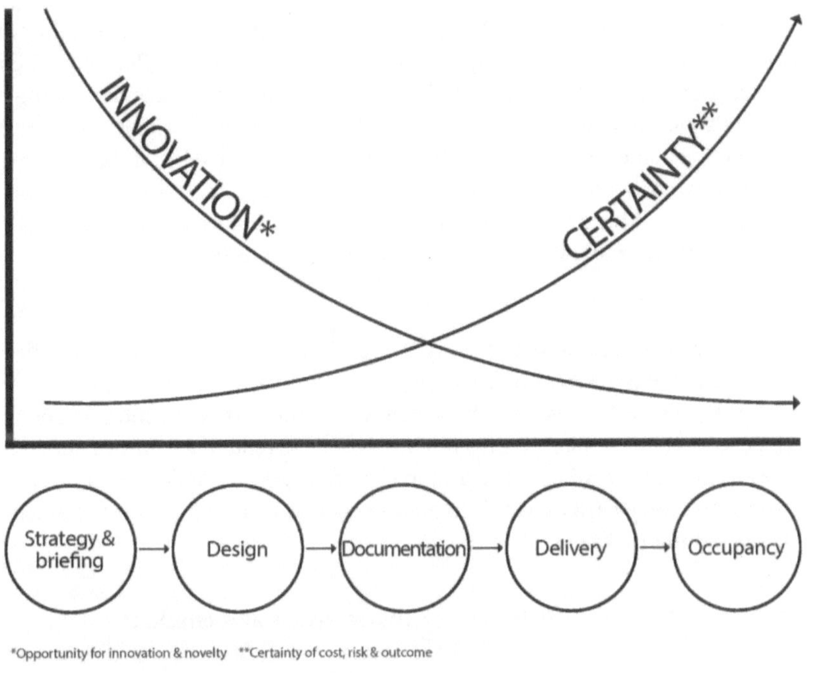

Figure 17.1 Innovation vs certainty through project stages. (Adapted from Blythe & Worthington, 2010 and MacLeamy, 2023)

their honest experience of work and the role the organisation plays in their personal career goals and aspirations.

These conversations about the future of Arup created the moment in which they could collectively influence their future workplace, own it, and articulate the type of workplace that was needed. Likewise, for Hassell, these conversations gave the designers a tacit insight into Arup's business, an opportunity to learn about their client through osmosis, and to arrive at that point of understanding needed to translate strategy into design.

Focus on what's important

A singular, connecting theme emerged in all interactions: Arup's strength is its people. The business lives its founder, Ove Arup's, belief that good people doing good work and enjoying it, is good for business.

> No matter how wonderful an organisation we can devise, its success depends on the people working in it – and for it
>
> (Sir Ove Arup, The key speech, 1970)

Arup people are driven by making a difference; their vision is to shape a better world.

Quality relationships are instrumental to organisational success, and for this workplace it was essential to create a fertile environment to foster deeper connection and for relationships to flourish – between Arup people, with clients and collaborators, and with their local communities. To achieve this Arup had to make themselves more permeable and accessible and make their people and work more visible for broader participation. Physically and culturally this meant bringing their various disciplines closer together and challenging people to think and behave differently. The team began questioning traditional ways of thinking to find solutions that inspire the lateral thinking essential for navigating the dynamic, complex, and ambiguous problems they solve each day. They needed to shift away from a traditional consulting model of working (where creative work is done away from the client) to a co-creative consulting model (where solutions are developed side-by-side with the client), and to do all this while not losing sight of commerciality and the need to run a profitable business.

The type of workplace Arup needed was perfectly captured by an employee during the engagement:

> In Arup we pride ourselves on engineering design and excellence, being at the forefront of these areas within the industry; however, our offices do not reflect this.
>
> Our offices should be used as a tool by which we can highlight to architects, interior designers, developers, and project managers the progressive and ingenuitive nature of our design work.
>
> We need to look at investing in the design of our offices as 'marketing' as well as a good place to work. It is very hard to justify to our clients good/sustainable design when our own offices do not exhibit these elements.

Part 2 – The how: workplace vision and enablers

Articulating the workplace vision

Like many global organisations, Arup wanted to strike the right balance between a globally consistent and recognisable 'Arup office' brand and workplaces that were unique representations of the business in each location. To achieve this balance, the workplace strategy was approached at two levels. The first level set a regional vision and series of objectives that would be applicable to all offices, and the second level would bring in the 'localness' so that each new office would fit the people and priorities in its specific geography. Both levels provided opportunities for co-creation between Arup and Hassell. The regional guidelines were co-authored with a group representing Arup across Australasia, and at a local level each office would be co-designed with a group representing that geography.

The regional workplace guidelines set the overall intent for Arup's workplaces in Australasia, but importantly without prescribing the functionality or design language in detail. The idea being that, in practice, when the guidelines were followed, all Arup workplaces would have a certain 'Arupness' about them, be recognisable manifestations of the brand and ethos, without being a roll-out of the same design typically associated with retail chains.

Seven workplace objectives were developed as the foundation of the guidelines and describe a future workplace that:

1. Allows employees and visitors to experience Arup at work and celebrates Arup thinking, expertise, and excellence through a layered and rich experience.
2. Supports the full spectrum of working modes and offers the choice to work where it best suits the task.
3. Makes Arup people visible to each other and to visitors.

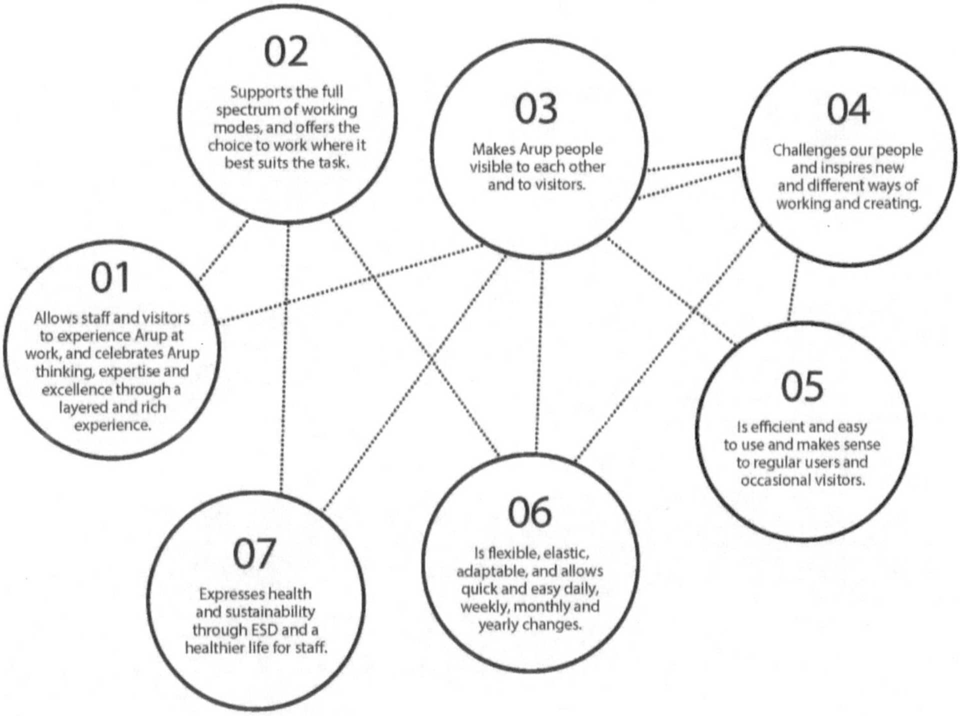

Figure 17.2 Workplace objectives, as captured in regional workplace guidelines.

4. Challenges Arup people and inspires new and different ways of working and creating.
5. Is efficient and easy to use and makes sense to regular users and occasional visitors.
6. Is flexible, elastic, adaptable, and allows quick and easy daily, weekly, monthly, and yearly changes.
7. Expresses health and sustainability through ESD and healthier options for Arup people.

These objectives captured the aspiration that would inform each local office, drive the design direction, and serve as a decision-making framework throughout the design process.

From vision to reality – workplace enablers

While the objectives paint a picture of Arup's ideal workplace, they don't define the actions that will make it possible to achieve this type of workplace. When considering each objective, and how one would go about making it a reality, it is clear that a few workplace systems need to work together.

For example, when thinking about the first objective and making it possible to experience Arup at work, there are various ways to achieve it. At the most visual level one can create views into the workspace and onto people while they're working, meeting, collaborating, etc. One can also put the work in progress on display, so others can see ideas as they are generated and explored, either on whiteboards around the place or through digital boards. One can make some parts of the design process, for example, design reviews, visible and inviting, so passers-by can stop and interact with the work while it is being created. All of this of course would rely on having the right technology to display the work while it is happening and make it possible to actually do the work in real time. It also relies on people having the right attitude towards being 'on display', not one of

Figure 17.3 Design review space.

feeling watched in a negative way, but of showcasing the smarts and deep expertise that is embedded within the workforce. At a work-flow level, it also necessitates a change, whereby the design review process itself is altered so that it can be experienced by more people.

To realise each of these objectives, this interrogative way of thinking is required about the implication for workplace design. The questions to be answered are: 'How can we make this objective real?', 'What would it take to enable this objective?', 'What workplace systems do we need to align to bring this objective to life at all levels?'

These 'enablers' fall into four broad categories:

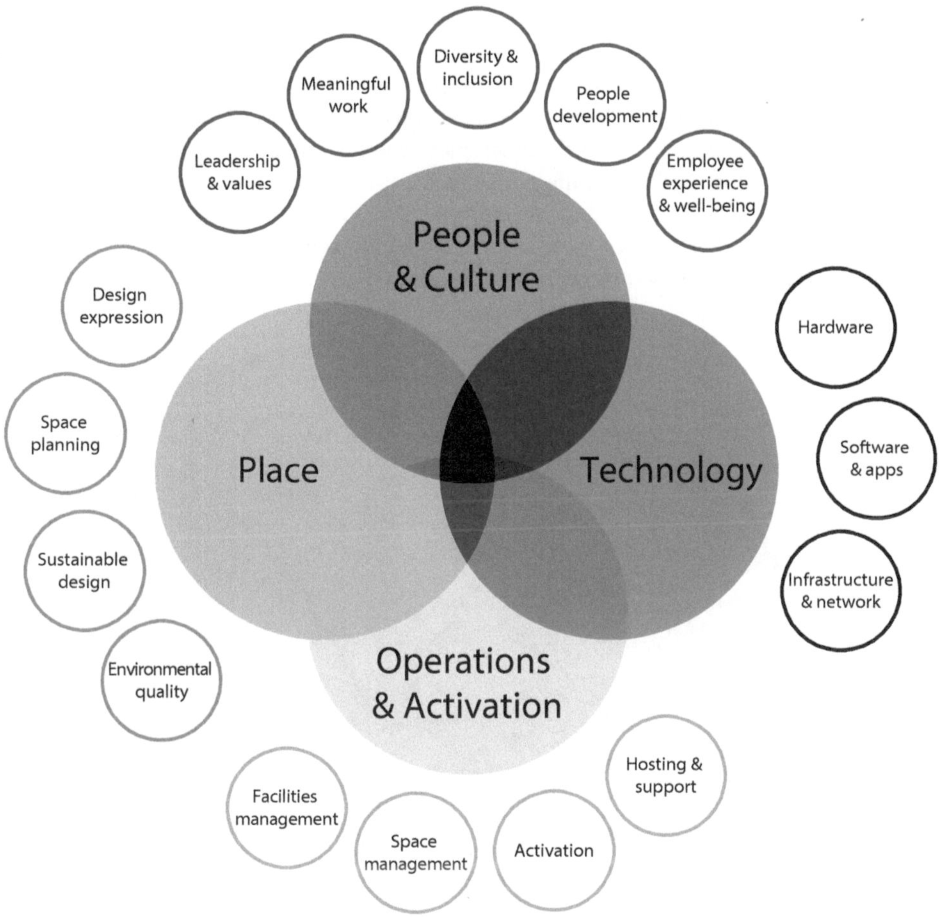

Figure 17.4 Workplace enablers.

1. Places and spaces

Firstly, those relating to place and the types and arrangements of spaces that will create the best environment for high-performance work.

At the macro level, it involves thinking logically through zoning and how the space is layered from public to private and noisier to quieter activities. At a micro level, it considers all the activities Arup people do and what the right spaces are for these tasks. Critically, it also considers how work is changing, or how it should change, and aligning space types to those new ways of working. Coming back to the design review of earlier, this type of open review was not part of the work process at that time, but it was desired; hence, the design review space was created to encourage this activity and make it possible.

When thinking about the place one also thinks about how the organisation's personality is brought to life through the built form, what 'look and feel' expresses Arup's culture and ethos. And at a human comfort level, the quality of the environment and positive impact on people's health and well-being, is an essential consideration.

2. **Technology**
A second set of enablers relates to technology and the crucial importance of a human-centred and frictionless experience when performing all work activities, whether in person, virtual, or hybrid. A technology strategy that aligns all technology streams, from network solutions to hardware, software and apps, with the workplace objectives is critical.

It's essential to consider the human experience when using technology, how easy it is for people and what value it adds. Setting performance criteria is essential at this point to make sure that the technology solutions deliver what's needed. For example, Arup gave their technology team a '30 second' brief – any room or system had to be operational within 30 seconds of starting the system, otherwise a simpler solution should be found. Coming back to the design

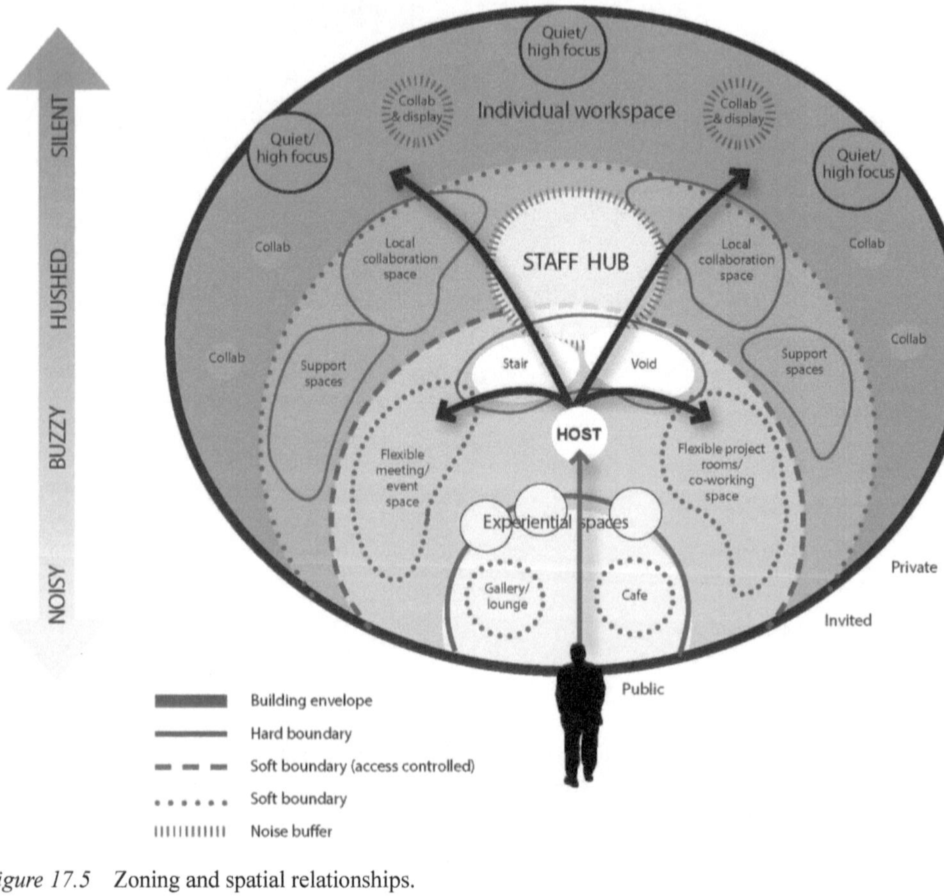

Figure 17.5 Zoning and spatial relationships.

review, if the technology doesn't make it easy for people to share work and to co-create in real time, all within a few seconds of starting the review session, it will fail.

3. **People and culture**

   Thirdly, a set of enablers that relates to people. People are Arup's most valuable asset, and creating an environment where there's room for everyone to grow in their career is essential to its success. What this means is that an experience of well-being must be at the heart of the workplace offer, informed by a deep understanding of the diversity of people.

   Diversity is a broad term that relates to personality, ethnic and cultural groups, gender, and generations. As a global business that encourages employee mobility between geographies, Arup is well versed in embracing this type of diversity. A newer form of diversity is in the types of work and ways of working, and the new types of (non-engineering) people in the business. Arup recognised that new ways of thinking and working are as diverse as the countries and nationalities Arup people represent.

   In a high-performance workplace these cultural factors are aligned and lived every day, through leadership and employee behaviours, as well as in the systems, policies, and programmes that people reference to do their work.

4. **Operations and activation**

   The final set of enablers relate to the ongoing operation and activation of the workplace. Attention to these enablers keeps the workplace alive, always fresh, relevant, and responsive to the needs of its users.

   They include the day-to-day smooth running of the workplace, the management and performance of the space, the cleaning and maintenance, the food and drink offers. They also include the special events, the activations, and support systems people have access to. These are the unnoticed elements that make or break the experience of a day in the office.

What stands out about these enablers, and their common denominator, is that they are dynamic in nature. These are not criteria that are ticked off as 'done' when the workplace is handed over after construction, they are the ingredients that need to be maintained, and constantly tweaked, for the life of the workplace. For Arup to achieve and maintain this type of workplace, it was always clear that it would have to be a living workplace. One that, at a micro level, would never be finished and would be tweakable and adjustable to grow and change with the business over time.

Part 3 – The what: design outcome and results

Bringing it to life – the living workplace

The concept for Arup Melbourne not only informed the design of the workplace but also set the foundation for how it would be used and operated. The concept 'living.arup' means living Ove Arup's philosophy, Arup's culture and principles. It is a workplace that grows, adapts, responds, and is always applicable. It implies and forces a new way of thinking about the workplace – as a living organism that requires ongoing care to perform optimally and to deliver on its promise.

Spatial design

Physically, Arup's workplace in Melbourne is an experience created through careful curation of the spatial sequences, lighting quality, indoor plantings, and service aspects to create a welcoming, calming, and friendly environment.

Figure 17.6 Arrival zone and café.

Every feature of the spatial design is pinned back to the 'living.arup' concept. Arriving at Arup, one enters the workplace via a sky garden.

The reception area intentionally looks nothing like a corporate office space, with an abundance of plants and greenery adding a sense of calm and wellness in this busy zone.

Beyond this initial arrival zone, the visitor is greeted with the volume and dynamism of the central zone. This multi-connected space uses voids and various mezzanines to create a cascading, terraced effect that opens views and access between three floors and five levels. The clever engineering required, selection of materials and finishes, and the exposed services all demonstrate Arup's ingenuity and intentionally puts their smarts on display.

This central zone is about connection and collaboration. A variety of visually and/or physically open meeting and collaboration spaces surround the void, giving passersby that ability to look in, to be part of what is happening in these spaces, and to participate momentarily.

A few of the specialised labs are also deliberately placed in this zone to invite views into the inner workings of the business.

As one moves deeper into the space, one enters the zones that are primarily for individual or focused work. In these neighbourhoods, teams work together in fluid and organic ways, and people move around to work with whomever they need to without being encumbered by fixed desks and technology. At the very edges of the neighbourhoods, as far away from the noise as possible, are the quiet zones, the areas dedicated to highly focused work where people can work uninterrupted.

Non-spatial design

Underpinning the physical design is the thoughtful, deliberate, and equal implementation of the non-spatial enablers.

The arrival experience is as much created by the friendly host who approaches you as you enter and settles you in. The café is more than just a trendy place for coffee, it is run by a social enterprise that helps disadvantaged young people who need help to get back into the workforce (https://streat.com.au/). The central atrium, and series of mezzanines and spaces that surround it, changes moods during the day and accommodates a range of events, from intimate coffee catchups to client parties and everything in between. Most of the spaces have this dual functionality to increase

Figure 17.7 Central zone and working neighbourhoods beyond.

their use. Furthermore, they are also available for use by Arup's extended network, thus further welcoming their local communities into their world.

A somewhat unusual objective is the notion that the workplace should challenge people and that it should push Arup towards an unknown, uncomfortable place. This objective, together with Arup's desire to be more open and welcoming, pushed them to redesign the way security is managed. Here, people do not use swipe cards to pass through speed stiles to enter the workplace. Visitors do not carry lanyards identifying them as 'not from here'. This approach to security is part of a carefully crafted experience. The front door is deliberately positioned to make sure people are seen as they approach, visitors are met and greeted as soon as they step into the space, and they are

Figure 17.8 Variety of collaboration spaces surround the central void.

Figure 17.9 Large event.

looked after every moment they are in the space. Security is still tightly managed, as it should be, but it is out of the public eye.

At the very heart of this workplace is a proactive team of office managers whose passion it is to keep the workplace relevant and fun to be in. They are the often invisible 'fairies' that host and care for visitors and Arup people and that carefully curate displays, events, and happenings to express and maintain the liveliness of this dynamic business.

Figure 17.10 Thoughtful detail.

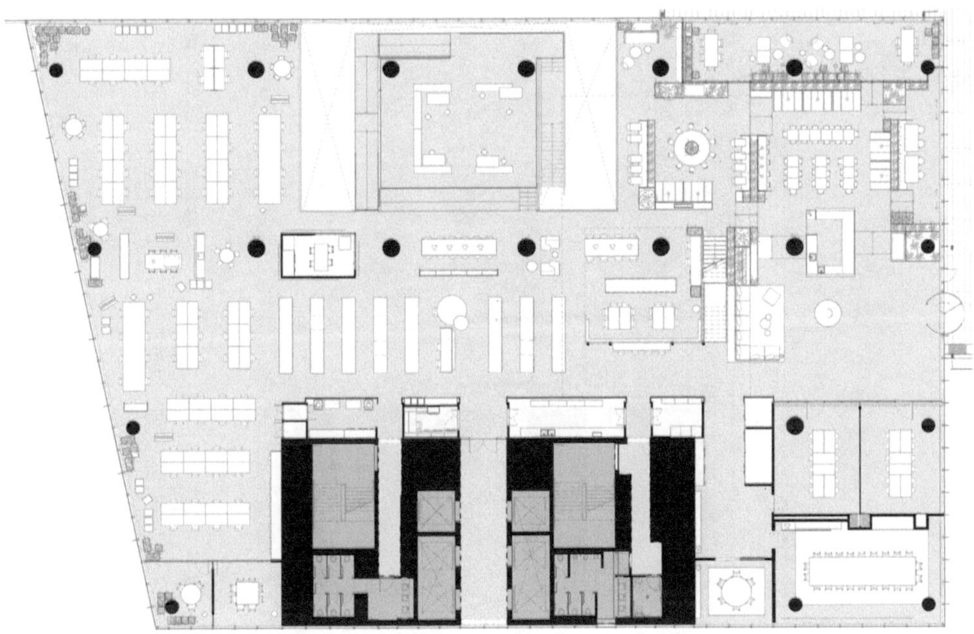

Figure 17.11 Floorplan – L02 arrival floor.

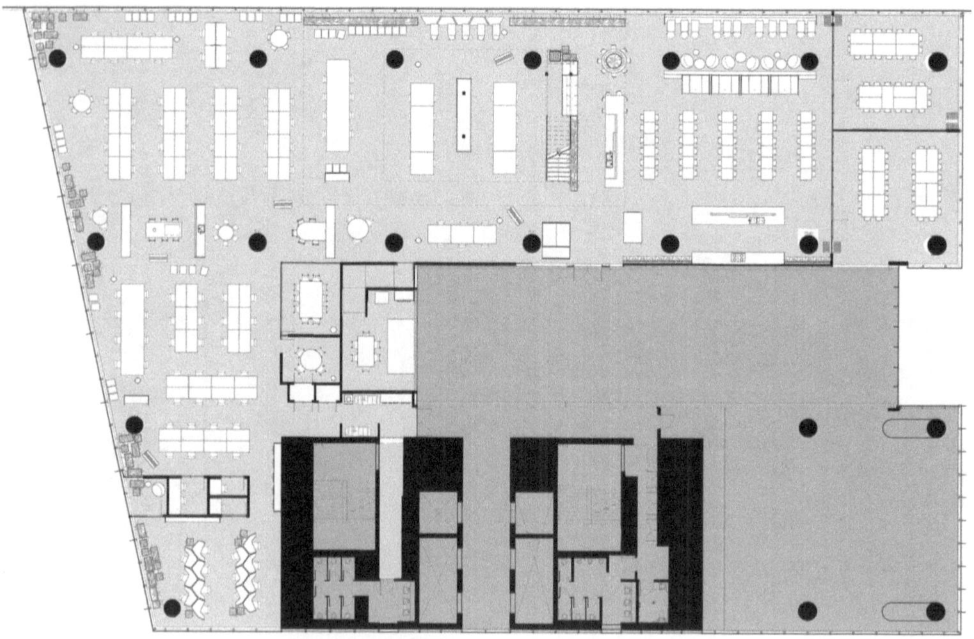

Figure 17.12 Floorplan – L01 kitchen hub floor.

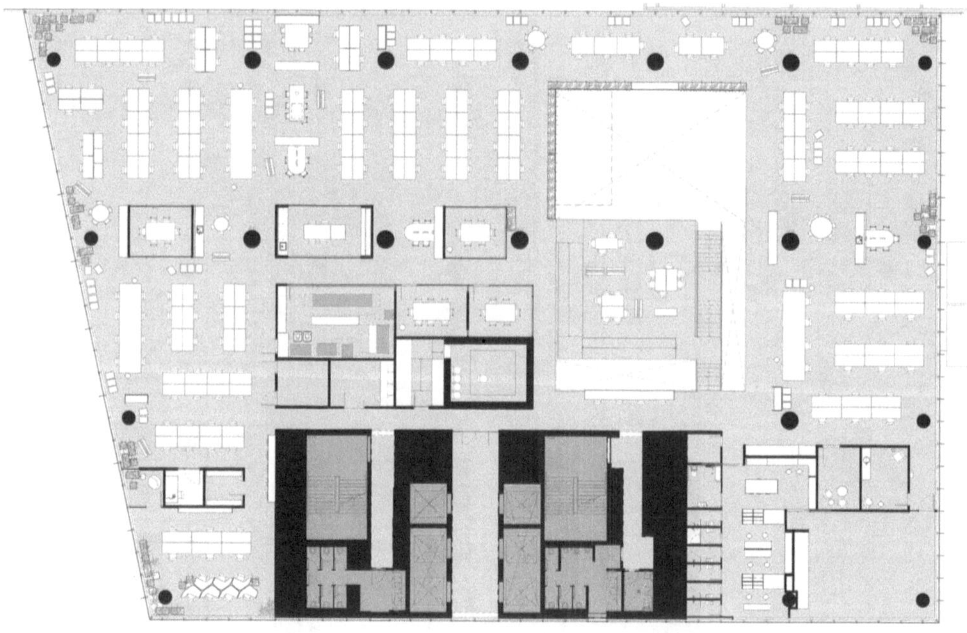

Figure 17.13 Floorplan – L03.

Measuring success

Arup moved into their new workplace in September 2018, seven years after the small, volunteer-run, workplace pilot, in which new ways of working were explored. The new workplace had immediate impact for Arup people and the workplace community alike. In addition to many accolades and industry awards, its success has been experienced, felt, and measured on many levels.

The workplace expresses an organisation and a brand that is successful, cutting-edge, and people-oriented, reflected in the 'feeling' one gets in the space.

Two of Arup's workplace objectives are centred around being visible and accessible and working as peers and partners with clients and the professional community. Arup desired for people to come to them and experience their world. In the first year of the new workplace, external people visiting Arup increased by 165%, from 23 to 61 people per day. Similarly, Arup hosted events with external people nine out of every 10 days. These events ranged from small to large, but all focused on making Arup more accessible to its community.

Spatially the workplace achieved measurable successes with a new spatial model. Historically workplaces have been largely dedicated to individual work, with most workplaces dominated by desks in open-plan and/or enclosed offices. In these historic workplaces an average of about 80% of floor area was allocated to individual work. As work evolved into being more collaborative this proportion started reducing, but even in the more progressive offices, the proportion of space for individual work still outweighed that of collaboration space. The new Arup workplace dedicated only 43% of the overall area to individual work and 57% to space for collaboration, co-creation, and connection.

Several operational successes have also been measured. The business saw desired improvements in office utilisation, technology use and support, energy and water use, and in details such as the use of environmentally sustainable cleaning products.

In the year after moving to the new workplace, 98% of people were happy with it, 95% of people were happy with the choice and diversity of spaces in which they could work, and 94% felt that their well-being was supported. These, and many similar statistics, provide us with the voice of the employee and are further evidenced through their Leesman Index (Lmi) results. The Leesman Index is a standardised and global workplace evaluation tool, comparing user experiences across organisations globally. In September 2019, a year after moving in, the Lmi score for Arup Melbourne was 78.3, 15.8 points above the Leesman benchmark of 62.5 (good), and 4.1 points above the Leesman+ (outstanding) benchmark of 74.2.

Conclusion

Today, years after Arup moved into their living workplace, and as we find our feet again following the global pandemic, the workplace remains a relevant and essential tool to enabling their people and business.

The legacy of the pandemic, while it is arguably still being shaped, is a significant change in how, when, and where we work. While knowledge work has been able to be performed 'anywhere, anytime' for some years now, in reality the physical workplace remained the centre of the 'anywhere, anytime' philosophy for most people. As discussed in Chapter 1 on office layout, office design has slowly been changing for decades, but it has taken a pandemic to accelerate the change towards diverse and varied office designs.

Going to the office is now no longer something one does on autopilot. It is done with intent, and for new and different reasons. For most people the 'post-pandemic workplace' is now somewhere to connect with colleagues, to learn from each other, to collaborate, and yes, to do some individual work too. The post-pandemic workplace is a place for togetherness, and as explored in Chapter 16 on belongingness and professional identity, the physical place is critical to the success of high-performing workplaces.

Arup created their post-pandemic workplace pre-pandemic. They leaned into new ways of working and new expectations of the experience of work long before the pandemic, and it is this initiative and foresight that has resulted in a resilient workplace design. For example, Arup trialled flexible hours of working, whereby individuals could choose when they wanted to work across the workweek to balance their personal needs with business needs, pre-pandemic. Similarly, the Melbourne office was designed with collaboration in mind, and the spatial design enhances the notion of 'togetherness' in the post-pandemic world. Like all organisations they too are exploring hybrid work and what that means for their workplace, but from an enviable starting point.

Today, the notion of co-creating the workplace with and for an organisation's people, has gained traction. The workplace is no longer a place one has to be, but a place employees choose to be. Each organisation is on a journey to determine the role of their workplace and why their employees will choose to go there. Co-creation as an approach provides the structure for this type of exploration. Engaging people in the conversation and the development of workplace solutions leads to ownership, empowerment, and commitment. And in a world where the future of work and organisations seem to be in constant flux, these are the exact attributes that will see our world of work succeed.

Acknowledgements

Thanking Arup and Hassell for their assistance and contribution to this case study. Specifically, Cameron McIntosh, Sue Seymore, and Nicole Neal at Arup, and Matty Kapeleri at Hassell.

References

Arup. (1970). *The key speech*. Retrieved July 3, 2023, from https://www.arup.com/perspectives/publications/speeches-and-lectures/section/ove-arup-key-speech

Arup. (2010a). *Arup corporate report 2010*. Retrieved July 3, 2023, from https://www.arup.com/perspectives/publications/corporate-reports/section/arup-corporate-report-2010

Arup. (2010b). *Arup group strategy 2010*.

Blythe, A., & Worthington, J. (2010). *Managing the brief for better design* (2nd ed.). Routledge.

Leesman Index. Retrieved July 3, 2023, from https://www.leesmanindex.com/

MacLeamy, P. (2023). *The effort curve or MacLeamy curve*. Retrieved July 3, 2023, from https://macleamy.com/

18

CASE STUDY

Universal Store – Brisbane, Australia

Annabel Khoo and Christian Pistauer

An engaged and aligned leadership team, holds the greatest single influence on how successfully an organisation adapts to and adopts changes in their way of working and workplace.

– Authors

Introduction

Universal Store is a leading retailer that specialises in trend-led and casual men's and women's fashion, shoes, accessories, lifestyle and gifting. Their vison is to "make the world a more welcoming place, creating memorable and positive experiences for all". This case study focuses on Universal Store's support office in Brisbane, Australia, that was being relocated as part of a move to their new custom-built distribution centre (DC). It covers the methodology undertaken through workplace strategy and change management processes, to transform Universal Store's workplace into a high-performance, hybrid way of working and flexible work environment, and how the pandemic affected – and perhaps assisted – this process.

Universal Store engaged Athena Blue Global in 2021 to develop a workplace strategy that would help guide the design of their workplace to support both current requirements and future growth. Workplace strategy can be defined as "the dynamic alignment of an organisation's work patterns with the work environment to enable peak performance and reduce costs" (Savage, 2005). For Universal Store, the focus of their workplace strategy was on enabling productivity and facilitating culture whilst considering sustainability in the way the workspace could be future-proofed.

Transforming a workplace to a high-performing workplace is more than just about improving the design of spaces. It also requires bringing an organisation's people along the journey, to successfully learn, adapt to and adopt changes. Kubler Ross's Change Curve Model (Kübler-Ross, 1969) identifies how individuals naturally move through the emotions of denial, anger, bargaining, depression and finally acceptance as they process changes. Universal Store implemented a change management process led by the outcomes of their workplace strategy, to ensure alignment of the workplace vision with their space and people. This resulted in a workplace satisfaction score increase of 2.7, to 8.1 out of 10, in a pre-to-post survey comparison of Universal Store's workplace, completed by employees. This score ranked Universal Store as a "world class" workplace on the Athena Blue Global Workplace Experience Index.

DOI: 10.1201/9781003328728-22

This chapter has been made available under a CC-BY-NC-ND 4.0 license.

In this chapter, we will explore Universal Store's office transformation to a new way of working, from workplace and technology strategy through to design of the workplace and change management, to supporting and embedding their new way of working and become a high-performance workplace. This case study will cover three key areas over their transformation:

1. Development of Universal Store's workplace strategy, including analysis of their existing workplace and pre-move satisfaction rating by employees.
2. Key challenges and opportunities identified and experienced in transforming Universal Store's workplace and way of working.
3. Transformation of the workplace across culture, space, behaviours and technology through change management, and what the impact of these changes have been on Universal Store's support office since moving into their new workspace.

1. Developing a workplace strategy

Universal Store recognised their move to a new purpose-built distribution centre and support office would also be an opportunity to address how their new workplace could support their business, people and processes. While there was a common sentiment that they had outgrown their existing workspace and it was no longer fit for purpose, they lacked the quantitative (measurable) and qualitative (sentiment) data to help articulate the "why" and to then develop the "what", "how" and "who" this would affect.

The workplace strategy for Universal Store brought together four key elements that influence and are influenced by the workplace: space, technology, work processes and culture. Some common aspects a workplace strategy seeks to understand for each organisation include:

- **Space:** What are the current workplace challenges? How is the space being utilised? What works well in the existing workplace? And what are the opportunities in a new workspace?
- **Technology:** What is the current state of technology? What is the level of technology standards? Where does an organisation see prioritisation of their technology spend?
- **Work processes:** How do teams/the organisation currently work and how would team/organisation like to work? Are there any department-specific special requirements?
- **Culture:** What is the current culture? What does an organisation want to retain or change in their culture? How can this be better supported?

Understanding each of these elements helps to articulate the "why" and, subsequently, how each of these elements informs the "what", "how" and "who" of a workplace strategy.

These elements are further discussed in the following three-stage breakdown of Universal Store's workplace strategy, being:

1. Understanding the current workplace status quo – across space, technology, work processes and culture.
2. Engaging with Universal Store's leaders and its people to develop a workplace vision, as well as understand functional details unique to each organisation.
3. Defining workplace scenarios and approaches, supported by data gathered, for leaders to take an informed decision.

Understand

This first stage of a workplace strategy process is focused on understanding and benchmarking how Universal Store's existing workspace performed, across space, technology, work processes and culture. This creates a baseline understanding of an organisation's workplace and way of working that is then built on through the following Engage and Define stages.

From an initial desktop review, Universal Store had an assigned seating approach to their workplace with an overall workpoint density of approximately 12.4sqm/WP. While considered quite a reasonable workpoint density for an office in Australia and New Zealand, having their workplace split across 3 buildings and multiple floors made it a very inefficient workplace and limited Universal Store's ability to grow – both from a workpoint perspective and an ability to bring everyone together.

In the pre-move Workplace Experience Survey, employees had an average satisfaction rating of 5.4 out of 10. This is considered an underperforming workplace, based on Athena Blue Global's Workplace Experience Index. Top opinion-based aspects from the survey correlated with overall satisfaction, from highest correlation (Pearson's r), included:

- "My workplace is functional and practical", scoring 3.24/5, considered average.
- "I am proud to invite customers and/or business partners to my workspace", scoring 2.78/5, considered underperforming.
- "The workplace interior reflects who we are and what we stand for as an organisation", scoring 2.5/5, considered underperforming.

This means that if Universal Store were to improve the aspects with the highest correlation to satisfaction, this would likely have the highest impact on improving overall employee satisfaction.

Having already experienced a few rounds of lockdowns in Brisbane by late 2021, a level of hybrid working was already being practised by office-based employees. When asked to comment on "what would be the number one factor to make a hybrid working a success" at Universal Store, technology and technology-related processes to support hybrid working were the most commented factor, at 40% of manually assigned "tags" to comment responses. As shown in Figure 18.1, "clear expectation and flexible working policies" ranked 4th in the topics tagged, at 12%. When the same question was posed in a survey with over 1000 participants across Australia and New Zealand, the highest-ranked response to making hybrid working a success was "clear boundaries and communication" (Pistauer, 2022). This difference in the number 1 key factor to Universal Store could be attributed to a. Universal Store having already communicated their approach to hybrid working as flexible working, to be a team-based approach and guided by line managers; and b. different technology (software and hardware) being used by different teams and individuals making virtual collaboration and communication challenging.

While Universal Store did provide swipe data over a period to identify high-level workplace occupancy (i.e. approximately how many people were in the office), data from a 5-day manual onsite Utilisation Study provided much more insight into how the different spaces within the office were used. For example, the utilisation data shown in Figure 18.2 shows an average of 26% utilisation of meeting rooms over the 5-day study period. This is far lower than the average target occupancy of 65%, which indicates meeting rooms are significantly underutilised. However, "access to formal meeting spaces" scored as underperforming in the Workplace Experience Survey. So why is access to formal meeting rooms considered underperforming when meeting spaces were mostly vacant? When correlated with other utilisation and survey data, and interview information from Universal Store, limited visibility of what rooms were and weren't available across the 3 office

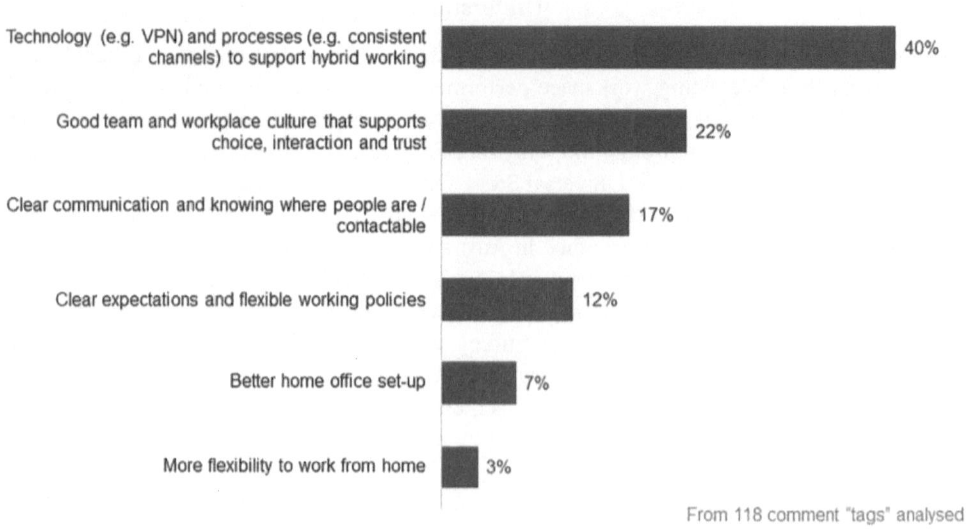

Figure 18.1 Key factors to make hybrid working a success at Universal Store, identified from employee comment topics and percentage of "tags" per comment. Graph by Athena Blue Global, Universal Store Pre-Occupancy Workplace Experience Survey (2021).

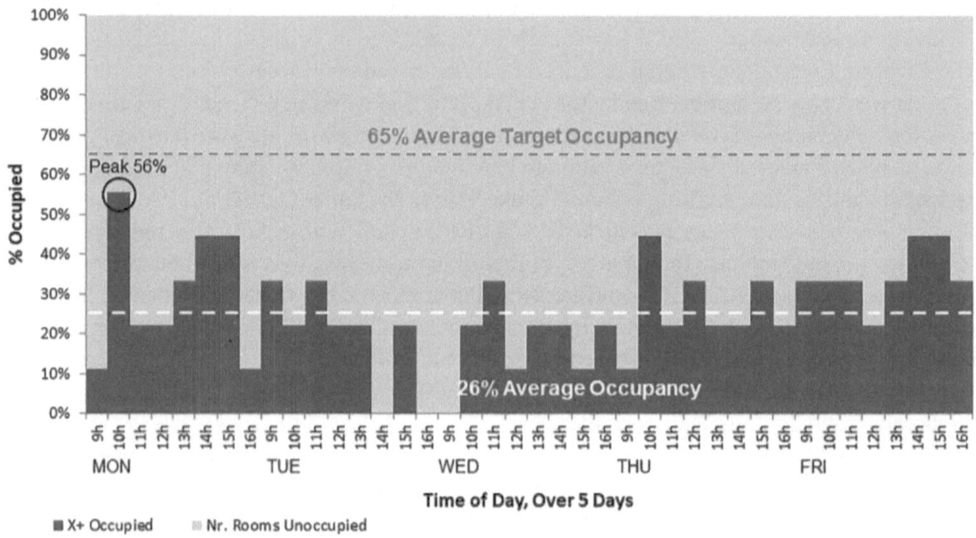

Figure 18.2 Average hourly occupancy of all formal meeting rooms in existing workplace, obtained from a 5-day onsite utilisation study of the Universal Store's office. Graph by Athena Blue Global, Universal Store Workplace Utilisation Study (2021).

spaces, employees not cancelling re-occurring room bookings in the system when not required, no access to the right size of meeting room required and limited AV equipment for virtual calls in some rooms were considered aspects that made these rooms less popular.

Engage

A lot of times, people don't know what they want until you show it to them.

– *Steve Jobs (1998)*

The engagement stage is centred around education, alignment and further gathering of information that is unique to how each organisation and their teams' function. While the output of a workplace strategy defines the key changes for a change management framework to be developed around, the engagement with leadership and employees during this stage can be considered an informal introduction to the change management process. Engagement activities, such as leadership and employee workshops, site visits to other workplaces, and interviews, help to provide perspective, as well as a 2-way platform for people to feel involved, and can have some input into their future workplace, beginning that initial "buy-in" process to the project.

For Universal Store, site visits to other workplaces and a Workplace Trends and Approaches session provided a platform for leaders to look innovatively at their future workplace and consider all the different possibilities inherent within it. Leadership's workplace vision and key objectives were then developed and aligned through the Leadership Vision Workshop.

Employee Engagement Workshops were also held with a cross-section of all teams and experience levels to understand what employee aspirations were for the workplace. Employee aspirations and leadership workplace vision were then compared to understand where there was alignment and potential misalignment on the workplace objectives between leadership and employees. Overall, Universal Store's leadership and people were considered aligned on the key objectives for their future workplace, with 3 key themes emerging:

- One Team – social connection and culture
- Technology as an enabler
- Functional spaces that reflect the Universal Store brand

Finally, detailed information from organisation-wide considerations, involving technology, people and culture, through to department-specific requirements, are gathered through department and functional interviews. Some requirements identified during interviews with Universal Store's department leads included mock store set-up for testing, ranging rooms with hanging solutions to available wall space, increased level of acoustic separation required to certain rooms, "Instagram" moments close to the photo studio, a multi-purpose training space for retail employees and priority to locate the logistics team closer to the distribution centre (DC) instead of with the rest of the office-based teams. This detailed overlay ensures organisation and department-specific spaces and processes that impact space requirements or considerations are captured in the workplace strategy.

Define

This 3rd stage involves consolidating and filtering all data gathered in the 1st and 2nd stages, to develop a comprehensive workplace strategy. Key outcomes of a workplace strategy include a workplace vision and objectives, recommendations to support an organisation's way of working and a breakdown of workplace requirements to help achieve the vision and objectives. It sets a clear direction that leaders can take key workplace decisions against, and clearly articulates "why" an organisation is changing their way of working or workplace.

Universal Store's vision and key objectives centred around:

- Showcasing the Universal Store brand
- Supporting its people and how they work
- Social connection and culture – One Team
- An inclusive workplace that supports sustainability and well-being
- Effortless and fit-for-purpose technology
- A future-proof workspace

The location of Universal Store's new office, adjacent to their new DC and away from Brisbane's central business district, meant certain future proofing options – such as taking additional tenancy space within the same office building or utilising shared building or co-working spaces, weren't available to Universal Store. Future-proofing options to support growth needed to be accommodated within their new available workplace.

From the accommodation scenarios presented to Universal Store, the leadership team decided to proceed with a new workplace designed to accommodate 80% of the company's 5-year growth forecast. Workspaces would be divided into "neighbourhoods" by teams. This concept helped alleviate concerns that were raised around not being able to sit within teams in the new flexible activity-based working approach and allowed for team-related items to be stored in particular neighbourhoods. Individuals would still be free to move between neighbourhoods to suit their work and who they may need to work with at any one time.

Neighbourhoods would be supported by a number of alternative informal and formal spaces, ranging from quiet spaces to more collaborative settings, rooms for focused work, to meeting rooms and more sociable "break-out" spaces. This neighbourhood addresses the concerns of managers who felt they would still need areas for confidential working.

Once the workplace strategy and approach were ratified by leadership, the direction and context for Universal Store's new workplace and changes were ready to be shared with employees through a change management process.

2. Transforming the workplace and way of working

Such a paradigm shift within an organisation's way of working always presents challenges and opportunities, and Universal Store was no different. Some of these are practical, involving the physical space of the office. If there are to be no more fixed desks, how will the office look? How much of the space should be dedicated to collaborative working? How much to focused working or meeting rooms? How will it support the organisational culture? And how much space does an organisation actually need?

Other challenges and opportunities are less tangible. For example, it is easy to create a new activity-based working (ABW) space; convincing those who are wedded to the idea of fixed desks is often a more complex problem. Universal Store were aware from the outset that they would have to address these cultural as well as the physical challenges through a change management process in order to maximise opportunities and create the high-performance workspace they were aiming for.

The change management framework for Universal Store's change to a new way of working was developed and implemented over a 10-month period that encompassed all team members. The following sections highlight the key areas considered in the change management process.

Leadership, culture and behaviours

The most important thing in communication is hearing what isn't said.

– *Peter F. Drucker (1988)*

The Universal Store leadership team were aware that the success of any organisational change is often down to the approach taken by leaders. An engaged and aligned leadership team holds the greatest single influence on how successfully an organisation adapts to and adopts changes in their way of working and workplace.

Such a significant cultural shift within an organisation must be leadership driven – not so much in terms of instruction but in behaviour – to develop a high-performance workplace. Therefore, from the outset the leadership team at Universal Store were committed to "walking the talk"; to using the new office space in the intended way and working in a hybrid, flexible manner. It was important that management were not just setting the new protocols but visibly adopting them; for example, adhering to the new "clean desk" policy rather than assuming a certain location within the office as their own.

Figure 18.3 Multi-purpose breakout and work hub space, for Universal Store employees and visitors.
Source: Lucy RC Photography, Universal Store Office [2023]

Clear, two-way communication was also important. Athena Blue Global worked closely with Universal Store's Change Lead and Change Champions to develop and implement a change framework, with key comms and activities planned throughout their workplace project. This ensured multiple touchpoints from teams through to individual employees to engage and familiarise themselves with the changes on how the new office space was to be used. For example, team members were encouraged to think about planning their days in or out of the office depending on the type of work they needed to do, rather than simply sticking to a fixed pattern.

Employee groups respond better if they feel as though they have been involved in the process and have had some say on the direction of change. Therefore, implementing a transparent process that allowed Universal Store's people to understand the change and the reasons behind it, as well as creating a feedback culture in which individuals have the means to ask questions and express concerns, was imperative to the success of the project. If successful, this process would mean that employees would understand how the new office space was to work, and the expectations around their behaviour, well in advance of the change taking place.

Organisations often underestimate the value of a change management process or fail to allow enough time to properly engage with their people. Universal Store's project programme ensured there was adequate time to engage with team members, ensuring concerns and challenges at all levels could be identified and addressed, prior to moving into the new space and making the transition smoother.

Design – a neighbourhood model

In line with the cultural changes brought about by the move to ABW, Universal Store's physical office space underwent a significant redesign from what had been proposed to Universal Store prior to Athena Blue Global commencing the workplace strategy. As previously outlined, Universal Store's workplace vision included being connected and collaborative and supporting their people. As a result, kitchen and breakout spaces were moved to window areas for access to natural light and increased in size to support well-being and double as alternative workspace settings. Offices were removed, the size of meeting spaces was adjusted and more quiet and focus rooms were added to support Universal Store's new way of working and functional requirements. Seas of desks were split into smaller groups, to a maximum 8 desks per pod, and informal drop-in spaces were used to break up the workspace with added acoustic elements to help absorb and break up noise in the open workspace. Well-being was a key consideration in design; thus, greenery was made abundant, warm textures and timbers were used throughout and access to natural light was maximised for workspaces and social spaces.

While the idea of neighbourhoods was something already incorporated into many ABW offices pre-pandemic, there has been a shift in the composition of neighbourhoods since the pandemic. The rise of virtual meetings meant an increased demand for smaller 1–2-person enclosed spaces with good acoustics and a monitor or screen that a laptop could be plugged into. Open focus zones for individual workspaces are now uncommon in hybrid-ready workplaces, with employees generally planning the majority of their individual focus work to be completed from home. The broad adoption of hybrid working since the pandemic has also resulted in many organisations implementing higher sharing ratios for individual workspaces, compared to standard ABW workplaces pre-pandemic.

To function as a high-performance workplace, the office also needed to naturally facilitate bringing people together. Amenities such as kitchen spaces are shared and central, thus encouraging "bump spaces'. These bump spaces are even more important in a hybrid work and ABW environment for organisations to foster communication and collaboration within and between teams, providing opportunities for both ad hoc and informal engagement while also building rapport amongst employees in person.

Technology

In recognition of the need for a connected workforce, a significant investment in technology was made to enable the new, hybrid model of working to be implemented. Standardised technology was incorporated across personal devices and throughout all office spaces, which allowed any employee to work from any location within the building and elsewhere. This included standardised portable technology, such as laptops and personal IT tools, as well as fixed technology, such as docking stations and monitors in the office. The Wi-Fi was upgraded to allow for seamless connections, and high-quality, user-friendly virtual meeting technology was installed in meeting rooms to support hybrid (in-person/virtual) meetings.

Part 3: impact

In order to measure the less tangible, qualitative elements, such as employee satisfaction and the way that teams and individuals were now using the space, Athena Blue Global carried out a post-occupancy survey 3 months after Universal Store had officially moved into the new office. This was enough time to allow the workforce to settle and embed the new way of working in their new office space. Some headline results from this survey were:

- 95% of respondents were happy or very happy about the workplace transformation (both the new space and the way of working).
- "Fresh" was the term most commonly used to describe how respondents felt about their new workplace.
- Mondays recorded the highest office occupancy during the week, 84% of respondents typically going into the office on Mondays.
- Top 3 things people enjoyed most about going into the new office were "face to face collaboration" at 21.6%, "in person time with my team" at 20.7% and "socialisation and 'buzz' in the office" at 15.7%.

As seen in Figure 18.4, Universal Store's workplace scored "good" or "excellent" across all aspects of the workplace surveyed in their post-move Workplace Experience Survey, from 50 individual attributes grouped into each key aspect under the following topics:

- Culture
- Functionality and comfort of the workspace
- Technology
- Spaces that support workflows and activities

The lowest-scoring individual aspect was "thermal comfort & air quality", which at 3.2 was the only aspect to score "average". Being a new build, at the time of the post-occupancy survey, contractors were still working on balancing the mechanical units within the building, with the intent of improving thermal comfort. This perhaps highlights a challenge for all organisations that may be moving into a new building.

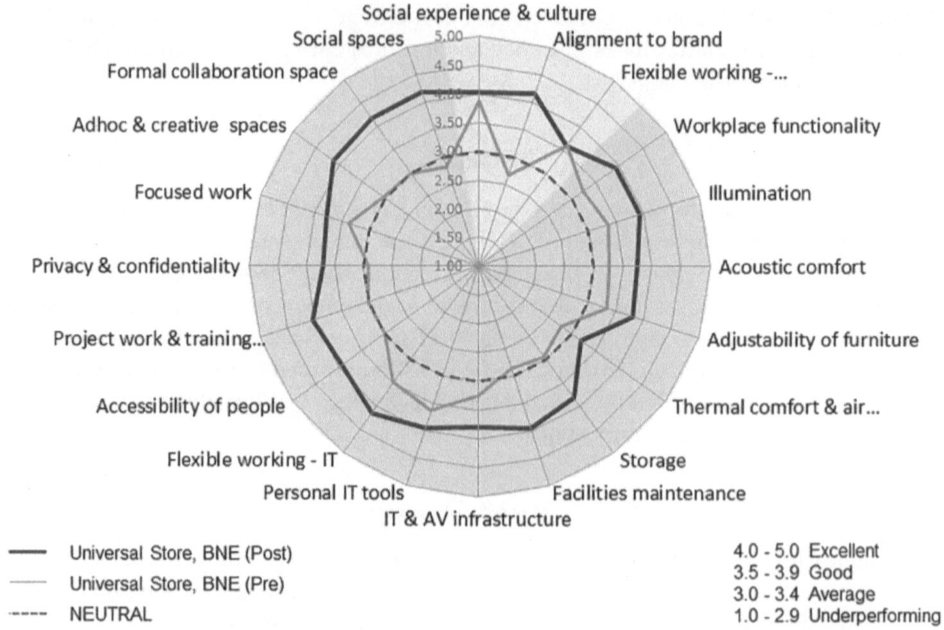

Figure 18.4 Comparison of average employee sentiment, from pre-move to post-move, of opinion-based questions. Clustered by aspect groups across culture, functionality and comfort of the workspace, technology and spaces that support workflows and activities, where 1 is the lowest and 5 is the highest possible result achieved. Graph by Athena Blue Global, Universal Store, Post-Occupancy Workplace Experience Survey (2023).

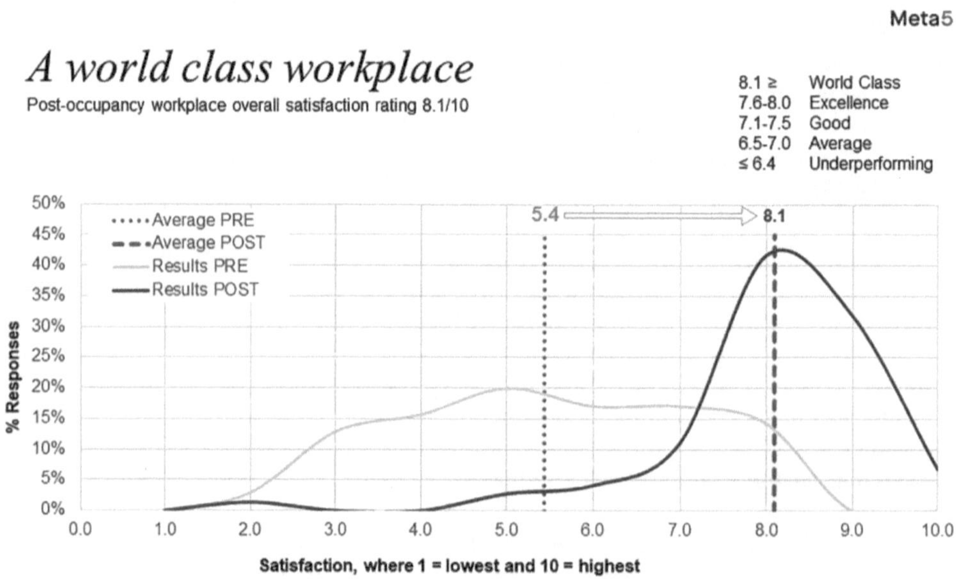

Figure 18.5 Overall workplace satisfaction rating by employees 3 months after moving into new workplace. Graph by Athena Blue Global, Universal Store Post-Occupancy Workplace Experience Survey (2023).

Interestingly, in the pre-survey, Universal Store employees indicated their preference to work 3.5 days (70%) in the office per week. In the post-survey, office-based team members indicated they were now working an average of 3.5 days (70%) in the office per week. This result still sits higher than the average 2–3 days (40–60%) working from the office preferred by many employees (CoreNet, 2020). So while many organisations grapple with how to bring their people back into the office more often since the pandemic, Universal Store office staff are coming in, on average, for their preferred amount of time spent working from the office.

Overall, the transformation to the flexible way of working, with a combination of hybrid working and ABW when in the office, can be seen as a resounding success for Universal Store's office. Universal Store's new workplace scored an overall satisfaction rating of 8.1 on the Athena Blue Global Workplace Experience Index, which puts the organisation in the "World Class" category, as shown in Figure 18.5. Perhaps most importantly, the aspect "Univeral Store's leadership team are engaged in our new way of working" was the most highly correlated aspect to the overall satisfaction score, with a 0.674 effect size (Cohen's f). This reflects the significant impact leadership had on the success of this workplace project.

Conclusion

Universal Store's new office demonstrated the positive impacts of their workplace approach through the overall workplace satisfaction of employees. While the pandemic may have assisted the shift from a traditional way of working to a more flexible hybrid way of working, there were still challenges in space expectations, technology and behaviours that needed to be addressed through the project, to ensure the new workplace would be used effectively as a flexible working environment.

The successful adoption of Universal Store's new ABW approach by neighbourhoods, together with hybrid working, was based on a combination of several factors:

- A strong project vision, with leadership that walked the talk.
- A new fit-for-purpose workspace that supported the project vision for how Universal Store wanted to work.
- Intuitive and standardised technology that was easy to use and supported seamless connectivity anywhere within the office, whether in-person or virtual engagement, and connectivity when working remotely.
- Clear communication through a change management process to ensure Universal Store's people understood the why, what and how things were changing.

As noted by Universal Store's leadership team, "key to designing our new support office and DC was ensuring the space aligned to our store retail network and represented our values of working together to get things done. Creating productive workplaces and trust in technology that 'just works' was critical for us."

These lessons from Universal Store's transformation to a new way of working in a new workplace are relevant for all organisations seeking to achieve a high-performance workplace. In order for a high-performance workplace to effectively support its organisation and its people, leaders need to be aligned in the intent for their workplace, and their people need to be brought on the journey to successfully understand, learn from and adopt changes in their way of working or workplace.

References

CoreNet NZ. (2020). *CoreNet global New Zealand, working from home*. CoreNet NZ.
Drucker, P. F. (1988, November 17). *Peter Drucker: Father of modern management*. Interview by Bill Moyers, *A World of Ideas*. https://billmoyers.com/content/peter-drucker/
Jobs, S. (1998, May 25). *Steve Jobs: 'There's Sanity Returning'*. Interview by Andy Reinhardt. *Business Week*.
Kübler-Ross, E. (1969). *On death and dying*. Routledge.
Lucy RC Photography. (2023). Universal Store Support Office. https://lucyrcphotography.com.au/
Pistauer, C. (2022). *Hybrid working, what employees really want*. Meta5. Retrieved October 28, 2022, from https://www.meta5group.com/insights/hybrid-working-what-employees-really-want-whitepaper
Savage, A. E. (2005). Workplace strategy: What it is and why you should care. *Journal of Corporate Real Estate*, 7(3), 222–233.

19
CASE STUDY
City of Casey – Melbourne, Australia

Eoin Higgins and Ivy Li

> We learned that the majority of people work best when empowered to work where and how they want, rather than being directed to certain locations. We embrace hybrid working, with limited expectations – we don't want our people to return to the traditional workplace mindset.
>
> – *Glenn Patterson, CEO City of Casey*

What is Activity-Based Working?

The Activity-Based Working (ABW) approach recognises that people perform different activities in their day-to-day work and therefore need a variety of work settings (physical) supported by the right technology (virtual) and culture (behavioural) to carry out these activities effectively. By creating a work environment based on this principle, ABW creates a space that is specifically designed to meet the physical and virtual needs of individuals and teams.

ABW reframes work into something one does, rather than somewhere one goes (Veldhoen + Company, 2020). One of the inherent characteristics of ABW is also what makes it so difficult to pin down. That is, its inherent malleability. Central to the concept is the idea that end users are provided with a range of settings that supports their needs. As such, if the work employees do is highly interactive, fast-paced, and dynamic then types of settings provided will tend towards informal collaboration. In contrast, a different range of settings would be required if the work is characterised by high degrees of deep concentration and low levels of interaction.

Unlike most organisational changes, a transition to an activity-based way of working is typically a systemic change. Everyone in the system must fundamentally change how they work. As such, it is often referred to as a transformational change. Perhaps even existential.

> Only when the strangeness of what-is forces itself upon us does it awaken and invite our wonder . . . does the "Why?" spring to our lips.
>
> (Heidegger, 1948)

Most individuals and teams take so much for granted in their ways of working. They are not aware of the rhythms and rituals (team norms, meeting habits, recognition practices, etc.) that bind them as a team and an organisation. When confronted with the prospect of adopting a new way of

DOI: 10.1201/9781003328728-23

This chapter has been made available under a CC-BY-NC-ND 4.0 license.

working, one must first consider the patterns of the current way of working. This fits nicely into a definition of an existential disruption as "those kinds of disruptions in which a practitioner's habits or conventional ways of doing things are threatened and can no longer be taken for granted" (Rolfe et al., 2016).

From this perspective, an ABW transformation is much more than an office design change. It can be an enabler to deconstruct a current way of working, challenge fundamental assumptions, to reconstruct it in a new way that is more closely aligned with the achievement of organisational goals and aspirations.

How, then, does one define a typical activity-based workplace? For the reasons outlined earlier, it may be a moot question. Perhaps it is better to focus on the factors that can lead to a high-performing ABW outcome. In short, ABW is more likely to be successful when the workspace provides a range of settings to support different tasks, technology and infrastructure supports mobility, and organisational culture supports the ways of working (Leesman, 2017). Additionally, taking a holistic approach, which includes a focus on change management, rather than a partial implementation will increase the likelihood of success (Marzban et al., 2022).

ABW has its roots in Europe. It was originated by Veldhoen + Company in the Netherlands (Leesman, 2017), who in 1995 partnered with the Dutch insurance company Interpolis for the first major implementation of the approach. The first ABW transformation in Australia was in 2009 with Macquarie Bank in Sydney (Hajkowicz et al., 2012). Again, Veldhoen + Company was an instrumental partner in developing the bank's approach to ABW and the implementation plan, which paid close attention to the cultural and behavioural aspects of the change.

From there, ABW quickly captured the imagination of CEOs and corporate real estate managers alike, to the point where the approach is now part of the fabric of Australian knowledge work (Cheung, 2019), with estimates that up to two-thirds of Australian workplaces were adopting the strategy by 2020 (Luff, 2018). However, the rapid uptake led to many cases of formulaic change, rather than transformational. This resulted in 'cookie cutter' approaches which had an inordinate focus on the implementation of change in the physical and virtual environments and not enough on the cultural and behavioural changes required (Marzban et al., 2022). Some ABW rollouts lost sight of the core principles of providing choice, autonomy, and equity of experience to a point where the approach has become synonymous with other workplace strategies like 'hot desking' (Bleby, 2022), which only provides low levels of choice and equity of experience. Despite the mixed results, the disruptive effect of the 2020 pandemic has meant that ABW has been 're-discovered' by many, in part due to the inherent organisational adaptability that it offers (Marzban et al., 2022).

Case study: City of Casey – Bunjil Place

> We have adopted a purposeful approach to our ways of working in the office and remotely, taken a team-based approach and an increasingly outcomes-oriented approach to working. This workplace transformation has positively impacted productivity, well-being and effectiveness.
>
> – *Glenn Patterson, CEO City of Casey*

The City of Casey is a local government municipality located 30km southeast of the Melbourne CBD, and is home to over 350,000 residents from more than 150 cultural backgrounds. It is one of Victoria's fastest-growing local council areas and is expected to grow by over 40% in the next 20 years. They are known as an innovative and progressive organisation. They were the first metropolitan growth area council to establish a design excellence programme to support their community vision (Mirage, 2022). They have funded innovative, interactive artworks that help minimise noise pollution in community spaces (Lacey, 2017). They were the first local government in Victoria to introduce electric waste vehicles (Bosworth, 2018). In 2022 the City of Casey was recognised as an ABA100 Winner in the Australian Business Awards 2022 for Change Management (National Tribune, 2022).

In 2013, the City of Casey began creating the Casey Cultural Precinct, a multipurpose development that aimed to co-locate arts, learning, and community facilities such as an art gallery, library, and meeting facilities. The plans included the construction of a new Council office building, named Bunjil Place, and aimed to accommodate the projected headcount of 725 City of Casey employees by 2027. Bunjil Place opened in October 2017 (Bailey, 2017).

The establishment of the new physical space presented the City of Casey with the opportunity to carefully reconsider their way of working to best support the local community well into the future. The next two subsections will chart the evolution of the City of Casey workplace, the workplace strategies it deployed and how it progressed to an ABW approach.

Workplace strategy 1: a revolutionary change

The first iteration of the City of Casey ABW evolution was seen by many in the organisation as a disruptive opportunity to achieve new goals. Of specific interest was how the new way of working could enable the council's strategic direction in both organisational and cultural terms; how it could help integrate the rapidly evolving nature of its technology, systems, and processes; and how it could address the appetite for change within the organisation at leadership, management, and frontline employee levels. This first attempt culminated in a strategy reminiscent of ABW; however, it was not developed in partnership with Veldhoen + Company.

The project was also viewed as an opportunity to stimulate fresh thinking about work and the need to design not just for today's work practices but to 'futureproof' the workplace and way of working to be flexible, adaptable, and resilient in the ever-changing context that is the 21st century.

To develop the strategy for the new way of working, a number of steps were taken. The state of the workplace and way of working at the City of Casey was first thoroughly understood through a combination of qualitative and quantitative means. The findings from qualitative methods such as executive interviews, accommodation tours, and observation studies were complemented by quantitative data gathered from an all-employee survey. These findings formed the basis for which

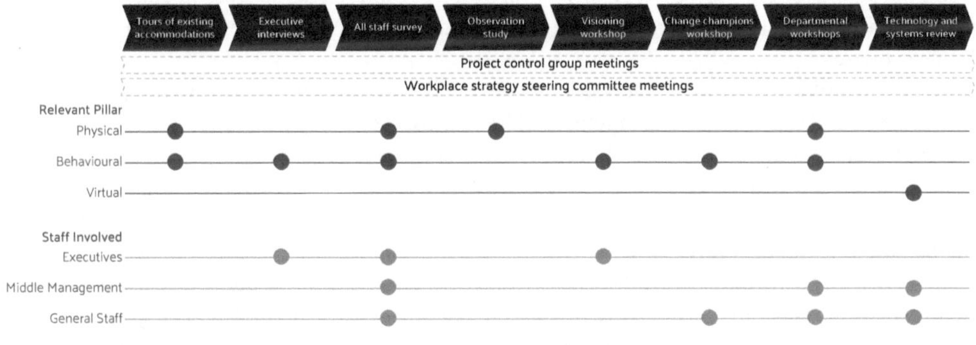

Figure 19.1 Strategic process.

the future vision was defined by senior leaders and then functionally envisioned through a series of departmental workshops. The concurrent initiation of change management and technology initiatives helped to further enrich the development of the new way of working.

The City of Casey developed a workplace vision "To provide staff with a great place to work that empowers you and gives you choice in how and where you work to support your health, wellbeing and productivity" and a set of six objectives:

1. Supporting our customer focus
2. Supporting our people
3. Creating a place to be proud of
4. Flexible, adaptable, futureproof
5. Being connected and collaborative
6. Being efficient and effective

As outlined earlier, a way of working can be characterised by three interdependent enabling elements; the physical, the virtual, and the behavioural/cultural.

The physical component of this workplace strategy centred around flexible working, which translated to a practical goal of the provision of 8 desks per 10 employees, and the organisation of employees into team zones. The zones reflected the desires raised in the employee survey, as it provided teams with settings designed for collaborative, confidential, concentrative, and creative work activities. With employees having no assigned desk, but rather an assigned team area where a variety of settings were provided, the City of Casey were beginning to formulate a workplace strategy where the physical environment hinted towards the ABW principle of aligning work activities with specific settings.

A workspace pilot was established to communicate the intent of the workplace strategy, to test design proposals, and to gather feedback. The pilot space provided staff with a tangible experience to understand the practicalities of the new ways of working, including how settings were to be accessed and used, and how technology was to be leveraged in these spaces. Giving employees the opportunity to explore new ways of working in a highly supported environment enabled individuals and teams to practise new behaviours, which underpinned the broader cultural change.

When Bunjil Place was completed in October 2017, the real number of employees working from Bunjil Place had surpassed the forecasted figures. On a monthly average, 925 unique employees were recorded to work at Bunjil Place, well above the projected figure of 725 employees by 2027. Despite the 28% increase in headcount, Bunjil Place was still able to meet demands, highlighting the adaptiveness the new way of working offered. There was success in enabling employees to work in time- and place-independent ways, and in reducing storage space requirements by 637 linear metres.

The virtual pillar of the workplace strategy was addressed through two programmes focusing on technology and information management. The workplace strategy included an award-winning approach to information computer technology (ICT) solutions, regarded as "a world-class, first of its kind solution for local government" (Rees, 2018).

The technology programme centred around essential aspects of the user journey to ensure that the appropriate hardware, software, and technological practices were adopted to seamlessly support the new way of working. The information management programme addressed the behavioural impediments that accompany the shift towards a digital-forward way of working and involved thoroughly understanding the practical needs and emotional attachments to physical resources and paper usage.

The benefits of these two programmes were observed six months after the move into Bunjil Place, when both office-based and offsite employees were reported to be able to work from anywhere and at any time. Customers also benefitted from the IT reformation, with customer service employees being able to resolve issues through the newly adopted smart mobile devices.

Supporting the cultural and behavioural changes required is central to the success of any workplace change. With the relocation of hundreds of employees to a new office building and the adoption of a new way of working, a change management programme was deployed to ensure that the shift in work styles and location could be made as seamless as possible. There were two main change management goals:

1. Employees needed to feel that the Council was trusting and empowering them to work effectively from multiple locations.
2. Managers had to address the notion of needing to see their team to know they are working and to redefine the manager–team relationship.

These goals were achieved through robust communications and experimentation. Employees were made aware of the new workplace strategy for Bunjil Place through multiple channels, with informative messaging around key dates, initiatives, and a general overview of the new concept. Feedback channels were also established so questions, concerns, interest, and enthusiasm could all be captured.

Research at six months post move-in highlighted that the change management programme successfully transformed the manager–team relationship, with a 15% increase in agreement that supervisors were able to maintain contact with teams, regardless of location.

Despite the various achievements of the new workplace strategy on all three physical, virtual, and behavioural aspects, it was not immune to growing pains.

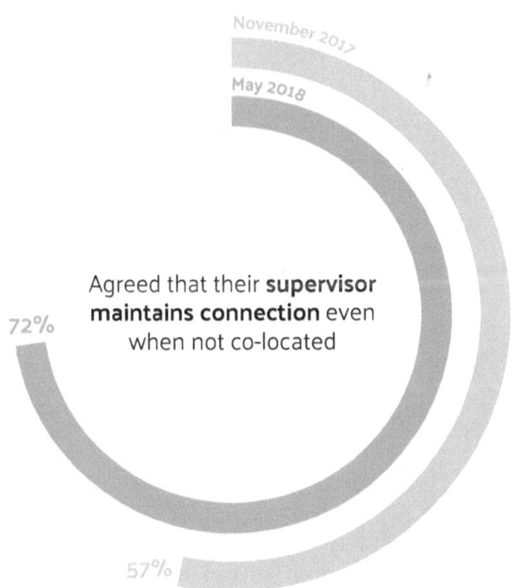

Figure 19.2 Post-move comparison – supervisor–team connection.

Whilst Bunjil Place was intended to provide 8 desks per 10 employees, this desk-to-person ratio was observed to be regularly exceeded during peak hours and was paired with a limited variety of individual work settings offered. Thus, there was minimal impetus and benefit for employees to work at different settings for different activities. Over time, this translated to a 23% perceived reduction in flexibility offered and a 31% perceived decrease of choice available. Such dramatic regressions undesirably fostered the behavioural issues of camping and becoming territorial with spaces. This also negatively impacted employees who typically worked in satellite spaces. When

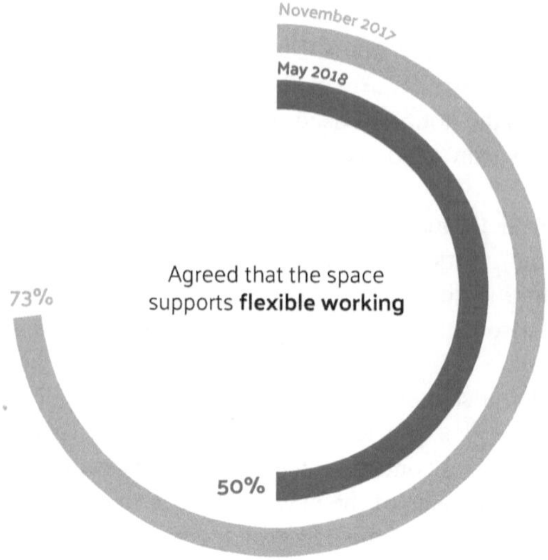

Figure 19.3 Post-move comparison – flexible working.

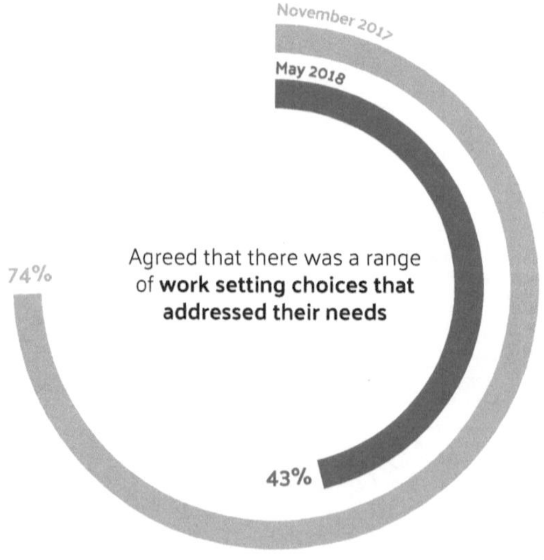

Figure 19.4 Post-move comparison – work settings.

they worked at Bunjil Place, it was not clear to them what spaces they could use, impacting their sense of inclusion and belonging.

Team zones were assigned in a one-size-fits-all approach. With some teams growing faster than others, sharing ratios became varied across teams, leading to vastly different experiences of the new strategy.

Whilst information management and efforts to go paperless were carried out well, only 39% of survey respondents agreed that technology enabled them to connect seamlessly, with some describing it as 'clunky' and 'unreliable'. The technology was also not perceived to support efficient work by 57% of survey respondents.

Despite leaders and supervisors being perceived to have maintained connection with their teams, 46% of survey respondents felt the general level of team connectedness had gotten worse. Similarly, the percentage of respondents agreeing that their team was functioning well declined by 13%, and the perceived ability for collaborative work to be undertaken well/very well fell by 14%.

Therefore, the City of Casey was eager to learn from the experience of the Bunjil Place employees and soon set their sights on improving it.

Workplace strategy 2: adapt to the pandemic, position for the future

No strategy should be a one-off exercise. Organisational context and circumstances are in a constant state of flux. The starkest example of this was the continued workplace disruption caused by the pandemic. Context changes, and so must the strategy.

> The pandemic revealed that flexible working was both possible and popular. We learned that the majority of people work best when empowered to work where and how they want, rather than being directed to certain locations. We embrace hybrid working, with limited expectations – we don't want our people to return to the traditional workplace mindset.
>
> – Glenn Patterson, CEO City of Casey

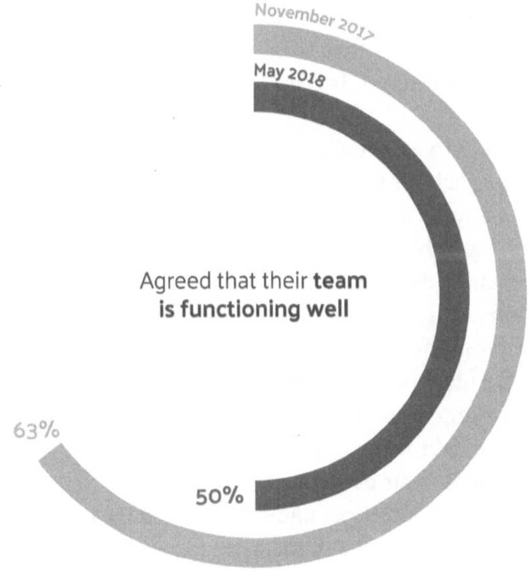

Figure 19.5 Post-move comparison – team functioning.

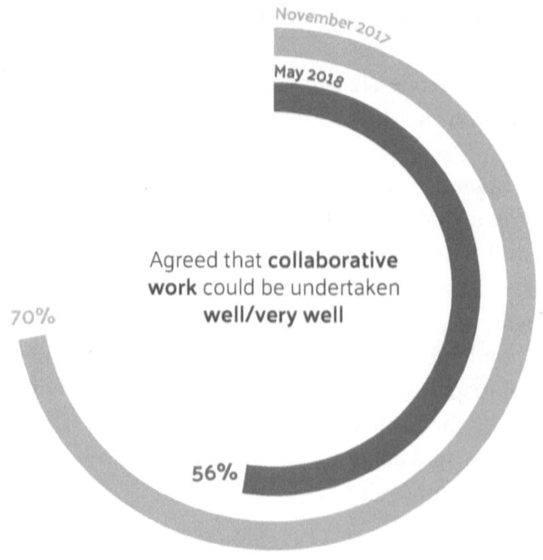

Figure 19.6 Post-move comparison – collaboration.

In 2019, City of Casey had begun to explore the need for a workplace strategy revision. This began with a review and then by early 2020 a decision was made to revise the overall workplace strategy.

Then the disruption of the pandemic was felt, forcing people to work from home and disrupting the 'normal' way of working and necessitating a workplace pivot that would ensure a continuity of service to the local community. However, instead of putting everything on hold indefinitely, once the remote-working challenge was addressed and, later, when 'return to office' planning was underway, the workplace strategy revision began in earnest.

As such, by Q3 2020, at a time when many organisations in Australia and around the world were still grappling with mass working from home, the City of Casey was positioning itself to devise a new workplace strategy, one that would address the short- to medium-term workplace challenges relating to the pandemic whilst simultaneously setting a strategic trajectory for their post-pandemic workplace.

The first workplace strategy was developed in a pre-pandemic context; the City of Casey was keen to take an iterative approach for the second. The original workplace objectives were retained, allowing the focus to be on how the way of working would support the achievement of those objectives, what elements could be kept from the original strategy, and what elements needed to be reimagined. The approach to develop the new strategy included executive team engagements, an all-employee survey, and a series of co-design workshops with a cross-functional representative group of employees. The programme was renamed 'Our Ways of Working' (OWOW). This was done to move away from the idea that a workplace strategy that was a 'set and forget' exercise and to reframe their ways of working as an iterative process (Westberry, 2022). The new language also assisted in expanding the mindset from simply focusing on changing the traditional office workspace to thinking about the behaviour of working.

The executive engagement focused on understanding how they envisioned the approach to hybrid work at the City of Casey, using the models described in Figure 19.7 (Veldhoen + Company, 2021) as a way to guide the discussion. This enabled a shared understanding that the City of Casey would take an approach to hybrid working that was characterised by a model that encouraged

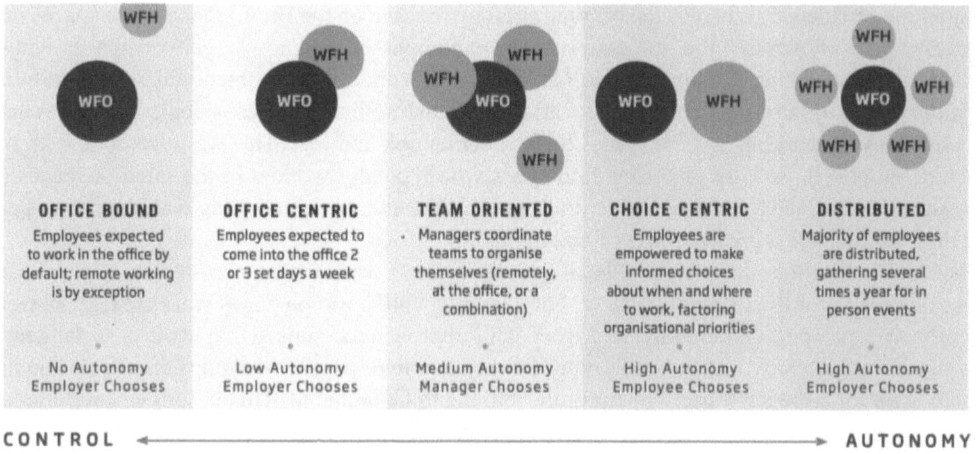

Figure 19.7 Workplace models framework.

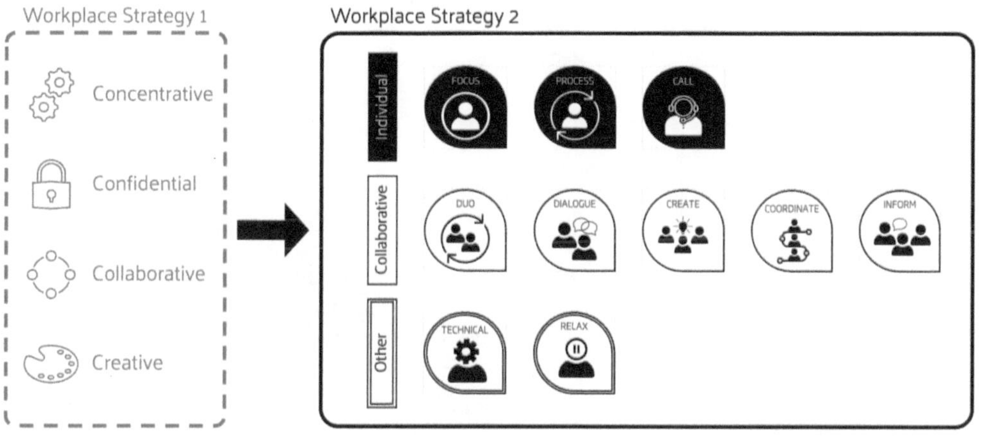

Figure 19.8 Revised activity definitions.

employees to regularly attend the office but provided teams with a level of trust and autonomy to make those decisions for themselves.

The co-design workshops were with a representative group of employees, charged with developing concepts for the different elements (the physical, the virtual, and the behavioural) of the new activity-based way of working. The process also broadened activity definitions from 4 to 10. Activity definitions are critical to ABW, as they are used to analyse the types of activities people do and the proportions they do them in. Increasing them to 10 allowed for a much more nuanced 'workstyle' to be measured and understood, particularly on the different forms of collaborative work that people do. This approach also enabled them to better understand the similarities and differences in workstyles across different role types, teams, and departments.

The process resulted in a range of changes and refinements related to the physical, the virtual, and the behavioural elements of the workplace. For the built environment, the scope of the OWOW programme broadened. Whereas the original strategy focused on the Bunjil Place office spaces and a nearby space known as Vibe, the new strategy encompassed all knowledge workspaces within the City of Casey remit. This meant that City of Casey workers could potentially access satellite locations in addition to the centralised locations and that no matter where people were, they had the same way of working and the spaces had the same look and feel. This was also done with the intent to support those City of Casey employees who typically worked in the satellite spaces so that when they needed to work at the centralised locations the way of working would be consistent and they would have a greater sense of belonging.

For larger locations like Bunjil Place, activity 'zones' were introduced, replacing the 'team zones' approach for the original strategy. For example, collaboration zones were created, as were 'focus' zones to support quiet individual work. This approach recognised that in the post-pandemic way of working there would be much more fluidity in where people worked (i.e. office or home) and allowed for a greater variety of furniture settings to be included. This in turn ensured that all activity types were supported (as per the office workstyle).

In the area of technology, the pandemic had already precipitated a greater shift to the adoption of cloud-based platforms to support knowledge management and connectivity. But the City of Casey developed their capability further. All medium to large meeting rooms were upgraded to include hybrid meeting technology, and additional training was provided in how to use all the tools and collaborative platforms available.

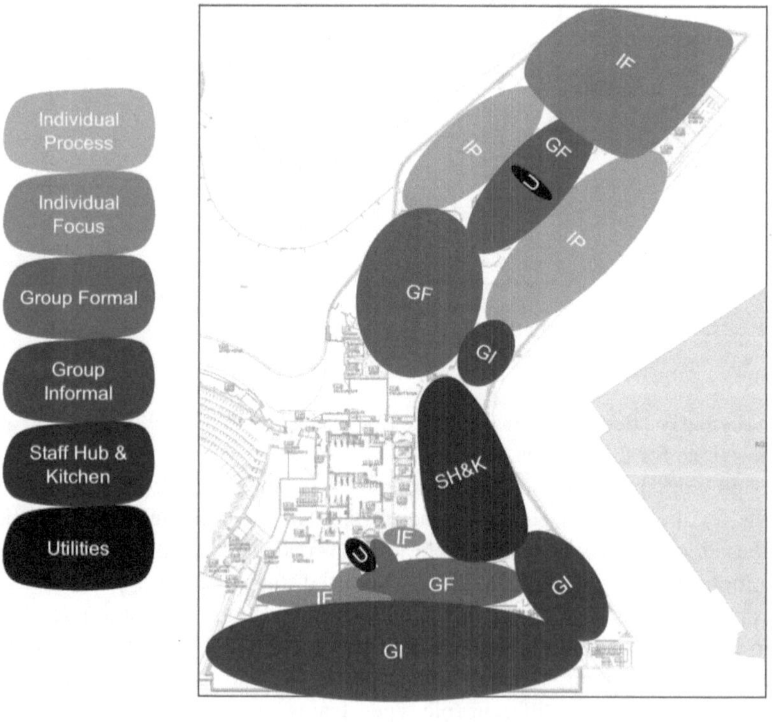

Figure 19.9 Example zoning plan.

The implementation of the new strategy required a large focus, because when employees were returning to the office, it would be in the aftermath of extended lockdowns and new behavioural norms (or office etiquettes) would be required for the ABW approach. The increase of the activity definitions provided a much clearer understanding of the types of activities people performed and the proportions in which they performed them. This allowed for 'office workstyles' and 'remote workstyle' to be developed. That is, profiles of activities that would be typically performed in the office and remotely. On average the office workstyle had a higher proportion of collaborative/communicative activities, whereas the remote (or home) workstyle had a higher proportion of individual activities. The revised workstyles informed decisions on office layout changes that could be made to better a post-pandemic way of working. Additionally, the activity definitions enabled each team to create a 'Team Agreement'. A Team Agreement is a set of rhythms (meeting cadence, email response times, etc.) and rituals (types of meetings, meeting etiquettes, recognition practices, knowledge sharing, etc.) that a team agrees on to be successful in the new ways of working.

From a change management perspective, the City of Casey was very active to ensure a successful transition to the new way of working and to support employees out of the extended working from home period.

> We have observed that our attraction of talented people wouldn't have occurred if they had been required to commute every day and we didn't offer high employee satisfaction with tools and resources, a strong sense of productivity from employees and flexibility to support employee well-being.
>
> – Glenn Patterson, CEO City of Casey

They launched OWOW Weeks, a programme based on the same 'o-week' principle that higher education institutions use to help new students orientate and acclimatise to their new surroundings. City of Casey OWOW Weeks included workplace tours, OWOW information sessions, well-being sessions, and workpoint ergonomic assessments. They also offered employees specific training offerings for how to use the new technology available and more generalised capability-building sessions like 'building positive workplace relationships'. In addition, people in leadership roles were offered a range of capability-building opportunities such as 'leading through change', 'leading in a hybrid work environment', and 'coaching for growth'. They also offered a range of forums to help all employees create new connections and rekindle old ones. This included initiatives like daily coffee groups, morning teas, and lunchtime walking groups.

Feedback gathered after the OWOW Weeks in March 2022 saw 92% of respondents confirm that the events were helpful in allowing them to feel comfortable attending Bunjil Place or Vibe. The in-person connection and informational aspect of this change management initiative were valued by employees, with one stating their highlight of the OWOW Weeks was "seeing old and new faces working on site at BP [Bunjil Place], especially others who you don't work with". The technology information sessions were also appreciated, with employees noting that "it was very valuable to see the hybrid meeting room demonstration and see how easy the technology is to use".

A survey and focus group engagements conducted in July 2022 gathered that the revised way of working was being positively received. A member of staff recorded that "it gives me the best of both worlds and my work–life balance has never been better", whilst others highlighted interpersonal benefits of feeling "that my supervisor and manager have trust and confidence in my ability to work effectively and efficiently regardless of the workplace". This enjoyable change to the way of working was also perceived to bring benefit to the public, as stated by one employee that "for the community I am more effective, quicker to respond/support and enjoy in-person meetings even more than ever, valuing their time and the interactions I have with them".

Some areas were also identified as requiring further work with the new way of working. The experience of newcomers was one such area, as it was noted that "new employees have limited opportunity to experience the wider organisation . . . [which] leads to less organisational understanding and few opportunities . . . to establish and build relationships when only speaking and meeting online". Corridor conversations and spontaneous collaborations were also perceived to be negatively impacted, with one employee identifying that "as you are not having bump in conversations or overhearing conversations on the floor, the opportunity to collaborate or exchange ideas/learnings has fallen away".

The OWOW approach is now embedded in the City of Casey 'business as usual' processes. Ongoing monitoring processes are being implemented on a monthly and quarterly basis to assess the ongoing relationship between the workplace strategy and key behavioural and performance indicators. The next phase of their iterative approach to workplace strategy will be a move towards an outcomes-based operating model, with the associated behaviours, practice, and policy. The focus will be on developing systems for better measuring organisation performance.

> Our changed ways of working have proven merit in optimising collaboration, communication and satisfaction. Activity-based working has benefits for workers' health, work performance and perceptions of the work environment, when complemented with appropriate leadership and organisation support. This is a crucial element of our EVP to attract and retain talented people. All of this leads to improved productivity and a higher-performing organisation.
>
> – Glenn Patterson, CEO City of Casey

Broader applications

The City of Casey approach to workplace strategy and workplace transformation has many applications. Key drivers of a high-performance approach are:

- Ensuring that the new way of working is seen as an opportunity to challenge assumptions, innovate processes, and provide improved benefit to the community/customers being served, rather than an opportunity to reduce space and modernise office design.
- A clear vision and set of goals that is based on organisational outcomes rather than design-based targets.
- Fostering ground up ownership of the change, using co-creative approaches.
- Supporting employees with what they need to do their best work – contributing to productivity, well-being, and strong talent attraction.
- Focusing on not just physical space but also culture and technology to enable the right behaviours and mindset.
- Adopting an iterative process, considering the changing organisational environment, behaviour shifts, and performance metrics.
- Driving strong leadership engagement.
- Providing internal capacity and capability to manage the change thoroughly.
- Integrated programme management that aligns the different streams of the programme to the core goals of the implementation.

Conclusion

ABW is an ideal workplace strategy for any organisation aspiring to be a high-performing workplace and providing employees with a range of work-setting choices while empowering them to make informed decisions as to how to work is central to the strategy. Operationally, this enables individuals, teams, and entire organisations to configure and reconfigure how they work as circumstances and contexts change. Strategically, it is amenable to an iterative approach, as described in this case study, whereby the way employees use space and the types of settings provided can be modified as expectations regarding when and where work is done changes over time.

The inherent malleability and elasticity of the approach provides for high levels of organisational adaptability, which supports business continuity and resilience in times of disruption, such as in a global pandemic. Furthermore, the workplace capabilities afforded by an activity-based way of working are directly applicable to the opportunities and challenges emerging from the exploration of hybrid ways of working. Leading dispersed and highly mobile teams, collaborating asynchronously, creating new organisational rhythms and rituals, and providing equitable and inclusive workplace experiences are some of the key focus areas for delivering high-performance in hybrid ways of working. There are also key areas that need to be addressed in developing and implementing a world-class ABW model.

References

Bailey, M. (2017). *Bunjil place library officially opens, half a million visitors a year expected*. Retrieved October 2022, from The Herald Sun: https://www.heraldsun.com.au/leader/south-east/bunjil-place-library-officially-opens-half-a-million-visitors-a-year-expected/news-story/5bbf472c378f2607b38a227512c2a0ea

Bleby, M. (2022). *Workers at home will be replaced by robots: Charter Hall CEO*. Retrieved October 2022, from https://www.afr.com/property/commercial/workers-at-home-will-be-replaced-by-robots-charter-hall-ceo-20220919-p5bj5h: Australian Financial Review

Bosworth, T. (2018). *First electric waste trucks go into service in Victoria*. Retrieved October 2022, from The Driven: https://thedriven.io/2018/10/04/waste-trucks/

Cheung, A. (2019). *Australian researchers to put activity-based working to the test*. Retrieved October 2022, from Commercial Real Estate: https://www.commercialrealestate.com.au/news/australian-researchers-to-put-activity-based-working-to-the-test-44807/

Hajkowicz, S., Cook, H., & Littleboy, A. (2012). *Our future world: Global megatrends that will change the way we live*. CSIRO.

Heidegger, M. (1948). What is metaphysics. In W. Brock (Ed.), *Exisance & being*. Regnery/Gateway Inc.

Lacey, J. (2017). *Let cities speak: Reclaiming a place for community with sounds*. Retrieved October 2022, from The Conversation: https://theconversation.com/let-cities-speak-reclaiming-a-place-for-community-with-sounds-76998

Leesman. (2017). *The rise and rise of Activity Based Working*. Leesman.

Luff, M. (2018). *Australia is leading the world in the adoption of activity based working*. Retrieved from Insight: https://workplaceinsight.net/australia-leading-world-adoption-activity-based-working/

Marzban, S., Candido, C., Mackey, M., Engelen, L., Zhang, F., & Tjondronegoro, D. (2022). A review of research in activity-based working over the last ten years: Lessons for the post-COVID workplace. *Journal of Facilities Management*, *21*(3), 313–333. https://doi.org/10.1108/JFM-08-2021-0081

Mirage. (2022). *Casey design excellence awards 2022*. Retrieved from Mirage News: https://www.miragenews.com/casey-design-excellence-awards-2022-854327/#google_vignette

National Tribune. (2022). *City of Casey wins Australian Business Award*. Retrieved from The National Tribune: https://www.nationaltribune.com.au/city-of-casey-wins-australian-business-award/

Rees, G. (2018). *CRN 2018 impact awards: Thomas Duryea Logicalis and City of Casey*. Retrieved from CRN: https://www.crn.com.au/feature/crn-2018-impact-awards-thomas-duryea-logicalis-and-city-of-casey-488264

Rolfe, B., Segal, S., & Cicmil, S. (2016). An existential hermeneutic philosophical approach to project management. *Project Management Journal*, 48–62.

Veldhoen + Company. (2020). *Activity based working*. Retrieved from Veldhoen + Company: https://www.veldhoencompany.com/en/activity-based-working/

Veldhoen + Company. (2021). *Veldhoen + Company*. Retrieved from On the Edge of Hybrid: lessons from the Australian experience: https://www.veldhoencompany.com/en/lessons-from-the-australian-experience-in-hybyrid-working/

Westberry, L. (2022). *Delivering a post-pandemic workplace strategy* (E. Higgins & H. Matharu, Interviewers).

20
CASE STUDY
Officeworks – Melbourne, Australia

Laurie Aznavoorian

The impact of the pandemic has been catastrophic and is likely to have a long-term social, cultural, and economic impact.

– *British Academy 2021*

Introduction

Since March of 2020, when the WHO declared COVID-19 a pandemic, society has demonstrated great ingenuity in reimagining how daily activities such as how we learn, shop and entertain ourselves were conducted. Organisations were not immune. Critical workplace activities like organising, connecting and collaborating demanded the rapid adoption of digital, with some aspects of work requiring completely novel approaches, e.g., Zoom happy hours. Companies reinvented service delivery models and in extreme cases pivoted to entirely new endeavours to survive.

Officeworks was no exception. Like many retailers the company was well on its way to building a stronger digital presence prior to the pandemic; the importance of this shift came to light during lockdowns as gaps in the market emerged that could be filled with Officeworks' products and services. What was widely seen as a global catastrophe became an opportunity to shift the brand. But to take advantage of the changing market communication between stores and with developers, marketing teams and digital designers all required improvement. These imperatives, already in place when the pandemic hit, aligned with a lease expiry, creating a perfect catalyst for the development of a physical environment capable of meeting the changing demands of team members and the brand.

This case study explores Chadstone Place and the new Officeworks headquarters. It is an example of one organisation's approach to developing a workplace taxonomy emerging from an overriding hypothesis that the way we occupy and use workplaces has been irreversibly impacted by the pandemic. The office relocation, which was scheduled to occur in March of 2023, offers a solution to feelings of disconnection within the organisation that were a natural consequence of occupying a rambling single-story environment with teams dispersed across multiple buildings. Chadstone Place not only offers Officeworks the ability to consolidate teams under one roof, but by nudging behaviours using subtle clues in the layouts and stacking arrangement the environment is designed to promote connection and build individual and organisational resilience. The

DOI: 10.1201/9781003328728-24

This chapter has been made available under a CC-BY-NC-ND 4.0 license.

approach borrows on forms of behavioural design and the theory of 'libertarian paternalism' – a system that encourages individuals towards selecting a particular outcome without removing the freedom of choice. Additional positives for the new location include lease flexibility offered for expansion or contraction if the expected up-take or prevalence of hybrid proves to be different than expected. The biggest challenges posed by the new location are acknowledged to be the ability to acquire digital talent from a demographic predominantly residing in the city. Therefore, to attract digital workers and establish a thriving community, the new workplace had to be highly energised and act as a vibrant hub worthy of the commute.

Notions of what constitutes an environment worth going to have evolved over the course of the pandemic; in the early days of the return to work, simply providing a safe place where social distancing could be practised was enough. But as society settled into living with COVID and organisations like Officeworks gave employees greater choice, design briefs adjusted. In parallel, the rise of an activist workforce that holds businesses accountable for making a difference (Atlassian, PWC, 2021) have necessitated the inclusion of considerations for the workplace that go beyond simple adjustments to temporal changes taking place. Organisations, and in turn the workplaces they occupy, must now acknowledge the external crises that lead to uncertainty in the workforce, such as escalating mental health challenges, loneliness, increased political instability and severe economic downturns (Carnevale & Hatak, 2020).

Exactly how the physical environment should respond is for the industry to test over the coming years, but from the data two implicit workplace directives emerge. The first is for next-generation workplaces to be highly flexible for both individuals and organisations to respond to the unknown; second, exploration in how space might be used to address external issues that affect people make sense. The pandemic has been described as a "human crisis" (Collings et al., 2021); therefore, helping the workforce adapt and cope with radical changes in the work and social environment is key to organisational performance and viability (Carnevale & Hatak, 2020).

During the pandemic routines and lives were thrown into disarray, workers were required to make rapid and monumental changes and employers had to rethink how they engaged with dispersed workers (Cheema-Fox et al., 2021). What made some organisations and some people able to respond better was their level of resilience. The Oxford dictionary defines resilience as "the capacity to recover quickly from difficulties"; what became clear during the pandemic was that people varied in how well they were doing and how much they improved over time (Park et al., 2021). The pandemic exposed a strong link between individual resilience and organisational resilience; consequently, to respond to future events, resilience must be cultivated (Ayoko & Ashkanasy, 2020).

The concept of building resilience for individuals and the organisation was an underlying theme for the design of the new Officeworks headquarters, the notion that the physical environment is a persuasive phenomenon (Ayoko & Ashkanasy, 2020), that acts as teacher and a catalyst to build the skills and behaviours set the foundations for the project. On that setting, key goals for the Officeworks headquarters unfolded during the strategic briefing phase:

The new workplace must:

- Facilitate magnetic connections.
- Be a hybrid heaven.
- Embrace diverse talent.
- Be a vehicle to showcase and share.
- Support environmental initiatives – green space/green impact.

As this chapter was written, the project was under construction, so there were no performance measurements available. Through internal surveys conducted during and after Melbourne's lockdowns, Officeworks learned employees hoped to return to the office two or three days per week, mainly to connect professionally and socially with colleagues, work with their teams and to attend special work or social events. Therefore, the typology of spaces provided in the headquarters reflects a shift away from individual focused work towards a larger number of togetherness places that are specifically designed to improve the performance and resilience of team members. An important point to note is that individual workplaces for employees unable to work at home are still required, but the overall percentage of individual to togetherness spaces favoured the latter.

Additional team members' expectations were a direct result of having easy access to food and beverages, fresh air, sunshine and outdoor spaces when working from home that needed to be mimicked. Similarly, typical workplace maladies like balancing noise and distraction that proved to be easier at home for some workers emerged as a focus of consideration once employees could compare their productivity to working in the office, which surveys indicated was frequently distracting. Since employees would be permitted agency over when and where work occurred, the space solution required provisions for oversubscription or, worse, undersubscription that would deliver an environment that felt and looked like a ghost town – extensively not the kind of place to attract employees with a choice.

The Officeworks site

The building is a low-scale commercial office tower sitting in a larger suburban retail precinct; Officeworks is segregated from the shopping centre but adjacent to it, allowing employees access to one of Melbourne's premier high-end retail complexes with associated food and beverage

Figure 20.1 The Officeworks site. (Rendered image by Bates Smart)

operators, grocers, and a new fresh food market. The workplace spans four levels, with floor plates ranging in size from 1,200m^2 to 1,500m^2. The largest floor, Level 1, comprises the existing tower footprint and a New Link addition that connects the companies' dedicated parking to the workplace tower. Employees can enter and exit freely without the challenge of finding a parking spot in a crowded retail complex.

The Link acts as a portal that employees and most visitors will traverse to reach the office space. Access will be either directly from the parking area, or through a spiral stair that connects the ground floor where the pedestrian walkways to the shopping centre and the End of Trip facility are located. Limited formal visitors are expected; when they do come to the headquarters, they will take the lifts to a reception area on Level 2, bypassing The Link.

Following design thinking methodology, multiple spatial arrangements were graphically prototyped; the process generated project objectives that became the criteria to analyse pros and cons of the direction being tested against its ability to meet the agreed directives. The inclusive process made decision makers aware of all necessary changes to technology, process and leadership along with any habitual changes required to successfully adopt the ideas. Illustrated pain versus gain metrics offered a simple analysis of the highlights of each idea, along with what would be required from a technology or leadership position to ensure the space achieved its potential. Such analysis is a nuance often omitted from the traditional briefing process, but critical to consider when organisations are making significant shifts to deliver higher performance, which cannot be achieved using space alone.

The value of the methodology relies on the consideration of outlier ideas that may be strange or confronting alongside safer, familiar options. This bracketed approach builds an awareness of what could be and what is, testing how far the organisation is prepared or able to go to achieve its goals. It is not uncommon for companies to bite off more than they can chew or abandon ideas they're not ready to implement that may be better for them in the long run. An advantage of this approach is it highlights measures that can be put in place for a future adoption, and it pinpoints conflicting priorities or necessary compromises that are part of every project. Understanding how decisions are made and clearly articulating the logic used to team members, the board and shareholders is a key benefit of using this framework for accountability. Importantly, the process appreciates the phenomenology of a space, reminding us that successful solutions come from a combination of responsive spaces, new behaviours, policy shifts, process reconfiguration and adopting the right technology.

Incorporated into the design briefing process was consideration of human science manifested through notions of choice architecture. In choice architecture, "Behavioural economics (or nudge theory) appears to provide an alternative in design for behaviour change by accounting for intuitive thinking to help people make better decisions" (Mejía, 2021). It is an approach retailers adopt to encourage behaviour change in customers, for example, making it easier to eat healthier by providing nutrition information on menus or prominently positioning stairs over escalators or lifts to promote movement (Trafford & de la Hunty, 2021). The concept is built on well-established behavioural research conducted by Kahneman, Simon & Amarilli and Vlaev et al. (Trafford & de la Hunty, 2021) and our human propensity to stick with the status quo. By incorporating nudges into workplace design occupants can be gently steered towards choices that they, or the company, will benefit from, such as bumping into colleagues and seeing important messages. With choice architecture and nudging there are ethical considerations, neither should ever be used to manipulate or exploit workers; nevertheless, it is a concept worthy of further examination for workplace designers.

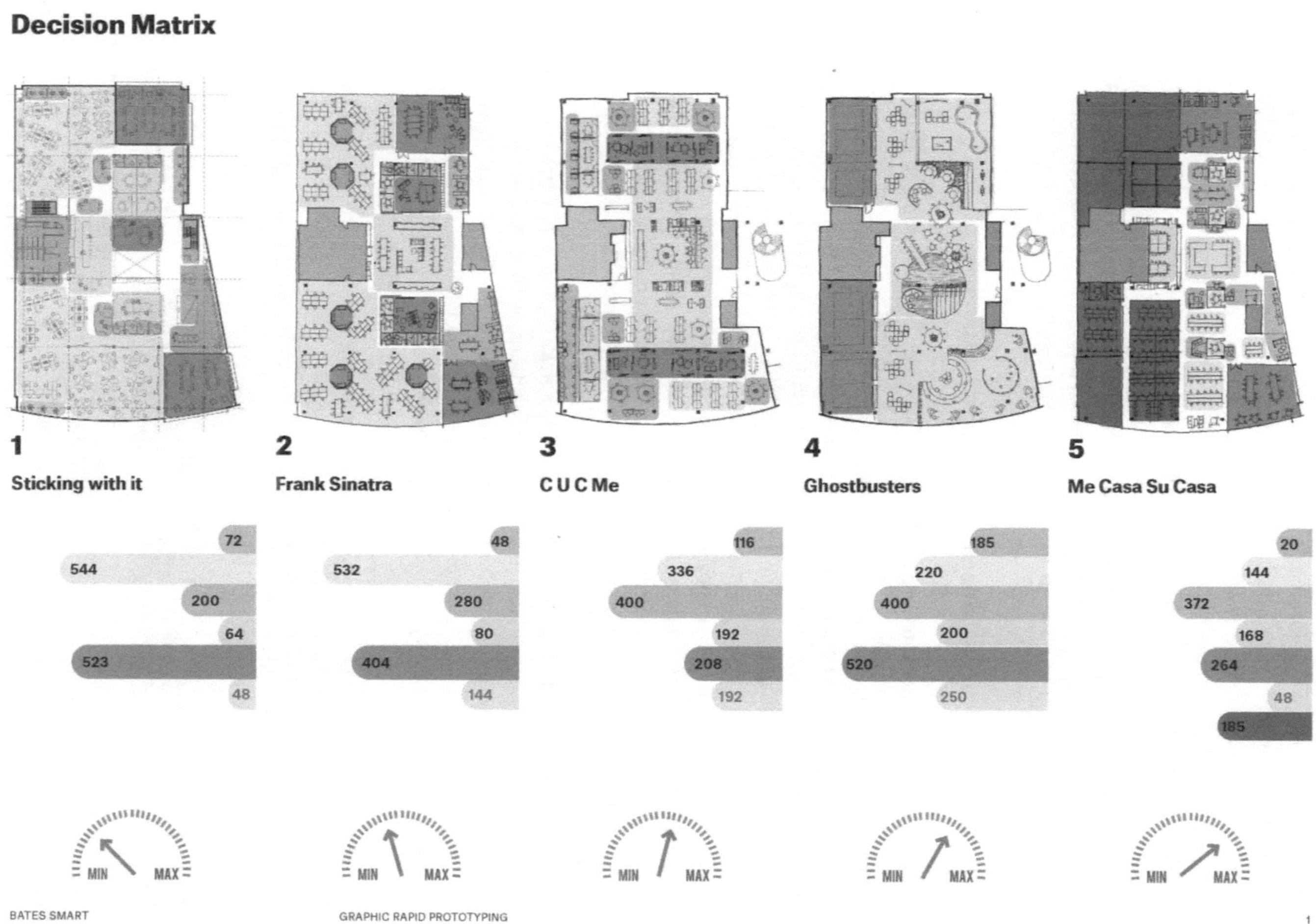

Figure 20.2 Decision matrix showing five directions considered, associated headcount and amenities included and an indication of the organisational change required for adoption. (Image created by Bates Smart)

Using the workplace to nudge team members' behaviours is a goal beyond the scope of most workplaces; this area is generally considered the domain of human resources. Nevertheless, Officeworks took on the challenge by incorporating the concept of building resilience into the design brief in hopes the new workplace would not only satisfy the pragmatic requirements of the brief but also work to help team members learn to adapt and cope with the unknown. During the pandemic employees had to embrace new technologies and ways of working, and adaptive organisations sought solutions that kept their businesses running. Believing uncertainty will become the norm for the future, Officeworks' headquarters proposes spatial solutions to tackle resilience in three ways. First is a layout that reduces distraction and unwanted noise. Second, the design and operations seek to build workers' tenacity by teaching them the skills to cope with the unknown, and, finally, thought has been given to how space can be used to support work activities and tap into the ideas and concepts that will intrinsically motivate workers.

Resilience is impacted by noise and distraction

Solution – an alternative stacking philosophy that gives employees more choice

In the book *Stolen Focus – Why You Can't Pay Attention*, author Johan Hari (2022) talks about the hidden forces that steal focus and drain our energy. He argues we are living in the most distracted world in human history, and these distractions pose a threat to our ability to achieve goals and solve problems. "Noise is a major problem in the modern office" (Oseland & Hodsman, 2018), studies have found acoustics to be the highest cause of dissatisfaction (Jensen & Arens, 2005) and noise and distraction are known to be major stressors in open-plan offices, influencing employees' satisfaction, annoyance and performance (Brocolini et al., 2016). Officeworks' internal survey results noted that employees desire to return to work to interact and connect with colleagues, which will exacerbate noise and distraction and these are already a pressing issue for Officeworks team members.

To combat noise and distraction an alternative building stacking philosophy has been adopted that features different floors being dedicated to different functions, with spatial designs, furniture selections and layouts supporting the desired activities for the floor. The spatial approach will gently nudge behaviours aligned to four activities: socialising and learning, collaborating, working in teams on projects and working solo. The stack and design philosophy has an added benefit

Figure 20.3 Destination strategy, each floor serves a unique purpose. (Graphic created by Bates Smart)

of laying the foundation for Officeworks to shed floors if occupancy patterns do not increase as anticipated, cultivating greater resilience through leasing options.

Attributes of the environments are as follows:

Level 1 – a floor for social interactions

The Link is a new architectural addition to the Chadstone complex that has been designed by Bates Smart Architects that acts as a front door and portal to the office. Functioning as a talisman of the Officeworks brand and experience, the intention of this space is to nudge employees to socially and professionally interact with one another while taking advantage of the café/barista, break out areas and an outdoor terrace. The social theme initiated in The Link flows to the remainder of the first floor that is positioned beneath the existing office building. Featuring a town hall, games area and multiple large studio spaces, the entire area is completely reconfigurable to support office events, showcase new product and encourage team members to play/experiment. The only fixed spaces are media and recording studios, additional large-capacity studios are reconfigurable for training or team events, spilling out to informal lounge settings. The floor is visible and physically connected to Level 2, where formal visitors are received, offering a glimpse of Officeworks' inner workings, including new products and store displays being tested. Importantly, there is a chance to glean the dynamic interactions and vibe that is the glue of Officeworks' culture.

This floor houses the reception area where limited external visitors arrive, although it is expected most external visitors will be project partners treated as team members and given credentials to enter through The Link. The formal front door connects the boardroom, large meeting rooms and small enclosed spaces for interviews and phone calls in a zone suitable for formal seminars and meetings. A reheat kitchen and external waiting area/partner lounge located in the first of the Mixed Mode Spaces services this client and partner zone.

Mixed Mode Spaces are a feature that repeats on Levels 3 and 4, providing access to fresh air when weather permits, and when conditions are not favourable mechanical ventilation takes

Figure 20.4 The Link. (Image provided by Bates Smart)

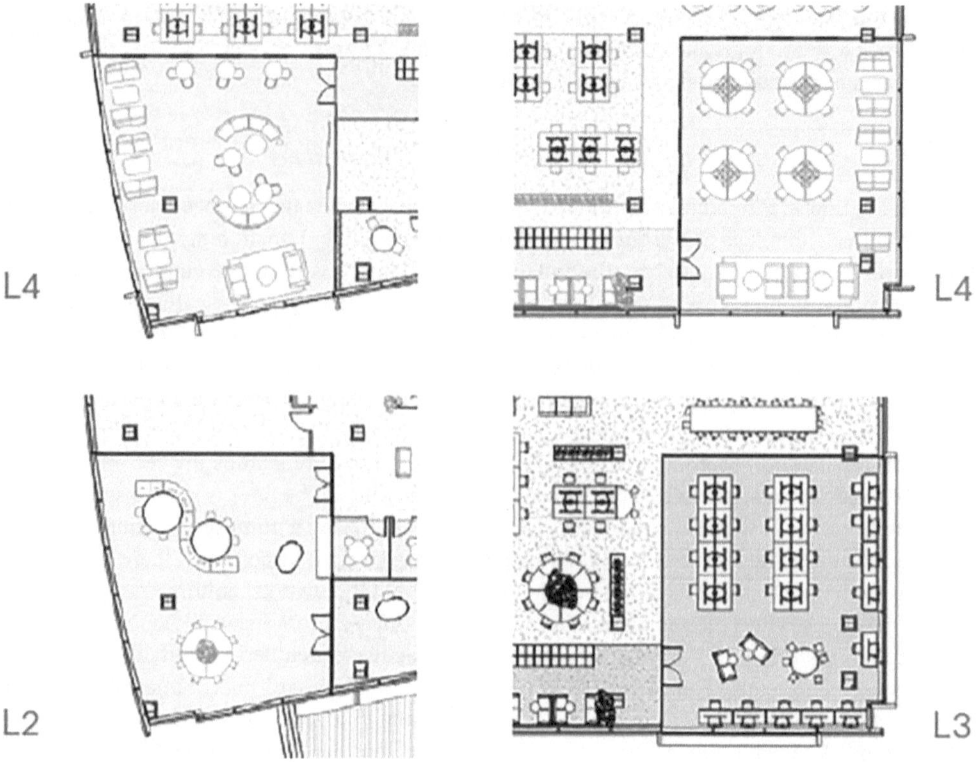

Figure 20.5 Variations of multimodal space layouts to match the destinational theme of the floor they're on. (Floor plans by Bates Smart)

control. The spaces offer a marked departure from other parts of the workplace through an introduction of biophilia expressed through the introduction of curves, planting, natural wood and fibres and access to the outdoors. The design of these environments creates places within the workplace where employees can retreat without entering a lift to travel off floor. Escaping the everyday work environment is linked to innovation, novel thinking and creativity (Elsach & Stigliani, 2020). With direct access on each floor, the immediacy of the Mixed Mode Space mimics the access and ease team members have to outdoor spaces at home and offer a different type of outdoor experience to what one would have visiting the terrace on The Link.

Mixed Mode Spaces adopt a chameleon-like design language that borrows the guiding principles and feel of the floor they occupy.

Level 3 – supporting project teams

Project spaces or labs are the dominant feature of Level 3; they contain internal moveable walls that team members can move themselves to expand or contract the amount of space their team needs, making the labs fully hackable. Some labs are fully enclosed with solid sliding partitions that separate what happens in them from adjacent open work areas, while others afford visibility to the inner workings and artefacts of a project team. Flexibility is made possible by overhead rigging that supports the movable walls, lighting and power and data receptacles that hang within reach of users, allowing them to make adjustments and mould spaces as they require.

Level 4 – a place for quiet contemplation

Designed for the individual, the top level of the workplace is a contrast to the togetherness nudges occurring on the lower levels. Layout and furniture choices on this floor make clear it is a place for dedicated, focused work with the highest proportion of enclosed rooms and individual workspaces. There are no meeting spaces beyond smaller rooms to facilitate conversations between two or three team members. The Mixed Mode Spaces on the floor follow suit and act as refuges for reading, retreat and relaxation. The goal of the floor is simulating a 'flow experience', or optimal state where the team member is fully immersed in their work, which implies 'focused attention' and an increased cognitive performance or 'cognitive rush' (Csikszentmihalyi, 1996).

Increasing employee tenacity to build resilience

Solution – building coping skills through experimentation and agency

Lenore Skenazy the author of "Free-Range Kids" (Skenazy, 2010) began working with social scientists in 2017 to gather insights into why children lacked resilience and discovered what she believed was the key – children are no longer allowed to play, and through play they develop the coping skills required to survive in the world. The same could be said of our workplaces. Over the past decade we have focused on creating 'frictionless environments'; many turned out to be benign workplaces that neither challenged nor provoked occupants. To survive today's challenges organisations must innovate and adapt; this is unlikely to happen in spaces that are dull and familiar.

Theories on innovation, including the design thinking methodology (Auernhammer & Roth, 2021), suggest breaking habitual moulds is critical to develop new ideas, but human nature dictates we follow the path of least resistance; this is the course many facility managers and workplace designers take. Repeating what is easy, comforting and was done in the past is a recipe for low-friction workplaces that do nothing to engage workers. In a post-COVID, pressure-filled world where some have boldly questioned the validity and purpose of the workplace, the safe approach could be considered irresponsible; at the very least it is a denial of what current data indicates. The path of least resistance is not the path Officeworks intends to take, beginning with granting permission and providing an infrastructure for team members to change where and how they work. The Chadstone precinct and headquarters workplace offers a variety of ecosystems to work from augmented by team workers' homes and other places they prefer to work. The landscape within the headquarters will change day by day, providing interest, provocation and inspiration to team members who prefer to revert to the same desk on the same floor.

Borrowing from Skenazy's Let Grow programme designed to build children's resilience through unsupervised play in semi-controlled environments, Officeworks team members are free to roam and encouraged to experiment or play in hackable space. The architectural infrastructure coupled with leadership's mindset grants permission; spatial flexibility is made possible through access to mobile wall units, sliding display panels, light fixtures and drop-down power/data points. Team members decide when visual access to a project lab is beneficial or better denied if confidence in the teams' progress does not warrant sharing.

Figure 20.6 View of an open collaborative space on Level 2. (Rendered image by Bates Smart)

Labs are located behind a spine element that acts as an orientation device and anchor point. The repeating element occurs on every floor and contains shared amenity: copy areas, meeting rooms, storage and quiet rooms. The types and quantities of spaces vary, as does visual permeability of the spine element's design, which is dictated by the theme of the floor and the spaces that surround it. For example, a larger proportion of quiet rooms comprise the spine on Level 4 given the floor's dedication to focus, while the spine on the collaboration floor is designed for groups, providing separation between rooms with loosely defined curtains or screens rather than walls.

The design nudges team members to engage and take control. Ownership, agency and belonging result from the investment they have made in fashioning the space their way. The importance of investment is described in the book *Hooked: How to Build Habit-Forming Products* where author Nir Eyal describes the Hook Model (Eyal, 2019). This is a formula that encourages habits and behaviours with the ultimate objective of making users return to a product; it has been used quite successfully and somewhat nefariously by technology designers. Moral implications aside, the Hook Model is based on five questions that, once satisfied, send customers into a loyalty loop. Clearly Officeworks headquarters is an experience, not a product; nevertheless, the concept of considering how workplace design might borrow some of the concepts is a way to expand ideas of how place might be leveraged to shift habits and behaviours.

Improving resilience by tapping workers' motivation

Solution two – engaging space to build a shared narrative, purpose and meaning and focus on issues that matter to employees

As a society we have reached a tipping point in the role we believe business should play in impacting the world around them (Atlassian, 2021). Employees expect more. When an organisation's actions or inactions are incongruent with stated values, there is a negative impact on employee sentiment. And it is through the physical workplace that culture is formed and where teams engage

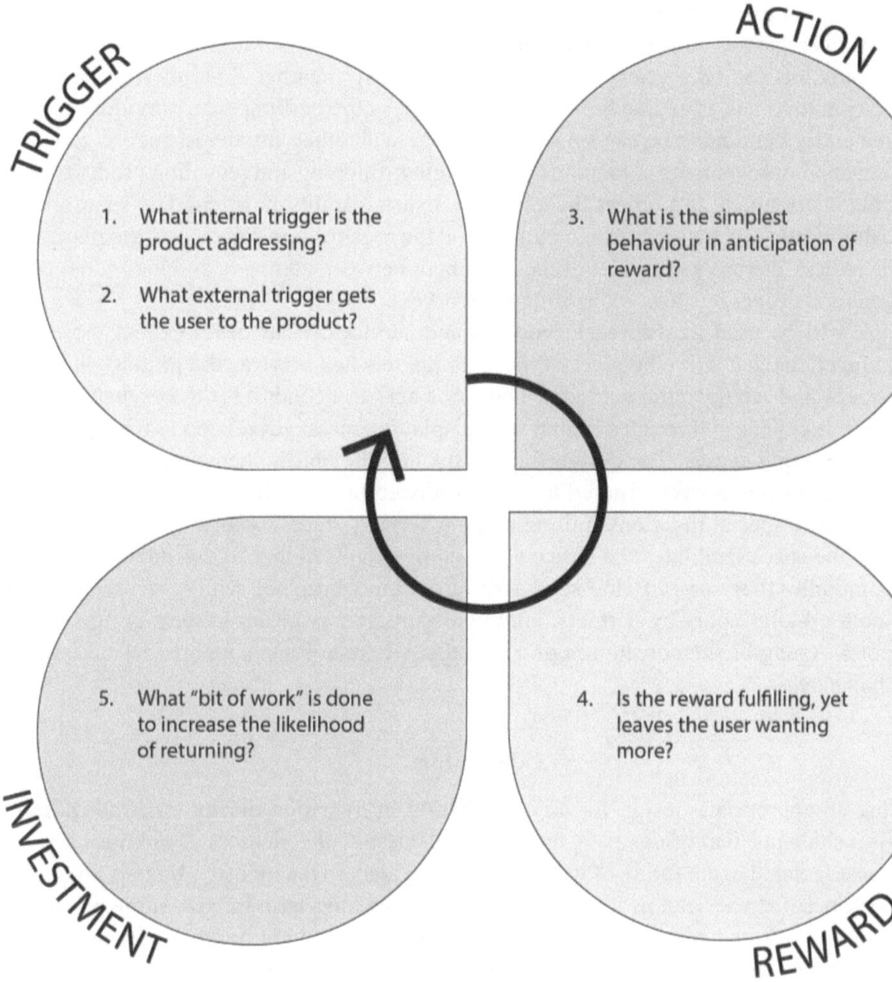

Figure 20.7 Hook Model created by Nir Eyal – tech entrepreneur, investor and Stanford Graduate School of Business professor. (Recreated by editors for case study)

in the processes needed to deliver business results. The space that will most embody this concept in the new Officeworks headquarters is The Link.

This new architectural addition acts as the front door and threshold for the company, a place to connect team members to Officeworks' mission and act as a billboard communicating what the organisation is doing. It will be the glue binding the company to team members and to the broader surrounding community they care for. The space tangibly supports three of the five stated project objectives: magnetic connection, showcase and share, and green space/green impact. Lease conditions dictated a carbon-neutral building along with outdoor access. Property developer Vicinity responded by directing the architects to convert unusable outdoor balconies to large Mixed Mode Spaces on Levels 2, 3 and 4, as well as include an exterior terrace adjacent to and accessible through The Link.

While The Link is the first space employees enter, it is not their first exposure to the company or the issues they care about – this happens when they park their car. Not normally a place for inspiration – parking lots can be soulless – but Officeworks team members journey from car to front door under a photovoltaic array that has been added to the entire parking area, providing shade and enabling the entire building to be carbon neutral. In line with other initiatives, such as a corporate tree planting and improvements to methods of producing, shipping and recycling products that are better for the environment, all reflect the company's sustainability position. The solar array is a physical manifestation of an issue team members and the organisation care about: the planet. From automobile to desk there is a reminder of the alignment between company and individual purpose that will generate deeper intrinsic motivation for workers.

The Link will be used to showcase products and services under development, host special events and functions that will take place at the headquarters and serve as the primary location for food, beverages and access to the outdoors. The space acts as a conduit for the exchange of information, which is enhanced through a digital wall displaying messages related to the company and social and community causes. The design follows the high flexibility theme with furnishings that can be removed entirely or reconfigured to support numerous activities: exercise classes, parties, training events and special functions spilling to the external terrace, weather permitting.

Critically, the space facilitates the Officeworks community's ability to extend and blend to the broader community they serve. Being segregated from the workplace with a secure barrier, The Link can be used after hours by partners, community guests or special interest groups the company supports. A tangible demonstration of a way that workplace can support societal issues and external challenges.

Conclusion

Anticipating an appropriate design for an organisation in transition during a period of extreme volatility is a challenge that brings risks for designers. Despite the plethora of opinions and direction hypotheses related to the future of work that are prevalent in the industry, there is no precedent to follow or clues that will lead us to answers related to the long-term impact of the pandemic on society, organisations, the economy or people. It is this not knowing of what humans will think and feel that poses the real obstacle for architects and designers who want to create places for people but find themselves ill equipped to address significant social and cultural disengagement and societal concerns that workers experienced and now influences their expectations. Existing workplaces have low impact for an organisation today who must contend with shifting occupancy patterns, users who want to do different activities in the workplace and have a strong desire for their organisation to leverage workplace to address external issues they care about. Designers have lost their ability to leverage workplace to help companies combat the socio-psychological issues they and their employees face.

This uncertainty on its own is a strong indication that future environments must become far more fluid than they have been in the past, even more than what was touted as 'flexible' but only adjustable by tradesmen. Office space typologies need to be recalibrated to support activities workers will come to the office for, which is to work with others in spaces designed to support collaboration both physically and digitally. The ones that don't will remain vacant hulls, coming in second place to better-equipped, quieter and more convenient work environments at home or in third places. Adding to the challenge, provisions for focus work cannot be ignored, and appropriate adjustments are necessary to remedy noise and distraction that rob individuals of their ability to focus; in addition, a wide range of diverse workers who will desire less stimulating environments, such as those with disabilities, neurodiversity, etc., and whose entry into the workforce was a positive aspect of the pandemic, will need to be considered. Inclusion must move from all talk to action.

Time will tell where this leads us, but from uncertainty two clear ideas come into view. The first is a need for an acceptance and tolerance of experimentation; the future will be a time of reimagination, trialling, measuring and adjusting. New workplaces must have the ability to adjust to users' changing needs; therefore, they will continuously evolve, and for that to happen designers' expectations of aesthetic control requires adjustment. Second, the future does not signal a waning of the importance of space; on the contrary, space is closely aligned with personal and professional identity and rituals; as a result, the importance of well-designed space escalates. But for architects and workplace designers to deliver the quality of spaces that will make a difference to the people that occupy them, they need to understand people, and at the moment design education generally only touches on the way that space impacts human behaviours and the development of workplace strategy. To acquire the skills necessary, more coordinated efforts between designers and environmental psychologists, psychologists, behavioural scientists and humanistic geographers should filter into both education and practice so designers can get a better understanding of ourselves.

Organisations play a part too in demonstrating the wisdom and courage to demand more than the status quo and resist the temptation to set the bar at satisfying pragmatic functional requirements. The world is facing too many existential problems for us ignore what physical environments might do to deliberately guide experiences in a way that will help humans and organisations thrive. The Officeworks headquarters is a start; many more companies need to follow a similar path.

References

Atlassian 2021 return on action report. (n.d.). *Return on Action report: the new social contract for business.* Atlassian-2021-return-on-action-report-australia.pdf

Auernhammer, J., & Roth, B. (2021). The origin and evolution of Stanford University's design thinking: From product design to design thinking in innovation management. *Journal of Product Innovation Management*, *38*(6), 623–644. https://doi.org/10.1111/jpim.12594

Ayoko, O. B., & Ashkanasy, N. M. (Eds.). (2020). *Organizational behaviour and the physical environment.* Routledge.

Brocolini, L., Parizet, E., & Chevret, P. (2016). Effect of masking noise on cognitive performance and annoyance in open plan offices. *Applied Acoustics*, *114*, 44–55. https://doi.org/10.1016/j.apacoust.2016.07.012

Carnevale, J. B., & Hatak, I. (2020). Employee adjustment and well-being in the era of COVID-19: Implications for human resource management. *Journal of Business Research*, *116*, 183–187. https://doi.org/10.1016/j.jbusres.2020.05.037

Cheema-Fox, A., Seerafim, G., & Wang, H. (2021). Corporate resilience and response to COVID-19. *Journal of Applied Corporate Finance*, *33*(2), 24–40.

Cheese, P. (2021). *The new world of work: Shaping a future that helps people, organizations and our societies to thrive*. Kogan Page.

Collings, D. G., Nyberg, A. J., Wright, P. M., & McMackin, J. (2021). Leading through paradox in a COVID-19 world: Human resources comes of age. *Human Resource Management Journal*, *31*(4), 819–833. https://doi.org/10.1111/1748-8583.12343

Csikszentmihalyi, M. (1996). *Flow and the psychology of discovery and invention.* Harper Collins.

Elsach, K. D., & Stigliani, I. (2020). The physical work environment and creativity: How creative workspaces support and encourage design thinking. In O. B. Ayoko & N. M. Ashkanasy (Eds), *Organisational behaviour and the physical environment.* Routledge.

Eyal, N. (2019). *Hooked: How to build habit-forming products.* Portfolio.

Hari, J. (2022). *Stolen focus – Why you can't pay attention.* Bloomsbury.

Jensen, K., & Arens, E. (2005). *Acoustical quality in office workstations, as assessed by occupant surveys.* Indoor Air.

Mejía, G. M. (2021). Theory-driven or theory-informed? A review of behavioural economics in design. *The Design Journal, 24*(4), 567–587. https://doi.org/10.1080/14606925.2021.1935089
Oseland, N., & Hodsman, P. (2018). A psychoacoustical approach to resolving office noise distraction. *Journal of Corporate Real Estate, 20*(4), 260–280. https://doi.org/10.1108/JCRE-08-2017-0021
Park, C. L., Finkelstein-Fox, L., Russell, B. S., Fendrich, M., Hutchison, M., & Becker, J. (2021). Psychological resilience early in the COVID-19 pandemic: Stressors, resources, and coping strategies in a national sample of Americans. *American Psychologist, 76*(5), 715–728. https://doi.org/10.1037/amp0000813
Skenazy, L. (2010). *Free range kids: How to raise safe, self-reliant children*. Jossey-Bass.
Trafford, E. P., & de la Hunty, A. (2021). A gentle nudge: Can choice architecture play a role in retailers' efforts to promote healthier choices? *Nutrition Bulletin, 46*(1), 98–109. https://doi.org/10.1111/nbu.12484

21
CASE STUDY
Mirvac – Sydney, Australia

Lisa Munao

For Mirvac, taking this step and taking it early provided a foundation which enabled adaptation to the changing needs and diversity of their business and a natural evolution taking place through the change of a generation. This was just the start of an evolution as the workplace will keep evolving. Agility, ease of collaboration and camaraderie are key to effectiveness. Emphasis on teams, how and where they work and are supported is in focus. An increased desire of employees (a new generation) for increased levels of flexibility, mobility and autonomy drives this natural evolution.

– *Author*

Introduction

This case study chapter features the Australian property developer Mirvac Ltd. Mirvac is an owner, developer and manager of a portfolio of properties with a purpose to consciously create and curate unique places and deliver outstanding services and experiences for employees and customers. Mirvac supports commercial customers to deliver successful workplaces through active listening, engaging with the community within its buildings, identifying pain points and opportunities, then addressing these through human-centred design, focused on problem solving and ideation. The outcome of this approach stretches beyond the benefits of Mirvac's business by also influencing better-quality places to work for the employees of their customers and partners.

Mirvac's innovative culture is the basis of its success across the broader markets of commercial, residential and retail. Mirvac's approach to the workplace is an example of high-performance due to an ongoing openness to explore new ideas and in their early adoption of new ways of workplace reform – an evolution from a static to an adaptive, flexible approach. In addition, the organisation focuses on creating inspiring and healthy environments that are unique and that support a variety of workstyles. Crafting a new way of working not just for Mirvac team members, but the workplaces of others by sharing their insights with the broader community.

Mirvac shows leadership, confidence and resolve in Australia with its experimental approach to ideate, iterate, test and learn through the process of workplace evolution. In this case study we explore the evolution of Mirvac's workplace through the lenses of physical design, technology integration and management.

DOI: 10.1201/9781003328728-25

This chapter has been made available under a CC-BY-NC-ND 4.0 license.

This case study discusses the key drivers which influence and shape the workplace, emphasising the benefits, satisfaction, health and productivity of workers. Differences pre and post pandemic will be highlighted, and benefits outlined to demonstrate what this kind of focus on workplace and employees has on ongoing business success and positive employee experience.

Mirvac's openness to an ever-evolving workplace will be illustrated by examining completed workplaces and workstyle approaches which evolved from static environments, through the unique 'agile' way of working, to the team-based, adaptable environments being tested today. Insights and observations along with changes in the physical space will be illustrated.

Image 21.1 The Adaptive Workplace project – Mirvac.

The (non)static workplace (1990–2016)

A static approach to workplace design as most of us know holds a prominent place in history.

Some businesses opted to remain static, whilst the majority have evolved the way they work in a physical sense. A workstation was a necessary tool for work, as it accommodated large CPUs, monitors and keyboards. Work was independent in nature and hierarchically driven. Enclosed offices and workstations with high screens offered a sense of privacy and noise control. Open and informal collaboration was limited, and meetings were held in enclosed spaces, providing privacy and confidentiality by acoustic separation. The workplace layout was made up of predominantly workstations and offices, with a small proportion of the area allocated to support such as printing, storage and kitchenettes or tea points (a necessary amenity to provide a place for employees to take a break and have tea, coffee or lunch). There was a large proportion of space for individual work per person, with a small amount of space dedicated for employee interaction – a far cry from the inspiring vibrant connected spaces of today. Management of space requires continual physical change to the environment as a result of business needs, growth and contraction. The environment requires continual property and facilities team management with regular construction work. Such churn is a costly process to business and disruptive to its occupants. While this static and cellular way of working was generally accepted and suited a hierarchical organisational structure, the late 90s saw an increase in the speed of change. Business models were evolving (driven largely by the growing tech industry), new technologies were emerging, there was a fascination and optimism about the future, in turn sparking the beginning of change in the way we were working.

Mirvac was one such business that did not remain static nor cellular, saw change as inevitable and envisioned the future and the impact that changing business models would have (were already having) on the way we work and adopted the 'open office'. Mirvac's General Manager, Strategy & Customer, Paul Edwards, said Mirvac's established 'lean into disruption' approach allowed the company to lead through innovation, engagement, iterate and learn. Mirvac's physical open-office environment supported the business through a simple set of workpoint types and support spaces. Primary factors that set Mirvac apart from and ahead of other organisations during this time include: (i) an office-free approach; (ii) a non-hierarchical, all-team-occupied, open-plan environment; and (iii) an experimental approach towards unassigned seating where people could share space and drop in and out.

The agile workplace: transforming the way we work (2016–2022)

The next phase of evolution in the way we work was Activity-Based Working (ABW), a philosophy that would 'untether' us from our desks and provide us the freedom to engage in collaboration and connect with each other like never before. An activity-based workplace supports individuals to work in focused and collaborative ways. Workstations are no longer allocated to an individual; the workstation or workpoint is now known as 'unassigned' (open to all). There are a variety of workpoint types providing and encouraging employees to choose the setting that best suits their task: 'freedom of choice for how and where you want to work'. Individual space which was once vacant due to leave or other factors is now highly utilised. The factor of being able to allocate more people than seats in the physical workplace means that otherwise underutilised space can now be re-deployed for individuals and teams to share. Shared space needs are evolving, a diverse range of meeting space is in demand from formal enclosed to informal open and ad hoc interaction.

Space use is more effective, more efficient and results in advantages for the employee and the business.

Paul Edwards noted, 'Our CEO focused on ensuring the business moved within the workspace, so people met new people, engaged with different environments and people'. To do this Susan Lloyd-Hurwitz insisted people didn't sit at the same desk. 'Our customers visiting the office were always amazed to learn that Sue didn't have an office and encouraged people to move'.

The shift to ABW from static or indeed a cellular environment is bold, it's a dramatic 'step change' in the way we work, it is synonymous with organisations who have a mindset to embrace change, to innovate, to adapt. There was some resistance to ABW implementation, in large part due to the intense change in mindset and behaviour that individuals no longer had a seat that they 'owned'; space was now there to 'share'. There was a nervousness that 'a sense of belonging' would be diminished and damage corporate culture and the ability to 'get work done'.

The increase in business adopting the digital business tool of 'agile methodology' further influenced the way we work. It requires space for teams to gather and work together on tasks yet retreat for focused work. This approach is property team–led with now greater input from human resources, people and culture. Change management becomes vital and permanent to encourage, guide and support employees in a new and exciting way to work.

While many organisations remained static amidst the ground swell and growing popularity of ABW, Mirvac was already 'leaning into the disruption'. The idea of untethering and unassigning was too much for some; to Mirvac this was exciting and certainly an opportunity to evolve, recognising that there is no 'one size fits all' approach. Mirvac had utilised its open-office environment in an unofficial pilot to test the idea of being 'unassigned', creating 'neighbourhoods' of teams, encouraging collaboration and adopting new technologies to enable them to 'untether'.

Mirvac skipped the ABW wave in Australia by launching a test pilot and designing their next workplaces to support a new agile environment with a unique set of principles which encouraged movement to be highly connected and collaborative. Being true to their approach of early adoption was a central motivator. The team would continue to innovate, iterate, test and learn to evolve and create a supportive and inspiring workplace.

Mirvac launched its own unique agile way of working pilot in 2015 – 'Transforming the way we work' – and their workforce moved into the new agile workspace one year later in 2016. Not only adopting the relatively new principles of ABW but forging their own path to develop their own unique spaces and tools. A high level of engagement with the team was needed to develop these and to ensure they feel supported, engaged and enjoy the experience of the environment to perform at their best. One of those projects was 200 George Street, Sydney and Australia's first WELL Certified[1] office at Gold level. It is also one of the healthiest places to work.

The primary factors underpinning Mirvac's agile environment include:

- Promoting agility and encouraging movement
- Encouraging flexible working
- Diversity and inclusion focus
- Providing more space for connection and collaboration

These tenets have resulted in connecting everyone in the organisation, not just by floor but across the whole workplace; improving the efficiency in the use of space, recognising that not all employees are in the workplace at any one time due to a variety of factors.

For Mirvac, taking this step and taking it early provided a foundation which enabled adaptation to the changing needs and diversity of their business and a natural evolution taking place through the change of a generation. This was just the start of an evolution as the workplace will keep evolving. Agility, ease of collaboration and camaraderie are key to effectiveness. Emphasis on teams – how and where they work and how they are supported – is in focus. An increased desire of employees (a new generation) for increased levels of flexibility, mobility and autonomy drives this natural evolution. These were just some of the drivers impacting the way we approached workplace and well-being before COVID-19.

In the management of space Mirvac's teams of property, people and culture are working collaboratively to provide effective solutions. Technology is quickly advancing to support greater mobility and agility. A drive-in technological innovation that is critical to enable the 'untethered' workforce demanding not only to be mobile and highly connected in the physical workplace but from wherever they are.

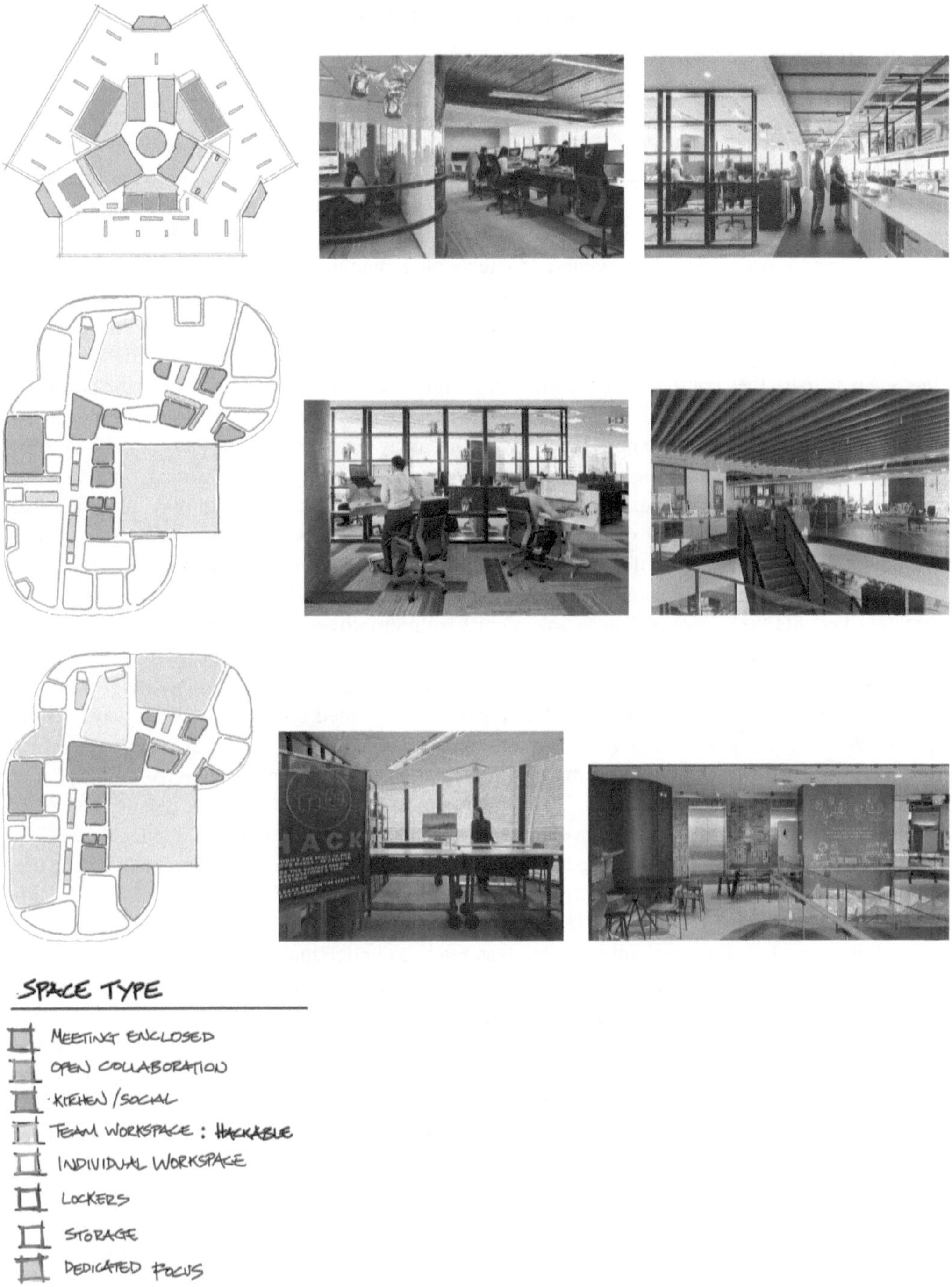

Figure 21.1 Key differentiators – proportions of workspace typologies and social space.

Lisa Munao

The adaptive workplace 2022

A shift from employer led to employee driven.

The impact of the pandemic for all is a turning point. Its mark on how we approach workplace is indisputable. In early 2020 the 'work from home' mandate threw (in particular) the corporate world into a spin. Some businesses and organisations were ready, many were not. Mirvac is one of those organisations that was well positioned, having taken the bold step to ABW and flexible work practices many years before with a workforce enabled by technology and approximately seventy-five percent of people with flexible arrangements in place. This enabled Mirvac to transition with speed to remote working. As we entered the pandemic, leaders focused on two critical factors to sustain performance: culture and technology. The two elements were crucial as leadership worked to ensure that while everyone was apart, they could still be together and continue to innovate and deliver for the customer.

This shared experience for all to work away from the primary workplace was irreversible. As lockdowns eased, this shared experience of working away from the primary workplace and the desire for employees to continue to enjoy the benefits of flexibility while valuing time together at the office sparked Mirvac's leaders to explore what role workplace should play, now and into the future. The emphasis being on finding purpose, fostering strong company culture, connection, innovation and learning (informal and formal), creating a physical workplace where people want to be, where success can be found in what works for the individual, the team and which ultimately benefits the business. There was a shift from employer led to employee driven. Post-lockdowns, there was a palpable change in how people think about work and life, from the pursuit for work–life balance to decisions based on lifestyle. Mirvac's approach recognises the benefits for all in a partnership between employer and employee: a continued consultation both ways, listening, empathising, being open, open-minded and ready to adapt to new ideas. An approach which promotes continued evolution and ultimately creates an exceptional experience for employees to thrive into the future.

Mirvac developed a new set of workplace criteria through the creation of a pilot floor, 'The Adaptive Workplace', with the purpose of creating a live test and learn environment. With the disruption of the pandemic, Mirvac, already working in a flexible and agile way, were able to quickly adapt to a workforce that would work from home and elsewhere. The year 2021 saw the return to the workplace, and characteristically Mirvac was ready to understand and action a modified way of working to build upon the positives of the recent experience. From 'a way of working' perspective, the overarching objective was to gain a deeper understanding of the various workstyles within their business, see how the needs of their people may have changed and how this 'work from home experience' would influence the types of spaces and tools they would need as they return to the workplace and ultimately understand the purpose of their physical workplace.

Mirvac's proposition to its employees through the Adaptive Workplace pilot was encapsulated in a White Paper:

> The Adaptive Workplace is a highly flexible, dynamic work environment that responds in real – time to the specific task, people, or team using it. It is embedded with a kit of parts and design components that allow it to oscillate between a variety of settings based on the changing needs of a workforce in the short-term and over time, capturing insights and data that allow it to constantly evolve.
>
> (Mirvac, 2022, p. 5).

The challenge facing the Adaptive Workplace is bringing together a hybrid workforce nurturing positive workplace culture and understanding the opportunities and implications. Hybrid working puts the employee at the centre, self-determining how they work, where, when and with a choice of collaborators.

This was supported by 5 key factors for the purpose of the Adaptive Workplace pilot

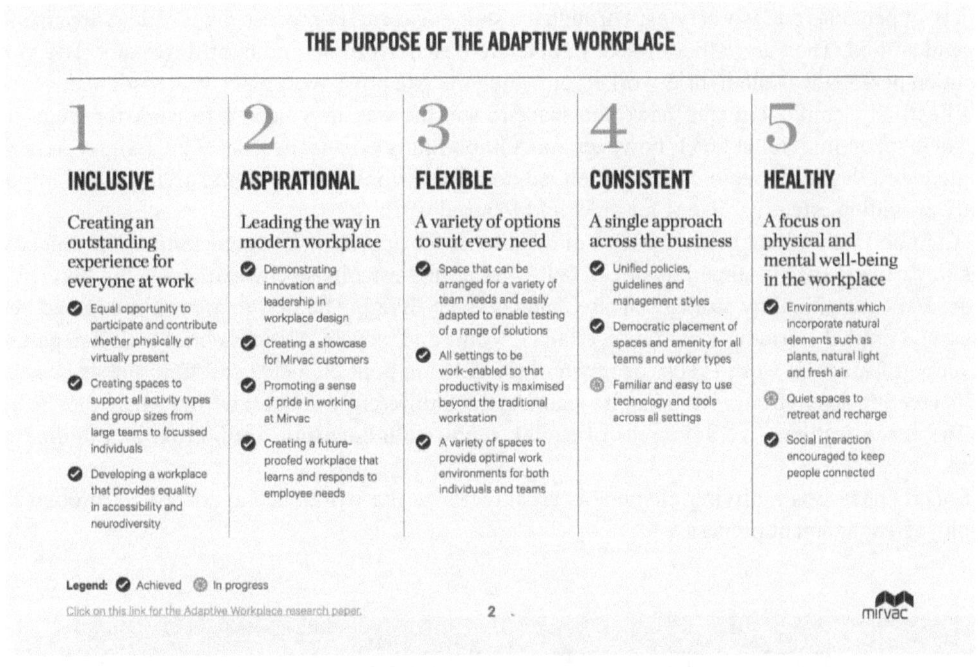

Key operational lessons

The engagement process gave clarity to the problem, which in turn enabled success. This engagement process comprised two key activities:

The first part was a process of workshops to discover the various workstyles that make up the Mirvac workforce, the primary discovery being that the hybrid worker was the most prominent of the various workstyles, and this provided the context for the design evolution.

The second was applied research. Five cohorts rotated through the pilot for four weeks. The teams were encouraged to experiment through hacking the space and giving feedback on their experience. These included working together, increased socialising, challenges in team organisation, booking space and discovering how various roles might find their place.

A standout discovery or lesson was that giving guidance, a framework rather than a set of rules, encourages people to embrace the freedom to truly feel licence to experiment and provide feedback. The result is highly engaged teams utilising the space exactly as they need it to be to support the way they work.

Behavioral change – the benefits of bringing people together – were evident. There was a significant increase in employees coming into the office. Brainstorming and creative work, learning from colleagues and creating meaningful connections were of benefit to all and were certainly an attractor. Continued encouragement and support from community managers and colleagues assisted many of the teams to move on from traditional workplace behavioral traits and to embrace the benefits this environment had to offer.

From a physical environment perspective, the Adaptive Workplace pilot space has been designed for ultimate malleability and operationally supports a way of working which is inherently flexible and adaptable. The design reflects Mirvac's purpose for the workplace by enabling a variety of personas and workstyles. Through the staff engagement process, five workstyle personas were identified. They are: office-based, in-out, site-based, freedom and hybrid workers. The most common persona was the hybrid worker, on which the Adaptive Workplace was modelled.

Effectively, employees can 'hack' the space to suit the way they need it to work for them. It's hackable on an individual level; however, most importantly on a team level. The design caters for an increased desire for team collaboration, ad hoc discussions and problem solving while importantly providing effective spaces for quiet and focused work.

An important element in the creation of the pilot is the approach to sustainability. The objective was to carry on the sustainability focus that Mirvac had established. In particular the objectives of the 2014 sustainability strategy 'This Changes Everything'. The design approach targeted zero waste and limited consumption – reuse, retain, relocate and recycle. Mirvac's brief to design partner Davenport Campbell was to reuse as much of the existing built elements and furniture as possible while creating an environment to inspire teams to think differently about how and where they work.

The space features five key areas of **social**, **team**, **collaboration**, **individual** and **dedicated focus**.

Social space was a driving element as an attractor to the workplace as identified through the employee engagement process.

Image 21.2 Social space – connect setting seated.

Image 21.3 Social space – connect setting high table.

Image 21.4 Team space – 'hackable' workpoints.

The existing kitchenette, which was central yet land locked by built elements, was opened up and tripled in size. This effectively created an open and inviting arrival experience from the lift lobby. Its central location provided an important pivot point for people traversing the floor, creating energy and enabling serendipitous connections. The space provided a location for casual and social events while also providing space to work individually, collaborate or meet with the team.

Team space provides workspaces for people working together or individually. Pockets of individual workspace were removed. The fixed workstations were replaced with individual work points 'daisy chained' together from a single point of power. This allowed the users of the space to easily reconfigure the layout of the workstations ('a hack'), yet they were still equipped with an adjustable monitor and docking station. A project/team table was introduced central to the team zone, a location to bring your own device (as there is no fixed equipment). This space became popular as a drop-in point for people between meetings and other activities. It became a place where leaders could be visible and approachable for their team to connect and work together.

The most common 'hack' was the 'horseshoe' configuration. Working side by side, yet individually, easily coming together at the central team table to meet. This is not a common planning solution due to potential inefficiencies; however, an important observation and reminder in focusing on what people need and how they want to work, not just on space efficiency and what looks good.

Open and informal **collaboration** spaces were increased and located adjacent to the team spaces. The furniture selection indicates to the user that it is easily reconfigurable (hackable) and can be intuitively rearranged to suit their workstyle needs. The spaces are equipped with both digital and analogue tools, such as mobile whiteboards and digital surface hubs that can be easily moved around. Across the duration of the pilot, these spaces were continually reconfigured to a variety of setups.

Image 21.5 Team space – team tables.

Image 21.6 Collaboration space – flexible and reconfigurable.

Image 21.7 Collaboration space – flexible and reconfigurable.

Image 21.8 Individual workspace.

Image 21.9 Dedicated focus zone.

Image 21.10 Individual desk within dedicated focus zone.

The team engagement workshops highlighted an important need for space to work individually by breaking away from the team space. **Individual** style workpoints are in areas that feel protected for the user, yet the occupant is still visible and connected. Importantly these spaces should be separate enough from the team space so that people working individually are not interrupted and people in the team space do not feel that they are interrupting. An individual desk offers privacy, height adjustability, adjustable monitor arms and docking stations.

The ability to carry out focused work within the workplace is a crucial element. While flexibility allows people to work both in and out of the office, a day will entail many tasks. A dedicated focus space to enable quiet work has been located in the most protected space on the floor. This location signals that those using this space have sought to retreat into a quiet environment and would like to remain uninterrupted. The space accommodates a variety of workpoints from an individual desk which offers privacy, adjustability and tech to a cocoon-like enclosed workpoint where the user is hidden from view and the acoustic separation is increased.

Key lessons

The type of spaces, their position and proportion and the furniture and tools within them provide the structure for flexibility.

Social connection is one of the most important elements of work. A large central place that is open and welcoming, a place where you can base yourself to be visible, accessible and enable serendipitous connections, is necessary. Space for informal collaboration to brainstorm and team space to work together is an attractor to the workplace. Permission to 'hack' team spaces to suit team needs offers freedom and creates positive team camaraderie, a sense of belonging, ownership

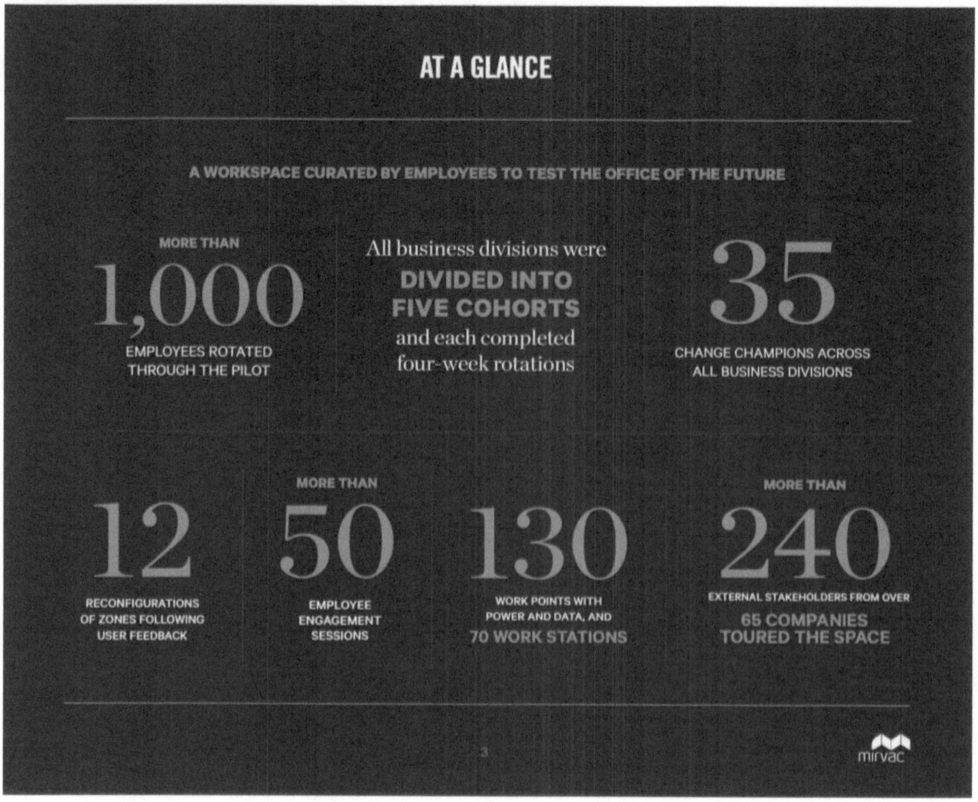

Figure 21.3 The Adaptive Workplace facts and figures. (The Adaptive Workplace Insight Report, March 2023, p. 3)

and autonomy over the space where you work. This then balances with carefully located individual workspace and a destination for uninterrupted focused work.

The results of digital data, utilisation studies, focus groups, feedback loops and observation were used to continuously adapt the pilot for its duration. Not only will this information show the utilisation and effectiveness of the physical space but will provide insight into how teams collaborate, what spaces different teams utilise and how they 'hack' to suit their needs. Insights are gathered for how leaders manage their teams in this new environment, how teams respond to working in a new way and what new behaviours might be created. Importantly, what might be missing and that require solutions are also revealed. Data-driven insights will assist change.

Conclusion

The workplace will continually evolve, and Mirvac has responded, leading through providing its network of teams and customers with the tools to work flexibly and with the ability to adapt. The spaces teams occupy can continue to change without major upheaval or startling change. Paul Edwards stated at the launch of The Adaptive Workplace Insight Report, March 2023, that Mirvac will continue to seek input and feedback, review data and iterate their workplaces.

Further, a recent (Mirvac, 2023; Durakovic et al., 2023) study six months after occupation of the second pilot shows the Adaptive Workplace is showing successful impact across most assessed areas of productivity. These include feedback, joint decision making, task coordination, brainstorming, cross-collaboration, learning, autonomy over how you do your work and being able to work undisturbed.

The Adaptive Workplace pilot

Design: Mirvac in partnership with Davenport Campbell
Size: 1300 sq metres

Note

1 https://www.wellcertified.com/

References

Durakovic, I., Munao, L., & Finlayson, S. (2023). *Supporting social capital in an omni-channel workforce. Research report*. Swayn Open Research. Retrieved June 26, 2023, from https://alastairswaynfoundation.org/funded-research/supporting-social-capital-in-an-omni-channel-workforce/

Mirvac. (2022). *The adaptive workplace: Designing the workplace of the future*. Retrieved February 22, 2023, from https://mirvac-cdn-prd.azureedge.net/-/media/Project/Mirvac/Corporate/Main-Site/Corporate-Theme/images/Office/Campaigns/Mirvac-AdaptiveWorkplace-WhitePaper.pdf?la=en&hash=BC64048F4DF33C1A98A8C4019B9FF3B4D658B6B9

Mirvac. (2023). *The adaptive workplace insight report*. Retrieved April 2, 2023, from https://mirvac-cdn-prd.azureedge.net/-/media/Project/Mirvac/Corporate/Main-Site/Corporate-Theme/images/Office/Campaigns/Adaptive-Workplace-Insight-Report-March-2023.pdf

CONCLUSION

Christhina Candido, Iva Durakovic, and Samin Marzban

The evidence explored in this book shows that high-performance workplaces are those that have a positive effect on individuals, organisations and the community more broadly. The interpretation of what defines high-performance as explored here comes from the workers' perspective and how the design, performance and experience of workplaces can be harnessed to enhance satisfaction, productivity and health in practice. Evidence harvested from research and practice over time shows that the successful delivery of high-performance requires a commitment to three pillars – physical, human and organisational. This book is the fourth publication added to the Transdisciplinary Workplace Research and Management Series led by Prof. Rianne Appel-Meulenbroek and Dr Vitalija Danivska.

Fundamentals covered in this book are intended to be relevant to static, untethered and adaptive workplaces, and considerate of the needs of the unshackled workforce post-COVID. Whilst the thread of the pandemic permeates this volume, its impacts on the workplace and every aspect of society have been of a scale not seen since the invention of the internet; therefore, a timestamp of one the biggest disruptors of our time was inevitable. However, what we hope readers will understand and take away are the core principles of high-performance workplaces which still stand, illuminated, tried and tested by the pandemic, and will continue to be the markers/bearers/roadmaps for designers, developers, researchers and leaders through the challenges of times that follow. Whilst the way people work, as well as where, when and how they work and want to work has changed over time, the evidence shows that high-performance can effectively be achieved if the three pillars are carefully considered, interpreted and implemented from inception.

From a physical environment perspective, lessons discussed in Part 1 reinforce the crucial role user-centred and evidence-based interior design plays in achieving high-performance workplaces. Results from static, untethered and adaptive workplaces consistently show that the overall quality of performance, and most importantly experience of workplaces, can only be lifted if the space matches the needs of the workforce. Evidence shows that landscaped designs able to accommodate and properly support a variety of work tasks are a must, but workers also need to buy into the idea and change their behaviour to harness the office infrastructure as whole. Findings also dispel the notion that different layouts are superior by default, especially when it comes to desk ownership provision. Authors make a strong call for open-plan offices not to be referred to in generic terms, especially in research, and for results to be better contextualised from an interior design

DOI: 10.1201/9781003328728-26
This chapter has been made available under a CC-BY-NC-ND 4.0 license.

perspective. Further, the evidence shows that healthy and environmentally conscious workplaces are front of mind to workers, with these concerns elevated from a "nice to have" to a "must have" in recent years. The rise of the unshackled workforce means that offices need to work harder to accommodate changes in space needs and to be able to support and bring together physical and virtual tribes of workers through seamless integration and experiences. Designers, industry and governments need to be better educated and able problem solvers to effectively meet the challenges of the coming decades and centuries, where artificial intelligence (AI), augmented reality (AR) and virtual reality (VR) are a given. Leveraging physical and digital space to support learning will lead to commitment.

From a human perspective, Part 2 shows that the workplace environment as a whole needs to be inclusive and participative by design to be able to cater for the needs of people from all walks of life. This global workforce composition means that workspaces need to be able to understand and respond to the workforce, shifting from a reactive to an anticipative approach, meaning that it is not enough to respond to the needs of an individual or a group of individuals, usually by demand, but to be inclusive to all by default. Diversity brings strength, resilience and greater capabilities to organisations' agency with which to positively impact society through formulating and implementing strategic environmental, social and governance commitments and principles synergistic with organisational ways of working. The expansion of labour pools possible through technology also allows for greater inclusion of introverted employees and those with disabilities and neurodiversity. The opportunities of technology and an untethering from spatial-temporal definitions of workplace participation, accelerated through the pandemic, must continue to be leveraged in increasing equality and diversity in the workplace.

From an organisational environment perspective, Part 3 shows that the workplace is a tool for business, a tool of work and a powerful tool in the wider ecosystem of our societies, economies and cities. There is shared responsibility between employees and the organisation to ensure safe, healthy and inclusive working practices wherever work is undertaken. Whilst not the focus of the book, the vital role that organisational management and human resource management (HRM) plays in this context must be acknowledged. Empathic leadership and consultative approaches to management built on trust enhance motivation to achieve our potential, in turn giving deeper purpose and meaning to our work. Alignment between organisations' purpose and individual purpose in the workplace fosters belonging, connectedness and strong community through shared values. This not only drives well-being but supports productivity and desire to be in the office and re-activates social systems and precincts surrounding work. Creating togetherness places that support a collective and augmenting our building asset services will create the unique places that act as anchors for attachment, reinforce company values and build group identity that all humans need. But we must accept that the landscape is not and will never be static, evolution must continue to occur through a process of testing, monitoring, learning and adjusting with and within our environments.

Cases studies featured in Part 4 show how workspaces can achieve high-performance in practice. Combined, these case studies demonstrate the value of considering the three pillars of high-performance workplaces from inception. They also demonstrate how Australian workplaces changed to accommodate the recent changes in ways of working, including findings from before and after the onset of COVID-19. Similarly, in other parts of the Western world, organisations are undergoing the same processes and facing comparable challenges. These examples once again show the crucial role of interior design in achieving high-performance workplaces and how a user-centred and evidence-based approach can be implemented in practice. These chapters celebrate some of the best workplaces in Australia, supported by achievements in terms of workers' satisfaction, productivity and health.

At the time this book was written, workplaces were navigating a "whole system crisis". Alignment between business purpose and wider functional, economic and social needs that high-performance workplace principles can achieve has never been more important. Viewing this dramatic step change in work and workplace as an opportunity rather than threat to what we know is imperative to resilience, agility and success. To do this, we must leverage the holistic picture of scientific and practical knowledge on improving work and life to design high-performing workplace environments – after all, we spend a third or more of our lives in them.

INDEX

Note: Page numbers in *italics* indicate figures and page numbers in **bold** indicate tables on the corresponding pages.